Jude and the Relatives of Jesus
in the Early Church

Jude and the Relatives of Jesus in the Early Church

BY

RICHARD BAUCKHAM

T&T CLARK
EDINBURGH

T&T CLARK
59 GEORGE STREET
EDINBURGH EH2 2LQ
SCOTLAND

Copyright © T&T Clark, 1990

T&T Clark is an imprint of HarperCollins Publishers

First Published 1990

ISBN 0 567 09573 8

British Library Cataloguing in Publication Data
Bauckham, Richard
Jude and the relatives of Jesus in the early church.
1. Bible N. T. Special subjects: Jews
I. Title
225.890904924

Typeset by C. R. Barbers (Highlands) Ltd, Fort William
Printed and bound in Great Britain by Billing & Sons Ltd

To Charlie Moule
who by his generous encouragement
and his example
introduced me to New Testament scholarship

Contents

Introduction

This book is a contribution to the history of Palestinian Jewish Christianity in the New Testament period. It examines only one aspect of that history: the activity and influence of the relatives of Jesus. Because the most important of these relatives, James the Lord's brother, is the only one whose role in the early church has received any serious attention up till now – and because James requires a book to himself – he has been largely omitted from this study. His eminent figure is here kept deliberately in the background, so that his lesser known relatives may emerge from the shadows for once into the foreground. Important as James was – surely as important in his time as Paul or Peter – the other relatives of Jesus should not be seen merely as obscure members of his circle. When Paul instanced the brothers of Jesus as especially good examples of travelling missionaries, to be mentioned in the same breath as Peter (1 Cor 9:5), he was not thinking of James but of the other three brothers. For Paul it was a well known fact – well known even in Corinth – that they played a major role as influential Christian leaders in their own right. Moreover, other members of the family became, after James' martyrdom, the most prominent Christian leaders in Jerusalem and Galilee until at least the early second century. This study is dedicated to recovering what can be recovered of the role of these brothers and other relatives of Jesus from the neglected evidence which survives here and there in early Christian literature. These fragments of evidence have never before been brought together and thoroughly and critically studied. In some cases they yield less than at first sight they seem to offer, but in other cases we can learn more than we might have expected to know. Owing to the fragmentary nature of the evidence which has survived, the emergent picture is a very incomplete one: there remain huge blank areas, where even speculation has no basis, but there are also some clear broad outlines and some patches of vivid detail.

The traditions of the early church about these relatives of Jesus, examined in the first two chapters of this book, give us some insight into their important role as missionaries and leaders of the church, but offer very few clues as to their understanding of Christian faith. Therefore the rest of the book is devoted to two texts which, it will be argued, derive from the circle of the brothers of Jesus and from which a surprising amount can be learned about the character of the Jewish Christianity they preached and promoted and about the important theological contributions they made to the early development of Christianity. One of these texts is the letter of Jude, that most neglected of the books of the New Testament, which will prove to be a much more interesting document of early Christianity than New Testament scholars have usually realized. As a glimpse of the theological creativity of the circle of the brothers of Jesus it is invaluable. This book has in fact grown out of an interest in the letter of Jude, on which I published a commentary[1] a few years ago – the only really detailed commentary on Jude to appear for over sixty years. There I already argued for the authenticity of the letter as actually written by Judas the brother of the Lord and showed how consistent it is with an early Palestinian Jewish Christian context, rather than with the late 'early Catholic' context to which recent scholarly tradition tends to assign it. It might have been expected that I could have no more to say on these mere twenty-five verses of the New Testament, even though they have always been among the least studied verses in the New Testament. I thought so myself when I finished the commentary, but since then I have surprised myself by finding there is more to be said about

[1] Bauckham (1983A).

Jude. The detailed exegetical work which I published in the commentary is not repeated in this book. Instead, in chapter 3, a detailed review of scholarship on Jude is offered, and in chapters 4, 5 and 6 the importance of Jude for our understanding of early Palestinian Jewish Christianity is explored by way of certain issues and themes.

Thus Jude's letter lies at the centre of this book, but the circumference encompasses the role of all the relatives of Jesus in the early church about whom we have information, James only excepted. A focus on the letter of Jude provides a different approach to the role of these relatives from the usual approach by way of the figure of James. The significance of the letter is illuminated by placing it within the context of what we can discover about the leadership exercised by the relatives of Jesus in the early church, while conversely the activity of the relatives of Jesus can be given a considerable amount of theological content from careful study of the letter of Jude. What we already know from James about the kind of Christianity promoted by the circles in which the relatives of Jesus were leaders can be considerably augmented and enhanced by fresh understanding of his brother Jude's letter.

Martin Hengel has remarked on the importance of particular leaders in early Palestinian Christianity: 'Individual figures kept standing out in the earliest community, despite its collective constitution. They – and not the anonymous collective – exercised a decisive influence on theological developments.'[2] Among those who played a creative theological role in the crucially important earliest decades of Christianity were the relatives of Jesus. Not only the letter of Jude provides us with insight into that role. The conclusion which took me most by surprise during my work on this book was the discovery that the genealogy of Jesus recorded in Luke's Gospel can be shown to derive from the same circle as Jude. Properly understood, it is a sophisticated theological document, a precious relic of the messianic-apocalyptic Christology which the brothers of Jesus preached on their

[2] Hengel (1983) 149 n. 124.

missionary travels throughout Palestine. Such a conclusion, baldly stated, may initially sound like the kind of sheer speculation which gets some forms of New Testament scholarship a bad name. I hope the final chapter of the book will show that it is a well-grounded conclusion. If so, some entirely fresh light will be shed on that early Palestinian Jewish Christianity to which all subsequent Christianity was indebted.

1

Who Were the Relatives of Jesus?

The identification of relatives of Jesus is a topic on which speculation has been rife. A surprisingly large number of persons mentioned in the Gospels have been supposed, by one author or another, to be related to Jesus,[1] while four of those who were undoubtedly related to him – his so-called brothers – have been the subject of exhaustive, but inconclusive, discussion, aimed at establishing precisely what their relationship to Jesus was. Since we cannot discuss the role of the relatives of Jesus in the early church without first ascertaining who they were, this first chapter attempts to find a way through the maze of scholarly discussion of this topic, distinguishing the more probable identifications of relatives of Jesus from the untenable and improbably speculative theories.

I. Who's who in the Gospels?

It will be convenient to begin by identifying the relatives of Jesus who are known from the New Testament and other reliable early Christian sources. Jesus' presumed father Joseph[2] appears alive in the Gospel narratives only in the birth and

---

[1] The record must belong to Wenham (1975), who finds no less than twenty named relatives of Jesus in the Gospels (excluding the ancestors in the two genealogies of Jesus).

[2] The topic of the virginal conception is beyond the scope of the present investigation, though I take the historical case for it to be better than is now often supposed.

infancy narratives of Matthew and Luke, though he is also named as Jesus' father in Luke 3:23; 4:22; John 6:42. Only in Matthew 13:55 is he called a carpenter (τέκτων),[3] a term which in the Markan parallel (6:3) applies to Jesus himself. From Joseph's absence from the Gospels in the period of the ministry and the Gospels' references to Jesus' mother and brothers together but without Joseph (Matt 12:46; Mark 3:31; Luke 8:19; John 2:12; Acts 1:14; cf. also GNaz 2), it is generally concluded that Joseph must have died before the outset of Jesus' public ministry. This argument from silence has some weight, but it is not as conclusive as is often supposed.[4] Jesus' mother Mary, though often unnamed, appears a number of times in the Gospel narratives of the ministry (Matt 12:46; Mark 3:31; Luke 8:19; John 2:1–5, 12; 19:25–27; cf. Matt 13:55; Mark 6:3; John 6:42): after Acts 1:14 she disappears from reliable sources (cf. John 19:27). Her presence in Acts 1:14 may indicate that she was known as an active figure in the early church, but if so, we know nothing of her role. Joseph, whether or not still alive, certainly played no part in the beginnings of Christianity. Luke alone attests a family relationship, no more precisely specified, of Mary the mother of Jesus with Elizabeth the mother of John the Baptist (1:36).

Mark 6:3 names four brothers of Jesus: James, Joses, Judas and Simon. In the Matthean parallel (13:55) the names are: James, Joseph, Simon and Judas. On the assumption of Markan priority, Matthew has made two changes. First, he has changed the name of the second brother Ἰωσῆς to Ἰωσήφ. Ἰωσῆς represents Jose (יוסה or יוסי), which was a common abbreviated form of the common Jewish name Joseph (יוסף). The abbreviated name was that of several rabbis,[5] before and after the New Testament period, occurs in a letter of the early second century A.D. from Muraba'at (Mur 46 line 1), and is found ten times in Palestinian synagogue inscriptions

---

[3] On the meaning and significance of this term, see McCown (1928); Furfey (1955); Albright and Mann (1971) 172–173; Batey (1984).

[4] Cf. Oberlinner (1975) 73–78, who allows it no weight at all.

[5] Blinzler (1967) 22 n. 6.

from the centuries after the New Testament period.[6] The Greek form Ἰωσῆς is found not only in Mark 6:3; 15:40, 47 (and as v.l. at Matt 13:55; 27:56),[7] but also in inscriptions[8] and as a variant reading at Acts 1:23; 4:36; and Josephus, *BJ* 4:1:66. The same variation between the full name Joseph and the abbreviated form occurs in the two versions of the Jerusalem bishops list (Ἰωσήφ and Ἰωσίς: see chapter 2 section III below). Matthew prefers the full form Ἰωσήφ to Mark's Ἰωσῆς not only in Matthew 15:33 ‖ Mark 6:3, but also in Matthew 27:56 ‖ Mark 15:40. Presumably, in both cases he simply preferred the full form as the more familiar form of the name, especially outside Palestine. His preference for the full form of the *name* in both cases indicates nothing about whether he thought the Joseph/Joses of Matthew 27:56 ‖ Mark 15:40 to be the same person as the Joseph/Joses of Matthew 15:33 ‖ Mark 6:3.[9]

Matthew's other alteration of Mark is that he has reversed the order of the last two brothers. This is less easy to understand.[10] It may mean that Matthew thought he knew better than Mark the actual order of the brothers in seniority and so corrected Mark. Whether the tradition on which he relied was actually more accurate than Mark's at this point we cannot tell. But if Matthew was correcting Mark from the list of the brothers he knew in his own tradition, then at least this tradition confirms Mark as far as the seniority of James and Joses goes. We may therefore be fairly sure that James was the eldest of the four and Joses the second, though we cannot be sure whether Simon or Judas was the youngest.[11]

---

[6] Mur 46 in Benoit, Milik & de Vaux (1961) 165. Synagogue inscriptions in Fitzmyer & Harrington (1978) 254 (text A4), 256 (A9), 260 (A22: twice), 262 (A25, A27), 264 (A29), 266 (A33, A36, A38). Cf. also ossuaries mentioned in Milik (1956–57) 243 and n. 21.

[7] For the text of all five verses, see Blinzler (1967) 30, 82–85.

[8] Frey (1936) 271 (no. 347), 426 (p. 581); cf. Latin on p. 441 (no. 614).

[9] Oberlinner (1975) 96–97.

[10] The suggestion of Oberlinner (1975) 353, that it is stylistic – Matthew wishes to avoid a sequence of three names beginning with 'I' – is not very convincing.

[11] Oberlinner (1975) 355, strongly denies that such precise information is available from the Gospels, but this is because he presumes the Evangelists to

All four names, it is worth noting at this point, were among the commonest Jewish names of the period. Simon is used, as by many Jews, as the Greek equivalent of Symeon. (In English Judas is often known as Jude, a form of the name which is conventionally reserved for this Judas, the brother of Jesus and the author of the letter of Jude. In this book he will usually be called Jude.)

Sisters of Jesus are explicitly mentioned in the Gospels only in Mark 6:3 ‖ Matt 13:56, though their existence may also be implied in Mark 3:35 ‖ Matt 12:46. To Mark's 'his sisters' (6:3) Matthew adds 'all' (πᾶσαι: 13:56), but the addition may be purely stylistic. In Greek 'all' can refer to only two.[12] We cannot tell whether there were more than two sisters. Of the names which later tradition gives to sisters of Jesus, the best attested are Mary and Salome.[13] In the Additional Note at the end of this chapter we shall show that there is some degree of probability that these names are authentic. If two sisters of Jesus were remembered by name in at least one branch of early Christian tradition, then the probability is that they played some part in the early Christian movement, though they cannot have been as prominent as those women disciples of Jesus whose names are preserved in the Gospel traditions.

know nothing, on this subject, but the actual traditional *Vorlage* of their text, which itself is not necessarily in touch with historical fact. I presuppose, on the contrary, that information of this kind, about prominent members of the early church, would be widespread in the early church and available to the Evangelists in a variety of ways. It would not always be entirely accurate (as in this case, where Matthew and Mark differ), but has a good chance of accuracy.

[12] Bauer, Arndt & Gingrich (1979) 632 (2γ); Blinzler (1967) 35–36; against Zahn (1900) 334; Gunther (1974) 39.

[13] These names are given, probably from some apocryphal work, by Epiphanius, *Pan.* 78:8:1; 78:9:6: by his previous marriage Joseph had four sons and these two daughters. I think it likely that the Salome who appears in ProtJas 19:3–20:3 is this daughter of Joseph, in which case the tradition of her name goes back to the mid-second century. A witness, earlier than Epiphanius, to the name Mary for a sister of Jesus is GPhil 59:10–11. In the History of Joseph the Carpenter, Joseph's daughters are called Lydia and Lysia. For other names given to the sisters of Jesus in patristic tradition, see Blinzler (1967) 36–38.

By contrast, the preservation of all four names of the brothers of Jesus in Matthew and Mark indicates that all four brothers were well-known figures in the early church.[14] Elsewhere in the Gospel tradition they are collectively called Jesus' 'brothers' (Matt 12:46; Mark 3:31; Luke 8:19; John 2:12; 7:3–10; Acts 1:14; GNaz 2), while the phrase 'his mother and his brothers' seems to be a stereotyped expression in the Gospel tradition (Matt 12:46; Mark 3:31; Luke 8:19; John 2:12; Acts 1:14; GNaz 2; EpApp 5; cf. GThom 99), indicating, presumably, his closest relatives as they were known in the early church. The brothers were known in both Jewish and Gentile Christianity as 'the Lord's brothers' (1 Cor 9:5; Gal 1:19; Hegesippus, *ap.* Eusebius, *HE* 2:23:4; 3:20:1; cf. GNaz 2). The precise relationship intended by the term 'brothers' has been very much discussed. We shall take up the question in the next section, but we should notice at once that the only plausible case for considering them neither sons of Jesus' presumed father Joseph nor sons of his mother Mary, but more distant relatives, depends upon identifying the two eldest brothers James and Joses with the James and Joses to whom Mark 15:40 refers. But this issue is best considered in relation to the wider issue of the names of the women at the cross and at the tomb in the four Gospels, and their possible relationships to Jesus.

The names given are as follows:

Mark 15:40 (cross):   Mary Magdalene
                       Mary the mother of James the little
                           and Joses
                       Salome

---

[14] I regard it as a good general rule – not without exceptions – that where the early Gospel tradition preserves the names of characters in the Gospel story (other than those of public figures such as Pilate and Caiaphas), these named people were Christians well known in the early church. In circles where they ceased to be known, their names often dropped out of the tradition (e.g. the name Bartimaeus, given in Mark 10:46, is dropped in Luke 18:35, doubtless because Luke's readers would not have known the name).

Mark 15:47 (burial):   Mary Magdalene
                            Mary [the mother?] of Joses

Mark 16:1 (empty tomb):   Mary Magdalene
                            Mary [the mother?] of James
                            Salome

Matt 27:56 (cross):   Mary Magdalene
                            Mary the mother of James and
                                Joseph
                            the mother of the sons of Zebedee

Matt 27:61 (burial):   Mary Magdalene
                            the other Mary

Matt 28:1 (empty tomb):   Mary Magdalene
                            the other Mary

Luke 24:10 (empty tomb):   Mary Magdalene
                            Joanna
                            Mary [the mother?] of James

John 19:25 (cross):   Jesus' mother
                            his mother's sister
                            Mary [the wife?] of Clopas
                            Mary Magdalene

John 20:1 (empty tomb):   Mary Magdalene.

It may seem obvious that the second Mary in each of Mark's three lists is the same person, but this has sometimes been doubted. Some have thought that the traditions taken over by Mark named 'Mary [the wife?] of Joses' (at 15:47) and 'Mary [the wife?] of James' (at 16:1), and that Mark himself harmonized these two traditions in 15:40 by a creating a Mary who was mother of both James and Joses.[15] This suggestion can be countered on redaction-critical grounds.[16] But it can also be criticized, probably more securely, on the grounds that it neglects the probability that the names which Mark retains from the Gospel traditions were not mere names to him, but people who, because of their prominence in the early church, were known, at least by reputation, to him and his readers. This probability is confirmed by the fact that in 15:40 Mark calls James 'the little', to distinguish him from the other Jameses well known in the early church. This James is no mere name to him, but a person whose distinguishing nickname he knows. So just as Mark identifies Simon of Cyrene by calling him the father of Alexander and Rufus (Mark 15:21), since these two men were known, at least by reputation, to his readers (cf. Rom 16:13), so he identifies this Mary by calling her the mother of James the little and Joses, since these were known, at least by reputation, to his readers. In circles in which this Mary had become completely obscure, she was dropped from the Gospel tradition (John 20:1; GPet 50; cf. EpApp 9–11). There is no difficulty in supposing that Mark first describes her fully (15:40), and then, having established her identity, refers to her briefly as either 'Mary of Joses' or 'Mary of James'. Evidently neither of her two sons was in Mark's mind a more prominent figure than the other, and so, when he needs a brief identification, he thinks of her as the mother of Joses as readily as he considers her the mother of James.

If we now compare the lists of women in the various Gospels, it will be seen that Mary Magdalene, the best known woman disciple of Jesus in the early church, appears in every group in every Gospel. We may also be sure that the second Mary in Mark's lists, the mother of James the little and Joses,

---

[15] References in Bode (1970) 21.

[16] So Oberlinner (1975) 97–117, who concludes (111–112) that pre-Markan tradition had 'Mary the mother of James the little and Joses' (15:40) and 'Mary the mother of Joses' (15:47), while the names at 16:1 are Markan composition.

is the same as the second Mary in all three of Matthew's lists and as the 'Mary of James' of Luke 24:10. (Matthew has substituted the more familiar form 'Joseph' for the less familiar 'Joses', just as he has at Matt 13:55.) However, there seems to be no firm ground for identifying any other woman in one Gospel with a woman in another Gospel. All three Synoptic evangelists state explicitly that many women who followed Jesus from Galilee were present at the cross (Matt 27:55–56; Mark 15:40–41; Luke 23:49), while according to Luke more women than the three he names went to the tomb on Easter morning (Luke 24:10). Even John's narrative suggests that Mary Magdalene was not the only woman at the tomb, though she is the only one named (John 20:2).[17] It is natural to suppose that the evangelists name different women, who for some reason were prominent in their own traditions, as representative of the group of women disciples. Thus Luke names Joanna, who featured in his special tradition at Luke 8:3. Salome appears only in Mark, though she is prominent in some extracanonical Gospel traditions (GThom 61; 1 ApJas 40:25; Secret Gospel of Mark 5; Clement of Alexandria, *Str.* 3:45, 63, 64, 66; *Exc. ex Theod.* 67; Pistis Sophia). But evidently she was not well-known in Matthew's church, and so he drops her name and at 27:56 substitutes 'the mother of the sons of Zebedee', who had already appeared in his Gospel (but nowhere else in the Gospel traditions) at 20:20. He cannot have thought that Mark's Salome was the mother of the sons of Zebedee, because at 28:1 he simply drops Salome from Mark's list of women at the tomb, without substituting the mother of the sons of Zebedee, as he would surely have done had he thought she was Salome. Presumably, since he knew that the mother of the sons of Zebedee was one of the women who travelled with Jesus to Jerusalem (20:20), he felt free to include her in the women at the cross, but not to add her, without any authority from tradition, to the witnesses at the empty tomb.

[17] However, the women at the cross in John (19:25) are not part of a larger group, but constitute with the beloved disciple a small group near the cross.

There is even less reason to identify Salome or the mother of the sons of Zebedee with the sister of Jesus' mother mentioned in John 19:25,[18] or to identify the second Mary of Mark and Matthew with the sister of Jesus' mother[19] or the Mary of Clopas mentioned in John 19:25.[20] Theories about the relatives of Jesus which depend on such identifications have no foundation.[21] But before turning to the women in John, we must pause further over the second Mary of Mark and Matthew, since a case might be made for her relationship to Jesus, independently of a theory of her identity with one of the women of John 19:25. Such a case depends on identifying her sons James the little and Joses with the two eldest 'brothers' of Jesus James and Joses.[22] We may first of all rule out the possibility that she is the mother of Jesus,[23] since it is incredible that Mark, Matthew or pre-Markan tradition should choose this way of referring to the mother of Jesus. But this Mary's sons James and Joses must have been known in the early church: this is why she is identified (distinguished from other Marys) by reference to them. Could it not be, therefore, that she was the mother of Jesus' so-called brothers

---

[18] The threefold identification – Salome (Mark 15:40) = the mother of the sons of Zebedee (Matt 27:56) = the sister of Jesus' mother (John 19:25) – is made by Zahn (1900) 341; others listed in Oberlinner (1975) 125 n. 395; Wenham (1975) 10–11.

[19] Most of those who make this identification take John 19:25 to refer to only three women, so that Jesus' mother's sister is Mary of Clopas (see next note). But McHugh (1975) 242–244, proposes the novel theory that John 19:25 refers to four women and that, not Mary of Clopas, but Jesus' mother's sister is identical with the second Mary of Matthew and Mark.

[20] This identification was made by Jerome, and has been followed by many: see Blinzler (1967) 113 n. 11; Oberlinner (1975) 121–122. Most of those who make it take 'his mother's sister' and 'Mary of Clopas' in John 19:25 to be in apposition, describing the same woman, so that the second Mary of Matthew and Mark becomes the sister (-in-law) of Mary the mother of Jesus.

[21] Cf. Blinzler (1967) 111–117; Oberlinner (1975) 121–125.

[22] This identification was made by Jerome and has been followed by many, including Blinzler (1967) 78–82; McHugh (1975) 239–242. On the question, with full bibliography, see Oberlinner (1975) 86–120.

[23] Trompf (1972); Gunther (1974) 30–35; but against these, see Oberlinner (1975) 117–120.

James and Joses, but not the mother of Jesus, so that these two were not strictly brothers of Jesus, but stood in a more distant relationship (such as cousins)? At first it might seem plausible to identify two sets of brothers, both named James and Joses and both known in the early church (specifically in the circles known to Mark and Matthew). However, there are two impediments to this view:

(1) James the Lord's brother, leader of the Jerusalem church, could certainly not have been called 'the little' in any sense other than a reference to his physical height,[24] but such a designation for him is nowhere else attested. The designations by which he was distinguished from other Jameses were 'the Lord's brother' (Gal 1:19; Hegesippus, *ap.* Eusebius, *HE* 2:23:4) and 'the just' (GHebr 7; GThom 12; Hegesippus, *ap.* Eusebius, *HE* 2:23:4, 7, 16; 1 ApJas 32:2–3; 2 ApJas 44:14; 59:22; 60:12; 61:14), though the latter designation could have originated later than Mark's Gospel.[25] Blinzler supposes that 'the little' was a very early designation of James, before 'the Lord's brother' became his firm title or 'the just' became his distinguishing epithet.[26] But this will not do, because 'the Lord's brother' was certainly the term in common use for him by the time Mark wrote his Gospel. If Mark retains the description 'the little' from his tradition, it will be because it could still serve, for his readers, the purpose of distinguishing this James from others. We must conclude that for Mark it serves precisely to distinguish this James from the Lord's brother to whom he refers in 6:3,[27] and this James' mother from the mother of Jesus.

It is true that neither Matthew (27:56) nor Luke (24:10) feel the need of this epithet 'the little'. They must have assumed that 'Mary the mother of James and Joseph' (Matt 27:56) or, in Luke's case, just 'Mary of James' (24:10), was sufficient identification. While it is true that normally in the

---

[24] For this sense, see the parallels in Bauer, Arndt & Gingrich (1979) 521.

[25] Pratscher (1987) 115–116. But the saying in GThom 12 may indicate a fairly early origin.

[26] Blinzler (1967) 76 n. 6.

[27] Oberlinner (1975) 112.

early church only James the Lord's brother could be called simply James without risk of ambiguity (Acts 12:17; 15:13; 21:18; 1 Cor 15:7; Jude 1), it does not follow, as McHugh argues,[28] that the James of Luke 24:10 must be the Lord's brother, since it is not there a case of an otherwise unidentified James but of a James who is connected with a Mary. If Luke could assume, as surely he could, that no one would refer to the mother of Jesus as 'Mary of James', he may have known only one Mary and one James, so connected, who were well known in the early church.

(2) The Lord's brother Joses was an insignificant figure by comparison with his brother James. It is incredible that the mother of these two should be distinguished from other Marys as 'the mother of Joses' (Mark 15:47). She would always be 'the mother of James'. That Mark can call his second Mary either 'the mother of Joses' (15:47) or 'the mother of James' (16:1) suggests that, unlike the brothers of Jesus, these two brothers were equally well known figures.[29] We must conclude that no relatives of Jesus appear among the women disciples named by the Synoptic evangelists.

In John 19:25, however, the case is different.[30] It seems that, along with the indispensable Mary Magdalene (named here to anticipate her necessary appearance at 20:1), the Johannine tradition here focussed on the relatives of Jesus.[31] Unlike the Synoptic picture of a large group of women distant from the cross, John has, close to the cross, a small group of those

[28] McHugh (1975) 205, 210, 453–454.

[29] Zahn (1900) 348–350, identified this Mary as the Mary of Rom 16:6, who would be known to Mark's readers in Rome, and her son Joses as Joseph/Joses Barsabbas (Acts 1:23), who he supposes, on the rather dubious evidence of Martyrdom of Paul 2, was also known in Rome. Either or both of these identifications is *possible*. The Mary of Rom 16:6 was certainly a Jewish Christian whom Paul had known elsewhere before she went to Rome.

[30] On the women of John 19:25, see Blinzler (1967) 111–118; Brown (1971) 904–906; Oberlinner (1975) 120–135.

[31] McHugh (1975) 243–244, thus rightly distinguishes John's interest from that of Matthew and Mark in their lists of women. John's list is the context for 19:26–27; Matthew and Mark are interested in the women as witnesses to the death, burial and resurrection of Jesus.

who were closest to Jesus. But it is not certain whether he intends to refer to three or to four women.[32] His list is in the form: A and B, C and D. This could be read, more probably, as two pairs of women, the first pair unnamed but designated by their relationship to Jesus, the second pair named. Less probably, the list could be read as of three women, in which case Jesus' mother's sister would be the same person as Mary of Clopas. The second possibility is not entirely excluded by the extreme improbability of two sisters' having the same name Mary, since 'sister' could designate a more distant relationship such as sister-in-law.[33] A further uncertainty lies in the description 'Mary of Clopas', which could mean wife, mother or daughter of Clopas.

Clopas, since he is named, must have been a known figure in the early church. There is therefore little room for doubt that he is the Clopas to whom Hegesippus refers, as the brother of Joseph and therefore uncle of Jesus, and the father of Symeon or Simon who succeeded James the Lord's brother in the leadership of the Jerusalem church (Hegesippus, *ap.* Eusebius, *HE* 3:11; 3:32:6; 4:22:4). In that case, his Mary can scarcely be his mother. She could be his daughter,[34] but is probably most naturally taken to be his wife. In that case she would be the wife of Jesus' mother's brother-in-law. Perhaps 'his mother's sister' could cover this relationship. Thus it seems that John refers to either two or three women of Jesus' mother's generation of the family. If his mother's sister is not Mary the wife of Clopas we know nothing further of her.[35]

Finally, we must ask whether Clopas appears elsewhere in the Gospel tradition. He has sometimes been identified as Alphaeus the father of James, one of the twelve (Matt 10:3;

[32] The ancient versions already differ on this: Zahn (1900) 338 n. i; Blinzler (1967) 112. According to Oberlinner (1975) 124 n. 391, the majority of exegetes think four women probable.

[33] Cf. Gunther (1974) 29–30; McHugh (1975) 245 n. 19.

[34] So Bishop (1961–62).

[35] GPhil 59:8–9 ('Mary his mother and her sister') looks at first sight like a reference to her (though it could scarcely be treated as reliable information), but should probably be corrected to 'his sister,' in accordance with 59:10.

Mark 3:18; Luke 6:15; Acts 1:13; the father of Levi has the same name in Mark 2:14), on the grounds that the two Greek names (Κλωπᾶς, 'Αλφαῖος or, better, 'Αλφαῖος) are alternative Greek forms of the same Semitic name (Ḥalphai).[36] Even if this identity of the names were accepted, it would still be surprising for a particular individual to be known by two such different Greek forms of his name. But the identity of the names has always been doubtful on philological grounds.[37] Moreover, the Semitic original of the name Κλωπᾶς, which used to be very uncertain, has now been found in an Aramaic document of the early second century A.D. from Muraba'at (Mur 33 line 5).[38] It is a distinct name (קלופו)[39] from that of which 'Αλφαῖος is the Greek form (חלפי).

The name קלופו may be a Semitic imitation of the Greek name Κλεόπατρος or its abbreviated form Κλεόπας,[40] but whether or not this is so, the Clopas of John 19:25 is likely to be the same person as the Cleopas of Luke 24:18.[41] This Greek name, borne by a Galilean Jew, will be used as the Greek equivalent of Clopas, in the same way as Jason was used as the equivalent of Jesus (Joshua) and Simon of Symeon. Luke's Cleopas must be named (unlike his companion) because he was known in the early church. So he can be probably identified with the Clopas whose wife Mary had come with the group of Jesus' followers from Galilee (John 19:25). And if Luke calls Clopas Cleopas, we can take it that he does not also call him Alphaeus (Luke 6:15; Acts 1:13). A later church tradition named the other disciple on the road to

[36] Still maintained by Wenham (1975) 13–14; cf. Blinzler (1967) 135–136 n. 40 for other references. For an original but very improbable suggestion about the names, see also Harris (1927) 65.

[37] Blinzler (1967) 120–121; Gunther (1974) 25–26. See the many Greek forms of חלפי attested in Wuthnow (1930) 16–18, 61–62, 119, 141: all lack the long first vowel of Κλωπᾶς.

[38] Benoit, Milik & de Vaux (1961) 151.

[39] The name was already known as a Nabataean name (קלופא): Chabot (1897) 327.

[40] Milik in Benoit, Milik & de Vaux (1961) 151; cf. Zahn (1960) 343–344.

[41] Cf. Gunther (1974) 26–30.

Emmaus as Simon.[42] If this were trustworthy, he could be
Clopas' son Symeon, whom we know from Hegesippus. But
it may well be only a misunderstanding of Luke 24:34, or
merely a guess that Clopas' well-known son Symeon would
have been his companion. It is rather unlikely that someone
so important at the time when Luke heard the tradition and
wrote his Gospel should not be named.[43]

Various members of the twelve have, on various grounds,
been identified as relatives of Jesus.[44] We have already rejected
the identification of the mother of the sons of Zebedee (Matt
27:56) with Jesus' mother's sister or with Mary of Clopas (John
19:25), which would make James and John the cousins of Jesus.
We have also already rejected the identification of Clopas with
Alphaeus, which would make James the son of Alphaeus a
cousin of Jesus. The fact that three of the names of the brothers
of Jesus (James, Judas, Simon) recur in the lists of the twelve
(Judas only in Luke 6:16; Acts 1:13; cf. John 14:22) is no
argument at all for identifying the persons so named: all three
were among the most common Jewish names at the time.
Because the names were so common, each of these three among
the twelve is distinguished in some way from others of the same
name: James as the son of Alphaeus (Matt 10:3; Mark 3:18; Luke
6:15; Acts 1:14), Simon as 'the Cananaean' (Matt 10:3; Mark
3:18) or 'the Zealot' (Luke 6:15; Acts 1:14), and Judas as '[son]
of James' (Luke 6:16; Acts 1:14). These – plainly traditional –
ways of distinguishing the members of the twelve give no
ground for identifying them with the brothers of Jesus,[45] or for
identifying Simon with the son of Clopas. Moreover, the
Gospel tradition several times distinguishes the brothers of Jesus
from the twelve (Mark 6:13–35; John 6:66–7:10; Acts 1:14),
which would be just tolerable if one of the brothers were a
member of the twelve, but not if more were. We conclude that
it is unlikely that any of the twelve were related to Jesus.

---

[42] Zahn (1900) 350–352.

[43] The same objection can be made to the suggestion of Gunther (1974)
28, that Cleopas' companion was James the Lord's brother.

[44] For references, see Oberlinner (1975) 121–122. Most recently Villegas
(1987) identifies three brothers of Jesus among the Twelve.

[45] Cf. Lightfoot (1892) 14–15; McHugh (1975) 231–232.

The information which survives about later generations of the family, a few members of which are known by name, will be discussed in chapter 2.

II. What kind of brothers?

The relationship to Jesus of the four men known in the early church as the 'brothers of the Lord' has been extensively discussed,[46] mainly because of its bearing on the traditional doctrine of the perpetual virginity of Mary. In the Greek patristic and eastern Orthodox tradition this doctrine has been accompanied by the view that the 'brothers of the Lord' were the sons of Joseph by a marriage prior to his marriage to Mary. Since Jerome the Latin western and Roman Catholic tradition has preferred the view that they were not brothers in any modern sense, but first cousins of Jesus. Only in modern Protestant scholarship, with no commitment to and often deeply suspicious of the idea of the perpetual virginity of Mary, has the view become at all common that the 'brothers of the Lord' were sons of Joseph and Mary, though probably the majority of exegetes, including a few Roman Catholic scholars,[47] now take this view. The three views have come to be known by the names of fourth-century proponents of each, as the Helvidian view (sons of Joseph and Mary), the Epiphanian view (sons of Joseph by his first marriage) and the Hieronymian view (cousins).[48] All three views have been ably defended in modern times: for example, the Helvidian view by Mayor,[49] the Epiphanian view by Lightfoot,[50] and variants of the Hieronymian view by

---

[46] Such discussions nearly always assume that the 'sisters' of Jesus (Matt 13:56; Mark 6:3) must be related to Jesus in the same way as the brothers.

[47] Notably Pesch (1976) 322–324.

[48] The three terms were perhaps first used by Lightfoot (1892) 5. McHugh (1975) 200–233 gives a useful account of the three views, with criticism from his own perspective. For patristic views, see Blinzler (1967) 130–136.

[49] Mayor (1897) vi–xxxvi; (1898) 320–326.

[50] Lightfoot (1892).

Blinzler[51] and McHugh.[52] For full discussion, readers are referred to these treatments. Here it will only be possible to touch on the major issues involved in a decision between the three views.

Of the three views the Hieronymian is the least plausible. The meaning of the word ἀδελφός is not decisive here. Leaving aside uses which do not refer to family relationships (fellow-countryman, co-religionist, etc.) and are clearly not relevant to this case, the word normally refers, like the English 'brother', to those who are related as sons of the same parent(s)' (including, of course, adoptive and step-relationships), but there is good evidence that it could sometimes be used more loosely of other close kinship relationships.[53] However, since ἀδελφός was regularly used for the 'brothers' of Jesus in the early church and no other kinship term is ever used to describe their relationship to Jesus, we should need positive evidence that in this case the term is not being used in its normal sense. Such evidence the Hieronymian theory finds in a series of identifications between various people mentioned in the Gospels.

In its traditional form, as proposed by Jerome and followed by many others,[54] the theory involves the following identifications: (1) The Lord's brothers James and Joses (Mark 6:3) are the same people as 'James the little and Joses', the sons of Mary (Mark 15:40). (2) This Mary is the same person as Jesus' mother's sister, Mary of Clopas (John 19:25). (3) James 'the little',[55] the Lord's brother, is the same person as James the son of Alphaeus, one of the twelve.[56] (4) Alphaeus and

---

[51] Blinzler (1967).

[52] McHugh (1975) 200–254.

[53] The evidence is well presented and assessed by Oberlinner (1975) 16–49; cf. also Blinzler (1967) 39–48.

[54] See Lightfoot (1892) 6–9; McHugh (1975) 223–226, 230; Oberlinner (1975) 121–122.

[55] Jerome uses the Latin *minor*, 'the less', and so gives the epithet a comparative force not required by the Greek (ὁ μικρός, 'the little'). He therefore supposed that this 'James the less' must be compared with just one other, greater James. So he must be the second James in the list of the Twelve, 'less' by comparison with James the son of Zebedee.

Clopas are the same person.[57] These identifications produce the following relationships:

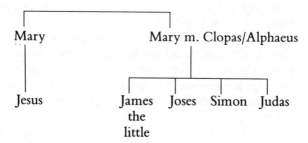

A variant of this view eliminates the improbability of the two sisters both called Mary, by considering Mary of Clopas to be not the sister but the sister-in-law of Mary, and adding a further identification: (5) The Lord's brother Simon is the same person as Symeon the second leader of the Jerusalem church, who according to Hegesippus was the son of Clopas the brother of Joseph:

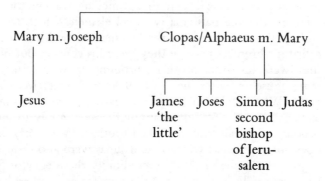

McHugh's modern variant of the Hieronymian view[58] de-

[56] Two further identifications have frequently been added: that the Lord's brother Simon is Simon the Zealot, one of the Twelve, and that the Lord's brother Judas is 'Judas of James' (understood as 'Judas the brother of James'), one of the Twelve. But these are inessential to the theory.

[57] This identification was not made by Jerome, who did not take Clopas to be the husband of 'Mary of Clopas' (cf. Lightfoot [1892] 8), but many of Jerome's followers have made it.

[58] McHugh (1975) 234–254.

pends on the following identifications: (1) The Lord's brothers James and Joses (Mark 6:3) are the same people as 'James the little and Joses', the sons of Mary (Mark 15:40). (2) This Mary is the same person as Jesus' mother's sister, understood as sister-in-law (John 19:25), but not as Mary of Clopas. (3) The Lord's brother Simon is the same person as Symeon the second leader of the Jerusalem church, who according to Hegesippus was the son of Clopas the brother of Joseph. These produce the following relationships:

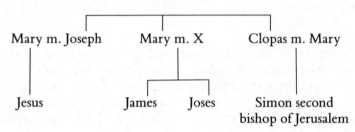

This leaves the relationship of the Lord's brother Judas to Jesus indeterminate: McHugh assumes he was another close relation. But the particularly novel element which McHugh adds to this scheme is that the brothers of the Lord were not called his brothers because they were his cousins, but because they were his foster-brothers, brought up with Jesus in the same household after the death of Joseph's sister Mary's husband. What McHugh apparently fails to realise is that this explanation, to have any plausibility, must apply to all four brothers, since all four are called brothers (Mark 6:3), but he does not explain why Simon and Judas were also brought up in Joseph's household.[59] Any credibility the theory of foster-brothers might have is lost if the four foster-brothers are not the sons of the same parents.

Blinzler's variant of the Hieronymian view[60] is the most economical with identifications. It requires only two: (1) The Lord's brothers James and Joses (Mark 6:3) are the same people as 'James the little and Joses', the sons of Mary (Mark

[59] Cf. McHugh (1975) 246–248, where he leaves it uncertain whether Simon and Judas were foster-brothers of Jesus.

[60] Blinzler (1967).

15:40). (This Mary or her husband was related to the family of Jesus, but Blinzler leaves the relationship indeterminate. Her husband may, he suggests, have been a brother of Mary the mother of Jesus.[61]) (2) The Lord's brother Simon is the same person as Symeon the second leader of the Jerusalem church, who according to Hegesippus was the son of Clopas the brother of Joseph. The relationships are therefore:

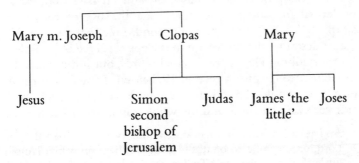

Mary m. Joseph   Clopas   Mary

Jesus   Simon   Judas   James 'the   Joses
       second   little'
       bishop of
       Jerusalem

It will readily be seen that the indispensable lynchpin of all forms of the Hieronymian view is the identification of the Lord's brothers James and Joses with the James 'the little' and Joses of Mark 15:40. This identification we have already rejected in section I above, along with the other identifications on which the traditional form of this view depended. The second key identification in the modern variants – the identification of the Lord's brother Simon with Symeon the son of Clopas – would have no plausibility if there were not already ground for supposing James and Joses to be related to Jesus more distantly than as actual brothers.

In fact, Hegesippus seems to distinguish the relationship to Jesus of Symeon the son of Clopas, whom he calls 'cousin of the Lord' (ἀνεψιός τοῦ κυρίου: *ap.* Eusebius, *HE* 4:22:4; cf. 3:11), from that of James and Jude, for both of whom he uses the traditional description 'brother of the Lord' (*ap.* Eusebius, *HE* 2:23:4; 3:20:1). Modern advocates of the Hieronymian view counter this evidence by the claim that Hegesippus (in Eusebius, *HE* 4:22:4) refers to Symeon as 'a second (i.e. anoth-

---

[61] Blinzler (1967) 145.

er) cousin of the Lord' (ὄντα ἀνεψιόν τοῦ κυρίου δεύτερον) with the implication that his predecessor James (whom Hegesippus has just mentioned) was also a cousin of the Lord.[62] However, if this is what Hegesippus meant to say, his whole sentence is an awkward way of saying it. The phrase in question is best understood by analogy with Eusebius, *HE* 3:22, where the word δεύτερος describes first Ignatius as second bishop of Antioch and then Symeon as second bishop of Jerusalem, without in either case the use of the word ἐπίσκοπος, which must be understood. Like that passage, *HE* 4:22:4 describes the succession in the episcopal see of Jerusalem (purportedly in Hegesippus' actual words, but summarized by Eusebius: see chapter 2 section IV below). In such a context, δεύτερον should be taken, not with ἀνεψιόν, but with ἐπίσκοπον understood, and the whole passage translated:[63]

> And after James the Just had suffered martyrdom, as had also the Lord, on the same account, the son of his [i.e., probably, James'] uncle, Symeon the son of Clopas, was next appointed bishop, whom, since he was a cousin of the Lord, they all put forward as the second [bishop].

In that case, Hegesippus' evidence must be held to count against the Hieronymian view. While he clearly describes Symeon as the Lord's cousin, he does not explain James' relationship to Jesus in the same way, but remains content with the traditional term 'brother of the Lord'.

It is much harder to decide between the Helvidian and Epiphanian views, despite the fact that most modern exegetes seem to treat the former as virtually self-evident. The references to the brothers of Jesus, including their association with his mother, in the Gospels and other early Christian literature are perfectly consistent with the view that they were his step-brothers. Positive evidence that they were the sons of Mary, as well as of Joseph, is lacking. The following points have been regarded as such evidence, but in fact are not: (1) Matthew 1:25

---

[62] Blinzler (1967) 96–98, 105–108; McHugh (1975) 245–246; for other literature, see Oberlinner (1975) 140 n. 457.

[63] For discussion and justification of this translation, see Lightfoot (1892) 29–30; Zahn (1900) 236–237.

(Joseph 'knew her not until she had borne a son'). Matthew's interest here is in the fulfilment of the Isaianic prophecy that a virgin shall conceive and bear a son (1:23), and so he states that Mary remained a virgin up to the birth of Jesus. This is the extent of the information he intends to convey.[64] His words cannot be pressed to imply that Joseph and Mary had sexual relations after the birth of Jesus, but even if they could it need not follow that they had children. (2) Luke 2:7 ('she gave birth to her firstborn son'). The term firstborn (πρωτότοκος) can specify the firstborn child in relation to other children born later, but in Jewish usage need not do so.[65] The 'first to open the womb' (Exod 13:1, 12; Num 3:12) was the firstborn, consecrated to God and requiring redemption by sacrifice, whether or not other children followed. Luke did not need to state that Jesus was born before other children of Mary, if there were such, since he has already made it clear that Mary was a virgin when she conceived Jesus. His interest in Jesus' status as Mary's firstborn in 2:7 is in anticipation of 2:22–24 and with reference to his consecrated status, as 2:23 makes clear. The question of other children of Mary does not come into Luke's view here.[66] (3) No argument can be built on the silence of the infancy narratives of Matthew and Luke as to children of Joseph already living at the time of the birth of Jesus. The evangelists have no interest in providing such information.[67]

In the absence of positive evidence for the Helvidian view, it may still be regarded as the most natural assumption, unless there is evidence against it and for the Epiphanian view. The only serious evidence for the Epiphanian view is that it is the only view positively attested in Christian tradition before Tertullian, if Tertullian is correctly interpreted as holding the Helvidian view, or before the late fourth century, if he is

---

[64] Oberlinner (1975) 51 57; cf. Blinzler (1967) 50–56; against, e.g., Mayor (1897) xxiii–xxv.

[65] See Blinzler (1967) 57; Oberlinner (1975) 58, for a Jewish grave inscription referring to a woman who had died giving birth to her firstborn child (πρωτοτόκου)!

[66] Oberlinner (1975) 57–61; McHugh (1975) 203–204; Blinzler (1967) 56–61; against, e.g., Mayor (1879) xxv.

[67] Cf. Oberlinner (1975) 65–68.

not.[68] It appears around the middle of the second century in the Protevangelium of James (9:2; 17:1–2; 18:1), in the Gospel of Peter (in the part of this work which is no longer extant, according to Origen, *In Matt.* 10:17), and in the Infancy Gospel of Thomas (16). Probably through the influence of the first two of these works, it was then accepted by Clement of Alexandria, Hippolytus, Origen and many subsequent writers.[69] To assess the value of this tradition, we need to investigate its second-century origins.

In the Protevangelium of James the view that the brothers of Jesus were his step-brothers, sons of Joseph by a previous marriage, is combined with two other beliefs concerned with the human origins of Jesus, which are not found in the New Testament: the Davidic descent of Mary (10:1) and the miraculous birth of Jesus (19:2–3), whereby Mary's virginal condition was unimpaired by childbearing (the *virginitas in partu*). Clearly all three notions are connected with the virginity of Mary. Emphasis on this must have seemed to require that Jesus' descent from David must be traced through Mary, not (as in Matthew and Luke) through Joseph. Regarding the brothers of Jesus as step-brothers and the story of the miraculous birth both ensure that Mary's virginity was preserved: her *perpetual* virginity, though not explicitly stated, is already implied. The Protevangelium of James is clearly interested in glorifying the figure of Mary as consecrated virgin.[70] But it is unlikely that any of these three beliefs originate with the Protevangelium of James. That the brothers of Jesus were sons of Joseph by his previous marriage is taken for granted (as it is also in InfGThom 16) as though the readers are already quite aware of it. This is also the case with Mary's Davidic descent, which in any case is already found in traditional credal formulations in Ignatius of Antioch (*Eph.* 18:2; *Trall.* 9:1; *Smyrn.* 1:1) and occurs in a number of other second-century works (AscIsa 11:2; 3 Cor 3:5; Justin, *Dial.* 45:4; 100:3; cf. TJos 19:8). The story of the miraculous birth

[68] For differing interpretations of Tertullian, see Lightfoot (1892) 31–32; Blinzler (1967) 139–141; McHugh (1975) 448–450.

[69] See Lightfoot (1892) 32–40; Blinzler (1967) 131–133.

[70] Smid (1965) 17–19.

is found in a simpler and probably earlier form in Ascension of Isaiah 11:9–14[71] and Odes of Solomon 19:8–9 (cf. 28:17)[72] and is implied by Ignatius' reference to the birth of Jesus in *Ephesians* 19:1.[73] Thus all three beliefs were probably already traditional when the Protevangelium of James took them up.

If we compare all the second-century works in which either the miraculous birth of Jesus or the view that the brothers of Jesus were step-brothers is found, we get the following pattern:

	Davidic descent of Mary	Miraculous birth[74]	step-brothers
Ignatius	✓	✓	
AscIsa	✓	✓	
OdesSol		✓	
GPet			✓
InfGThom			✓
ProtJas	✓	✓	✓

Since the extant section of the Gospel of Peter is quite closely related to traditions in the Ascension of Isaiah,[75] it is quite possible that it had something similar to the latter's birth narrative and so included, along with the identification of the brothers of Jesus as step-brothers, the Davidic descent of Mary and the miraculous birth. What is of particular interest is that all six of these works are either certainly or quite probably of Syrian origin.[76] It looks as though we have here a complex

[71] Cf. Aldama (1970) 204–206.

[72] Cf. Aldama (1970) 207–211.

[73] Since Ignatius here refers to Mary's virginity and her giving birth (τοκετός) as two distinct mysteries, he probably refers to two miraculous acts by which the Son of God entered the world: the virginal conception and the miraculous birth. See the discussion and this conclusion in Aldama (1970) 189–203.

[74] This is also found in Acts of Peter 24 (dependent on AscIsa 11) and probably in SibOr 8:472, which may not be as early as the second century.

[75] The most striking parallel is AscIsa 3:14–17 with GPet 28–42.

[76] As well as Ignatius of Antioch, the Gospel of Peter and the Ascension of Isaiah probably come from the west Syrian area around Antioch, the Odes of Solomon are associated with east Syria, the Infancy Gospel of

of traditions which dates from the very beginning of the second century in Syria. The tradition about the brothers of Jesus may therefore seem condemned as unhistorical by association with the other two traditions: it looks like part of a doctrinal or hagiographical development of the theme of the virginity of Mary. On the other hand, it is possible that the brothers of Jesus were correctly remembered not to have been sons of Mary and that this made possible the development of the idea of Mary's perpetual virginity as a result. Good historical tradition certainly was still available in the early second century, even if mixed with much legendary material.

This view of the brothers of Jesus would have more probable historical value if it could be plausibly traced to Palestinian Jewish Christian tradition. None of these six Syrian works can be very closely associated with such tradition. But we must, finally, consider three possible witnesses to Palestinian Jewish Christian tradition about the brothers of Jesus.

(1) The early medieval Irish writer Sedulius Scotus attributes to a 'Gospel according to the Hebrews' an account of the arrival of the magi at the cave in Bethlehem, in which Joseph addresses Simon – clearly his son, one of the brothers of Jesus.[77] This has been treated and discussed as a possible fragment of the second-century Jewish Christian Gospel, which scholars usually call the Gospel of the Nazarenes.[78] In fact, it is an extract from chapter 89 of the Latin Infancy Gospel published by M. R. James.[79] Another Irish reference to the same passage, in a twelfth-century manuscript, also attributes it to the Gospel according to the Hebrews, but may be dependent on the quotation in Sedulius Scotus.[80]

Thomas may also be east Syrian in origin, while the Protevangelium of James may be probably located in Syria because of its affinities with these other works.

[77] Latin text in Bischoff (1974) 203–204; Klijn (1988) 4027; English translation (as frag. 28 of GNaz) in Vielhauer (1963) 151.

[78] Klijn (1988) 4028, 4030, treats it as questionable.

[79] James (1927) 82–83.

[80] James (1927) xxviii, 99–100; Gijsel (1976) 300. The same manuscript (Harl. 1802) contains an Irish poem on the magi (Stokes [1887] 346–351) which is dependent on this passage in the Irish version of James' Latin Infancy Gospel (see Stokes [1887] 360–361; James [1927] 112).

James' Latin Infancy Gospel is a (probably Carolingian)[81] compilation from the Protevangelium of James, the Infancy Gospel of Pseudo-Matthew, and an otherwise unknown ancient source (followed in chapters 59–76, 81–85, 89–95). This unknown source, from which the passage attributed to the Gospel according to the Hebrews by Sedulius Scotus comes, could well be as early as the second century: it has affinities with the Protevangelium of James. Joseph's son Symeon is prominent in this source. It is possible that Sedulius Scotus knew this *source* itself as the Gospel according to the Hebrews and that it was in fact the second-century Gospel of the Nazarenes.[82] On the other hand, it may be the *compilation* (James' Latin Infancy Gospel) which he called 'the Gospel according to the Hebrews,' a title which was sometimes used inaccurately in the medieval period. The matter deserves further study, but in the present state of investigation it would be hazardous to use this material as evidence of early Jewish Christian tradition.

(2) The Second Apocalypse of James from Nag Hammadi, despite its Gnostic and anti-Jewish character, certainly has taken over some Jewish Christian tradition. Its account of the martyrdom of James the Lord's brother (61:1–62:14) is probably independent of Hegesippus' account but derived ultimately from the same Jewish Christian tradition.[83] It also has a curious account of a meeting of James with Jesus (50:5–51:22), which looks as though it is based on an account of the resurrection appearance to James like that in Gospel of the Hebrews 7.[84] As in the latter, Jesus addresses James as 'my brother' (50:11–12), but this apparently astonishes James. James' mother (unnamed) then explains that 'both of you were nourished with the same milk. Because of this he calls me "My mother." For he is not a stranger to us. He is your [step-brother . . .]' (50:18–22).[85] But Jesus himself goes on to explain a better reason for calling James his

---

[81] Gijsel (1976) 301–302.

[82] So Gijsel (1976) 300–301.

[83] Brown (1975) 227–231; Pratscher (1987) 241–251, 255.

[84] Bagatti (1971B) 72.

[85] Translation from Robinson (1977) 251. Unfortunately for our purposes, the restoration of the end of line 22 is problematic: see Funk (1976) 120–122.

brother: his divine Father has become a Father to James (51:19–22). This passage expresses the rather common Gnostic view[86] that Jesus had no real human origin and that neither of his supposed parents were really his parents[87] (cf. 51:19–20), but it also regards James as the son of Jesus' supposed mother. It might be suggested therefore that it reflects a Jewish Christian tradition which held the brothers of Jesus to be sons of Mary. However, this is rendered very unlikely by the quite unparalleled name Theuda[88] which this Apocalypse of James gives to James' father (44:20), which indicates that the author either depended on a very eccentric tradition about the family of Jesus or had no traditional information about the parents of James or Jesus at all. Probably the tradition he used in 50:5–22 informed him only that Jesus called James his brother (as in GHeb 7): the rest is his own attempt to explain this, given his Gnostic presupposition that Jesus could have no real human parents.

(3) If the view held by Hegesippus about the brothers of Jesus could be ascertained, it would probably be our best chance of access to Palestinian Jewish Christian tradition on the subject. But from the fragments of Hegesippus extant in Eusebius it is not possible to be sure whether he held the Helvidian or the Epiphanian view. Significance has sometimes been attached to his reference to Jude 'who was called [the Lord's] brother according to the flesh' (*ap.* Eusebius, *HE* 3:20:1). But, on the one hand, 'according to the flesh' (κατὰ σάρκα; also used of the relatives of Jesus by Eusebius, probably following Hegesippus, in *HE* 3:11; Julius Africanus, *ap.* Eusebius, *HE* 1:7:11; Didascalia 24; Ap. Const. 8:35:1; HistJos 2)[89] does not distinguish blood-relationship from, say, mere adoptive or step-relationship (so that, given the virginal conception, Jude would have to be the son of Mary), but distinguishes natural, earthly relationship from spiritual relationship. On the other hand, the word 'called' (λεγόμενου; cf. Eusebius, *HE* 2:1:2; ClemHom 11:35) does not mean that

---

[86] Brown *et al.* (1978) 269–270.

[87] Funk (1976) 120; Pratscher (1987) 168.

[88] Against attempted identifications see Brown (1975) 225 n. 4; and cf. Funk (1976) 90.

[89] On the phrase see Blinzler (1967) 108–110.

Jude's brotherhood of Jesus was reputed rather than real[90] (since, on the Epiphanian view, he was not a blood-relative), but merely indicates that Hegesippus is reporting a common usage.

However, Lawlor argues that two passages of Epiphanius himself, which clearly support the Epiphanian view, derive from Hegesippus.[91] The first (*Pan.* 78:7) states that Joseph's first wife was of the tribe of Judah and bore him four sons and two daughters. The second (*Pan.* 78:8) gives the names of the four sons in the Matthean order (Matt 13:55) as the order of birth, and the names of the two sisters as Mary and Salome. Joseph is said to have been about forty when his eldest son was born, and over eighty when, as a widower, he married Mary. But elsewhere in this chapter Epiphanius clearly draws, directly or indirectly, on the Protevangelium of James, and although the information in these two passages does not come from the Protevangelium of James, it more plausibly comes from some apocryphal account, perhaps dependent on the Protevangelium of James, than from Hegesippus. Much more plausibly dependent on Hegesippus[92] is a passage in *Pan.* 29:4, which begins, 'For he [James] was Joseph's firstborn son': but this statement, of course, is consistent with the Helvidian as well as the Epiphanian view.

The most that can be said with confidence about Hegesippus is that, if he had clearly stated the Helvidian view, we should expect other writers to have respected his authority on this point and to have followed him, but none do. Eusebius, who relied heavily on Hegesippus' information about the family of Jesus and shows no sign of crediting apocryphal infancy literature such as the Protevangelium of James, himself takes the Epiphanian view for granted (*HE* 2:1:2). But, of course, Hegesippus may not have clarified the relationship of the brothers to Jesus further than in the extant fragments.

In conclusion, the Epiphanian view has a better claim to serious consideration than is often nowadays allowed. The second-century tradition could preserve an accurate historical memory. On the other hand, it could be a legendary construct

---

[90] As Lightfoot (1892) 30, suggests.
[91] Lawlor (1917) 11–12; the two passages are printed on p. 98.
[92] Lawlor (1917) 10.

in favour of the perpetual virginity of Mary. We cannot be sure. Fortunately, whether the Helvidian or the Epiphanian view is preferred will make no difference to our discussion, in the following chapters, of the role of the brothers of Jesus in the early church.

III. Judas Thomas the twin brother of Jesus?

Some attention must be given to the tradition that appears to identify Jude the Lord's brother with the apostle Thomas, known in the East Syrian tradition as Judas Thomas. Some recent scholars have appeared to favour the historicity of this tradition[93] and to associate the letter of Jude with it.[94] However, this tendency is based on an insufficiently critical view of the tradition.

In the east Syrian tradition of Edessa and its region, the apostle Thomas was known as Judas Thomas (GThom title; ActsThom 1; 2; 11 etc.; BkThom 138:1; John 14:22 in the Curetonian Syriac; Abgar legend *ap.* Eusebius, *HE* 1:13:4, 11; 2:1:6; Doctrine of Addai; Ephraem; the additional name Didymus, the Greek equivalent of Thomas,[95] is also given in GThom; ActsThom 1). Only in works from this particular geographical area of the early church is the name Judas given to the apostle Thomas.[96] The church of Edessa claimed some special connexion with this apostle, who in the Abgar legend was responsible for sending Thaddaeus/Addai to evangelize Edessa. Moreover, in just two works which originate from this area, probably c. 200,[97] the sur-

---

[93] Koester (1965) 296–297.

[94] Layton (1987) 359. Koester (1982) 247, suggests that the letter of Jude was written in Syria under the pseudonym of Jude the brother of Jesus, chosen for anti-Gnostic polemical purposes, because Judas Thomas was an authority for Gnostic circles in Syria.

[95] Cf. John 11:16; 20:24; 21:2.

[96] For the east Syrian origin of the Gospel of Thomas, see Fallon and Cameron (1988) 4227–4228.

[97] For the date of the Book of Thomas, see Turner (1975) 233–237. The Acts of Thomas seem to have influenced Mani before his break with the Elkasite Christian group in which he grew up, i.e. before 240 (Lieu [1985] 29–32, 51–53, 61), and so cannot be dated much after 200.

name Thomas, which is the Aramaic word for twin (תאומא),[98] is taken to indicate that the apostle Judas Thomas was the twin brother of Jesus (ActsThom 11; 31; 39; BkThom 138:4, 7, 19) and so presumably the same person as Jude the Lord's brother.[99] Again, this identification of Thomas as a brother of the Lord is known at an early date only in the east Syrian area, appearing elsewhere only in much later works under the influence of the Acts of Thomas.[100] It should also be noticed that in this tradition Judas Thomas was *not* identified with the apostle 'Judas of James' (Luke 6:16; Acts 1:13; cf. ActsThom 1), so that such an identification cannot be the reason why he was called Judas.[101]

What has not been sufficiently noticed is that in several of the sources which attest the name Judas Thomas there is no hint of his identification with the Lord's brother. In particular, Ephraem distinguishes Judas Thomas from both the apostle Judas of James and Jude the Lord's brother, but regards the last two as the same person.[102] The explicit identification of Judas Thomas as Jesus' twin brother is confined to the Acts of Thomas and the Book of Thomas, though it may well be presupposed in the Gospel of Thomas.[103] These three works are closely associated both in theology and in traditions (they seem all to be dependent on the Gospel tradition which

[98] Another etymology, deriving the name from תהומא ('abyss') was also current in Syria: Poirier (1981–82).

[99] The Infancy Gospel of Thomas is problematic in this connexion. Attributed to 'Thomas the Israelite', rather as the Protevangelium of James is to James the Lord's brother, it mentions James as Joseph's son (16:1–2), but Thomas himself does not appear in the stories at all and is not called Judas Thomas. Its traditions were known to the author of the Acts of Thomas. Probably it did not originate in the east Syrian Judas Thomas tradition, but was adopted into it because of its attribution to Thomas.

[100] For these occasional later traces of the idea, see Harris (1927) 54–56; Blinzler (1967) 32.

[101] Bauer (1909) 444; against Blinzler (1967) 32–34.

[102] Harris (1894) 37–38, gives an extract (preserved in Armenian) from Ephraem's commentary on Acts 1:13, where in the list of the Twelve he identifies the apostle Judas of James (understood as Judas the brother of James) with Judas the Lord's brother, but neither with Thomas. He also identifies the apostle Simon the Zealot with Simon the Lord's brother.

[103] Cf. Gunther (1980) 114–115.

was transmitted in east Syria under the name of Thomas[104]). Moreover, the identification of Thomas as the twin brother of Jesus serves a highly theological purpose in these works: it makes Thomas the model of Christian selfunderstanding.[105] To know oneself is the way to know one's divine double or twin (BkThom 138:7–21; cf. GThom 13; 108). The understanding of the twins Jesus and Thomas in the Acts of Thomas has also been influenced by the Greek myth of the Dioscuri.[106] Thus it may be that the tradition of the name Judas Thomas preceded his identification as the brother of Jesus and assisted it, but that the main impetus to this identification came from the theory of spiritual twinship with Jesus.

Although the Greek word for twin, Didymus, was sometimes used as a personal name, its Semitic counterpart Thomas seems not to have been so used in New Testament times.[107] So it is unlikely that Thomas, the name by which the apostle was exclusively known in the Christian traditions of the first and second centuries outside east Syria,[108] was actually his personal name. For some reason his actual name was not used or remembered, and he was known simply by the nickname or surname 'Twin.' Similarly, the apostle Simon/Symeon Peter, whose personal name was a very common Jewish name and also borne by another of the twelve (Mark 3:18), was often known simply as Peter or Cephas, while Joseph Barnabas (Acts 4:36) was almost always known simply as Barnabas. The most likely reason for the disuse of Thomas' personal name is that it was a common name also borne by at least one other prominent early Christian leader.[109] From this point of view, the east Syrian tradition that his personal name was Judas is entirely plausible.[110] In that case, he would have

[104] Turner (1975) 233–237; cf. also Bauckham (1987A).
[105] Layton (1987) 159–160.   [106] Gunther (1980) 117.
[107] Harris (1927) 25–27; Klijn (1970) 89 n. 3. The only examples are much later: Fitzmyer and Harrington (1978) 268 (text A40); Wuthnow (1930) 55, 174.
[108] For extracanonical traditions see Bauer (1965) 59.
[109] The two other reasons suggested by Gunther (1980) 124 (that Thomas' personal name was Jesus, or that Thomas in fact resembled Jesus in appearance and so was called his twin) are less likely.
[110] Koester (1982) 152.

been commonly called Thomas in order to distinguish him from other disciples called Judas, including two among the twelve (Luke 6:16) as well as the Lord's brother and Judas Barsabbas (Acts 15:22). It is also credible that in east Syria, where the Gospel tradition in some sense derived from him and was transmitted under his name, his personal name should have been remembered, whereas elsewhere it was forgotten. As for the reason for his surname Thomas, he probably was actually a twin. To argue, as Rendel Harris does, that his twin must have been a more important person than he, because 'the less is defined with reference to the greater,'[111] is fallacious. He would have been called twin simply because this was a characteristic which distinguished him from other disciples with the name Judas. His twin would no doubt have been someone known to the circle who first gave him the nickname, but need not have been prominent in the early church and could be completely unknown to us. Other later traditions of the church, other than the east Syrian tradition, gave him an otherwise unknown twin brother Eliezer (Clem-Hom 2:1:2) or twin sister Lysia.[112]

That the name Judas was actually Thomas' name is more probable than that he was so called in east Syria as a result of his identification as a twin of Jesus and therefore with Jude the Lord's brother. Considering him the twin brother of Jesus would not necessarily identify him with *Jude* rather than with another of the brothers. In any case, it is somewhat doubtful whether the notion of Thomas as Jesus' twin was originally intended to refer to a *physical* relationship at all. It is hard to imagine how the idea of a twin brother of Jesus could have been taken seriously in circles where the tradition of the virgin birth was current (cf. OdesSol 19).[113] In Acts of Thomas 11–12 Jesus appears in the form of Thomas – i.e. as

[111] Harris (1927) 45.

[112] Blinzler (1967) 34. Thomas' twin sister Lysia appears in *Chron. paschale* 9.

[113] Possibly, as in 2 ApJas 50:2–23, Jesus was not thought to have a real human origin at all, but was fostered by his supposed mother along with her real son. But the Valentinian view that Jesus 'passed through Mary as water runs through a tube' (Irenaeus, *Adv. haer.* 1:7:2; cf. Brown *et al.* [1978] 270) is scarcely compatible with his having even an apparent twin.

his identical twin – but this may be only one of his 'many forms' (48).[114] The real interest is in Thomas as the spiritual twin of Jesus, Jesus' 'twin and true companion' (BkThom 138:1), 'fellow-initiate into the hidden words of Christ . . ., fellow-worker of the Son of God' (ActsThom 39), the apostle who knows Jesus best and most resembles him. Even the depiction of Thomas as a carpenter like Joseph (ActsThom 2–3), though no doubt inspired by the idea of literal brotherhood to Jesus, finds its real significance as a spiritual metaphor (cf. 17–24). It is possible that a tradition of Thomas' physical twinship to Jesus was later exploited theologically, but it is at least equally possible that an interpretation of his name as implying his spiritual twinship with Jesus later brought with it the idea of physical twinship.

To associate the letter of Jude with the east Syrian tradition about Judas Thomas the twin brother of Jesus, as some have done,[115] is most implausible. Even in that tradition the apostle is usually known as Judas Thomas or as simply Thomas (GThom13; BkThom 138:4, 19, 21, 36; 139:12, 22, 25; 140:5, 37; 141:2, 19; 142:3, 18). Only in the Acts of Thomas is he sometimes called simply Judas, but only after his identity as Judas Thomas has been left in no doubt. He is never called 'Judas, the brother of James.' But it is the phrase 'brother of James' which is used in Jude 1 to distinguish its author from other apostles or disciples called Judas. Anyone in the east Syrian tradition writing a pseudepigraphal letter of Judas Thomas would have used the surname Thomas to identify its author. Anyone outside that tradition would not even have known that the apostle Thomas was called Judas. Even the apostle Judas Thomas himself would surely have distinguished himself from other Judases by means of his wellknown surname Thomas, rather than as 'brother of James,' even assuming he was a brother of James!

---

[114] Klijn (1970) 93–96, thinks that the idea of Thomas' physical resemblance to Jesus as his twin arose from the name Thomas understood in the context of a 'morphē-Christology' in which Jesus appears successively in different forms.

[115] Koester (1982) 247; Layton (1987) 359.

Additional Note on the Names of the Sisters of Jesus

The best attested of the names[116] which post-canonical Christian tradition attributed to the sisters of Jesus are Mary and Salome.[117] These are given by Epiphanius (*Pan.* 78:8:1; 78:9:6; cf. *Ancoratus* 60:1[118]) as the names of the two daughters of Joseph by his first wife.[119] Although Lawlor argued that in *Pan.* 78:8:1 Epiphanius was dependent on Hegesippus,[120] it seems more likely that he drew these names, along with other information about Joseph's first marriage, from some apocryphal source which is no longer extant, probably one which bore some relation to the Protevangelium of James, on which Epiphanius seems also to be dependent (directly or indirectly) in this context.[121] These names for the sisters of Jesus are not found very often in early Christian literature. References to them in later patristic and early Byzantine writers (Sophronius of Jerusalem, Anastasius of Sinai, Theophylact, Euthymius Zibagenus, Nicephorus Callistus)[122] are probably dependent on Epiphanius. But the names can probably also be traced in two writings prior to Epiphanius: the Gospel of Philip and the Protevangelium of James.

The Gospel of Philip is a Valentinian work of probably the third century. It contains the following statement:

There were three who always walked with the Lord: Mary his

---

[116] For other names, see Blinzler (1967) 36–38.

[117] In Epiphanius, *Pan.* 78:8:1 the order is Mary, Salome; in *Pan.* 78:9:6 the order is Salome, Mary.

[118] The text of *Ancoratus* 60:1 gives the names Anna and Salome. Ἄνναν may be a textual error for Μαρίαν (so Holl [1915] 70 n.), but if so it was an early error known to Sophronius of Jerusalem, who knew of three daughters of Joseph: Mary, Anna and Salome (Blinzler [1967] 36–37).

[119] The extant text of Epiphanus gives no name to Joseph's first wife, but Anastasius of Sinai, *Quaest.* 153 (PG 89:812), purporting to quote Epiphanius (*Pan.* 78:7:6) calls her Salome. Other late writers identify her with Mary the mother of James and Joses (Mark 15:40): see Blinzler (1967) 36.

[120] Lawlor (1917) 11–12.

[121] *Pan.* 78:7:2; cf. ProtJas 9. The references to Joseph's age in *Pan.* 78:8:1–2, which do not derive from the Protevangelium of James, correspond roughly, but not exactly, to History of Joseph 14.

[122] For references, see Blinzler (1967) 36–37.

mother[123] and her sister and Magdalene, the one who was called his companion. His sister and his mother and his companion were each a Mary (59:6–11).[124]

If the two lists of three women are to be made consistent, then 'her sister' in the first list must be corrected to 'his sister', as in the second list. The scribal error may be due to the fact that Jesus' mother's sister is mentioned in John 19:25, and on a possible (though not the more probable) reading of that verse could be thought to be named Mary. This fact has also misled some modern scholars into supposing the original text of the Gospel of Philip referred to Jesus' mother's sister,[125] but this is impossible: if 'his sister' in the second list were corrected to 'her sister' the reference would be to Mary Magdalene's sister, not Jesus' mother's sister. The original reference must have been to Jesus' sister Mary.[126] The notion that she was a constant companion of Jesus might be the result of identifying her with one of those Marys (other than Mary Magdalene)[127] who appear in the Gospels as disciples of Jesus (Matt 27:56, 61; 28:1; Mark 15:40, 47; 16:1; Luke 24:10; John 19:25).[128] But it is worth noting that the Apostolic Constitutions (3:6), which certainly did not make this

[123] For Mary the mother of Jesus as his constant companion, see Epiphanius, *Pan.* 78:13:1; *contra* Tertullian, *Carn.* 7:9.

[124] Translation from Robinson (1977) 135–136.

[125] Cf. Buckley (1986) 108.

[126] Cf. Wilson (1962) 97–98.

[127] For the constant attendance of 'the other Marys' (including Mary Magdalene) on Jesus, see Tertullian, *Carn.* 7:9.

[128] For some later writers who identified Mary the sister of Jesus with Mary the mother of James and Joses (Mark 15:40), see Blinzler (1967) 36. According to Anastasius of Sinai, *Quaest.* 153 (PG 89:812), Mary the sister of Jesus, Joseph's daughter, married her uncle, Joseph's brother Clopas, and was therefore known as the sister of Mary the mother of Jesus (John 19:25) (so also Hippolytus of Thebes, quoted by Blinzler [1967] 36). This information purports to come from Epiphanius, *Pan.*, but is not in the extant text of *Pan.* 78:7–8, and probably represents a later elaboration of Epiphanius (perhaps on the basis of Epiphanius' claim that the Gospels of Mark and John are evidence that Joseph had four sons and two daughters: *Pan.* 78:7:6). It makes sense of the extant text of GPhil 59:6–11: Mary the sister of Jesus was, on this view, also Jesus' mother's sister! But it is unlikely that this view is really presupposed by the Gospel of Philip.

identification, supposes the sisters of Jesus to have been among his women disciples.

The significance of the statement is probably allegorical, in accordance with a common Valentinian manner of allegorizing the Gospel narratives.[129] The three Marys are no doubt seen as symbolizing feminine spiritual powers (such as the Holy Spirit and Sophia), who are related to Jesus as his mother, his sister and his consort.[130] (For Mary Magdalene as Jesus' consort, see also GPhil 63:32–36.) The allegorical significance of these three relationships explains why these three Marys are mentioned, while the other Marys who appear in the Gospel narratives as disciples of Jesus are not mentioned. But the sister of Jesus called Mary is not likely to have been invented for the sake of the allegory. Rather, the allegory is possible because Jesus' mother, sister and closest female disciple were known to share the same name, Mary. The Gospel of Philip is therefore evidence of the same tradition as we find later in Epiphanius. Of course, we cannot tell whether the tradition behind this Gospel also knew of a sister of Jesus called Salome, since this particular passage provides no occasion for her to be mentioned. In favour of dependence by the Gospel of Philip on an apocryphal tradition about the relatives of Jesus, like that known to Epiphanius, is the fact that apocryphal traditions about the family and the childhood of Jesus are also used elsewhere in the Gospel (63:25–30; 73:9–15).[131]

If Jesus' sister Mary appears in the Gospel of Philip, it is arguable that the other sister Salome appears in the Protevangelium of James. We have already noticed how this late second-century account[132] of the family background and birth of Jesus treats the brothers of Jesus as sons of Joseph by his first marriage (9:2; 17:1–2; 18:1; 25:1). The narrative tells how Joseph leaves Mary, who is about to give birth, in a

---

[129] Cf. Layton (1987) 272–274; and the examples in Irenaeus, *Adv. Haer.* 1:3:2–4; 1:8:1.

[130] Cf. the discussion of female symbolism in the Gospel of Philip in Buckley (1986) 105–125.

[131] The tradition in 73:9–15 is otherwise unknown. The tradition in 63:25–30 is a variant of a story about the child Jesus which is found in some Infancy Gospels: see James (1924) 66–67; Cullmann (1963A) 400–401.

[132] For the date, see Strycker (1961) 412–418; Smid (1965) 22–24.

cave, in the care of his sons, while he goes to find a midwife
(18:1). When he returns with a midwife, they witness the
miraculous birth of Jesus.[133] Leaving the cave, the midwife
meets Salome (19:3), who appears at this point in the narrative
without any explanation of who she is. Salome refuses to
believe that a virgin has given birth unless she can test Mary's
condition with her finger and find her to be still a virgin.
When she goes to do so, her hand is burned (20:1). When she
prays, an angel appears and tells her that if she touches the
child she will be healed. She does so, is healed, and is told not
to tell of the miracle she has seen (20:4). This story is clearly
modelled on that of Thomas, who refused to believe in the
resurrection until he could put his finger in the wounds of
the risen Christ (John 20:24–29). Salome's role is that of a
witness of the miracle of the virgin birth.[134]

   This may in part account for the fact that Salome is named,
by contrast with the midwife, whose witness is less dramatic.
But the abrupt introduction of Salome in 19:3, not even as 'a
woman called Salome', but simply as 'Salome', requires that
the writer expected his readers to know who she was. The
best explanation is that she is Salome the daughter of Joseph,
who could naturally be supposed to have accompanied her
father and brothers on their journey to Bethlehem. This is
much more plausible than Morton Smith's assumption that
she must be Salome the disciple of Jesus (Mark 15:40; 16:1),[135]
whom the Protevangelium's readers would hardly expect to
find loitering outside a cave on the road from Jerusalem to
Bethlehem at the time of the birth of Jesus. The introduction
of Salome without identification would be similar to the
abrupt appearance of James, as the writer of the work, in

---

[133] In chapters 19–20, in which Salome appears, the text in the earliest
manuscript (P. Bodmer V) is considerably shorter than that in other manuscripts. Strycker (1961) 377–389, and Smid (1965) 7, 131, agree that here
the text of P. Bodmer V is not the more original form, but is an abridge-
ment of the longer text. This issue makes no decisive difference to our argument.

[134] Smid (1965) 139, points out that the midwife and Salome together
fulfil the Deuteronomic requirement of two witnesses (Deut 19:15; cf.
Matt 18:16).

[135] Smith (1973) 190–191.

25:1, with no explanation that he is the son of Joseph. In these cases, and probably also in 17:2, where the name Samuel is most likely a corruption of Symeon, the writer takes it for granted his readers know the names of Joseph's children.

If the name of Salome the sister of Jesus was well known in the circle from which the Protevangelium comes, it was evidently not well known in the early church as a whole. The unexplained appearance of Salome therefore caused difficulty for later readers of the work, and the Greek textual tradition of the Protevangelium of James already shows attempts to identify her with the midwife or as another midwife.[136] Later birth narratives dependent on the Protevangelium solve the problem by means of one or other of these options. In the Latin Infancy Gospel of Pseudo-Matthew, which tells basically the same story about Salome (13), she is a second midwife, while the first is called Zelomi (a variant of her name). In two closely related Coptic narratives – a Sahidic fragment on the birth of Jesus[137] and the Discourse by Demetrius of Antioch on the Birth of our Lord[138] – there is just one midwife who is Salome. In these narratives the story of Salome's unbelief, testing and healing is omitted. As soon as she arrives with Joseph and sees the mother and child, she believes the miracle of the virgin birth. Both accounts say that she became a follower of Mary and Jesus from that moment until after his resurrection. According to the Discourse by Demetrius,

> this woman Salome was the first who recognized the Christ, and who worshipped Him, and believed on Him when He came upon the earth; and she did not return to her own house until the day of her death. Whithersoever Christ went to preach, with His mother the Virgin, there she followed Him with His disciples

[136] The abridged version of chapter 20 in P. Bodmer V alone calls Salome the midwife (μαῖα) at 20:2. Most manuscripts of the longer text conclude Salome's prayer in 20:2 with a reference to her performance of her duties as a midwife (τὰς θεραπείας), but this is missing in manuscript C. Clearly, these are two different attempts by scribes to identify Salome as a midwife and so to explain her appearance in the narrative. Smith's view ([1973] 191) that the reading of P. Bodmer V at 20:2 shows that in an older form of the text Salome was the (one and only) midwife is quite implausible.

[137] Translation in Robinson (1896) 196–197.

[138] Translation in Budge (1915) 652–698.

until the day when they crucified Him and [the day of] His holy resurrection. She saw them all, with His mother the Virgin.[139]

The Coptic History of Joseph, which gives the two daughters of Joseph the names Lysia and Lydia (2:3), briefly alludes to the same Coptic tradition about Salome when it says that Salome followed Mary, Joseph and Jesus on the flight into Egypt (8:3).[140]

This Coptic tradition[141] has evidently identified Salome the midwife with Salome the disciple of Jesus known from the Gospel traditions (Mark 15:40; 16:1), but this identification is clearly a late development in the tradition. It is an instance of the common Jewish and Christian exegetical practice of identifying people with the same names. The same practice led later writers (Theophylact, Euthymius Zigabenus, Nicephorus Callistus) who knew Salome the sister of Jesus from Epiphanius to identify her with the Salome of Mark 15:40, whom they also identified as the mother of the sons of Zebedee (Matt 27:56).[142] Occasionally such later writers also identify Salome's companion at the cross, Mary the mother of James and Joses (Matt 27:56; Mark 15:40), with Joseph's other daughter Mary.[143] But it is very unlikely that the tradition of these names for the sisters of Jesus *originated* as an interpretation of Mark 15:40, as Swete[144] and Blinzler[145] suppose. There would be no reason to suppose that the women mentioned in Mark 15:40 were sisters of Jesus unless the sisters of Jesus were already known as Mary and Salome. The tradition of the names of the sisters of Jesus must antedate their identification with the women of Mark 15:40.

---

[139] Budge (1915) 674.

[140] No doubt as a result of this Coptic tradition, Salome later appears in this role as constant companion of the holy family in Arabic and Ethiopic literature about the infancy. James (1924) refers to 'a Coptic text not yet printed in full' which tells the whole life story of Salome, but I have not been able to trace this.

[141] A further trace of this tradition is in the Coptic Book of the Resurrection by Bartholomew, where the women who visit the empty tomb on Easter morning include 'Salome who tempted him' (in James [1924] 183). This must refer to Salome's confession in ProtJas 20:1 ('I have tempted the living God').

[142] For references, see Blinzler (1967) 36.

[143] Blinzler (1967) 36.

[144] Swete (1909) 113.

[145] Blinzler (1967) 36.

So is there any degree of probability that the tradition known to the Protevangelium of James, the Gospel of Philip and the source used by Epiphanius correctly preserved the actual names of two sisters of Jesus? A recent study of the recorded names of Jewish women in Palestine in the period 330 B.C.–200 A.D.[146] finds that, although the 247 women whose names are known bore 68 different names in all, 61 of these 247 women were called Salome (including its longer version Salomezion) and 58 were called Mary (Mariamme or Maria).[147] In other words, these two names account for 47.7% of the women. Every second Palestinian Jewish woman must have been called either Salome or Mary. Individual sources for the names also show high percentages of these two names, making it likely that the sample is in this respect representative. The popularity of these names may derive from the fact that they were borne by members of the Hasmonean royal house, as were several of the most popular male names of the period.[148]

In the light of this statistical finding, it seems that the tradition which gives the names Mary and Salome to Jesus' sisters has a 50% chance of being correct, even if it was not based on historical memory! But the full significance of the statistic emerges only when we also consider the frequency of Jewish women's names *outside* Palestine. For this purpose, unfortunately, no such exhaustive collection of the surviving evidence is available. However, the list of 769 named Jewish women, from both Palestine and the diaspora, compiled by Mayer, includes at least 21 women named Mary living in the diaspora,[149] but only two women named Salome living in the diaspora (Rome and Beirut).[150] Salome seems to have been a peculiarly Palestinian name.[151] Thus it is unlikely that a Gentile

[146] Ilan (1989).

[147] In fact, this figure could be increased to 59, since Ilan (1989) 195, does not list Mary of Clopas (John 19:25), presumably – but probably incorrectly – considering her the same person as Mary the mother of James and Joses.

[148] Ilan (1989) 191–192.

[149] Mayer (1987) 104–106. The figure would be higher if the name Marion (and variant forms), used in Egypt, were included.

[150] Mayer (1987) 106–107, cf. 109–110.

[151] Cf. Mayer (1987) 42.

Christian living in the diaspora in the second century, wishing to invent names for the sisters of Jesus, would have hit on the two most common Palestinian Jewish women's names. He may well have called one sister Mary, but is unlikely to have called the other Salome. If the tradition is therefore to be traced back to Palestinian Jewish Christian circles, the chances of its being an accurate historical tradition are relatively high.

Simply to know, with some degree of probability, the names of two sisters of Jesus is in itself of very little historical interest. But if their names were preserved in Christian tradition, this must indicate that they were known figures in some early Christian circles. They must have played some part in the early Christian movement. That it cannot have been too prominent a part is shown by Mark's reference to a disciple of Jesus named Salome (15:40; 16:1). Whereas Mark knows that Jesus had more than one disciple called Mary and so refers to them in ways which identify the Mary in question (15:40, 47; 16:1), he evidently sees no need to distinguish the Salome in question from any other Salome associated with Jesus. That this disciple called Salome was the sister of Jesus is unlikely, both because she does not appear in the Johannine tradition which specifically remembers the women relatives of Jesus who were present at the cross (John 19:25), and because no early extra-canonical tradition about Salome the disciple of Jesus offers any hint that she was a relative of Jesus. So it seems that Salome the disciple of Jesus was known by name to Mark's readers, but her namesake the sister of Jesus was not. Moreover, we have observed that the tradition of the names Mary and Salome for the sisters of Jesus was not widely known at a later date. The probability is therefore that these two sisters of Jesus played some part in the early Christian movement, such that they were remembered in one branch of early Christian tradition, but were not as prominent in the early church as the brothers of Jesus or as some of those women who were disciples of Jesus during his ministry. This conclusion adds a little more evidence to the general picture (provided by the evidence surveyed in this and the next chapters) of the significant role the relatives of Jesus in general played in the early church.

2

The Relatives of Jesus in the Early Church

Serious and systematic study of the relatives of Jesus has hitherto been limited to only two of them: his mother Mary and his
brother James, who for quite different reasons have been the
subjects of major studies in recent years.[1] About Mary's role
in the early church after the death and resurrection of Jesus
the evidence allows little to be said. About James' role there is
a great deal to be said, but he is not the focus of this chapter,
which will take for granted what is generally known about
the major part he played in the first few decades of Christian
history and the reputation he had in subsequent Jewish Christianity. He will certainly not go unmentioned, because it is
impossible to write about the other relatives of Jesus without
reference to James, but when he appears in this chapter it will
be more for the sake of illuminating the role of the family of
Jesus in general than for his own sake. The information[2]

---

[1] On Mary in the New Testament: Brown *et. al.* (1978); McHugh (1975).
James: Pratscher (1987), with full bibliography of earlier studies.

[2] Some texts have been alleged to contain information about relatives of
Jesus which in fact they do not:
(1) A statement of Philip of Side about Julius Africanus, who lived at
Emmaus (de Boor [1889] 169: ἐν ᾗ οἱ περὶ Κλεόπαν ἐπορεύοντο) has been
taken by Harnack (1897) 220 n. 1, and Gunther (1974) 27, to refer to
descendants of Cleopas. In fact, οἱ περὶ Κλεόπαν means no more than
'Cleopas and his companion' (for the usage, see Bauer, Arndt & Gingrich
[1979] 645 2aδ), i.e. the two travellers to Emmaus in Luke 24. The information does not go beyond that in Luke 24:13–18.

available about the relatives of Jesus in general and particular relatives other than Mary and James has never previously been collected and studied in a properly critical way in order to build up a general picture of the role the family played in early Christianity. Some of the evidence is hard to assess, but some issues which have previously been debated will become clearer in the context of all the available evidence.

I. The Gospels

Of the evidence to be discussed in this chapter, only the references to the relatives of Jesus in the canonical Gospels have already been studied very thoroughly by others.[3] This does not mean that there are agreed results. It will be necessary in this section to agree with some scholars, to disagree with others, and to offer a few relatively new conclusions. Reasons for these judgments will be indicated briefly, with references to the full tradition-historical and redaction-critical discussions provided by previous writers. The focus, naturally, will be on the light the Gospels might throw on the role of the relatives of Jesus after his death and resurrection, but their historical relationship to him during the ministry will not be irrelevant to that.

(1) Mark's Gospel gives the impression of a complete rift between Jesus and his family. During his ministry Jesus no longer lives in Nazareth, but has made his home in Caper-

(2) Bagatti (1969) 13 (cf [1971B] 20) claims that an addition to Ap. Const. 2:63 reads: 'Jude and James were farmers. So narrate Hegesippus and Tertullian the Roman.' The text is: οἱ δὲ περὶ Ἰούδαν Ἰακώβου γῆς ἐργάται: 'those who belonged to Judas of James [were] workers of the soil'. The reference which follows to Hegesippus *and Tertullian* shows that the information comes from Eusebius, *HE* 3:20 (the reference to Tertullian in 3:20:7 has been misunderstood), i.e. from Hegesippus' story about the grandsons of Jude. Jude is called 'Judas of James' because he has been identified with the apostle so described in Luke 6:16; Acts 1:13 (so also Ephraem in Harris [1894] 37–38).

(3) Bagatti (1971B) 20, claims that, according to Epiphanius Monachus, *De vita B. Virg.* (PG 120:204), Jude returned to Nazareth to preside over the church. No such statement is found in the text.

[3] See the studies to which the following footnotes refer. For the Synoptics, there is a very full bibliography in Oberlinner (1975).

naum (Mark 2:1; 3:20; 7:17; 9:28). The house was perhaps
Peter's (1:29), but Mark treats it as Jesus' home. Only two
passages in the Gospel concern Jesus' relatives (3:19b–35; 6:1–
6) ...nd both portray them as disbelieving in Jesus' mission
from God.

Mark 3:19b–35 employs Mark's 'sandwich' method of
narration (cf. 5:21–43; 6:7–30; 11:12–25; 14:1–11) in which one
narrative is inserted between two phases of another. In this
case a narrative about Jesus' family (3:19b–21, 31–35) is inter-
rupted by the Beelzebul controversy (3:22–30). This structure
confirms the interpretation of οἱ παρ' αὐτοῦ in v 21 as Jesus'
family (rather than 'friends' or 'associates').[4] The effect of the
juxtaposition of the two incidents is to parallel the accusation
of Jesus' relatives ('he is beside himself,' v 21) with that of the
scribes ('he is possessed by Beelzebul,' v 22; 'he has an unclean
spirit,' v 30).[5] However, this does not make the family as
culpable as the scribes, since their motive is implied to be one
of concern for Jesus' welfare. Since he is not allowing himself
the opportunity even to eat (v 20),[6] they conclude that he
must be out of his mind and that it is their duty to protect
him from himself. They are not therefore condemned like
the scribes who misinterpret the work of the Spirit through
Jesus as the work of the devil.[7] But the parallel highlights the
two forms of opposition Jesus had to suffer: misunderstanding
from his relatives, slander from his religious opponents.

The response of Jesus to the news that his mother and his
brothers are in search of him is virtually to disown them. At
least, their blood-relationship gives them no right to remove
him from those who constitute his real family – those who
do the will of God. Given a choice between relatives who fail
to recognize his mission and those who throng to hear his
teaching in their eagerness to do God's will, the latter are
Jesus' true family (3:33–35). The natural family, we could

[4] Cf. Cranfield (1963) 133; Lane (1974) 138 n. 75, 139.
[5] For discussion of the parallel, see Brown *et al.* (1978) 54–58.
[6] I am not convinced by the attempt of Crossan (1973) 83–84, to discon-
nect 3:21 from 3:20; cf. Lambrecht (1974) 249.
[7] Against Crossan (1973) 87–96; cf. Lambrecht (1974) 244–246.

say, is replaced by the 'eschatological family' called into being by Jesus' preaching of the kingdom.[8]

The impression of a complete rift between Jesus and his family is confirmed by Mark's account of the visit to Nazareth (6:1–6). Here not only do the Nazarenes find it difficult to accept Jesus as a prophet because they know his family origins as one like themselves (6:3). It is also clear that the family of Jesus themselves do not believe. This is evident from v 4, where a saying known elsewhere in a shorter form (Luke 4:24; John 4:44; GThom 31; Pap.Oxy. 1:32–33) has been expanded probably by Mark himself in order to include reference to Jesus' family.[9]

We might wonder whether in fact Mark created the picture of a rift between Jesus and his family which was not in his sources. Might he not have constructed 3:19b–21, 31–33 in order to provide a setting for the saying in 3:34–35, which by itself need not imply such a rift?[10] (At least in its present form the saying presupposes some reference to Jesus' actual mother and brothers: otherwise there would be no reason for singling out these particular family relationships and omitting father.) However, the independent tradition (as I take it to be) in John 7:5 also attests that Jesus' brothers did not believe in him. So we may presume that the Markan picture has a historical basis, though Mark has presented the family's disbelief in Jesus in a heightened and peculiarly stark form.[11] As for Mark's motive in emphasizing this point, some have suggested that it is a polemical one, aimed against the jurisdictional role of the Jerusalem church in early Christianity, which Mark takes the relatives of Jesus to represent.[12] Mark was opposed

[8] Brown *et al.* (1978) 53.

[9] Cf. Crossan (1973) 102–104; differently Oberlinner (1975) 300–312.

[10] Lambrecht (1974) 249–251, who believes Mark used Q, suggests that the Q passage (if it is) in Luke 11:27–28 was Mark's sole basis in tradition for 3:20–21, 31–35. On the other hand, Oberlinner (1975) 154–183, considers only 3:20–21 and parts of the narrative framework of 3:31–35 to be redactional.

[11] Similarly Pratscher (1987) 15.

[12] Kilpatrick (1982) 7; much more fully Crossan (1973); others mentioned in Oberlinner (1975) 240–241 nn.

to the role which the relatives of Jesus, especially James, played in the early church. While this is possible, it is more likely that Mark is interested in portraying Jesus as a precedent for his followers, who have to face opposition and mis-understanding from their families and to renounce natural family ties which would hinder their discipleship (cf. 1:20; 13:12).[13] The saying in Mark 10:29–30 indicates that just as Jesus identified those who do God's will as his true relatives, so disciples of Jesus who have renounced their natural rela-tionships find new relatives in the community of Jesus' true brothers and sisters.[14]

(2) The Markan picture of Jesus' relationship with his family is not significantly altered by Matthew. He makes more explicit the fact that Jesus left the family home in Nazareth and made his home in Capernaum (4:13; cf. 9:1). At first sight his redaction of the two Markan passages about the relatives of Jesus might suggest that he deliberately plays down the family's disbelief, but in fact this is unlikely. It is true that he does not take over Mark 3:19b–21, with the result that in Matthew 12.46 (‖ Mark 3:31) no motive is attributed to Jesus' mother and brothers in asking to see him. But Mark 3:19b–21 is probably simply a casualty of Mat-thew's conflation of his sources. In Matthew 12:22–50 Mat-thew is combining two blocks of material in his sources: Mark 3:19b–35 and the Q material which Luke reproduces in Luke 11:14–23 (cf. also Luke 12:10). These two sources overlapped in that both had a version of the Beelzebul con-troversy (Mark 3:22–27; Luke 11:14–23) and each had a saying about Jesus' mother of a similar nature (Mark 3:31–35; Luke 11:27–28).[15] Matthew conflates the two versions of

[13] Cf. Lambrecht (1974) 257–258.

[14] Cf. Crossan's account of Mark's redactional activity in 10:29–30 as a deliberate echo of 3:35: Crossan (1973) 98.

[15] I assume that Luke 11:27–28 stood in Q at the point where Luke has it. Alternatively, Luke may have substituted it for Mark 3:31–35, which he had already used in 8:19–21 (Marshall [1978] 481). Against this, however, is the fact that Luke's version of the Beelzebul controversy (11:14–26) seems to be pure Q, not (like Matthew's) a conflation of Mark and Q. So there is no reason to suppose that Luke is here following Mark 3 at all.

the Beelzebul controversy (12:22–32) and prefers the
Markan saying about Jesus' family (Matt 12:46–50 ‖ Mark
3:31–35) to the briefer Q version (Luke 11:27–28). But Mark
3:19b–21, which probably seemed to Matthew little more
than an introduction to the Beelzebul controversy, is
rejected in favour of the more relevant account of an exorcism which prefaced the Q version of the Beelzebul controversy (Matt 12:22–23 ‖ Luke 11:14). Thus Matthew's
failure to retain the Markan motive of the family of Jesus
in Matthew 12:46 may not have been very deliberate.[16] His
deliberate redaction of Mark 3:31–35 consists in applying
the saying to the disciples of Jesus (Matt 12:49) rather than
to the crowd (Mark 3:32, 34). This coheres with Matthew's
designation of the disciples as brothers of Jesus in 28:10 (and
25:40 according to one interpretation).

In the account of the visit to Nazareth (Matt 13:53–58 ‖
Mark 6:1–6) Matthew omits καὶ ἐν τοῖς συγγενεῦσιν αὐτοῦ
from Jesus' saying, but since he retains καὶ ἐν τῇ οἰκίᾳ αὐτοῦ
the meaning is not changed and Matthew may only be ab-
breviating. It is worth adding that, as well as retaining Mark
10:29–30 (Matt 19:29), Matthew includes Q sayings which
emphasize renunciation of family ties and division within
families (Matt 10:35 ‖ Luke 12:52–53; 10:37 ‖ Luke 14:26).

(3) The Markan impression of a rift between Jesus and his
family, which Matthew retains but with less emphasis, seems
to disappear in Luke.[17] It is hard to be sure whether this is
deliberate. Any suggestion of the family's disbelief is missing
from Luke's account of the visit to Nazareth (Luke 4:16–30),
but this may simply result from his following a different
source, which he here preferred to Mark for reasons which
had nothing to do with Jesus' relatives. Mark 3:19b–21 does
not appear in Luke, again no doubt because of his use of
sources. He prefers the Q version of the Beelzebul controversy
(11:14–23), and when he uses Mark 3:31–35 in a different

---

[16] Against Brown *et al.* (1978) 99.

[17] For a different view of Luke, see Kilpatrick (1982) 9–11. The relevance
of Luke 2:35 to this question is difficult to assess: cf. Kilpatrick (1982) 9–10;
Fitzmyer (1981A) 423, 429–430.

context from Mark's (Luke 8:19–21), he does so to reinforce the lesson of parables on hearing and doing the word of God (Luke 8:9–18). He redacts the Markan saying accordingly (Luke 8:21 || Mark 3:35). However, the suggestion that the Lukan version of this saying intends not to contrast the physical relatives of Jesus with his true relatives, but rather to cite his physical mother and brothers as examples of those who hear and obey the word of God,[18] is scarcely plausible because in the parallel Q saying, which Luke has in 11:27–28, there is indubitably a strong contrast (μενοῦν). It is those who hear the word of God and keep it who are blessed, *rather than* she who bore and suckled Jesus. The point is that blessedness in the kingdom of God depends not on physical relationship to Jesus but on obedience to God. In 8:19–21 and 11:27–28 the relatives of Jesus are mentioned only for the sake of this point: there is no interest in them themselves. At most one might suggest that Luke avoids any tension with his portrayal of Mary in the infancy narratives as one who did hear and obey the word of God.[19]

However, the absence of any hint in Luke of the family's opposition to Jesus means that the reader is not surprised and requires no explanation when they eventually appear in Luke's writings among the disciples of Jesus. Whereas Matthew and Mark never suggest that the family came to believe in Jesus (though their readers must, like everyone in the early church, have known that at any rate James did), Luke never suggests that they ever disbelieved in Jesus. So it is no surprise when Cleopas, who we have argued is probably Jesus' uncle, Joseph's brother Clopas, appears in Luke 24:18 as one of those followers of Jesus who had travelled with him from Galilee to Jerusalem. Admittedly, Luke does not mention his family relationship to Jesus, but the point of mentioning his name at all is probably that Luke's readers can be expected to

---

[18] Fitzmyer (1981A) 723, 725; Brown *et al.* (1978) 167–170.

[19] In the Lukan infancy narrative, Mary is 'blessed' (1:42, 45), not simply because of her physical relationship to Jesus, but because her motherhood of Jesus is her obedience to God's gracious choice of her. 11:28 is *consistent* with this, but it is going too far to say that it 'stresses that Jesus' mother is worthy of a beatitude' (Brown *et al.* [1978] 172).

know who he is. Then the mother of Jesus and his brothers are included, with the women disciples and the apostles, in the group of the followers of Jesus who stayed together in Jerusalem between the ascension and Pentecost (Acts 1:14). Finally, Jesus' brother James (not hitherto named by Luke) appears for the first time as leader of the Jerusalem church in Acts 12:17 (and subsequently in 15:13; 21:18): his relationship to Jesus was too well known for Luke to need to mention it.

(4) If Matthew and Mark gave the impression of a complete rift and Luke of complete harmony between Jesus and his relatives, John alone among the evangelists presents a more complex picture. At the beginning of the Galilean ministry, Jesus' mother and brothers are closely associated with Jesus and his disciples and travel from place to place with them (2:1–2, 12). In 7:1–10 Jesus is in communication with his brothers and it is expected that they should travel to Jerusalem for the feast together, but John also states that the brothers 'did not believe in him' (v 5), because they wanted him to make public proof of his claims in Jerusalem. John probably intends at this point to associate the brothers with the many disciples who had abandoned Jesus, according to 6:66. The brothers do not reappear in the Gospel,[20] but the group of women at the cross (19:25) include two or three relatives of Jesus: his mother, the wife of his uncle Clopas, and another aunt, his mother's sister, if this woman is distinct from 'Mary of Clopas.' Whatever else the words of Jesus to his mother and to the beloved disciple (19:26–27)[21] may indicate for the evangelist, they surely represent the full acceptance of Jesus' physical relatives into the circle of Jesus' disciples, who are called his brothers in 20:17. To argue that if James and the other brothers of Jesus had been sons or even step-sons of Mary, Jesus would not have entrusted his mother to the care of

[20] If this were a matter of polemic against Jewish Christianity (cf. Brown *et al.* [1978] 201; cf. Brown [1978] 13), it is odd to find 'Mary of Clopas' at the cross (19:25). She was the mother of the most prominent Palestinian Jewish leader, the successor to James in Jerusalem, at the time when the Fourth Gospel was written.

[21] For a brief discussion of suggestions, see Brown *et al.* (1978) 210–218.

someone else,[22] is beside the point. With Jesus' death his earthly relationships to his natural family no longer count. The risen Christ's brothers are his disciples (20:17). Mary, who loses her physical son Jesus as he dies on the cross, finds another within the community of the disciples. John 19:26 is an acted version of Mark 10:29–30.

(5) The canonical Gospels show little interest (at least outside the infancy narratives of Matthew and Luke) in the relatives of Jesus for their own sake. Their names are sometimes given because they were well known in the early church. But the traditions that concern them are recounted for the sake of their teaching about Christian discipleship. They function neither to support nor to oppose the role which the relatives of Jesus played in the early church. The Gospel of Thomas provides in this respect a contrast. It includes a saying of Jesus which explicitly legitimates the preeminent position of James as Palestinian Jewish Christianity understood it:

> The disciples said to Jesus, 'We know that you will depart from us. Who is to be our leader?' Jesus said to them, 'Wherever you are, you are to go to James the righteous, for whose sake heaven and earth came into being' (GThom 12).[23]

The presence of this saying in Thomas should be explained by the Jewish Christian origins of at least parts of the Gospel tradition which Thomas represents.[24] Presumably the saying must have originated during James' lifetime, and provides a most valuable insight into the position of unique authority which he was accorded in Jewish Christian circles which revered the mother church in Jerusalem and acknowledged the authority of its leader even over churches established outside Palestine. In its context in the Gospel of Thomas, this authority of James has been relativized by the saying which follows, in which, it would seem, higher authority is given

---

[22] Lightfoot (1892) 24–25; on this question, see Oberlinner (1975) 73, 125–135.

[23] Translation from Robinson (1977) 119. On this saying, see Wilson (1960) 124–126; Pratscher (1987) 151–157.

[24] For an account of the state of discussion on the origins of the Gospel's tradition, see Fallon and Cameron (1988) 4213-4224.

to the secret teaching attributed to Thomas. It seems we have evidence here of the development of the tradition behind this Gospel from Jewish Christian origins in a Gnostic – or at least encratite – direction. But it is noteworthy that the saying about James has not been dropped from the tradition.

The Gospel of Thomas is also notable for its parallels with Synoptic sayings about the renunciation or irrelevance of natural family relationships. Logion 99 is a parallel to Mark 3:31–35 and logion 79 is a parallel to Luke 11:27–28 (combined with Luke 23:29): both retain the sense that natural relationship to Jesus does not count in the kingdom of his Father. To the Q saying about the renunciation of family relationships (Matt 10:37 ‖ Luke 14:26) there are two parallels (both closer to the harsher Lukan form) in logia 55 and 101. In the latter Jesus declares himself the model for 'hating' father and mother:

> Whoever does not hate his father and his mother as I do cannot become a disciple to me. And whoever does [not] love his father and his mother as I do cannot become a [disciple] to me. For my mother [. . .], but [my] true [mother] gave me life (GThom 101).[25]

(This version in logion 101 may be a development from the version in logion 55, where 'as I do' is used of taking up the cross, cf. Matt 10:38 ‖ Luke 14:27.) In this version Jesus rejects his earthly parents in favour of his heavenly Father and Mother: his disciples are to do the same. GThom 105, which has no parallel in the canonical Gospels, should also be considered along with these sayings:

> He who knows the father and the mother will be called the son of a harlot.[26]

This suggests that the Jewish charge of illegitimacy against Jesus was due to his acknowledgment of his heavenly Father and Mother (rather than – presumably – his supposed earthly parents). Again Jesus is taken as a model for his disciples preferring heavenly to earthly relationships. The prominence

---

[25] Translation from Robinson (1977) 128–129.
[26] Translation from Robinson (1977) 129.

of such sayings in Thomas reflects the ascetic and encratite tendencies of the East Syrian Christian tradition in which this Gospel belongs. What is noteworthy for our present purpose is that they coexist with logion 12. Admittedly, caution is needed in drawing conclusions from this, because the sayings in Thomas may derive from more than one source. Some at least of the sayings we have just discussed may derive from the canonical Gospels. We cannot be sure how far back in the oral tradition the coexistence of these sayings with logion 12 goes. However, it does seem likely that, within a tradition which retained a high regard for the authority of James, the preeminence of the Lord's brother was not felt inconsistent with sayings that sharply devalue physical relationship to Jesus. This should warn us against interpreting the presence of sayings of the latter type in the Synoptic Gospels as polemic against James and his circle.

(6) Finally, one of the fragments of the second-century Jewish Christian Gospel of the Hebrews (fragment 7),[27] offers an account of the resurrection appearance to James, which is otherwise known only from Paul's bare reference to it in the traditional list of appearances in 1 Corinthians 15:7 (where the Lord's brother must be meant, as the only James to whom such a reference would be unambiguous). In this narrative James is represented as having already been, before the crucifixion of Jesus, not merely a disciple of Jesus, but a disciple whose faith extended to a vow, made at the last supper, to fast until such time as he saw the risen Lord. There is also a clear implication that James was the first person to whom Jesus appeared after his resurrection. All these details seem due to the strong later Jewish Christian tendency (evident also in the traditions recorded by Hegesippus) to glorify the figure of James. There is probably no conscious polemical intention of exalting James above, say, Peter (who appears first in 1 Cor 15:5). Rather it is taken for granted that the preeminent position James later held, for those who attributed

[27] Latin text in Klijn (1988) 4011 (from Jerome, *de vir. ill.* 2); English translation in Vielhauer (1963) 165. For the significance of the account, see Pratscher (1987) 46–48.

supreme authority to the Jerusalem church, must date back to the time of Jesus' ministry and resurrection.

From this analysis of the Gospels we may draw the following conclusions:

(1) During his ministry Jesus' relationship with his family was not entirely smooth (Mark 3:19b–21; 6:4; John 7:5). At least for part of the ministry they were not among his followers. This point has perhaps been often overstressed, through an excessive and uncritical reliance on the Markan redaction, but it undoubtedly has some genuine historical basis.

(2) According to both the Markan and Q traditions Jesus expected renunciation of family relationships as part of the cost of discipleship (Mark 10:29; Matt 10:35 || Luke 12:52–53; Matt 10:37 || Luke 14:26; cf. GThom 55, 101), and it is not unreasonable to suppose that this was also the cost to himself of his own mission. In addition, both the Markan and Q traditions attest that Jesus taught that in the kingdom of God what counts is not natural relationship to himself, but doing the will of God (Mark 3:31–35; Luke 11:27–28; cf. GThom 99, 79). (The Johannine tradition also seems to suggest that natural relationship to Jesus is transcended in the community of his disciples [John 19:26–27; 20:17], and may here be reflecting in its own way the same theme in the Gospel traditions as Mark 3:31–35; Luke 11:27–28 do.)

(3) At least by the time of his last visit to Jerusalem, Jesus' relatives – his mother, brothers, his uncle Clopas and his wife, and probably another aunt – had joined his followers. This is in fact better attested than (1), since independent traditions in the Lukan writings (Luke 24:18; Acts 1:14) and John (19:25–27) are confirmed by Paul's reference to a resurrection appearance to James (1 Cor 15:7; cf. GHeb 7). If James were in no sense a follower of Jesus until he met the risen Christ, this resurrection appearance would be comparable only to the appearance to Paul. It is more likely to imply that James already belonged to the circle of the disciples of Jesus.

(4) The references to and naming of relatives of Jesus in the Gospel traditions indicates that they were well-known figures in the early church. This applies not only to the four

brothers of Jesus, but also to his mother Mary, his mother's sister, his uncle Clopas/Cleopas and Clopas's wife Mary.

(5) However, though they were clearly people who would be known by reputation to the readers of the Gospels, in the canonical Gospels interest in them for their own sake is very limited. The traditions in which they are mentioned or named are retained and developed by the evangelists for paraenetic purposes with reference to the nature of Christian discipleship. The traditions which denigrate natural relationship to Jesus probably have this significance, rather than the intention of polemicizing against the role which the relatives of Jesus played in the leadership of the Palestinian church. The canonical Gospels are neither critical of this role nor interested in providing it with support from the Gospel traditions. This circumstance probably indicates that by the time the canonical Gospels were written and in the areas in which they were written, the authority of the relatives of Jesus was no longer a live issue. The leaders of the Palestinian churches were no longer influential in the churches from which the canonical Gospels come, and the *de facto* independence of these churches from the mother church of Jerusalem was now taken for granted. By contrast, the Gospel of the Hebrews and the Gospel of Thomas come from circles which had always been more closely attached to the Jerusalem church leadership and where the relatives of Jesus were figures of real influence in the period of the development of the Gospel tradition.

II. Travelling missionaries

Only once in his letters does Paul mention the brothers of Jesus other than James, but this reference (1 Cor 9:5), at first sight merely incidental, proves very informative. Paul is maintaining that, although he has waived his right as an apostle to be supported by his converts at Corinth, he has this right, just as much as the other apostles do. It was an accepted principle in the early church that travelling missionaries had a right to food and hospitality on their travels, from the Christian communities among whom they worked. Evidently, it was also accepted that such support should be extended to their wives, if they accompanied them on their travels. Both rights, to food and drink and to be accompanied by a wife, Paul attributes to 'the rest of the apostles and the brothers of the Lord and Cephas.' The apostles, in Paul's terminology, are certainly a larger body than the twelve: they include all who had received a commission to preach the Gospel from the risen Christ himself.[28] Whether Cephas (Peter) was personally known to the Corinthians is disputed (cf. 1:12): the reference to him here need not imply that. Rather Paul here wishes to associate himself not only generally with the rest of the apostles, but specifically with people whose claim to apostleship and its rights was unquestioned and unquestionable. Peter, who by this time had become very much an itinerant missionary, had impeccable apostolic credentials, disputed by noone, and was much the best-known name among the twelve. For Paul to mention Peter in this context was an obvious choice.

That the other individuals singled out for mention are the brothers of Jesus is of considerable interest. Like Peter, they must have been engaged in travelling missionary work from the early days of the church, so that their status as apostles and accepted right to support as apostles were as well-known as Peter's. We may wonder whether James is included here. People, like perhaps some of the twelve, whose mission was confined to Jerusalem would be no less apostles because they did not travel, and they were not really excluded from the principle to which Paul appeals: they had a right to support from the Jerusalem church and even from visitors to Jerusalem converted through their ministry. Yet Paul does speak specifically of *travelling* (περιάγειν) with a wife, because his concern is with the principle as it would apply to himself and Barnabas. He is unlikely to have thought of referring, as particularly weighty instances of his point, to people who were not known as *travelling* missionaries. This makes it unlikely that when he refers to the brothers of the Lord he has James primarily in mind. Our knowledge, of course, is not sufficient to rule out the possibility that James did engage

[28] Dunn (1975) 272–275.

in some travelling missionary work within Palestine. But his rise to eminence in Jerusalem must have been partly due to the fact that, unlike many of the twelve, he remained in the city and devoted himself to ministry there. Certainly by the time Paul wrote 1 Corinthians James cannot have been known in the church at large primarily as a travelling missionary. So it is likely that the brothers of the Lord come to Paul's mind as particularly good examples of his point because of the reputation of the *other brothers* as travelling missionaries.

That Paul includes the brothers of the Lord within the general category of apostles is clear (and resolves the rather more ambiguous language of Gal 1:19[29]). Since he certainly cannot mean that Cephas is not an apostle, it is natural to take 'and the brothers of the Lord and Cephas,' not as additions to 'the rest of the apostles,' but as examples of them. Moreover, Paul's point that he as an apostle has the same rights as other apostles could not be advanced by referring to people who were not apostles. It is true that in early Christian literature the brothers of the Lord are never explicitly called apostles, but this is doubtless because they were generally known by another term − 'brothers of the Lord' − which not only described them more closely but also indicated that they ranked with the apostles in status and ministry. Because they were recognized as exercising apostolic authority, the term 'brother of the Lord' became a reference to that authority, as well to their family relationship to Jesus. Just as the Provost of King's College, Cambridge, holds an equivalent position to the Masters of most other Cambridge colleges, but is not correctly called Master because in his case his title is Provost, so the brothers of the Lord had the same authority as the apostles, but were not normally called apostles.

It is worth noting that, if Paul regarded all four brothers of the Lord as apostles, then probably this means they had all received an apostolic commission from the risen Lord himself in a resurrection appearance. We know that James, like Peter, was the recipient of an individual resurrection appearance (1 Cor 15:7). It is not unlikely that the other brothers were

[29] Cf. Bruce (1979) 89; (1982) 100-101.

present with other disciples on another occasion, such as the appearance to five hundred disciples (1 Cor 15:6). This throws doubt, therefore, on Stauffer's argument that James' unique position in the early church, which he exploited in his rise to leadership of the Jerusalem church, lay in the combination of the two facts that he was a brother of the Lord and that the risen Lord had appeared to him.[30] Stauffer's argument could be modified, however, by qualifying both of the facts: James was the eldest brother of the Lord, and the Lord had appeared to him *individually*, as not to the others.

That the Lord's brothers and Peter had the right to be accompanied on their missionary journeys by a wife does not prove that all of them exercised that right, but it is likely, from Paul's specific mention of this right and his instancing them as examples, that some of them did. Their travels must have been extensive enough, in distance and time, for this to be a common practice. We cannot tell from Paul's language whether they had homes, from which they made missionary journeys for periods long enough to wish to take their wives with them, or whether they were permanently on the move from place to place, with no fixed home base, as Theissen envisages the wandering charismatic preachers of early Palestinian Christianity to have been.[31] At any rate, the model Theissen derives from the Gospels, of people who had completely abandoned homes and families cannot quite apply to missionaries who took their wives with them. 1 Corinthians 9:5 throws perhaps a little doubt on the view that the circumstances of the disciples during the ministry of Jesus, as the Gospels depict them, are an exact reflection of the way of life of the early Christian missionaries in Palestine after the resurrection. Specifically with regard to the Lord's brothers, our next piece of evidence will indicate that they did retain homes, from which they undertook missionary journeys. Paul's language is not inconsistent with this.

During the first half of the third century, Julius Africanus, in his *Letter to Aristides*, wrote of the *desposynoi* ['those who

[30] Stauffer (1952) 198.
[31] Theissen (1978) 8–16; cf. Schottroff and Stegemann (1986) 45–51.

belong to the Master'] – a term which, he explains, was used to designate the relatives of Jesus – that they preserved their family genealogy and interpreted it wherever they went on their travels throughout Palestine:

> From the Jewish villages of Nazareth and Kokhaba they travelled around the rest of the land[32] and interpreted the genealogy they had [from the family tradition] and from the Book of Days [i.e. Chronicles] as far as they could trace it [or: as far as they went on their travels] (*ap.* Eusebius, *HE* 1:7:14).

This sentence and the longer report about the genealogy of Jesus to which it belongs will be fully discussed in chapter 7 (section III), where reasons will be given for supposing that Julius Africanus is closely following a Palestinian Jewish Christian source which claimed to preserve tradition from the relatives of Jesus. In its context it is natural to take the sentence about the travels of the *desposynoi* as referring to the first Christian generation in the earliest period of the church, or at least as referring to a period from that time onwards. In that case its reliability can be supported from its coherence with Paul's information about the brothers of the Lord. The travels of which it speaks will certainly not have been exclusively for the purpose of expounding the family genealogy, although, as we shall see in chapter 7, the genealogy probably played a significant part in their presentation of the Christian message. The reference is to the same missionary travels which are presupposed as well-known by Paul in 1 Corinthians 9:5, but whereas Paul's statement allows no certain deduction about the area of the missionary work of the Lord's brothers, the tradition quoted by Julius Africanus gives some geographical precision. Their field of mission was in Palestine, and the home bases from which they undertook missionary journeys were Nazareth and Kokhaba. As in 1 Corinthians 9:5, James can scarcely be included, since he was based in Jerusalem. But whereas 1 Corinthians 9:5 refers only to the brothers of the Lord, the tradition known to Africanus probably intends to refer to a wider circle of Jesus' relatives (which would include,

---

[32] Surely not, as Schoeps (1949) 283 supposes, the whole world.

for example, Clopas and Symeon). Since the term 'brothers of the Lord' was itself the standard term in use in Palestinian Jewish Christianity for Jesus' brothers, the term *desposynoi* must have been used for the sake of its wider reference. It occurs only in this passage of Julius Africanus, but since it is not the term he himself uses for the relatives of Jesus when composing freely (cf. *HE* 1:7:11) and when he does use it here he finds it necessary to explain its meaning, it must have been the term used in Palestinian Jewish Christian circles.

Some scholars, most notably Harnack,[33] have correctly read Africanus' statement as referring to the earliest period of the Palestinian church, but probably a majority have supposed that Africanus is referring to his own time or at least a period much later than the first generation. The reasons for this seem to be two: (1) Earlier in the *Letter* Africanus reports another Jewish Christian tradition, allegedly from the relatives of Jesus, about the genealogy of Jesus. This tradition concerns the reconciliation of the two divergent genealogies of Jesus which we have in the Gospels of Matthew and Luke. Whether or not this tradition presupposes the existence of the canonical Gospels, rather than simply the circulation in Palestine of the two genealogies which they contain, the tradition would seem to be a relatively late one. If the tradition Africanus reports, in the sentence quoted above, means that the *desposynoi* travelled around Palestine explaining the way in which the two divergent genealogies of Jesus should be reconciled, then it would almost certainly have to refer to a period after the first generation. In fact, however, as we shall see in chapter 7, Africanus has brought together two quite distinct traditions about the family of Jesus and their genealogy. The sentence quoted above, which refers simply to the family genealogy, not to two divergent genealogies, has no original connection with the explanation of the two genealogies Africanus had reported earlier. Its date and reliability can be assessed quite independently.

(2) The name Kokhaba (Κωχαβα), given by Julius Africanus as one of the two villages from which the *desposynoi*

[33] Harnack (1908) 99.

travelled throughout Palestine has sometimes been identified with Kokhaba in Batanea,[34] to the East of the Jordan, which was a centre of Jewish Christianity at a later date. To associate the *desposynoi* of the first Christian generation with this Kokhaba would be most improbable. But the matter requires more careful consideration.

A place called Kokhaba (Κωκάβη: Epiphanius, *Pan.* 29:7:7; 30:18:1; 30:2:8–9; 40:1:5; in 29:7:7: 'Κωκάβη, called Χωχάβη in Hebrew') occurs in Epiphanius as one of the main centres of both Nazarene and Ebionite Jewish Christianity. It is located in Basanitis or Batanea,[35] and should be identified with the modern Kaukab, just north of the northern border of modern Jordan.[36] Eusebius (*Onomasticon* 172) refers to another place with the similar name of Khoba (Χωβά) as an Ebionite village. Eusebius locates it fairly precisely: 'Khoba which is to the left of Damascus. There is also a village of Khoba in the same district in which there are Hebrews who believe in Christ, called Ebionites.' This appears to distinguish two places called Khoba in the area of Damascus. The first may be modern Kabun, just north ('to the left') of Damascus.[37] It is possible that the second, Ebionite Khoba is actually the same as the Kokhaba of Epiphanius[38] and that Eusebius mistook its location (Batanea can hardly be accurately described as in the area of Damascus), as well as perhaps confusing its name with the Khoba north of Damascus. But it is also possible that Eusebius' Ebionite village is the modern Kaukab which is fifteen kilometres southwest of Damascus[39] (it is the place where medieval Christians located Paul's conversion[40]). In that case we should have to suppose that

---

[34] E.g. Lohmeyer (1936) 53–54; Meyer and Bauer (1963) 424; Gunther (1973) 94; Freyne (1980) 352–353.

[35] Epiphanius, *Pan.* 30:2:8. This clear and accurate geographical statement by Epiphanius indicates that he is unlikely to be purely dependent on Eusebius for his knowledge of Kokhaba, as Klijn and Reinink (1973) 29, 37, 71, think.

[36] Bagatti (1971B) 25; cf. Harnack (1908) 103 n. 2.

[37] Harnack (1908) 103 n. 2.

[38] Schoeps (1949) 273.

[39] Bagatti (1971B) 25.

[40] Harnack (1908) 103 n. 2.

Ebionites spread from their main centre in Batanea north to Khoba/ Kokhaba near Damascus. This would not be surprising, apart from the coincidence of the names, to which we shall return.

Julius Africanus, however, associates Kokhaba with Nazareth, and there are two places of this name not far from Nazareth. One, to the southwest, is modern Kokhav Hayarden or Kaukab el-Hawa, site of the Crusader fortress of Belvoir,[41] but closer to Nazareth, in the hills north of Sepphoris, sixteen kilometres from Nazareth, is the modern village of Kaukab, which should surely be identified as the Kokhaba of Julius Africanus.[42] (According to Bagatti, there are remains which indicate occupation in the Byzantine period, and perhaps a church on the site of the present mosque.[43]) That this, rather than the transjordanian Kokhaba, must be the home of the *desposynoi*, along with Nazareth, would never have been disputed, had it not seemed too much of a coincidence for both Kokhabas to be Jewish Christian centres.[44] The coincidence is less remarkable when it is observed that Kokhaba was a rather common Palestinian place name, but there is a further consideration which may make us wonder whether in fact the apparent coincidence does not reflect a deliberate choice by the Jewish Christian émigrés who established their centre at Kokhaba in Batanea.

The Semitic name, of course, means 'star,' a word fraught with messianic significance in the period (as Bar Kokhba, the messianic pun on the name of Simon bar Kosiba, reminds us). It would have suggested Balaam's prophecy of the star (*kôkāb*) of Jacob in Numbers 24:17.[45] But we also know that Nazareth was probably related, by means of the pesher-like pun, to the prophecy of the messianic branch (*nēṣer*) from the roots of Jesse (Isa 11:1). By means of this pun, Jesus' otherwise

---

[41] Bagatti (1971A) 291–296.

[42] So Harnack (1908) 103 n. 2; Bagatti (1969) 19; (1971A) 124–125; (1971B) 21.

[43] Bagatti (1971A) 122–125.

[44] Lüdemann (1980) 254 n. 70.

[45] On the messianic use of this text in Judaism, see Daniélou (1964) 102–123 = Daniélou (1957).

distinctly unmessianic home town (cf. John 1:46; 7:41–42) was given messianic prophetic significance (Matt 2:23).[46] Probably also the term Nazarenes as a designation of the Jewish Christians (Acts 24:5) was accepted because it was associated with this messianic pun and so later became the standard term for the non-Ebionite Jewish Christians.[47] Not only were the two texts Number 24:17 and Isaiah 11:1 individually popular messianic texts both in pre-Christian Judaism (for Num 24:17 see: CD 7:18–21; 4QTest 9–13; 1QM 11:6–7; TLevi 18:3;[48] and for Isa 11:1 see: 4QPBless; 4QFlor 1:11–12; 4QpIsa[a] frag. A; cf. allusions to other parts of Isa 11:1–5 in 1QSb 5:24; PssSol 17:35–37; 1 Enoch 49:3; 62:2) and in early Christianity (for Num 24:17 see: Matt 2:2, 9–10; and the archeological evidence for the star as a Palestinian Jewish Christian symbol;[49] for Isa 11:1 see: Rom 15:12; Rev 5:5; cf. allusions to other parts of Isa 11:1–5 in John 1:33; 2 Thes 2:8; Rev 19:15).[50] They were also sometimes closely associated (TJud 24:1–6; Rev 22:16; Justin, *1 Apol.* 32:12–13; *Dial.* 126:1; cf. *Dial.* 106:4).[51] It seems a remarkable coincidence that the two bases of the mission of the *desposynoi* should have names which could be connected with the two titles – Star and Branch – that these two prophecies gave to the Davidic Messiah. Perhaps some of the family did happen to live in Kokhaba, but it was its name which led the *desposynoi* to give this village the status, along with Nazareth, of a centre for their mission. Then, given the significance they would have seen in the name Kokhaba, we can readily suppose that the Kokhaba of Batanea became a centre for Jewish Christians who

[46] Cf. Lindars (1961) 194–196, on this text.

[47] Pritz (1988) 12–15.

[48] See also the Targumim in Levey (1974) 21–27.

[49] Testa (1962) 48–50, 282–288.

[50] Lindars (1961) 201–203, minimizes the role of Isa 11:1–5 in early Christianity, in line with his view that Jesus' Davidic origin was not a matter of Christian interest at first. But it is doubtful whether we can be so confident about which texts were or were not used in the earliest period.

[51] On these texts in Justin, see Daniélou (1964) 106–107; Skarsaune (1987) 50–52, 264–265. Skarsaune argues that Justin's use of these texts stems from Jewish Christian tradition.

moved east of the Jordan precisely because of its name.[52] The same can be said for the Khoba/Kokhaba which Eusebius locates near Damascus, if this is in fact a third Jewish Christian Kokhaba.[53]

The story of the Christian mission as Luke tells it in Acts is schematized according to the pattern announced in 1:8: 'in Jerusalem and in all Judea and Samaria and to the ends of the earth.' The mission of the apostles is confined to Jerusalem until the persecution following the martyrdom of Stephen scatters the Hellenists, at least, through Judea and Samaria (8:1) and further afield (11:19). Only in the wake of this scattering of the Hellenists are members of the twelve represented as engaged in mission outside Jerusalem (8:14–25; 9:32–10:48). This schematized account preserves an important aspect of the history, as Hengel's important essay on the origins of the Christian mission shows.[54] For the earliest Jewish Christian community Jerusalem had a special theological significance as the place of the coming of eschatological salvation, to which in the messianic age Israelites and Gentiles would come, according to such prophecies as Isaiah 2:2–3. Moreover this eschatological significance corresponded to the fact of Jerusalem's place at the centre of Judaism, to which not only Palestinian but also diaspora Jews were constantly coming on pilgrimage. It was to these that the mission of the apostles in Jerusalem was at first primarily directed. Luke's narrative also preserves, in somewhat muted form, the important contribution of the Hellenists to the extension of mission outside Jerusalem and especially to Gentiles.

Nevertheless, Hengel has not sufficiently recognized the onesidedness of Luke's scheme,[55] which obscures the probability of missionary activity throughout Palestine from the beginning. It is unlikely that Jesus' own missionary travels

---

[52] The claim that the first-century Samaritan sectarian Dositheus considered himself the star of Jacob of Num 24:17 and lived at Kokhaba (Daniélou [1964] 117) is based on a mistake: see Isser (1976) 8–9 n. 8, 119–120.

[53] For a very speculative treatment of possible links between Num 24:17 and this Kokhaba near Damascus, see Daniélou (1964) 116–123.

[54] Hengel (1983) 48–64.

[55] Cf. Hengel (1983) 60.

throughout his ministry and the mission on which he had sent out the disciples during his ministry, the historicity of which Hengel himself defends,[56] should have been entirely superseded by a mission purely in Jerusalem, until the Hellenists, rather than those who had participated in Jesus' own mission, extended it outside Jerusalem.[57] Not all of Jesus' Galilean disciples can have taken up permanent residence in Jerusalem or taken no interest in the apostolic commission to preach the Gospel. The evidence we have discussed for the missionary travels of the *desposynoi*, from their bases in Nazareth and Kokhaba, is an important qualification of the Lukan picture. It reveals an extensive Jewish Christian missionary activity which did not result from developments in Jerusalem, but could be regarded by Paul, writing to Corinth in the 50s, as a matter of common Christian knowledge. No doubt the *desposynoi* and other Galilee-based missionaries looked to Jerusalem as the mother church with a unique eschatological significance. But they also probably saw special messianic significance in the names of their own bases at Nazareth and Kokhaba.

It could even be said that Luke lends indirect support to the idea of an evangelization of Galilee independent of the movement of the Gospel out from Jerusalem which he depicts, in that he does not include Galilee in his notices of this movement (Acts 8:1, 5, 25, 40; 9:32, 38; 10:24; 11:19)[58] and yet, in his only mention of Galilee in Acts, indicates the presence of a well-established church there (9:31).[59] However, since the *desposynoi* are left so completely out of the Lukan story which constitutes our only systematic information about the early Christian mission, we can largely only speculate about the extent of their mission.[60] The tradition reported by

[56] Hengel (1981) 73–79.

[57] Cf. Theissen (1978) 7–11, who entirely rejects the Lukan scheme.

[58] Although 'Judaea' can sometimes be used of the whole of Palestine (Acts 10:37), this cannot be the meaning in 8:1, where Samaria is also mentioned.

[59] Cf. Lohmeyer (1936) 54. For suggested explanations of the silence of Acts on Galilee, see Freyne (1980) 345–346.

[60] Gunther, who (in [1980], despite his caution in [1974] 40) accepts the rather late patristic identification of the apostle Thaddeus with Jude the

Julius Africanus refers to the whole of Palestine: this must be seen as a later generalizing phrase, which need not include every part of Palestine nor exclude some missionary activity outside Palestine. Obvious places for missionary work based in Galilee would have been Phoenicia, Damascus, the Decapolis and other areas to the east of the Jordan. Schoeps suggested that an earlier evangelization of the Decapolis by Jewish Christian missionaries from Galilee may be the reason why refugees from the Jerusalem church later settled in Pella.[61] Lohmeyer[62] and Grundmann[63] suggested that the brothers of the Lord may have evangelized Damascus and account for the church which Paul found there more adequately than Hellenists recently fleeing from persecution in Jerusalem would do. At first sight this suggestion might seem to find support in a Coptic fragment of the second-century Acts of Paul, in which Paul, recalling his visit to Damascus after his conversion, says that he was there helped in the faith by Judas the Lord's brother.[64] However, this reference is probably no more than an imaginative identification of the Judas in whose house Paul lodged in Damascus (Acts 9:11) with Jude the Lord's brother. Like Jewish exegetes, later Christian readers of the New Testament loved to identify figures who bore the same name.

However, if these possibilities for the mission areas of the *desposynoi* outside Galilee must remain pure conjectures, there is one intriguing and neglected piece of evidence[65] which may indicate an even more extensive mission. In the list, given in medieval chronicles, of the early bishops of Ctesiphon-Seleucia on the Tigris, in central Mesopotamia, the three names following that of Mari, the late first-century founder of the church, are Abris, Abraham and Ya'qub

Lord's brother, draws on the traditions of Thaddeus' missionary travels ([1980] 140–144). But this identification is unlikely.

[61] Schoeps (1949) 270. Of course, this presumes some historical truth in the tradition of the flight of the Jerusalem church to Pella.

[62] Lohmeyer (1936) 54–56.

[63] Grundmann (1939) 45–46.

[64] Schneemelcher (1965) 388.

[65] Mentioned, without reflection, by Schoeps (1949) 283; Meyer and Bauer (1963) 425; Bagatti (1971B) 53.

(James).[66] Abris is said to have been 'of the family and race of Joseph' the husband of Mary, while Abraham was 'of the kin of James called a brother of the Lord' and Ya'qub was Abraham's son.[67] These persons should certainly not be dismissed as legendary simply because of their alleged descent from the family of Jesus.[68] Claims that particular individuals were descendants of the family of Jesus are extremely rare in Christian literature.[69] Such claims seem neither to have been made by historical individuals without foundation nor to have been attributed to legendary figures. So this feature is by no means obviously legendary. The name Abraham was not very common, but is by no means unknown,[70] among Jews of that period, while James, of course, was both a common Jewish name and a family name, borne not only by the Lord's brother but also by a grandson of Jude (see section V below).[71] Only if the three names had been Abraham, Isaac and Jacob would we have been justified in suspecting them!

Fiey has recently defended the basic historicity of the tradition that Mari, a disciple of Addai the apostle of Edessa, brought the Christian Gospel to Ctesiphon-Seleucia at the end of the first or beginning of the second century.[72] He considers the medieval lists of the bishops of Seleucia between Mari and Papa (310–329) to be to some extent artificial,[73]

---

[66] Fiey (1970) 64.

[67] Kmosko (1907) 666.

[68] Kmosko (1907) 666; Harnack (1908) 149 n. 3.

[69] Of course, apocryphal information about members of the family of Jesus of his own and previous generations is plentiful. But later descendants of the family are very rarely encountered. I know only of Symeon the son of Clopas, Zoker and James the grandsons of Jude, and Conon the martyr, all discussed in later sections of this chapter.

[70] Frey (1936) 693 (no. 504); Tcherikover and Fuks (1957) 204 (no. 50); (1960) 166 (no. 365), 167 (no. 374), 182 (no. 412), 215 (no. 428); (1964) 162 (no. 1530A); other examples in Wuthnow (1930) 10–11.

[71] Abris is perhaps Eber עבר = Ἔββρεος (Wuthnow [1930] 44, 154).

[72] Fiey (1970) 39–43. He argues that Mari must have come to Ctesiphon at some point before the Tigris changed its course, which happened some time between 79 and 116 A.D. Fiey's argument depends on his rejection of the authenticity of the *Chronicle of Arbela*.

[73] Between Ya'qub and Papa some lists have two names, some three.

though Papa certainly had predecessors.[74] The medieval chroniclers did have access to good older sources. Abris, Abraham and Ya'qub may not have been precisely bishops of Seleucia, but that they were Christian leaders in some capacity in that area in the second century seems entirely possible. The suggestion of a kind of dynastic succession is also strongly in favour of the historicity of the tradition, for it resembles the way leadership of the church had passed down in this family in Palestine, where James was succeeded in Jerusalem by his cousin Symeon and the grandsons of Jude are found presiding over the churches. Outside specifically Palestinian Jewish Christian tradition, this notion of a kind of dynastic tradition of church leadership by the relatives of Jesus is not found.[75]

The large Jewish diaspora in Mesopotamia and the close links between it and Palestinian Jews[76] means that there is nothing improbable in the idea that some of the *desposynoi*, in the late first or early second century, should have travelled there as missionaries and remained as church leaders. They would presumably have reached Ctesiphon-Seleucia quite independently of Mari's mission from Edessa, travelling no doubt along the major trade route through Damascus, Palmyra and Dura Europos.[77] In this way they would have continued the family tradition of missionary enterprise to which 1 Corinthians 9:5 testifies.

III. The Jerusalem bishops list

We must give some attention to the Jerusalem bishops list, since not only were the first two 'bishops' (James and Symeon) relatives of Jesus, but also it has been suggested that other names on the list may also be those of members of Jesus' family. The list is given by several ancient writers,

But this degree of uncertainty hardly throws doubt on the whole list of Papa's predecessors.

[74] Fiey (1970) 64–65.

[75] Cf. Stauffer (1952) 200.

[76] Neusner (1965) 41–43.

[77] For the development of this route from the first century B.C. to the second century A.D., see Rostovtzeff (1932) 31–32, 101–108.

	Jerusalem Bishops List		Letter of James to Quadratus	
	Eusebius	Epiphanius	Armenian	Syriac
1	Ἰάκωβος	Ἰάκωβος		
2	Συμεών	Συμεών		
3	Ἰοῦστος	Ἰούδας		
4	Ζακχαῖος	Ζαχαρίας		
5	Τωβίας	Τωβίας		
6	Βενιαμίν	Βενιαμίν		
7	Ἰωάννης	Ἰωάννης		
8	Ματθίας	Ματθίας		
9	Φίλιππος	Φίλιππος	Philip	Philip
10	Σενεκᾶς	Σενεκᾶς	Senikus	Senikus
11	Ἰοῦστος	Ἰοῦστος	Justus	Justus
12	Λευίς	Λευίς	Levi	Levi
13	Ἐφρής	Οὐαφρίς	Aphre	Aphre
14	Ἰωσήφ	Ἰωσίς		
15	Ἰούδας	Ἰούδας	Juda	

most importantly by Eusebius (*HE* 4:5:3–4; 5:12:1–2) and Epiphanius (*Pan.* 66:21–22).[78] Eusebius' list (which he gives in two parts at appropriate points in his narrative) consists of fifteen Jewish Christian bishops up to the Bar Kokhba war (*HE* 4:5:3) and fifteen Gentile bishops of the Gentile church of Jerusalem from 135 to c. 200.[79] The matching numbers show that the two parts of the list belong together and that it must have been compiled in the time of the fifteenth Gentile bishop, Narcissus. The duplication of some names (Maximus, Julian, Gaius) in the second part may indicate that the number of fifteen Gentile bishops has been artificially constructed to correspond to the fifteen bishops

[78] The two lists are set out synoptically in Harnack (1897) 223–225; Zahn (1900) 282–283. For variants in later versions of the list, see Harnack (1897) 220–221 n. 3.

[79] Though the list from Marcus to Narcissus in *HE* 5:12:1–2 claims to be of fifteen names, there are only thirteen in the extant text. But the names Maximus and Antoninus can be supplied, after Capito, from Eusebius' *Chronicon*.

from the circumcision.[80] In that case, the first part of the list must already have been a fixed tradition, inherited by the Gentile church of Jerusalem from Jewish Christian sources. Eusebius himself evidently obtained the whole list from the local records of the Jerusalem church (*HE* 5:12:2). Epiphanius' version of the list has some variations in the names, though not in the number, which probably indicate that his list is not derived from Eusebius.[81] Epiphanius, who lived much of his life in Palestine, had plenty of opportunity to obtain a version of the list from local sources.

Only the list of Jewish Christian bishops presently concerns us. Since the second person in the list, Symeon the son of Clopas, was martyred under Trajan (*HE* 3:32:1–6; and cf. section IV below), the thirteen names following his can scarcely be the names of thirteen bishops in linear succession before 134. Eusebius' explanation (which he claims to have from tradition, but which was probably only his own deduction from the fact that there were so many names in the list) that they were extremely shortlived (*HE* 4:5:1) will hardly suffice! Many other explanations of the list have been offered,[82] but new light has recently been thrown on the matter by van den Broek, who points out that six of the later names in the list occur in the apocryphal letter of James the Lord's brother to Quadratus, which is extant in Syriac and Armenian.[83] (The Armenian version has Philip, Senikus, Justus, Levi, Aphre and Judas; the Syriac lacks Judas: see the table.) The letter has no historical value itself, but van den Broek argues for its Jewish Christian character.[84] In any case, it seems to have drawn the six names from Jewish Christian tradition, independently of Eusebius. The six are described as 'respected scribes of the Jews,' converted to Christianity, 'to-

[80] So Ehrhardt (1953) 39–40.

[81] Cf. Harnack (1897) 225–226, against Schlatter's view that Epiphanius' list comes from Julius Africanus.

[82] Reported in Gunther (1973) 92–93; van den Broek (1988) 63–64; cf. also Schoeps (1949) 286–287; von Campenhausen (1950–51) 142.

[83] van den Broek (1988) 57–58, gives Vetter's translation of the Armenian, with variants from the Syriac.

[84] van den Broek (1988) 59–61.

gether with their other companions,' and now engaged in arguing from the Scriptures with non-Christian Jews in Jerusalem.[85] In other words, they are not later successors to James, but contemporaries of his, engaged with him in the Christian mission to Jews in Jerusalem. Even allowing for the chronological vagueness of many apocryphal works, it is unlikely that a reader of Eusebius' bishop list would have used these names in this way. If he was really thinking of men who later succeeded to James' position, one would expect him to use earlier names from Eusebius' list, whereas the names he gives are all but one of the last seven in Eusebius' list. We must conclude that these names were known to him in tradition as coworkers with James, rather than as later bishops of Jerusalem.

If we suppose the third name in Eusebius' list (Justus) to be the last Jewish Christian leader of the church in Jerusalem, who occupied the position between Symeon's martyrdom and the Bar Kokhba revolt, we are left with *twelve* names. These can then readily be understood as a college of twelve elders who presided over the Jerusalem church along with James. A list of these will have been subsequently misunderstood in the tradition as successors to James. With only Eusebius' list to guide us, we might have supposed, as Carrington suggested,[86] that the twelve were elders who presided along with the third bishop Justus immediately before the Bar Kokhba war, but the letter of James to Quadratus shows that they were known in tradition rather as coworkers with James.

As van den Broek points out, there is evidence, especially in the Jewish Christian traditions incorporated in the Pseudo-Clementines, for the idea that a monarchical bishop should have twelve presbyters associated with him in the leadership of a church (ClemRec 3:68; 6:15:4; ClemHom 11:36:2; cf. Testament of our Lord 1:34).[87] There were few, if any, such monarchical bishops in the New Testament period, but the

[85] van den Broek (1988) 58 (v. 10).
[86] Carrington (1957) 419.
[87] van den Broek (1988) 64–65 (including additional evidence).

preeminent position which James attained in the church of Jerusalem, if not precisely that of a later monarchical bishop, certainly came rather close to it. If James in fact had a college of twelve presbyters associated with him, it is understandable that later Jewish Christian tradition could have taken this as the model to which other churches ought to conform.

Whether James had a college of twelve presbyters and whether the tradition has correctly preserved their names are, of course, distinct questions. The first is not at all unlikely. From the narrative of Acts it seems that in the early years of the church the twelve apostles were based in Jerusalem, though some of them certainly made missionary journeys to other parts of Palestine, and were the effective leaders of the church in Jerusalem. James' rise to prominence, first in association with leading members of the twelve (Gal 2:9) and then in a more uniquely dominant position (Acts 21:18), was probably due to a number of factors, including his relative closeness to the more conservative wing of the church. But it cannot have been unconnected with the decline of the twelve as a body of leaders resident in Jerusalem. Some, like James the son of Zebedee, were martyred, others, like Peter and probably Thomas, engaged in more distant missionary activity in the diaspora, some may well have settled in other parts of Palestine.

A group of elders in the Jerusalem church is first mentioned in Acts 11:30. At the time of the council of Jerusalem, Acts repeatedly (15:2, 4, 6, 22, 23; 16:4) refers to the Jerusalem leadership as 'the apostles and the elders,' as does the decree itself (15:23), whence perhaps Luke derived his perception of the composition of the leadership at this stage.[88] In Luke's language, at least, the apostles must be members of the twelve: not necessarily all of them, but enough still to constitute a distinct body. By Acts 21:18, there appear to be only James

---

[88] Pratscher (1987) 75–76, thinks the role of the elders in Acts 11, 15, 16 unhistorical, but this judgment depends both on his view of the disputed issue of the correlation of events in Acts and Galatians, and on a dubious argument from silence (elders are not mentioned in Gal 2). But he correctly observes that the 'brothers' of Acts 12:17 are the church as a whole, not the elders or a special group around James.

and the elders. If any members of the twelve still played a role in the leadership of the Jerusalem church, they are presumably now included in the body of elders.

It seems at least plausible that, at any rate by this late stage, there was a body of twelve presbyters. The number twelve would be readily enough suggested by Jewish constitutional precedent[89] (at least as strong as the precedent which no doubt suggested the number seven:[90] Acts 6:3), as well as by the precedent of the twelve apostles themselves. We have no evidence to suggest that the twelve apostles *as such* were replaced (the loss of James the son of Zebedee, for example, was not made up). But on the other hand, the evidence does not suggest that the Jerusalem elders were first constituted as a body *alongside* the twelve apostles, since the number of the latter had already dwindled when the elders first appear in the narrative of Acts. So we are not to think of, say, a body of twenty-four – twelve apostles and twelve elders. Rather, what may have happened was that, at a point when the number of the twelve apostles resident in Jerusalem had become very small, a body of twelve elders was constituted, under the leadership of James, to succeed to their leadership function in the Jerusalem church. Any of the twelve apostles who were still part of the effective leadership of the Jerusalem church would now be included in this new body of twelve elders. But James, who was never, of course, a member of the original twelve and who already by Galatians 2:9 seems to have attained precedence in the Jerusalem leadership even over Peter and John,[91] would not have been included in the twelve elders. He consolidated the unique position he had already gained (cf. GThom 12).

If this conjecture is justified, we should not expect the

---

[89] Horbury (1986); Draper (1988). If 1QS 8:1–2 should be read, as it usually has been, to refer to a council of twelve laymen and three priests, one might conjecture a parallel situation in the Jerusalem church at the time when James was one of the three 'pillars' (Gal 2:9): three pillars and twelve elders. But Draper argues persuasively that the Qumran text intends a council of twelve *including* three priests.

[90] Hengel (1983) 15–16.

[91] But the point is debated: Pratscher (1987) 68–70.

names of the twelve elders to be all unknown to us. They would be some of the most prominent members of the Jerusalem church. They would include any of the twelve apostles still in the Jerusalem leadership, and no doubt also other disciples of Jesus from the period of his earthly ministry. From this point of view, the twelve names in Eusebius' bishop list look entirely plausible. Some of the names could be those of members of the twelve apostles (John, Matthias, Philip). Others may be disciples named in the Gospel traditions (Levi and Zacchaeus, if this name in Eusebius' list is preferred to Zacharias, which Epiphanius gives) and prominent members of the Jerusalem church in Acts (Justus[92] may be Justus Barsabbas: Acts 1:23; Papias, *ap.* Eusebius, *HE* 3:39:9). Doubtless not all of these identifications are correct, but there are sufficient such plausible identifications, along with a number of unknown names, which we should also expect, to make the list as a whole generally plausible.

Could any of the twelve names be those of relatives of Jesus? Harnack[93] and Gunther[94] suggested that Zacharias (preferring this name in Epiphanius' version of the list to Eusebius' Zacchaeus) could be the grandson of Jude whom Hegesippus calls Zoker (see section V below). But if the names are those of contemporaries of James this is not possible. More plausible is the suggestion that the last two names: Joseph/Josis and Judas may be the Lord's brothers of those names. Certainly the form Ἰωσίς in Epiphanius should be preferred to Ἰωσήφ in Eusebius. The former is not an assimilation to Mark's Gospel, where the form is Ἰωσῆς (Mark 6:3; 15:40, 47), but no doubt represents the same Semitic form of the name. Eusebius' version of the list has substituted the more familiar form of the name, just as Matthew has in Matt 13:55; 27:56. So the name in the list of twelve elders could refer to Jesus' brother Joses, but it might just as well refer to the Joses of Mark

---

[92] The name Justus given as that of a brother of Jesus in some late apocryphal accounts is only a corruption of Joses (from the genitive Ἰωσῆτος): Blinzler (1967) 34.

[93] Harnack (1897) 220 n. 2.

[94] Gunther (1973) 92.

15:40, 47 (whose mention in those verses indicates that he was a well-known figure in the early church). Even less certainty could attach to the identification of the Judas of the list as Jude the Lord's brother. A more probable identification would be Judas Barsabbas, whom we know to have been a prominent member of the Jerusalem church (Acts 15:23, 27, 32). The Judas son of James who appears in Luke's list of the twelve (Luke 6:16; Acts 1:13; also John 14:22) is also possible. In the case of such a very common name, only conjecture is possible. So we cannot rule out the possibility that one or even two of the Lord's brothers participated with James in the leadership of the Jerusalem church, or that other names in the list belong to relatives of Jesus whose names we do not know. But these are no more than possibilities. The list is consistent with the impression gained from Julius Africanus that most of the family who were active in Christian leadership and mission, apart from James himself, were based in Galilee rather than Jerusalem. We should note that the list certainly includes neither Clopas nor his son Symeon, who would later succeed James in Jerusalem.

Symeon will be discussed later in section IV. But we must conclude our discussion of the bishops list by considering Symeon's successor, the third person in the list, whom we have suggested was in fact the last leader of the Jewish Christian church in Jerusalem before the Bar Kokhba revolt. His name appears in Eusebius as Justus (Ἰοῦστος), but in Epiphanius as Judas (Ἰούδας). The difference is best understood as a transcriptional error in Epiphanius' list. Eusebius also refers to Justus in *HE* 3:35:1, though he there gives no information he could not have derived from the bishops list[95] and so we cannot postulate another source which would confirm the name Justus. Oddly enough, however, it is Epiphanius who indirectly confirms that the last Jewish Christian bishop of Jerusalem was Justus. Epiphanius adds to some of the names in his list indications of time, which he did not find in his list but must have added from other sources. For

---

[95] He is also apparently dependent on Acts 21:30 – which reveals his lack of genuinely relevant sources at this point.

example, he notes that Symeon was crucified in the time of Trajan, and to the name John he adds: 'until the nineteenth year of Trajan'. Presumably this is because he rather oddly supposes this John to be the apostle, whom he knows (as he says shortly before giving the list) to have survived into the reign of Trajan. Since he is interested in extending the generation of the apostles as far as possible, he puts John's death in the last, the nineteenth year of Trajan. Then, to the name Justus, the eleventh name on the list (the second Justus in Eusebius' list, but the first in his), he adds: 'until Hadrian'. This note is also odd, since Hadrian was Trajan's immediate successor and three names have intervened between John and Justus. The note must derive from information Epiphanius had independently of the list and which (unlike the note about Symeon) he could not have gained from Eusebius. He must have known a tradition in which Justus succeeded Symeon and was bishop until the time of Hadrian, i.e. until the Bar Kokhba revolt. (Possibly he knew this from Hegesippus, though it is debatable whether Epiphanius had access to Hegesippus' work independently of Eusebius.[96]) Since Epiphanius has only one Justus in his list, he has attached the note to this Justus, but clearly it really belongs to the third person on the list, whom Eusebius calls Justus.

We may conclude that the third and last leader of the Jewish Christian church in Jerusalem was Justus. He may have been, like his two predecessors, a relative of Jesus, but we have no way of knowing this.[97] Much later, despite the chronological impossibility, he was identified with Jude the Lord's brother.[98] We can see how this has happened. In *Apostolic Constitutions* 7:46, the third bishop of Jerusalem is said to be 'Judas of James'. This is not a more accurate version of the bishops list than Eusebius', still less an indication of the real author of the letter of Jude, as Streeter thought.[99] Rather,

---

[96] See Zahn (1900) 258–270; Lawlor (1917) 14–18, for arguments that he did, and Pratscher (1987) 103–104, for a cautious response.

[97] Cf. von Campenhausen (1950–51) 142–143.

[98] So the Menology quoted in Lawlor (1917) 44 n. 3.

[99] Streeter (1929) 180.

the author of the *Apostolic Constitutions* must be here dependent on the same form of the Jerusalem bishops list as Epiphanius knew (if not on Epiphanius himself), but has identified its third bishop Judas with 'Judas [the son] of James' in Luke's list of the twelve (Luke 6:16; Acts 1:13). He may or may not have considered this member of the twelve to be the same person as Jude the Lord's brother, but such an identification became common[100] and made Jude the third bishop of Jerusalem.[101]

IV. Symeon the son of Clopas

Apart from his appearance in the Jerusalem bishops list, all we know about Symeon the son of Clopas comes from the late second-century, probably Palestinian writer Hegesippus as quoted or reported in Eusebius. Since in both this and the following section the evidence of Hegesippus is extremely important, we must begin, not with a full discussion of all the problems involved in reconstructing and assessing Hegesippus' work, for which there is no space here, but with at least some preliminary indications of the nature of Hegesippus' work and its preservation in Eusebius.

(1) Hegesippus' work, though concerned with church history, was not primarily a history of the church, but an apology (Eusebius, *HE* 4:8:1). In part at least, it was a defence of the catholic faith as true apostolic tradition against the second-century Gnostic traditions, but it may also have involved apologetic against pagan charges against and misunderstandings of Christianity.[102] (2) Like Irenaeus, in the same period and for the same reason, Hegesippus was therefore concerned with the preservation of true apostolic teach-

[100] E.g. Ephraem (in Harris [1894] 37–38); EpTitus (de Santos Otero [1965] 151). Hence also the identification of Jude the Lord's brother with the apostle Thaddeus: in, e.g., the Ethiopic *Preaching of Judas Thaddeus in Syria* (Budge [1935] 296–305). Gunther (1980) still defends this threefold identification: Jude the Lord's brother = Judas of James (Luke 6:16) = Thaddeus.

[101] Cf. Zahn (1900) 293 n.

[102] Lawlor (1917) 2–4.

ing in the church through a succession of reliable teachers.[103]
He had a definite theory of church history, according to
which the church remained pure in its faith until the reign of
Trajan, i.e. during the period when the apostles and their
immediate disciples were alive. Heresy had its first beginnings
in the latter part of that period, but only gained a foothold in
the church after it (*HE* 4:22:4–6; 3:32:7–8).[104] (3) Whether or
not Hegesippus was himself a Christian of Jewish extraction,
as Eusebius deduced, but perhaps mistakenly, from his
writings (*HE* 4:22:8),[105] he certainly had access to Palestinian
Jewish Christian tradition, most likely a written source from
the first half of the second century.[106] He has reproduced
these traditions fairly faithfully,[107] but for his own apologetic
purpose. (4) Eusebius has selected and arranged the material
he drew from Hegesippus as he needed it for his own history.
In fact, he has probably reproduced most of what Hegesippus
said about the history of the Palestinian church, though without all of the apologetic argument for which, in Hegesippus,
it was the evidence. But he shared at least partly Hegesippus'
interests in the lines of succession of reliable teachers and in
the origin of heresy.[108] Even where he paraphrases or summarizes Hegesippus, he follows Hegesippus quite closely, as
can be seen in cases where the same passage is both quoted
and paraphrastically reported (*HE* 3:20:1 ‖ 3:19; 3:32:6a ‖
3:20:6; 3:32:6b ‖ 3:32:2).

Since Eusebius actually quotes from Hegesippus *two*
accounts of the martyrdom of Symeon the son of Clopas,
which were clearly in different contexts in Hegesippus' work,

---

[103] von Campenhausen (1950–51) 138–139.

[104] Lawlor (1917) 62–64.

[105] Cf. Pratscher (1987) 105 n. 11, with references to the debate.

[106] Pratscher (1987) 106–107.

[107] Gustafsson (1961) argues that Hegesippus' account of the martyrdom
of James is 'an oral, legendary but genuine tradition, that Hegesippus has
rendered as faithfully as possible' (228). The detailed study by Pratscher
(1987) of the three major, related Christian accounts of the martyrdom of
James (238–255) confirms this view, though he prefers to think of Hegesippus' source as written (106–107).

[108] Cf. Halton (1982).

one following an account of heretics (3:32:3; cf. 4:22:5–6), the other the account of the grandsons of Jude (3:32:6; cf. 3:20:1–6), it is clear that Hegesippus' information about the history of the Palestinian church after the death of James was not presented in a single chronological sequence. In fact if we leave aside the long account of the martyrdom of James (*HE* 2:23:4–18) and the notice of the seven Jewish sects which must have preceded it (4:22:7; cf. 2:23:8), all the rest of the material from Hegesippus about the Palestinian church can be plausibly arranged in two sequences, each ending with the martyrdom of Symeon.[109] My reconstruction of these two sequences cannot be justified in detail here, but it depends on both the connections between and the subject-matter of the material as Eusebius gives it. Where the details of the reconstruction are important in the argument that follows, they will be justified in that context.

The first sequence concerns the preservation of the Jerusalem church in apostolic teaching during the period of Symeon's leadership, the origin of heresy with Thebouthis and its success only after Symeon's death. In the following list the passages underlined are those in which Eusebius expressly quotes Hegesippus' words, and gaps are indicated where we have to presume material which Eusebius has not preserved:

<u>4:22:4a</u> ‖ 3:11
. . .
<u>4:22:4b–6</u>
. . .
<u>3:32:3</u>
<u>3:32:7–8</u>

The second sequence concerns the Roman persecution of Davidides in the reigns of Vespasian, Domitian and Trajan. Its main apologetic purpose seems to be to show that the relatives of Jesus who were accused and suffered as Davidides did so unjustly.

---

[109] My reconstruction of the two sequences is similar to that of Lawlor, but omits material which does not relate to the Palestinian church and which can only dubiously be assigned to Hegesippus: see Lawlor (1917) 18–62.

3:12
<u>3:20:1</u> ‖ 3:19
<u>3:20:2</u>
3:20:3–5
3:20:6 ‖ <u>3:32:6a</u>
3:32:2 ‖ <u>3:32:6b</u>
3:32:4a.

It is impossible to be quite sure that this was the second of the two sequences in the context of Hegesippus' work. It does refer to Symeon as 'The *aforesaid* Simon son of Clopas' (3:32:6b: ὁ προειρημένος Σίμων υἱὸς Κλωπᾶ), but this could be due to Eusebius' editing of Hegesippus' words. However, if the two sequences were in this order, then the first sequence makes clear who are the 'heretics' or 'heresies' who in the second sequence accuse the grandsons of Jude (*HE* 3:19) and Symeon (3:32:6b). They are not simply the seven Jewish sects who had been responsible for the death of James (2:23:8), but the Jewish Christian or Gnostic heirs of these Jewish sects, associated with Thebouthis in the time of Symeon's leadership of the church (4:22:5–6). It is clear that in the first sequence the accusers of Symeon (3:32:3) must be these Jewish Christian or Gnostic heretics, but the identity of the same accusers of Symeon in the second sequence (3:32:6b) would not be clear unless it followed the first sequence. Therefore the order of the two sequences which I have proposed is probable.

We turn to the material specifically about Symeon. His appointment as second bishop of Jerusalem in succession to James was recorded by Hegesippus in the opening of the first sequence of material we have identified. This is preserved by Eusebius in two versions:

(3.11) After the martyrdom of James and the taking of Jerusalem which immediately ensued, it is recorded that those apostles and disciples of the Lord who were still surviving met together from all quarters and, together with the Lord's relatives after the flesh (for the more part of them were still alive), took counsel, all in common, as to whom they should judge worthy to be the successor of James; and, what is more, that they all with one consent approved Symeon the son of Clopas, of whom also the book of the Gospels [i.e. John 19:25] makes mention, as worthy

of the throne of the community in that place. He was a cousin –
so it is said – of the Saviour; for indeed Hegesippus relates that
Clopas was Joseph's brother.[110]

(4:22:4a) And after James the Just had suffered martyrdom, as
had also the Lord, on the same account, the son of his [i.e.,
probably, James'] uncle, Symeon the son of Clopas, was next
appointed bishop, whom, since he was a cousin of the Lord,
they all put forward as the second [bishop].[111]

Although the second of these passages purports to be a direct
quotation from Hegesippus, it must in fact be regarded as a
highly condensed quotation of material which Eusebius paraphrases in 3:11. In 4:22:4 Eusebius is not interested in giving
an account of the appointment of Symeon for its own sake
(having already recorded it in its chronological place in book
3), but needs to refer to it in order to date the account which
follows, in direct quotation from Hegesippus, of Thebouthis
and the origin of heresy (4:22:4b–6). It would not be surprising if, while using Hegesippus' own words in 4:22:4a, he also
omitted some of what Hegesippus wrote about the appointment of Symeon. Moreover, it is noteworthy that he calls
him Symeon. Elsewhere where Hegesippus' actual words are
quoted the name given is *Simon* the son of Clopas (3:32:3, 6),
while Eusebius paraphrasing Hegesippus or writing freely uses
Symeon (3:11:1; 3:22:1; 3:32:1–2, 4; 3:35:1), as the Jerusalem
bishops list also does (4:5:3). Of course, both forms are correct, but evidently Hegesippus preferred the Greek name,
while Eusebius preferred the Semitic form, perhaps because
of its Jewish flavour as well as because it was the form used
in the bishops list. If he has changed Hegesippus' Simon to
Symeon in 4:22:4a, this may indicate that he is not here
reproducing Hegesippus' text exactly.

Whether 3:11 derives from Hegesippus is disputed.[112] The

110 Translation from Lawlor and Oulton (1927) 78 (slightly adapted).
111 My translation from the text in Schwartz (1903) 370.
112 For a lengthy defence of the view that it is, see Lawlor (1917) 21–39,
though I cannot accept all the details of his reconstruction of Hegesippus
there. Harnack (1897) 220 n. 1, denies that Hegesippus is the source, but
suggests Julius Africanus.

phrase 'it is recorded' (λόγος κατέχει) certainly indicates a source.[113] (In 3:19 the same phrase introduces a paraphrase of material from Hegesippus, whose actual words are then quoted [3:20:1].) There are a number of indications that the source was Hegesippus: (1) The opening reference to the martyrdom of James and the immediately following fall of Jerusalem certainly depends on Hegesippus (*HE* 2:23:18). (2) The essence of 4:22:4a is contained in 3:11, so that *another source* would be superfluous: if material in 3:11 does not derive from the fuller version of what is summarized in 4:22:4a, it must be regarded as Eusebius' own expansion of his source. (3) But one item of information, not in 4:22:4a, is explicitly said to be from Hegesippus: that Clopas was the brother of Joseph. This information does not occur in Hegesippus' accounts of the martyrdom of Symeon (3:32:2–3, 6). So if it were not in the fuller version of Hegesippus behind 4:22:4a, we should have to postulate a quite distinct Hegesippean passage about Symeon on which Eusebius does not otherwise draw. This is less plausible than that Eusebius found this information in the account of the appointment of Symeon from which he draws the rest of 3:11. (4) The description of the Lord's relatives as 'those who belong to the family of the Lord according to the flesh' (τοῖς πρὸς γένους κατὰ σάρκα τοῦ κυρίου) resembles the terminology used by Julius Africanus (*ap.* Eusebius, *HE* 1:7:11), Hegesippus (3:19; 3:20:1), and other sources dependent on Jewish Christian tradition (Didascalia 24; Ap. Const. 8:35:1). It could have been picked up by Eusebius from other contexts in Julius Africanus or Hegesippus, but it more plausibly derives from his source at this point. (5) The statement that many of the relatives of the Lord were still alive resembles what Hegesippus says about the grandsons of Jude (3:20:1; cf. 3:32:5). (6) The conjunction of the remaining apostles with the relatives of the Lord coheres with Hegesippus' statement about James and the apostles in 2:23:4. Although some have supposed the mention of the apostles in the latter text to be Eusebius' gloss on Hegesip-

---

[113]Lawlor (1917) 21–23.

pus' text,[114] the only reason for supposing this is the belief that the role of the apostles in 3:11 is Eusebius' free elaboration of Hegesippus. (7) The information which is in 3:11 but lacking in 4:22:4a – that the election of Symeon was by unanimous consent of all the surviving apostles, disciples of the Lord, and relatives of the Lord (in place of the un-explained πάντες of 4:22:4a) – well serves Hegesippus' purpose in the context of 4:22:4–6. It shows that Symeon was appointed and Thebouthis rejected by all who had any authoritative relationship to the Lord, and so deprives Thebouthis' heresies of any possibility of apostolic legitimacy. We may conclude that 3:11 derives substantially from Hegesippus.

Naturally this does not guarantee the historicity of the account. It must be admitted that it could be Hegesippus' own creation for the sake of his apologetic purpose. For example, it is possible that, historically, James had no successor as such, but that immediately after his death the leadership of the Jerusalem church was in the hands of the presbytery and that only gradually did Symeon emerge as principal leader, in the same way as James had done. But Hegesippus, knowing only that in his time Symeon was regarded as the second bishop of Jerusalem, assumed the appointment must have been as he describes it. On the other hand, as Stauffer has shown,[115] there is nothing historically improbable about Hegesippus' account of Symeon's appointment, and a number of considerations are in its favour:

(1) The role of the relatives of Jesus, along with the apostles and disciples, is unlikely to be Hegesippus' creation. It is true that it serves his apologetic purpose: the relatives of Jesus, including James, Symeon and the grandsons of Jude, feature in his account of the Palestinian church as, by virtue of their relationship to Jesus, guarantors of true Christian teaching. Though he stresses that they presided over the church in conjunction with the apostles (2:23:4; 3:11), they emerge as in fact more important than the apostles, principally because in their case he can establish a succession which continues to the

[114] Pratscher (1987) 104, with references to others.
[115] Stauffer (1952) 212–214.

reign of Trajan.[116] But Hegesippus would not have been able to give this role to the relatives of Jesus unless the Jewish Christian tradition on which he depends had already focussed on their leadership role in the first-century church. So it is likely that the role of these relatives in the appointment of Symeon derives from that tradition. Especially in extending the circle of these relatives beyond the four brothers of the Lord, it is entirely consistent with the account of the *desposynoi* given by Julius Africanus.

(2) All the evidence shows that by the time of his death James had attained a position of considerable preeminence in the Jerusalem church. Moreover, if, as our analysis of the evidence of the Jerusalem bishops list (section III above) suggests, James presided not as one of but along with a college of twelve presbyters, his unique position was already a formally constituted one. It would be natural for such a position not to lapse at his death but to be filled by the election of a successor. The notion of succession in such an office certainly does not need to be regarded as an early catholic one, but is deeply rooted in Jewish tradition, as Stauffer has shown in detail.[117] (3) Assuming (but this is an assumption which might not be correct) that the list of twelve presbyters we have extracted from the Jerusalem bishops list (section III above) is correct for the time of James' death, Symeon was not one of the elders of the Jerusalem church. So James' position was not filled by the elders themselves from among their own number. This suggests that the election must have been a matter of wider participation. (4) In any case the election of James could not, for Jewish Christians, be a matter of purely local concern. The status of Jerusalem as the mother church of the whole Christian community had given James an authoritative position not only throughout the Palestinian church but even further afield (Gal 2:12; Acts 21:35; GThom 12). The succession to the leadership of the Jerusalem church would be a matter of concern wherever this authority was acknowledged. So a gathering like the Jerusalem council of

---

[116] Cf. Lawlor (1917) 63–64.
[117] Stauffer (1952) 207–211.

Acts 15 is quite possible, even if Hegesippus' statement of its composition is somewhat idealized.

The fact that the election is dated after the fall of Jerusalem in A.D. 70 is the result of Hegesippus' belief that the siege of the city began immediately after the death of James (*HE* 2:23:18). He or the tradition he followed would simply have assumed that the earliest practical opportunity for an election would be after the capture of the city. Thus we cannot suppose this dating to be accurate.[118] If Symeon was in fact elected as successor to James, we must assume the appointment took place soon after the martyrdom of James in A.D. 62.

In the choice of Symeon as successor to James his family relationship to Jesus must have been at least an important factor. Since his reported age of a hundred and twenty at the time of his death (*HE* 3:32:3, 6) is certainly not to be considered accurate (see below), we do not know how old he was in A.D. 62. Calculating from a more plausible old age in the reign of Trajan, he would be perhaps between forty and fifty in A.D. 62, and if his father Clopas were a younger brother of Joseph, this is quite possible. He might have been just an adult at the time of Jesus' ministry, but is likely to have been still a boy. So it would not be because he was 'an eyewitness and actual hearer of the Lord' (*HE* 3:32:4) that he was elected. When Eusebius concludes that he must have been an eyewitness, he is explicitly doing no more than make his own deduction from Symeon's reputed age at the time of his martyrdom (3:32:4). Clearly Hegesippus did not say this, and had Hegesippus thought it it would have been very much to his purpose to say so. Had Symeon been known to have been his father's companion at the time of the resurrection appearance on the way to Emmaus (Luke 24),[119] one would also have expected Hegesippus to say this and Eusebius to have reported it. So the choice of Symeon cannot have been made because of his direct contact with the Lord, but must reflect

[118] And we need not, with Stauffer (1952) 212, speculate as to why the election was delayed.

[119] So Stauffer (1952) 212; cf. Gunther (1974) 27–28.

the general prominence of the *desposynoi* in the Palestinian churches, Symeon's individual prominence as a leader in the churches, and very probably the influence of a kind of dynastic feeling, to which it seemed right that the leadership of the church should remain in the hands of relatives of Jesus, passing from his brother James to another relative. It may not have been a matter of *strict* dynastic succession, in the sense that Symeon's claim was strictly based on his being next in line of succession after James. Nor would dynastic feeling have been influential at this point unless the other *desposynoi*, besides James, had been in any case prominent in the leadership of the churches in Palestine. But given this prominence, belief that it was appropriate for the succession to James to continue within the family must have been operative in the election of Symeon.

For Hegesippus, the full apologetic value of his account of the appointment of Symeon depended on its close connection with his account of the origin of heresy[120] which followed:

> (4:22:4b) For this reason they used to call the church a virgin; for she had not yet been corrupted by vain teachings. (22:5) But Thebouthis, because he was not made bishop, began secretly to corrupt her from the seven sects among the people, to which [sects] he himself belonged; from which [sects] came Simon (whence the Simonians) and Cleobius (whence the Cleobians) and Dositheus (whence the Dositheans) and Gorthaeus (whence the Gorathenians) and the Masbotheans. Springing from these, the Menandrianists and Marcianists and Carpocratians and Valentinians and Basilidians and Saturnilians, each by themselves and each in different ways, introduced their own peculiar opinions. (22:6) From these sprang false Christs, false prophets, false apostles, those who have divided the unity of the church by injurious words against God and against his Christ [cf. Ps 2:2].[121]

Hegesippus has a highly schematized view of the sects or heresies (αἱρέσεις)[122] which opposed the true church. At first

---

[120] Cf. von Campenhausen (1950–51) 140–141.

[121] Translation from Lawlor and Oulton (1927) 128 (slightly adapted).

[122] On Hegesippus' use of the term αἵρεσις, see Simon (1981) 820–824.

there were the seven Jewish sects (named in an early part of his account of the Palestinian church which Eusebius quotes at 4:22:7) whose opposition to Jesus and the church culminated in the martyrdom of James (2:23:8–9). Then from these developed various Jewish and Samaritan sectarian groups (Simonians, Cleobians, Dositheans, Gorathenians and Masbotheans), some of which were of a gnosticizing character. Finally, in the third stage of development, from these Palestinian groups developed the Gnostic heresies of the second century: Menandrianists, Marcianists, Carpocratians, Valentinians, Basilidians and Saturnilians. As a schematized account this is not entirely lacking in historical value.[123] But the relation of the second and third stages to Christianity is somewhat ambiguous in Hegesippus, as a result of his apologetic concern. He wishes to give the Gnostic heresies of his own time a pedigree which derives them from the Jewish sects which opposed Jesus and his immediate Jewish Christian followers, rather than the derivation from Jesus and some of his apostles, which these groups claimed. But he also recognizes that they make Christian claims, have an influence within Christianity and 'have divided the unity of the church'. So he seizes on the name of Thebouthis, which tradition must have given him as some kind of Jewish Christian opponent of Symeon, and attributes to him the secret beginnings of heresy in Christian circles. The artificiality of the connection of Thebouthis with his scheme is shown by the claim that Thebouthis belonged, apparently, to all seven Jewish sects,[124] as well as by the fact that the derivation of the Jewish Gnostics (Simon and the rest) from the seven Jewish sects is very loosely connected with the reference to Thebouthis, so that it is impossible to tell exactly what Hegesippus thought the connection to be.

The translation (with reference to Thebouthis' corruption of the church) of ὑποφθείρειν as '*secretly* to corrupt' can be justified by Eusebius' paraphrase of a later statement of Heges-

[123] Cf. Fossum (1985) 20–21.

[124] Isser (1976) 14–15, offers a rather speculative reconstruction of Hegesippus' text at this point, but destroys the genealogy of sects which Hegesippus must have intended.

ippus to the effect that during the time of Symeon, 'if there were any who were trying to corrupt the sound standard of the preaching of salvation, they were still then lurking, as it were, in some obscure and dark hole' (3:32:7). Only after the death of Symeon could heresy, in the form of second-century Gnosticism, gain a real foothold in the church. Clearly we are not likely to be able to recover any secure historical information about Thebouthis from Hegesippus.[125] The statement that he began to corrupt the church 'because he was not made bishop' (presumably at the time of the election of Symeon) may well have been taken by Hegesippus from his Jewish Christian tradition, but it is, of course, a standard way of discrediting an opponent and cannot be taken very seriously.

Since Thebouthis was evidently an important name in the tradition Hegesippus received, it is possible – though it cannot be proved – that the split between Ebionite ('heretical') and Nazarene ('orthodox') Jewish Christianity in Palestine stems from Thebouthis' split with Symeon. But the real importance of this material in Hegesippus for our enquiry is that it explains why Hegesippus attributes to 'the heretics' or 'the heresies' the accusations against both the grandsons of Jude (3:19) and Symeon (32:2-3, 6), which led to their arrest and in Symeon's case to his martyrdom. Evidently these are not the seven Jewish sects, which had been responsible for the death of James. Rather in this period, the second stage of the development of heresies, the church's opponents are the followers of Thebouthis, Simon, Cleobius and the rest. Such people – whose relationship to Christianity Hegesippus leaves very obscure – are the people who inform against the Lord's relatives on the grounds of their being Davidides, and in one case are themselves arrested on the same charge (3:32:4a). It is hard to see why the members of such groups, rather than other Jews, should have been particularly the opponents of the Jewish Christian leaders in that period between the two

[125] For suggestions about Thebouthis, see Schoeps (1949) 283–284. It is possible that he should be connected with the Masbotheans, whom Hegesippus' list leaves without a founder.

Jewish revolts. As with the stories of Peter's conflicts with Simon, there are probably real antagonisms reflected but no reliable historical information.

In the first sequence of material, following the account of the beginnings of heresy in Symeon's time, Hegesippus' only real concern with Symeon's martyrdom was to attribute it to the heretics and to represent it as the point after which heresy could flourish more freely. So his account is brief:

> (3:32:3b) Certain of these (plainly, the heretics) [cf. 32:2] accused Simon the son of Clopas of being of the house of David and a Christian; and so he was martyred at the age of a hundred and twenty years, when Trajan was Caesar and Atticus the governor.[126]

Evidently this is dependent on the tradition which Hegesippus reports more fully in the second sequence, following the account of the grandsons of Jude. These, having been accused by the heretics of being Davidides but then released,

> (3:32:6) remained until [the time of] Trajan Caesar; until the son of an uncle of the Lord, the aforesaid Simon son of Clopas, was informed against by the sects, and was likewise also accused on the same charge before Atticus the governor. And he bore witness through tortures of many days' duration, so that all, including the governor, marvelled exceedingly how an old man of a hundred and twenty years could thus endure. And orders were given for him to be crucified.[127]

This second passage has also been paraphrased by Eusebius in 32:2, according to his habit of first paraphrasing what he then goes on to quote from Hegesippus (cf. 3:19 ∥ 3:20:1), but in this case the paraphrase contains no information omitted from the quotation.

The account of Symeon's martyrdom is hagiographical, in its depiction of the Roman governor's astonishment and in

---

[126] Translation from Lawlor and Oulton (1927) 93 (altered). Smallwood (1962) 131, argues that the description of Atticus as ὑπατικός should not be taken as indicating consular rank, but in its later, general sense of 'governor', irrespective of rank.

[127] Translation from Lawlor and Oulton (1927) 93.

its attribution to Symeon of the age of one hundred and twenty. This was the biblical limit on human life, according to Genesis 6:3, which the most righteous people might therefore be expected to attain. Following the even longer lived patriarchs, it was attained by Moses (Deut 34:7), whose age at death was the limit set for later people (Josephus, *Ant.* 1:152;[128] cf. LAB 9:8). The tradition that Symeon was able to endure many days of torture at that age should be compared with the biblical statement that at the same age Moses' natural strength had in no way diminished (Deut 34:7; cf. also TIss 7:9). The same ideal age at death was later attributed in rabbinic tradition to Hillel, Johanan ben Zakkai and Aqiba.[129] It was no doubt part of the hagiographical tradition about Symeon which came to Hegesippus from Jewish Christian tradition of the decades following Symeon's death. That it was in the tradition Hegesippus used is shown by the fact that he makes nothing of the implication of this age which could have served his apologetic purpose: that Symeon was a contemporary of Jesus and old enough to have been an eyewitness of Jesus' ministry (cf. *HE* 3:32:4b). Thus, while Symeon's one hundred and twenty years are not historical, they testify to the veneration in which he was held in Palestinian Jewish Christianity in the first half of the second century. Little though we know of him, he must have been a major figure for the tradition.

Removing the hagiographical elements and Hegesippus' dubious identification of the informants, the reliable information about Symeon's death is probably that he was arrested on a charge of political subversion, as a Davidide supporter and relative of Jesus the alleged Davidic king, and was tortured and crucified in the reign of Trajan and under a governor called Atticus. This is the only evidence for a legate of Judaea of this name, but the names of only a few of the legates of that period are known.[130] Smallwood argues that he should probably be identified with Ti. Claudius Atticus

---

[128] Haacker and Schäfer (1974) 148.
[129] Carrington (1957) 417.
[130] Schürer (1973) 514–518.

Herodes, father of the orator Herodes Atticus,[131] and tentatively dates his governorship 99/100–102/103 A.D.[132] But a date later in Trajan's reign (between 108 and 117) is also possible: that the son of a brother of Joseph could have survived so long is less likely, but not impossible.

Symeon was therefore leader of the Jerusalem church and probably the most important figure in Jewish Christianity for nearly forty years, perhaps even longer. That we know so little about so important a figure is a salutary reminder of the limits of our evidence. It is, of course, of a piece with our general ignorance of the history of Christianity in the later decades of the first century, a period which we fill with traditions, theological trends and anonymous authors, but for which there is rather little concrete evidence about people and events. But we must probably also reckon with the declining influence of the Jerusalem church in the church at large during the period of Symeon's leadership. Whereas even Paul, so jealous of his apostolic independence vis-à-vis the Jerusalem church leaders, took considerable trouble, by means of his collection, to acknowledge a kind of special status for the Jerusalem church and to maintain a link between it and the churches he established, we hear of no such links in the later part of the century. The churches outside Palestine were growing more distant from their Palestinian roots, and although we should not exaggerate the extent to which leadership was passing from Jewish to Gentile Christians in this period, no doubt this will also have been a factor. But with the destruction of the Temple, the real (as distinct from the symbolic) significance of Jerusalem for Jews was also diminishing. While the Temple stood Jewish Christians from the diaspora would

---

[131] The identification itself is a very old one: cf Graetz (1885) 22–23; Zahn (1900) 242. Graetz also argued that Atticus is the Roman governor mentioned in rabbinic traditions by the name of Agnitus (and variant forms of the name), but this is quite doubtful: Schürer (1973) 519. Another possible identification of Atticus, suggested by Zahn (1900) 242, is with Sextus Attius Suburanus, whose name is erroneously given as Ἀττίκος Σουρβανός in the *Martyrdom of Ignatius* (Roman Acts) (Lightfoot [1885] 493).

[132] Smallwood (1962).

have been frequent visitors to Jerusalem on pilgrimage and this will have helped to maintain the influence of the Jerusalem church and a sense of its role as the theological centre of the Christian movement for many Jewish and probably even many Gentile Christians. After A.D. 70 this influence must have waned, until, after Symeon's death, the Bar Kokhba war and the end of the Jewish Christian church in Jerusalem will have deprived Palestinian Jewish Christianity of most of its influence elsewhere.

Of course, our evidence biases our view of Christianity up to the early second century. We see the church largely from the perspective of the churches of the north Mediterranean area from Antioch to Rome, and from this perspective Palestinian Christianity is rapidly marginalized during the second half of the first century. If we knew more about Christianity in Egypt, Arabia, Phoenicia, east Syria, and Mesopotamia the impression might be different – and specifically with reference to the *desposynoi*, there are tantalizing hints in Gospel of Thomas 12 (section I above) and in the presence of a 'dynasty' of Jesus' relatives in second-century Seleucia-Ctesiphon (section II above) which suggest the continuing influence of the Palestinian church leadership outside Palestine. Symeon's period of leadership may not have been a period simply of decline. It may have been a period of missionary advance for the Jewish Christian mission both within Palestine and in some areas beyond it. We have to admit our ignorance. Owing to the indubitable decline of Palestinian Jewish Christianity after Symeon's time, the evidence which might have illuminated the period of his leadership has not survived. But the next two sections will allow us just a glimpse of the churches of Galilee around the turn of the century.

V. The grandsons of Jude

For Hegesippus' account of the two grandsons of Jude, the main source is Eusebius, *HE* 3:19:1–3:20:7, where Eusebius directly quotes a section of Hegesippus' text and reports the rest, apparently faithfully:

(19:1) Now when this Domitian gave orders that those who were of the family of David should be put to death, it is recorded in an ancient authority that some heretics brought an accusation against the descendants of Jude, who was the Saviour's brother after the flesh, on the ground that they were of the family of David, and that they bore kinship to Christ himself. This is shown by Hegesippus, who speaks as follows in these very words:

> (20:1) But there still survived of the family of the Lord the grandsons of Jude, his brother after the flesh, as he was called. These they informed against, as being of the family of David; and the 'evocatus' brought them before Domitian Caesar. For he feared the coming of the Christ, as did also Herod. (20:2) And he asked them if they were of David's line, and they acknowledged it. Then he asked them what possessions they had or what fortune they owned. And they said that between the two of them they had only nine thousand denarii, half belonging to each of them; and this they asserted they had not in money, but only in thirty-nine plethra of land, so valued, from which by their own labours they both paid the taxes and supported themselves.

(20:3) And [he adds] that they showed also their hands, and put forward the hardness of their bodies and the callosities formed on their hands from continual working, as a proof of personal labour. (20:4) And that when asked about Christ and his kingdom, its nature, and the place and time of its appearing, they tendered the reply that it was not of the world nor earthly, but heavenly and angelic; and that it would appear at the end of the world, when he should come in glory and judge the quick and the dead, and render unto every man according to his conduct. (20:5) And [he says] that after this Domitian in no way condemned them, but despised them as men of no account, let them go free, and by an injunction caused the persecution against the Church to cease. (20:6) And that when released they ruled the churches, inasmuch as they were both martyrs and of the Lord's family; and when peace was established, remained alive until [the time of] Trajan. (20:7) Such is the account of Hegesippus.[133]

The information in Eusebius' introduction (19:1) is clearly

---

[133] Translation from Lawlor and Oulton (1927) 80–81.

drawn from the very text of Hegesippus which he then goes on to quote (20:1), but it contains one additional piece of information which must have been in the text of Hegesippus but which Eusebius omits from his citation of Hegesippus' words. This is that the grandsons of Jude were accused by 'some heretics' (τῶν αἱρετικῶν τινας). That Hegesippus said this is clear from *HE* 3:32:6, where Eusebius gives an actual quotation from Hegesippus which plainly followed immediately in Hegesippus' text the account of the grandsons of Jude. Here Hegesippus says that Simon the son of Clopas was 'informed against by the sects (τῶν αἱρέσεων) in the same way' – in the same way as the grandsons of Jude were, that is. By the 'sects' (αἱρέσεις) Hegesippus apparently means, as we have already seen (section IV above), not the seven sects into which he divided non-Christian Jewish religion (4:22:7; 2:23:8–9), but the Jewish Christian or at any rate Jewish Gnostic sects to which he refers in 4:22:5.

That in 3:20:3–6 Eusebius follows Hegesippus' text closely can be seen from the later passage, which we have just mentioned, in 3:32:5–6, where he takes up Hegesippus' narrative again at the same point, briefly summarizing the incident of the arrest of the grandsons of Jude, but then quoting the actual words of Hegesippus which correspond to 3:20:6:

> (32:5) And the same writer says that there were also other descendants of one of the Saviour's reputed brethren, whose name was Jude; and they survived until this same reign [of Trajan], after they had given their testimony before Domitian to their faith in Christ, as we have already previously recorded. He writes as follows:
>
> > (32:6) They came, therefore, and ruled every church, as being martyrs (μάρτυρες) and of the Lord's family; and, when profound peace was established in every church, they remained until [the time of] Trajan Caesar: until the son of an uncle of the Lord, the aforesaid Simon son of Clopas, was informed against by the sects. . . .[134]

Presumably in the context of Hegesippus' narrative it was

---

[134] Translation from Lawlor and Oulton (1927) 93.

clear that 'every church' meant no more than every church in Palestine. It is understandable that Eusebius omits 'every' in 3:20:6.

As well as these two overlapping reports by Eusebius of Hegesippus' account of the grandsons of Jude, we also have an ancient summary of the same passage of Hegesippus[135] which has come down to us in what looks like and in one of its two occurrences in the manuscripts is said to be a (summarized) extract from Eusebius.[136] *HE* 3:17:1 and 3:18:1 are first summarized, with close verbal resemblances to Eusebius. Then follows:

> When Domitian spoke with the sons of Jude the brother of the Lord and learned of the virtue of the men, he brought to an end the persecution against us. Hegesippus also reports their names, and says that one was called Zoker (Ζωκήρ) and the other James (Ἰάκωβος).[137]

If this were a summary based directly on the text of Hegesippus and independent of Eusebius, we should have to suppose that in *HE* 3:17:1–3:18:1 Eusebius draws from Hegesippus, without acknowledgement, material which immediately preceded Hegesippus' account of the grandsons of Jude. Lawlor argues that this is in fact the case,[138] and it is possible. However, in that case, we should expect the names Zoker and James, which Eusebius does not report, to be integral to the account in the extract, rather than appended as an additional piece of information. So it seems likely that the extract is dependent on Eusebius, but its author also had access to Hegesippus' work itself, from which he was able to add the information that Hegesippus gives the names Zoker and James. That he says Hegesippus *also* reports these is not a problem for this view,[139] since Eusebius makes very clear

---

[135] Paris MS 1555A, printed in Cramer (1839) 88, and Bodleian MS Barocc. 142, printed in de Boor (1889) 169. Lawlor (1917) 41–42, gives the text alongside *HE* 3:17–20, indicating the verbal agreements.

[136] de Boor (1889) 168.

[137] My translation.

[138] Lawlor (1917) 42–53, followed by Halton (1982) 690.

[139] Against Lawlor (1917) 43.

that the account of the appearance before Domitian comes from Hegesippus.

Another account of Zoker and James in Epiphanius Monachus, *De vita B. Virg.* 14 [PG 120:204],[140] agrees very closely with the extract just discussed and is very probably dependent on it rather than directly on Hegesippus. In particular the two accounts agree that Domitian was impressed by the virtue (Epiphanius adds the wisdom) of the two men. Hegesippus himself is unlikely to have said this, since it conflicts with Eusebius' account of what he said, but it is easily intelligible as a hagiographical improvement on Hegesippus' report that Domitian despised them as insignificant people.

That Hegesippus gave the names of Jude's grandsons and Eusebius omitted them is therefore very probable. More problematic is the fact that the extract and Epiphanius Monachus speak of sons (υἱοί) of Jude, whereas Eusebius' quotation of Hegesippus (3:20:1) refers to grandsons (υἱωνοί) of Jude. It is not possible to harmonize the sources, as Bagatti does,[141] supposing Zoker and James to be the sons of Jude, but the story in Eusebius to be not about them, but about Jude's grandsons. This is clearly impossible because both the extract and Epiphanius Monachus attribute to Zoker and James the sons of Jude the same interview with Domitian which the grandsons of Jude have in Eusebius' quotation from Hegesippus. It is also clear that grandsons rather than sons were in the text of Hegesippus which Eusebius used, since he speaks of grandsons not only in the quotation of Hegesippus' actual words, but also twice in his own summaries of Hegesippus (ἀπόγονοι: 3:19:1; 3:32:5). Thus if the extract is dependent on Eusebius, its 'sons' (υἱοῖς) must derive from a corrupt text of Eusebius. If it were dependent, as Lawlor thinks, on Hegesippus independently of Eusebius, its text of Hegesippus differed from that used by Eusebius. In that case, we could not be quite sure whether Hegesippus spoke of the sons or the grand-

---

[140] Quoted in Lawlor (1917) 45 n. 3. The Menology quoted by Lawlor (1917) 44 n. 2, also calls James and Zoker the sons of Jude and so seems to derive from the same source.

[141] Bagatti (1965) 259.

sons of Jude, but the latter would still be more likely, since textual corruption of υἱωνοί to υἱοί is more likely than the reverse.

Thus, if we add the names Zoker[142] and James to the two overlapping passages in Eusebius, we may be sure we have substantially all that Hegesippus wrote about the grandsons of Jude. But how far is his account historically trustworthy? It certainly requires a more critical assessment than it has previously been given.[143] There are, in the first place, a number of historical difficulties in the account of the arrest and appearance before Domitian:

(1) We have already noted, in section IV above, that the identification of the informants as Jewish Christian sectaries is not very probable and most likely due to the polemical intent of either Hegesippus or his source.

(2) The account is given legal verisimilitude by the two Latinisms (3:20:1: ἐδηλατόρευσαν, ἠουοκᾶτος). But the second of these, which represents the Latin *evocatus*, appears to be a solecism. An *evocatus* is a soldier recalled to military service. It does not seem to be an appropriate term in the context.[144]

(3) More seriously, the trial before the Emperor Domitian in person is very improbable.

(4) Also improbable is the claim that, as a result of discovering the grandsons of Jude to be harmless, Domitian ordered the persecution of Christians to stop. At this point the story seems to have a strong apologetic motive: the grandsons of Jude succeed in showing Domitian that Christianity was not a threat to Roman power (Zoker and James are not rebels but loyally pay their taxes) and the Emperor himself is represented as recognizing that persecution of Christians is therefore unnecessary and unjustified. Along with this apologetic motive there is also a hagiographical one: the cessation of the second great imperial persecution of the church is thereby

---

[142] The name Zoker is an abbreviation of Zechariah (cf. 1 Chron 8:31, where Zecher [זכר] = the Zechariah of 9:27). Cf. also שׂכר = Ζουχιρ in Wuthnow (1930) 170.

[143] E.g. by Carrington (1957) 335: 'There seems little reason for doubting this story, which is full of good detail and is devoid of legendary features.'

[144] Cf. Zahn (1900) 240.

attributed to the witness of the Lord's relatives Zoker and James. This is the same kind of hagiographical glorification as can be seen in Hegesippus' account of James the Lord's brother.[145]

(5) Finally, there is a difficulty about connecting the incident with a persecution of the church. According to 3:20:1, the grandsons of Jude were accused not of being Christians, but of being Davidides. This accusation fits well into the context Hegesippus himself has provided for it, according to Eusebius, *HE* 3:12. Eusebius there reports Hegesippus as saying 'that Vespasian, after the taking of Jerusalem, gave orders that all the members of the family of David should be sought out, so that none of the royal tribe might be left among the Jews; and that for this reason a most terrible persecution once more hung over the Jews.'[146] In this context, the people who, according to Hegesippus, inform against Zoker and James would be exploiting the Roman authorities' suspicion of Davidides, rather than a Roman policy of action against Christians. Leaving aside the vexed question of the extent of a Domitianic persecution of Christians, the connection of this story with such a persecution seems historically gratuitous and likely to be due to the apologetic and hagiographical motives already mentioned.

The reply of Zoker and James to Domitian requires fuller discussion. It is a statement designed to rebut a Roman political misunderstanding of Christianity, according to which the kingdom of Christ would be understood as a worldly kingdom in competition with Roman rule and for which Christians would therefore plot and fight to overthrow the Roman Empire. Consequently Zoker and James make clear that Christ's kingdom is not worldly (κοσμική) or earthly (ἐπίγειος), but heavenly and angelic (ἐπουράνιος δὲ καὶ ἀγγελική). Moreover, it is not a present rival to Roman power, but will appear only at the end of the age, when Christ comes in glory to judge all humanity. While not altogether evading the early Christian belief that the kingdom of Christ is in

---

[145] Pratscher (1987) 109–121.
[146] Translation from Lawlor and Oulton (1927) 78.

some sense an alternative to the Roman Empire, since it will replace all earthly kingdoms at the parousia, the statement succeeds in showing that allegiance to Christ's kingdom does not make Christians political revolutionaries intent on overthrowing the Roman state.

The description of the parousia is a series of conventional expressions. 'The end of the age' (συντέλεια τοῦ αἰῶνος) is characteristic of Matthew (Matt 13:39, 40; 24:3; 28:20; cf. ApPet E1, reproducing Matt 24:3), but is based on Daniel (συντέλεια τῶν καιρῶν: Dan 9:27 LXX; συντέλεια τοῦ καιροῦ: Dan 9:27 Θ; συντέλεια ἡμερῶν: Dan 12:13 LXX, Θ) and cannot be regarded as uniquely Matthean (cf. TBenj 11:3; TLevi 10:2; Heb 9:26; Hermas *Vis.* 3:8:9). The coming of Christ 'in glory' (ἐν δόξῃ) is common early Christian language (Matt 16:27; 24:30; 25:31; Mark 8:38; 10:37; 13:26; Luke 9:26; 21:27; 2 Thess 1:9; 1 Pet 4:13; AscIsa 4:13; EpApp 16; ApPet E1; SibOr 2:241; Justin, *1 Apol.* 52), as are the two expressions for his judgment: 'to judge the living and the dead' (Acts 10:42; 2 Tim 4:1; 1 Pet 4:5; 2 Clem 1:1; Barn 7:2; Polycarp, *Phil.* 2:1; ApocPet E1; EpApp 16; ActsPet [*Act. Verc.*] 28), and 'to reward everyone according to his conduct' (ἀποδώσει ἑκάστῳ κατὰ τὰ ἐπιτηδεύματα αὐτοῦ). Hegesippus' use of ἐπιτηδεύματα here, rather than ἔργα or ἔργον, is unusual, but otherwise the phrase, derived from Ps 61(62):12; Prov 24:12 (cf. LAB 3:10), is standard (Matt 16:27; Rom 2:6; Rev 22:12; 1 Clem 34:3; 2 Clem 17:4; Did 16:8 [Georgian]; ApPet E1, E6; Hippolytus, *Dan.* 4:10:1–2). Hegesippus himself used it (with the more usual ἔργα) also in his account of James (*HE* 2:23:9). Thus the whole description of the parousia has a stereotyped, almost credal character. It is particularly noteworthy that all four of these conventional elements are found in the opening section of the Apocalypse of Peter (E1),[147] partly owing to the latter's dependence on Matthew. But the combination of the two conventional phrases for Christ's judgment – 'judge the living and the dead and recompense every man according to his work' (ApPet E1) – seems to be found only in the Apocalypse of Peter and this text of Hegesippus. Since the

[147] On this passage see Bauckham (1985) 271–277.

Apocalypse of Peter is very probably a Palestinian Jewish Christian work of the early second century,[148] it may even be the source for the Palestinian Jewish Christian tradition here used by Hegesippus, or both may reflect the same tradition.

More significant, however, is the contrast between 'worldly or earthly', which the kingdom of Christ is not, and 'heavenly and angelic', which it is. This corresponds to the common second-century Christian understanding of the kingdom of God and Christ as heavenly and future.[149] That it is heavenly means that it is to come *from heaven* to earth, and so it is not to be established by earthly means like the kingdoms of this world. That it is angelic might refer to the common view that the life of the kingdom is a participation in the heavenly life of the angels (cf. Heb 12:22; Hermas, *Vis* 2:2:7; *Sim.* 9:12:8; 9:23:5; 9:25:2; 9:27:3; AscIsa 8:15; 9:9; Clement of Alexandria, *Eclog. Proph.* 57:4), but perhaps more likely in this context it refers to the hosts of angels expected to accompany Christ at his coming to establish his kingdom (Matt 16:27; 25:31; Mark 8:38; Luke 9:26; 1 Thess 3:13; 2 Thess 1:7; Jude 14; AscIsa 4:14; ApPet E1; SibOr 2:242; Justin, *1 Apol.* 52). Christ's heavenly kingdom will be established by heavenly, angelic power, not by human arms.

The contrast between the kingdom of Christ and an earthly kingdom can be found in a series of early Christian texts with a similar apologetic concern:

(1) John 18:36: 'My kingdom is not of this world (ἐκ τοῦ κόσμου τούτου). If my kingdom were of this world, then my servants would fight, that I might not be handed over to the Jews. But my kingdom is not from here.'

(2) Justin, *1 Apol.* 11: 'When you hear that we look for a kingdom, you suppose ... that we speak of a human kingdom; whereas we speak of that which is with God, as appears also from the confession of their faith made by those who are charged with being Christians, though they know that death is the punishment awarded to him who so confesses. For if we looked for a

---

[148] In Bauckham (1985) I argued for a date during the Bar Kokhba revolt; cf. also Bauckham (1988C) 4738–4739.

[149] Ferguson (1982) 669–671.

human kingdom, we should also deny our Christ, that we might not be slain . . .'[150]

(3) Hippolytus, *Dan.* 4:11:4: 'So that noone should suppose that it is a transitory or earthly kingdom that has been given to him [Christ] by the Father, the prophet says, "His dominion is an everlasting dominion, which shall not pass away, and his kingdom shall not be destroyed" [Dan 7:14].'[151]

(4) Martyrdom of Paul 1–4:[152] Nero's cupbearer Patroclus, who has become a Christian and has been resuscitated from death by Paul, declares to Nero his allegiance to 'Christ Jesus, the king of the ages', who will destroy 'all the kingdoms under heaven' and whose soldier he now is. Nero, supposing Christians therefore to be dangerous armed rebels in the service of an earthly king, orders all Christians to be put to death. Then Paul, condemned to death, explains to two Roman officials: 'we do not march, as you suppose, with a king who comes from the earth, but one from heaven, the living God, who comes as judge because of the lawless deeds that are done in this world' (4).[153]

These texts must reflect an actual Roman perception of Christians as armed rebels, arising from their talk of the kingdom of Christ and perhaps also from an association of them with Jewish messianic movements which took revolutionary form in the late first and early second centuries. They show, in response to this perception, an apologetic concern to make clear the real nature of the kingdom of Christ as heavenly rather than earthly. The martyrological context, not only in (1) and (4), but also in (2), is significant, when compared with Hegesippus' story of the grandsons of Jude. Moreover, the role of Nero in (4) compares to some extent with that of Domitian in Hegesippus.

The relation between Hegesippus' text and John 18:36 is of special interest, since the latter is the earliest of these texts and there is unlikely to be a literary relationship between it and Hegesippus. In Hegesippus both the grandsons of Jude and

---

[150] Translation from Dods, Reith and Pratten (1867) 14.

[151] My translation from the text in Bonwetsch (1897) 212.

[152] This is part of the late second-century Acts of Paul, but Rordorf (1982) 367–370, argues that it embodies much earlier material.

[153] Translation from Schneemelcher (1965) 384–385.

later Simon the son of Clopas (*HE* 3:32:3) are accused by *Jews* to the Roman authorities on the *political* charge of being Davidides and therefore presumably of favouring a political power alternative to that of Rome. The resemblance to the circumstances of the passion narratives not only of John but of all four canonical Gospels (cf. especially Luke 23:2) is striking. If Hegesippus' stories in any way reflect the reality of Jewish Christian life in Palestine in the tense period between the two great Jewish revolts, it is possible that some of the passion narratives reflect the apologetic concern of Jewish Christians in that period to dissociate the kingdom of Christ from the suspicion of political messianism (cf. Matt 26:52–53).

The apologetic concern in Hegesippus' story of the grandsons of Jude may go back to his Jewish Christian source, in which it is thoroughly plausible. But when we recognize the conventional nature of the language attributed to Zoker and James we can scarcely claim to have access to their own views. Allowing for the apologetic and hagiographical concerns of the tradition, we may accept as reliable that the two grandsons of Jude were prominent leaders in the Jewish Christian churches and that they came under suspicion by the Roman authorities because they were known to be (and their status in the churches was no doubt partly connected with the fact that they were) relatives of Jesus whom they claimed to be the Messiah, the son of David. Their appearance before Domitian and the connection of their arrest with a Domitianic persecution of Christians must be considered rather doubtful.

That Zoker and James were poor farmers is no doubt also accurately remembered, and the size of their smallholding (39 plethra, valued at 9000 denarii) is so precisely stated that perhaps this too is accurate tradition. (If the plethron is here used as equivalent to the Roman iugerum, the size is about 29 acres.)[154] Their farm was no doubt the inherited family property, which may have remained in the possession of the family and its size have been well known in the second-century Palestinian Jewish Christian circles in which the

[154] Carrington (1957) 334, calculates nine or ten acres.

tradition reached its present form. Though not located by Hegesippus, we can safely assume that the farm was in Galilee.[155] This information about Zoker and James is a valuable indication of the socio-economic position of the *desposynoi*, and so probably of Jesus' own socio-economic background. It should also be borne in mind in discussion of the rural, agricultural context of the letter of James (5:4, 7) and its denunciation of wealthy landowners (5:1–6).

Hegesippus' statement that Zoker and James 'exercised leadership over every church' (προηγοῦνται πάσης ἐκκλησίας: *HE* 3:32:6) may be an exaggeration (and presumably, since according to Hegesippus this leadership of the churches was contemporary with the leadership of the Jerusalem church by Simon the son of Clopas, he means only that they participated in the leadership of the churches throughout Palestine). Hegesippus' main concern in reporting the tradition about them is to show that reliable Christian leaders, who had known those who had known the Lord, were in charge of the churches of Palestine until the reign of Trajan. He may therefore have exaggerated the authority of Zoker and James. But their prominence in the Jewish Christian tradition he reports can assure us that they were at least important leaders in the churches of Galilee.[156]

No doubt the period in which Hegesippus places them is approximately correct. But we cannot be as precise as he is. The connection with Domitian may be quite artificial, and equally artificial is Hegesippus' other piece of temporal information about them: that 'they remained until [the time of] Trajan Caesar' (*HE* 3:32:6). For Hegesippus this information has more than a merely temporal significance, as is revealed by the immediately following words: 'until the son of an uncle of the Lord, the aforesaid Simon son of Clopas, was informed against by the sects . . .' (*HE* 3:32:6). Simon's martyr-

[155] Lohmeyer (1936) 54; Bagatti (1969) 13.

[156] Bagatti (1969) 14 (cf. Bagatti [1965] 261), by connecting this passage with Julius Africanus' report (*ap.* Eusebius, *HE* 1:7:14), deduces that they were heads of the two Christian communities at Nazareth and Kokhaba. However, Hegesippus' phrase seems not to localize them in specific churches but to give them a broad authority throughout Palestine.

dom in the reign of Trajan is the point at which Hegesippus assumes the influence of the grandsons of Jude must also have disappeared. This is because he sees the martyrdom of Simon, the last of the generation of Jesus and the apostles, as the point after which the pristine purity of the church succumbed to heretical teachers (*HE* 3:32:7–8). Heretical teaching in the Palestinian churches had already begun secretly with Thebouthis (*HE* 4:22:4–5), but was able to flourish only after the passing of the generation of the apostles and the generation of those who had known them (3:32:8).[157] It is this rather artificial scheme, hingeing on the date of Simon's martyrdom and serving Hegesippus' overall purpose of apologetic, that determines the limit he gives to the period of activity of Zoker and James. Thus, although it is probably approximately correct, it cannot be relied on precisely.

VI. Jacob of Sikhnin

The purpose of this section is to raise the possibility that James the grandson of Jude was also remembered in Jewish tradition. Our major concern will be with a story (which has been much discussed for the sake of its evidence about Jesus and Jewish Christianity) about the well known Rabbi Eliezer ben Hyrcanus and a certain Jacob of Sikhnin. It is found in three somewhat divergent versions. For ease of reference to Maier's discussion of these texts and for cross reference between them, I have divided each into sections A–H as in Maier's synoptic presentation[158] of them:

t. Ḥull. 2:24:

> (A) The case of R. Eliezer, who was arrested for *mînût*, and they brought him to the tribunal for judgment. The *hegemon* [governor] said to him, 'Does an old man like you occupy himself with such things?' He said to him, 'Faithful is the judge concerning me [i.e., I rely on the judge].' The *hegemon* [governor] supposed that he only said this of him, but he was not thinking of any but his Father in heaven. He [the governor] said to him,

[157] Cf. Lawlor (1917) 62–64.
[158] Maier (1978) 145–151.

'Since I am trusted concerning yourself, thus also will I be. I said, perhaps these societies err concerning these things [or: Is it possible that these white hairs should err in such matters?]. *Dimissus* [pardoned]. Behold, you are released.' (B) And when he had been released from the tribunal, he was troubled because he had been arrested for *mînût*. His disciples came in to console him, but he would not take comfort. R. Aqiba came in and said to him, 'Rabbi, shall I say to you why you are perhaps grieving?' He said to him, 'Say on.' He said to him, (C) 'Perhaps one of the *mînîm* has said to you a word of *mînût* and it has pleased you.' He said, 'By heaven, you have reminded me! (D) Once I was walking along the street of Sepphoris, and I met Jacob of Kephar Sikhnin, and he said to me a word of *mînût* in the name of *Yēšûaʿ ben Pntyry*, and it pleased me. (F) And I was arrested for words of *mînût* because I transgressed the words of Torah, *Keep your way far from her, and do not go near the door of her house, for many a victim has she laid low* [Prov 5:8; 7:26].' (H) And R. Eliezer used to say, 'Ever let a man flee from what is hateful, and from that which resembles what is hateful.'[159]

Eccles. R. 1:8:3:

R. Eliezer was once arrested because of *mînût*, and the *hegemon* [governor] took him and made him ascend a dais to be tried. He said to him, 'Rabbi, can a great man like you occupy himself with those idle matters?' He answered him, 'Faithful is the judge concerning me.' He [the governor] thought that he was alluding to him, whereas he said it with reference to God. He thereupon said to him, 'Since I have been acknowledged right by you, I too have been thinking and say, "Is it possible that these academies should go astray with such idle matters!" You are consequently acquitted and free.' (B) After R. Eliezer had left the dais, he was sorely grieved at having been arrested because of *mînût*. His disciples visited him to console him, but he would not accept [their words of comfort]. R. Aqiba visited him and said to him, (C) 'Rabbi, perhaps one of the *mînîm* expounded something in your presence which was acceptable to you.' He answered, 'By heaven, you have reminded me! (D) Once I was walking up the main street of Sepphoris when there came toward me a man named Jacob of Kephar Sikhnaya who told me something in the name of *Yēšû ben Pndr*' which pleased me, (E) viz.

---

[159] Translation from Herford (1903) 137–138 (altered).

"It is written in your Torah, *You shall not bring the hire of a harlot, or the wages of a dog, into the house of the Lord your God in payment for any vow* [Deut 23:18]. What is to be done with them?" I told him that they were prohibited [for every use]. He said to me, "They are prohibited as an offering, but is it permissible to destroy them?" I retorted, "In that case, what is to be done with them?" He said to me, "Let bath-houses and privies be made with them." I exclaimed, "You have said an excellent thing," and the law [not to listen to the words of a *mîn*] escaped my memory at the time. When he saw that I acknowledged his words, he added, "Thus said *Yēšû ben Pndr'*: From filth they came and on filth they should be expended; as it is said, *From the hire of a harlot she gathered them, and to the hire of a harlot they shall return* [Mic 1:7]. Let them be spent on privies for the public," and the thought pleased me. (F) On that account I was arrested for *mînût*. More than that, I transgressed what is written in the Torah, *Keep your way far from her, and do not go near the door of her house* [Prov 5:8] – *Keep your way far from her* – i.e. *mînût*, and do not go near the door of her house, i.e. immorality. Why? *For many a victim has she laid low; yea, all her slain are a mighty host* [Prov 7:26].'[160]

b. 'Abod. Zar. 16b–17a:

(A) When R. Eliezer was arrested because of *mînût*, they brought him up to the tribune to be judged. Said the *hegemon* [governor] to him, 'How can a sage man like you occupy himself with those idle things?' He replied 'I acknowledge the judge as right.' The *hegemon* [governor] thought that he referred to him – though he really referred to his Father in heaven – and said, 'Because you have acknowledged me as right, *Dimissus* [pardoned]. You are acquitted.' (B) When he came home, his disciples called on him to console him, but he would accept no consolation. Said R. Aqiba to him, 'Master, will you permit me to say one thing of what you have taught me?' He replied, 'Say it.' He said, (C) 'Master, perhaps some of the teaching of the *mînîm* came to you, and you did approve of it, and because of that you were arrested?' He exclaimed, 'Aqiba, you have reminded me. (D) I was once walking in the upper-market of Sepphoris when I came across one of the disciples of *Yēšû hannôṣrî*,[161] Jacob of Kephar Sikhnaya by name, who said to me,

---

[160] Translation from Cohen (1939) 26–28 (altered).
[161] The name is missing in some manuscripts.

(E) "It is written in your Torah, *You shall not bring the hire of a harlot* . . . *into the house of the Lord your God* [Deut 23:18]. May such money be applied to the creation of a retiring place for the high priest?" To which I made no reply. He said to me, "Thus was I taught by *Yēšû han-nôṣrî*,[162] *From the hire of a harlot she gathered them, and to the hire of a harlot they shall return* [Mic 1:7], they came from a place of filth, let them go to a place of filth." Those words pleased me very much, (F) and that is why I was arrested for *mînût*; for thereby I transgressed the scriptural words, *Keep your way far from her* – which refers to *mînût* – *and do not go near the door of her house* [Prov 5:8] – which refers to the ruling power.'[163]

Most discussion of this story has taken it for granted that it can be treated as a reliable historical account,[164] even though it should have been clear that this is a very questionable approach to a tradition of this kind. Neusner, is his study of the traditions about Eliezer ben Hyrcanus included it in the category he called 'the fair traditions' (following the 'best' and the 'better' traditions) and considered it difficult to say whether it had a foundation in historical fact.[165] But recently Maier has subjected the tradition to an extremely detailed tradition-historical analysis, which deprives the story not only of any claim to historicity but also, in his view, of any reference to Jesus or Christianity.[166] It will not be possible in the present context to discuss all the details of Maier's analysis and conclusions, which are also part of his broader argument that there are no authentic references to Jesus in early rabbinic traditions, but certainly his case cannot be ignored. His reconstruction of the tradition history of this story is unverifiably, as well as unnecessarily, complex, and his elimination of any reference to Christianity seems contrived, but he

---

[162] The name is missing in some manuscripts.

[163] Translation from Mishcon and Cohen (1935) 84–85 (altered).

[164] Graetz (1885); Laible (1893) 62–66; Herford (1903) 140–145; Klausner (1925) 37–44; Lieberman (1944) 20–24; Jeremias (1957) 10–12; Freudenberger (1968); Manns (1977) 187–189; Freyne (1980) 348; Simon (1986) 184; Pritz (1988) 96–97, 101–102.

[165] Neusner (1973) II 201–202, 366–367.

[166] Maier (1978) 144–181.

has rightly raised the tradition-historical questions which must be confronted if this tradition is to be used as evidence for anything and he has made important observations on many aspects of the tradition.

Maier regards the story of Eliezer's arrest and release (A) as an originally independent anecdote (probably with the addition of H, which draws the moral, but this is more dubious), which has been expanded later in several stages by the addition of further material. His reconstruction of the various stages of expansion is very speculative, but he may well be right that A was originally an independent unit of tradition[167] – an entertaining anecdote about Eliezer's escape from a charge of *mînût*. A rather similar tale of a rabbi who eludes a Gentile judge is told in b. Ber. 58a.[168]

Most interpreters have considered, in view of the later part of the tradition (C–E), that Eliezer was accused of being a Christian, but Maier argues that Eliezer was suspected of participating in a morally disreputable event – presumably some kind of orgy – such as would easily be associated with *mînîm* (Jewish apostates). Hence the moral drawn in H, which is a maxim usually cited in connexion with sexual immorality.[169] However, the problem with this interpretation is that it fails to confront the question: On what kind of charge of *mînût* would Eliezer have been tried before the Roman governor? This question does not presuppose that the story is a historical report. Even a purely fictitious anecdote from the second century A.D. (Maier himself dates A before 132) would need some degree of verisimilitude. As Liebermann has shown, the account of the trial accurately reflects contemporary legal procedure.[170] So it must be assumed that the charge is one that would have been heard in the Roman governor's court. On this assumption, an accusation of dissolute living is unlikely. The only kind of *mînût*

---

[167] So also Neusner (1973) II 199, 366–367.

[168] Cf. Neusner (1973) II 366: 'The primary element of the story therefore contains a commonplace motif.'

[169] Maier (1978) 157–160.

[170] Lieberman (1944) 20–24; cf. also Freudenberger (1968).

with which a Roman governor would have been concerned is Christianity. The maxim in H is of a kind which is naturally flexible in application, and H, which occurs only in the Tosephta version, may well be a late addition to that version of the tradition.

Since Eliezer is known to have lived in the late first and early second centuries, Herford associated the incident with the persecution of Christians in Palestine during the reign of Trajan, in which Symeon the son of Clopas was martyred.[171] In fact it is not at all clear from Hegesippus' account that this was a persecution of Christians as such, or indeed that it was a persecution, as distinct from an incident in the continuing Roman anxiety about Jewish political messianism between the two revolts. According to Hegesippus, presumed Davidides who were not Christians also came under suspicion (*ap.* Eusebius, *HE* 3:12; 3:32:4), and although, in one of his accounts of Symeon's martyrdom, the charge against him is said to have been that he was descended from David *and* a Christian (*HE* 3:32:3), in the context this must mean that his Christian allegiance aggravated the suspicion attached to his being a Davidide, not that he would have been arrested even if he had not been a Davidide. So we have no secure ground for associating this story of Eliezer with a specific persecution of Christians during his lifetime. On the other hand, we know that there was sporadic local action against Christians by the Roman authorities in other parts of the Empire even before the reign of Trajan and certainly during and after his reign. Pliny's correspondence takes it for granted that the profession of Christianity was illegal. So there is no difficulty in supposing this story to have been credible as an anecdote during or soon after Eliezer's lifetime. For our present purposes there is no need to attempt to decide whether an historical event lies behind it.

The addition of the rest of the material in the tradition to the anecdote turns it into a very explicit warning against any form of association with *mînîm*. The most important question about the significance of this material concerns the origin of

[171] Herford (1903) 140–142.

section E. This section, which is integral to the Babli version of the tradition, is missing in the Tosephta. The version in the Midrash is evidently a conflation of the two traditions, as can be seen from its repetition of the words, 'and it pleased me,' which it has both before and after section E (i.e. both as a conclusion to section D, as they are in t. Ḥull. 2:24, and as a conclusion to section E, as they are in b. 'Abod. Zar. 16b–17a), as well as its relative closeness to the Tosephta version before section E and its relative closeness to the Babli version from section E onwards. It may well, however, preserve a more original form of section E than the abbreviated form in b. 'Abod. Zar. 16b–17a.

Maier is undecided whether section E has dropped out of the Palestinian tradition preserved in t. Ḥull. 2:24.[172] It seems most likely that it has.[173] Section E is a standard piece of halakhic discussion. There is nothing unusual or 'heretical' about the conclusion. There is no reason why the conclusion in itself should not have pleased Eliezer. What is objectionable, according to the tradition, is not the conclusion but that Eliezer should have heard it from a *mîn*.[174] His apparently innocent halakhic discussion with Jacob was an infringement of the prohibition on even conversing with a *mîn*, which is explained as the meaning of Proverbs 5:8. Thus the moral of the story is that, just as this otherwise unobjectionable conversation with the *mîn* Jacob led to Eliezer's arrest for *mînût*, so any contact with *mînîm* is to be avoided lest it lead to guilt by association. Once the longer version of the story is understood in this way, the shorter version in t. Ḥull. 2:24 is intelligible as an abbreviation. In this version, what Jacob said to Eliezer is not reported, but it is not unexceptionable: it is 'a word of *mînût*.' The tradents of this version may have been unwilling to condemn Eliezer for approving of so unexceptionable a statement as the longer version attributes to Jacob. Alternatively, their problem with the longer version may

---

[172] Maier (1978) 168–170, 174–175.
[173] The opposite view in Schlatter (1925) 449 n. 360; Jeremias (1957) 12; Neusner (1973) II 199.
[174] Maier (1978) 168–169.

have been that Jacob gave his halakhic opinion in the name of Jesus. For these later tradents such an unobjectionable judgment could not be attributed to Jesus, nor was a halakhic discussion of this kind consistent with what they knew of Christianity. For them, a statement made in the name of Jesus must have been 'a word of *mînût*.'

The references to Jesus are different in the Palestinian and Babylonian versions of the tradition. In the first place, the name is different: *Yēšûaʿ ben Pnṭyry* in t. Ḥull. 2:24, *Yēšû han-nôṣrî* in b. ʿAbod. Zar. 16b–17a. Secondly, the references to Jesus occur at different points. Neither of these differences counts against the originality of a reference to Jesus in the tradition. The Babylonian tradition has substituted for the unfamiliar *Yēšûaʿ ben Pnṭyry* its normal form of reference to Jesus: *Yēšû han-nôṣrî* (i.e. Jesus the Christian). The difference of position has resulted from the abbreviation of the tradition in t. Ḥull. 2:24 through the omission of E (and perhaps also from the abbreviation of E in the present form of the Babli tradition).

Maier considers the references to Jesus in b. ʿAbod. Zar. 16b–17a to be entirely secondary,[175] but is less clear in his treatment of *Yēšûaʿ ben Pnṭyry* in t. Ḥull. 2:24. After throwing doubt on it as perhaps as introduction from the story in t. Ḥull. 2:22–23 (which has 'in the name of *Yēšûaʿ ben Pnṭr*''), resulting from the bringing together of the two traditions,[176] he seems eventually to consider the reference in t. Ḥull. 2:24 to be original, but to be a reference *not* to Jesus of Nazareth, but to an unknown 'halakhist.'[177] The problem he seems to find in supposing that the tradition attributed the halakhic discussion of section E to Jesus is not a real one. In second-century Palestine Jewish Christians might well be known to be interested in matters of halakhah. But in any case, the tradition is not really interested in reporting what Jacob might actually have said and need not presuppose any close acquaintance with the views that Christians ascribed to Jesus. Rather,

[175] Maier (1978) 165, 172–173.
[176] Maier (1978) 164.
[177] Maier (1978) 176, 264–265.

its point is to represent Eliezer as hearing an unexceptionable religious opinion from a well-known *mîn*. That Jacob of Sikhnin was a well-known Jewish Christian teacher is the only accurate information which need be presupposed for the purpose of the story.

However, that this *is* accurate information can be shown by a closer consideration of the name *Yēšûaʿ ben Pnṭyry*. Both parts of the name are unusual. Jesus of Nazareth in rabbinic literature is usually *Yēšû*, not *Yēšûaʿ*, while the patronymic which has been commonly regarded as designating Jesus of Nazareth is usually *Pandēraʾ*, not *Pnṭyry*. In this respect, Eccles. R. 1:1:8, which has *Yēšû ben Pandēraʾ*, has been assimilated to the more familiar form.[178] The only parallel – but not an exact one – to *Yēšûaʿ ben Pnṭyry* in t. Ḥull. 2:24 is *Yēšûaʿ ben Pnṭrʾ* in the adjacent story in t. Ḥull. 2:22–23, which will be discussed below. At any rate, this shows that *Yēšûaʿ ben Pnṭyry* in t. Ḥull. 2:24 is an *independent* tradition, not a secondary addition to the tradition by analogy with references to *Yēšû ben Pandēraʾ* elsewhere. Maier denies that the traditions about *Ben Pandēraʾ* originally referred to Jesus of Nazareth at all, or have anything to do with Celsus' report of a second-century Jewish tradition naming Panthera as the father of Jesus (Origen, *c. Cels.* 1:32).[179] But whatever may be thought about *Ben Pandēraʾ*, the significance of *Yēšûaʿ ben Pnṭyry* in t. Ḥull. 2:24 must be assessed on its own merits. *Pnṭyry* is closer to Πανθήρα than *Pandēraʾ* is, while *Yēšûaʿ ben Pnṭyry* is more likely to be identical with Jesus son of Panthera than with the otherwise unknown *Ben Pṭyrʾ* (b. B. Meṣ. 62a) suggested by Maier.[180] There seems a good case for the view that the tradition did regard Jacob of Sikhnin as a follower of Jesus of Nazareth.

Jacob will have been named in this tradition only because he was a well-known Galilean *mîn* contemporary with Eliezer. The historicity of his meeting with Eliezer must be very doubtful.[181] No conclusions about him can safely be drawn

[178] So Maier (1978) 176–177.
[179] Maier (1978) 265–266.
[180] Maier (1978) 181–182.
[181] Against the view that the historical Eliezer was sympathetic to Christ-

from his reported discussion with Eliezer, still less can the question of an authentic saying of Jesus be raised. Even the location in Sepphoris probably indicates no more than that that was the sort of place where one might meet a *mîn*.[182] However, the information we can draw from the tradition is not negligible: that Jacob came from Sikhnin (the place-name has no function in the tradition except to identify a well-known figure), that he was a Christian teacher and a very prominent one, well-known in the rabbinic circles in which this tradition originated. Apart from the rather dubious case of his namesake Jacob of Sama (to be discussed below), he is the only Jewish Christian between the immediate disciples of Jesus and the end of the third century whose name survives in Jewish literature. Attempts to identify him with a Christian of the first generation (James the Lord's brother,[183] James the son of Alphaeus[184]) have rightly been regarded as chronologically unlikely. It is not historically impossible[185] that Eliezer should have encountered even James the Lord's brother before his martyrdom in A.D. 62, though Sepphoris is not a plausible setting for such a meeting. But if the tradition is a second-century one, it will have associated Eliezer with a *mîn* who was remembered as active at a later period, in which the traditions about Eliezer himself are set, i.e. at the end of the first and beginning of the second century. But if Jacob of Sikhnin was not one of the followers of Jesus named in the New Testament, must we conclude, as most scholars have done, that he is 'completely unknown from Christian

---

ian teaching, see Neusner (1973) II 332–333. In other traditions Eliezer discusses the exegesis of Deut 23:18 (m. Par. 2:3; t. Par. 2:2B: see Neusner [1973] I 302–304) in a way which 'is consistent, in a general way' with the teaching Eliezer approves in section E of our tradition (Neusner [1973] 366), but this can have little value in indicating the historicity of the tradition.

[182] Maier (1978) 155. Goodman (1983) 74, thinks of a public disputation (with Rabbi Eliezer in the audience) in the market place of Sepphoris.

[183] Klausner (1925) 41–42.

[184] Schoeps (1949) 212 n. 1; Cohen (1939) 27 n. 4.

[185] Cf. Neusner (1973) II 294–295: Eliezer was probably educated as a Pharisee before 70.

sources.'[186] The possibility that he is James the grandson of
Jude, who must have been a fairly close contemporary of
Eliezer, has never been raised. Of course, the name was a
very common one. But Jude's grandson was a prominent
leader in the Galilean churches. Moreover Sikhnin (t. Ḥull.
2:24) or Sikhnaya (b. 'Abod. Zar. 16b–17a; Eccles. R.
1:1:8)[187] (Σωγάνη: Josephus, *Vita* 188, 265–266; modern
Sakhnin) is a mere six kilometres from Kokhaba, which, as we
have seen, was one of the two main centres of the mission of
the *desposynoi*. While the identity of Jacob of Sikhnin with
James the grandson of Jude cannot be proved, it could be said
to be somewhat probable.

Bagatti even claims to have identified his tomb. On a visit
to Sakhnin in 1961, he was shown a tomb known in local
tradition as that of 'James the Just' and venerated by Christians, Jews and Muslims. He considers that it could well date
from the second century. By the time of his second visit to
the village in 1966 the tomb had been restored and claimed as
that of Rabbi Joshua of Sakhnin.[188]

A puzzling tradition in the Babylonian Talmud (b. Giṭṭ.
57a) concerns a place called Kephar Sikhnaya of *Egypt*. Three
stories are told to illustrate how strictly the people of this
place adhered to *halakhah*, after which the question is asked,
'Since they were so virtuous, why were they punished?,' and
the answer given: 'Because they did not mourn for Jerusalem.'
Klein plausibly suggested that 'Egypt' (מצרים) be emended to
mînîm (מינים) or to 'Nazarenes' (נוצרים).[189] In that case, the
village's mysterious punishment, after A.D. 70, might be, as
Pritz suggests,[190] its general succumbing to *mînût*, in the form
of Jewish Christianity. Perhaps we may see here some
evidence of the success of the mission of the *desposynoi* in their
native Galilee.

Jacob of Sikhnin has usually been considered the same man

---

[186] Bagatti (1971B) 95.

[187] For the two forms of the name (Hebrew and Aramaic) see Maier
(1978) 164–165. On the place, see also Klein (1923) 20–21.

[188] Bagatti (1971A) 145–148.

[189] Klein (1909) 29–30 n.

[190] Pritz (1988) 100–101.

as a certain Jacob of Sama, who appears in another story set in the same period (t. Ḥull. 2:22–23; Eccles. R. 1:8:3; b. ʿAbod. Zar. 27b; j. ʿAbod. Zar. 40d–41a; j. Šabb. 14d–15a). Only two versions[191] need be given in this case:

t. Ḥull. 2:22–23:

The case of R. Eleazar ben Dama, whom a serpent bit. There came in Jacob, a man of Kephar Sama, to cure him in the name of *Yēšûaʿ ben Pnṭr*ʾ, but R. Ishmael would not allow it. He said, 'You are not permitted, Ben Dama.' He said, 'I will bring you a proof that he may heal me.' But he had not finished bringing a proof when he died. R. Ishmael said, 'Happy are you, Ben Dama, for you have departed in peace, and have not broken through the ordinances of the wise; for upon every one who breaks through the fence of the wise, punishment comes at last, as it is written, *Whoever breaks through a fence, a serpent shall bite him* [Eccles 10:8].'[192]

b. ʿAbod. Zar. 27b:

A man shall have no dealings with the *mînîm*, nor be cured by them, even for the sake of an hour of life. The case of Ben Dama, sister's son of R. Ishmael, whom a serpent bit. There came Jacob the *mîn* of Kephar Sikhnaya to cure him; but R. Ishmael would not allow him. And he [Ben Dama] said to him, 'R. Ishmael, my brother, allow him, that I may be cured by him, and I will bring a text from the Torah that this is permitted.' But he had not finished his discourse when his soul departed, and he died. R. Ishmael pronounced over him, 'Happy are you, Ben Dama, for your body is pure and your soul has departed in purity, and you have not transgressed the words of your companions, who have said, *Whoever breaks through a fence, a serpent shall bite him* [Eccles 10:8].' It is different in regard to *mînût*, which bites a man, so that he comes to be bitten afterwards.[193]

There are two differences between the two versions which are important for our purposes. First, in the version in the Tosephta Jacob is going to heal Ben Dama in the name of *Yēšûaʿ ben Pnṭr*ʾ (so also other forms of the Palestinian tradi-

[191] A synopsis of three versions is in Maier (1978) 183–186.
[192] Translation from Herford (1903) 103 (altered).
[193] Translation from Herford (1903) 104 (altered).

tion, with variations in the name), whereas this reference to Jesus is lacking in the Babylonian Talmud. Secondly, Jacob is differently described in the two versions, as 'a man of Kephar Sama' in the first, but as 'the *mîn* of Kephar Sikhnaya' in the second. It is important to notice that both these differences relate to a requirement in the story: the need to explain why Jacob's healing is unacceptable in R Ishmael's judgment. In the Tosephta version it is unacceptable because it is in the name of *Yēšûaʿ ben Pnṭrʾ*, while in the Babli it is unacceptable because Jacob is a *mîn*.

The reference to Jesus may be considered first. Maier suggests,[194] following Friedländer, that this may belong to a late stage of the tradition and have been introduced from another healing story (in j. ʿAbod. Zar. 40d; j. Šabb. 14d; Eccles. R. 10:5:1).[195] In that story, a grandson of R. Joshua ben Levi is healed by a man who speaks to him in the name of *Yēšû Pndyrʾ*; again, the Rabbi disapproves of the healing. Since this story in j. Šabb. 14d is immediately adjacent to the story of Eleazar ben Dama and the form of the reference to *Yēšû* is there the same in both cases, the suggestion is that the phrase has migrated from one story to another. To evaluate this suggestion we need to compare the name in the various versions of these two stories and that of Eliezer discussed above (in which it is used in the same phrase: 'in the name of . . .'):

	t. Ḥull.	Eccles. R.	j. Šabb.	j. ʿAbod. Zar.
Eliezer	Yēšûaʿ ben Pnṭyry	[Yēšû][196] ben Pndrʾ		
Ben Dama	Yēšûaʿ ben Pnṭrʾ	Yēšû ben Pndrʾ	Yēšû Pndrʾ	Yēšû ben Pndrʾ
Joshua b. Levi		Yēšû bar Pndyrʾ	Yēšû Pndyrʾ	Yēšû ben Pndrʾ

[194] Maier (1978) 190–191.
[195] Synopsis of the three versions in Maier (1978) 193–194.
[196] *Yēšû* is lacking in one manuscript: see Maier (1978) 296 n. 305.

It is clear that in all four works there is a tendency to assimilate the name in one story to the name in another. All forms of the name can be explained on the hypothesis that a different form of the name was original in each story: in the Eliezer story *Yēšûaʿ ben Pnṭyry*, in the Eleazar ben Dama story *Yēšû ben Pndrʾ*, in the Joshua ben Levi story *Yēšû Pndyrʾ* or perhaps just *Pndyrʾ*. In each work other occurrences of the name have been assimilated, not always completely, to one form, different in the case of each work. This hypothesis completely explains the variations, as the hypothesis of a transfer of the phrase from one story where it was original to another where it was not cannot do. The conclusion is important: that the name already existed, in different forms, in each of the stories prior to its incorporation in its present literary context. In other words the name belongs to the *oral tradition* of each story, independently of the others. (It remains *possible*, however, as Maier maintains,[197] that *Yēšû*, though not *Yēšûaʿ*, is a later addition in every case.)

Turning to the description of Jacob in the Ben Dama story, we should note that the version in Eccles. R. 1:8:3 (not given above) describes him as 'a man of Kephar Sikhnaya,' but in a reference to the story in Eccles. R. 7:26:3 he is 'Jacob of Kephar Sama.' Clearly 'Sikhnaya' in 1:8:3 is an assimilation to the immediately preceding story of Eliezer and Jacob, where the Eccles. R. version has 'Jacob, a man of Kephar Sikhnaya.' Similarly, the description of Jacob as 'the *mîn* of Kephar Sikhnaya' in b. ʿAbod. Zar. 27b (the Ben Dama story) must be borrowed from the Eliezer story (b. ʿAbod. Zar. 16b–17a), where Jacob of Kephar Sikhnaya is clearly a *mîn*. In this case, the identification of the two Jacobs serves to explain why Jacob's cure in the Ben Dama story is unacceptable: because he is Jacob the *mîn*. We must conclude that in this story Jacob of Sama was original, Jacob of Sikhnaya is secondary. It is very unlikely that the two have been assimilated because the tradition *knew* they were the same man. So there is no foundation for the easy assumption in many

[197] Maier (1978) 195, 197–198.

modern discussions of these stories that the same Jacob is described in two different ways.[198]

However, if the description of Jacob as 'the *mîn* of Kephar Sikhnaya' in b. 'Abod. Zar. 27b is removed as secondary, this version of the story would contain no indication why Jacob's healing was unacceptable to R. Ishmael. This suggests two possibilities: (1) In the original form of the story the reason for the unacceptability of the healing was unexplained, presumably because Jacob of Sama was well known to be a religiously unacceptable person. When this was no longer self-evident, the Palestinian tradition explained it by adding the phrase 'in the name of [*Yēšû*] *ben Pndr*',' the Babylonian tradition by identifying him with the Jacob of Sikhnaya who was known from the story of his meeting with R. Eliezer to have been a *mîn*. However, since Jacob of Sama is nowhere else mentioned in rabbinic traditions, this possible explanation is less likely than the second. (2) The phrase 'in the name of [*Yēšû*] *ben Pndr*'' belonged to the tradition from the start, but the patronymic *Ben Pndr*' was unfamiliar in Babylonia and so the tradition was changed. This explanation is coherent with our explanation (above) of the different ways Jesus is referred to in the Palestinian and Babylonian forms of the Eliezer story. We might, however, have expected the Babylonian tradition simply to change the name to *Yēšû han-nôṣrî*, as has happened in the Eliezer story. So perhaps it is likely that as the tradition came to Babylonia the patronymic was used without *Yēšû* (cf. the references to *Ben Pndyr*' in b. Šabb. 104b; b. Sanh. 67a).

Whether Ben Pandera was originally Jesus we need not decide here. For the tradition has proved in any case to be probably irrelevant to our subject. Firstly, even if the reference is to Jesus, it may not be original to the tradition (possibility 1 above) and may not imply that Jacob was a Christian, for others used the name of Jesus for healing.[199] Secondly, the identification of Jacob of Sama with Jacob of Sikhnin/Sikhnaya must be doubtful. It is not certain where Sama is.

[198] Laible (1893) 77–78; Herford (1903) 106; Bagatti (1971B) 22; Freyne (1980) 347–348.

[199] Maier (1978) 192.

Bagatti identifies it with modern Kefr Simai, which is thirteen kilometres north of Sikhnin.[200] That the same Jacob should have been associated with both places is quite possible, but very uncertain.

VII. Conon the martyr

It is not the purpose of this book to pursue the history of Palestinian Jewish Christianity beyond the New Testament period, but something must be said, little though there is to be said, about the subsequent history of the *desposynoi*. Symeon, James and Zoker, as we have seen, were the leaders of the Jewish Christian movement in Jerusalem and Galilee at the beginning of the second century. We do not know whether other descendants of the family succeeded them. We do not know whether the last of the leaders of the Jewish Christian church of Jerusalem, Justus, was a member of the family, like his two predecessors. We do not even know whether, after the Bar Kokhba war and the expulsion of all Jews from Jerusalem, the succession to James continued in some other location (Nazareth? Pella? Kokhaba in Basanitis?). Apart from the three descendants of Joseph who were Christ-ian leaders in Ctesiphon-Seleucia in the second century (section II above), only one further member of the family of Jesus is known to us by name.[201]

Probably during the persecution of Christians in 250–251, under the emperor Decius,[202] a certain Conon, a gardener on the imperial estate, was martyred at Magydos in Pamphylia

[200] Bagatti (1971A) 197–202.

[201] Julius Africanus, writing in the first half of the third century, speaks of two traditions handed down by the relatives of Jesus (*ap.* Eusebius, *HE* 1:7:11), one of which concerns the reconciliation of the two genealogies of Jesus (1:7:2–10), while the other concerns Herod's destruction of genealogies and the family's preservation of theirs (1:7:11–14) (see chapter 7 section III.1 below). But he probably had these traditions in written Jewish Christ-ian sources. Nothing is implied about the activity of the *desposynoi* at the time when he was writing.

[202] In the extant acts of his martyrdom (see next note) there is no date, because (as is clear from 1:1) they were closely linked to the *Acts of SS. Papias, Diodorus and Claudianus*, martyred at the same time as Conon. The

in Asia Minor. According to the acts of his martyrdom,[203] when questioned in court as to his place of origin and his ancestry, he replied: 'I am of the city of Nazareth in Galilee, I am of the family (συγγένεια) of Christ, whose worship I have inherited from my ancestors, and whom I recognize as God over all things' (Mart. Conon 4:2). Any suspicion that he might be speaking metaphorically of his *spiritual* family, as a Christian, rather than a natural family relationship to Jesus, is dispelled by his claim to come from Nazareth, along with the consideration that Nazareth at that time was a thoroughly Jewish community.[204] His Greek name Conon is not especially surprising:[205] Greek names were widely used by Jews, including Galilean Jews. His acts, as we have them, are probably post-Constantinian and much of the account may be fictional,[206] but the sheer unexpectedness of a record of a member of the family of Jesus in Pamphylia at a time when, to judge by extant Christian literature of the period, the church at large had lost all interest in living members of that family, argues for the authenticity of at least this part of the account. Conon's employment as a gardener is consistent with what we know of the socio-economic status of the *desposynoi*.

The martyr from Nazareth was honoured in his homeland. In the old (pre-Byzantine) Palestinian liturgical calendar, which has been preserved in a Georgian manuscript, his com-

latter, which presumably were dated, have not survived (see van de Vorst [1911] 254). However, not only does the Roman Martyrology date Conon's martyrdom under Decius (Musurillo [1972] xxxiii), but also the *Life of Conon the Isaurian* (a namesake of our Conon), the first chapter of which summarizes the *Martyrdom of Conon* the gardener, dates the latter under Decius (in Halkin [1985] 6).

[203] Greek text and translation in Musurillo (1972) 186–193.

[204] Meyers and Strange (1981) 57, 134; cf. Epiphanius, *Pan.* 30:11:9–10.

[205] Against Musurillo (1972) 189 n. 4.

[206] Harnack (1904) 469; Musurillo (1972) xxxiii. Cf. van de Vorst (1911) 254, who compares the *Martyrdom of Conon* with the Panegyric of Asterius on St Phocas. But his case for borrowing by the former from the latter is not very strong. There are other martyrs called Conon from the same area: Conon of Iconium, put to death with his son, and Conon the Isaurian. But if there is any question of 'duplication' of Conons, it is Conon the Isaurian whose historicity must be doubted, since his *Life* is entirely legendary (Halkin [1935] 370–374; Halkin [1985]).

memoration is given special prominence, along with other feasts of specially Palestinian interest, as a feast preceded by an eight-week fast.[207] It is also possible that there is archaeological evidence – from the site of the church of the Annunciation in Nazareth – for his cult at Nazareth from very soon after his death. Before the fifth-century Byzantine church was built on this site, there was a third-century building built above two small caves. Architectural fragments of the building resemble synagogues of the period, but inscriptions and graffiti identify it as Christian and so presumably as a Jewish Christian church/synagogue.[208] One of the caves is traditionally known as the Grotto of the Annunciation; the other, smaller cave[209] was identified by the Franciscan excavators as a martyrium, because they believed it to have been dedicated to the memory of the martyr Conon. The evidence for this is indirect. The cave was in use before the fourth century, since a coin of the young Constantine was found in its third coat of plaster. An inscription and decorations on the wall from the earliest phase of its use suggest an association with a martyr,[210] and no other martyr of Nazareth from that time is known. Moreover, outside the entrance to the grotto, at the foot of the steps which lead down from the church to the caves, a mosaic was laid in the fourth century, bearing the inscription 'Gift of Conon deacon of Jerusalem.'[211] This Conon cannot, of course, have been the martyr, and he must have been a Gentile Christian, but his gift of the mosaic may have been inspired by love of his namesake the famous martyr of Nazareth and placed where the latter was commemorated.[212] If the association of the cave with Conon the martyr is justified, it must have been

[207] Garitte (1958) 242–243, 434. Although there are other martyrs named Conon (cf. pp. 173, 244, 263, 338, 373, 380), the inclusion of the martyr commemorated on 5 June with the other Palestinian saints (pp. 433–434) shows that this one must be Conon of Nazareth.

[208] Strange (1983) 17; Meyers and Strange (1981) 130–135.

[209] On this cave, see Bagatti (1969) 185–213.

[210] Bagatti (1969) 193, 196–198; cf. also Testa (1969) 112–123, for the Jewish Christian character of the martyrium.

[211] Bagatti (1969) 100.

[212] Bagatti (1969) 198.

dedicated to his memory not very long after his martyrdom. But to conclude, with Bagatti,[213] that the cave was actually be- neath his family home is to carry uncertain speculation too far.

In any case, it seems clear that not simply Conon's ancestors, but Conon himself came from Nazareth, so that members of the family of Jesus were still living there in the first half of the third century. A passage of Epiphanius (*Pan.* 30:11:9–10), which some have taken to mean that there were no Christians at all in Nazareth before the time of Const- antine,[214] in fact refers only to the state of affairs at the time of Constantine, not in the previous century, but in any case clearly has only Gentile Christians in view.[215] But the fact that Joseph of Tiberias, a converted Jew, from whom Epi- phanius had this information, was himself compelled to leave the Jewish city of Tiberias and take refuge outside Galilee in the Gentile city of Scythopolis (Beth Shean) suggests that in the early fourth century some at least of the Jewish Christian communities of Galilee may have been finding it more diffi- cult to survive alongside their non-Christian Jewish neigh- bours. We can only guess that remaining members of the family of Jesus may have abandoned Nazareth at that time.

That Conon was revered as a martyr in the Catholic Church of the fourth century does suggest that the *desposynoi* had not thrown in their lot with those Jewish Christian groups, such as the Ebionites, who were regarded as sectarian and heretical by Catholic writers. They can most plausibly by placed among those 'Nazarene' Jewish Christians whose distinctness from Gentile Catholic Christianity was cultural rather than doctrinal, even to the extent of remembering Paul and the Pauline mission with full approval.[216] Such groups, however, were slowly dwindling, under the impact of the consolidation of rabbinic Judaism in Galilee, the success of Ebionite, Elkasite and Gnostic influences in Jewish Christ- ianity east of the Jordan, and cultural isolation from the Gen-

[213] Bagatti (1969) 198–199.
[214] Goodman (1983) 106, seems to think it proves there had never been any Jewish Christianity in Galilee.
[215] Bagatti (1969) 17–18.
[216] Pritz (1988) 64–65; cf. 44, 68–69.

tile church. We might have expected descendants of the family of Jesus to have retained the memory of such illustrious ancestry for many centuries. That they disappear so rapidly and completely from history can only be attributed to the marginalized status of the groups to which they belonged. Had the literature of those groups survived in more than the few fragments we have, we might know much more about the *desposynoi*. Meanwhile, while the Catholic church delighted in elaborating legends about the family background of Jesus, those who might have been able to seek out the surviving members of the family and record some really valuable traditions – Eusebius, Epiphanius, Jerome – seem to have had not the slightest interest in doing so.

VIII. A Christian Caliphate?

The observation that not only James, but also other members of the family of Jesus were prominent in the leadership of the churches of Palestine down to at least the early second century prompted a series of scholars from Harnack to Schoeps to speak of a Christian 'caliphate' or of a dynastic form of Christianity,[217] in which the highest authority in the church passed down from Jesus through dynastic succession of members of his family, much as the highest authority in early Islam passed down through the descendants of the family of the prophet Muhammed. This thesis of a dynastic succession in Palestinian Jewish Christianity was strongly attacked by von Campenhausen,[218] whose article provoked an equally strong defence and reaffirmation of the thesis by Stauffer.[219]

Our investigation in this chapter allows us to acknowledge some truth in the arguments of both von Campenhausen and Stauffer. The thesis of a strictly dynastic succession cannot be maintained, but it has to be admitted that family relationship to Jesus played some part in the prominence of the *desposynoi* in the leadership of the Palestinian churches:

[217] References in von Campenhausen (1950–51) 134–135; see also Elliott-Binns (1956) 56, 60.
[218] von Campenhausen (1950–51).
[219] Stauffer (1952).

(1) In the first place, it should be noted that neither James nor Symeon could have been regarded as successors to Jesus in a strict sense, as though Jesus himself were just one more successor to the throne of David, who could be succeeded by the next in line to the throne, as Solomon succeeded David. In the belief of the first Jewish Christians, Jesus was not just a successor to the throne of David, but the *eschatological* heir to the throne of David, who would himself reign for ever when he came in glory. He could have no successors to his throne. (That this is precisely how the brothers of Jesus saw the matter will be demonstrated in chapter 7, but in any case nothing we know about early Christianity permits us to think otherwise.) More plausible than the idea of successors to Jesus, as a model for the way the *desposynoi* may have been regarded, is the association of members of a ruler's family with him in government. It was normal practice in the ancient East for members of the royal family to hold high offices in government. Those places on the right and left side of his throne which the sons of Zebedee coveted (Mark 10:37) could readily be thought due to the brothers of Jesus. Prophecies could have been found which associated the Messiah's family, the house of David, with him in his rule (Ps 122:5; Zech 12:8).[220] The term *desposynoi* ('those who belong to the Sovereign': see chapter 6 section III below) could well have precisely this connotation of a royal family sharing in Jesus the messianic King's rule.[221] In this looser sense, the influence of a dynastic principle is plausible, especially when we consider how very deep-rooted in contemporary Jewish thinking was the association of authority with a family, rather than with an isolated individual.[222]

(2) But we should also take account of contrary indications. The authority of the brothers of Jesus was certainly not

[220] Stauffer (1952) 199.

[221] Cerfaux (1954A) 52–53.

[222] This point is well documented by Stauffer (1952) 194–197: he refers to the high priesthood, the Hasmonaeans, the dynasty of revolutionary leaders founded by Hezekiah and his son Judas of Gamala, and the 'dynasty' of Hillel. 1 Macc 5:62 is a striking indication of the way authority could attach precisely to a *family* (rather than merely a succession).

founded solely on their family relationship with Jesus. James certainly, and the other brothers of Jesus probably (see section II above), had received, like the apostles, a commission from the risen Christ himself. In this sense, their authority was not dynastic but apostolic – of the same kind as that of the twelve and the wider circle of apostles. Yet we have noticed (section II above) that they were not *called* apostles, since the title 'brother of the Lord' seems to have functioned in their case as the title 'apostle' did for others. It was a way of including them in the circle of authoritative leaders while acknowledging a certain distinctiveness in their case. Among the apostles they were marked out as 'the brothers of the Lord,' rather as 'the twelve' were also distinguished as a special category (Mark 14:10, 17, 43; John 5:70–71; 20:24; Acts 1:26; 1 Cor 15:5; Rev 21:14). While they would not have had the position of authority they had without a dominical commission in a resurrection appearance, their relationship to Jesus seems also to have had some weight.

(3) Thus the title 'brother of the Lord,' like the broader term *desposynoi*, bears witness to the fact that *some* importance was attached to their family relationship with Jesus. But there is also evidence that a need was felt to qualify the title lest it be misunderstood. While Palestinian Jewish Christian usage is no doubt reflected in the simple phrase 'brothers of the Lord' in Paul (1 Cor 9:5; Gal 1:19), other sources indebted to Jewish Christianity which preserve this usage also attest a degree of reservation about it. Hegesippus speaks of 'Jude, his brother according to the flesh, as he was called [λεγομένου]' (Eusebius, *HE* 3:20:1), presumably reporting Jewish Christian usage, while in another passage dependent on, though not explicitly quoting Hegesippus, Eusebius calls members of the family of Jesus 'those who belonged to the Lord's family according to the flesh' (τοῖς πρὸς γένους κατὰ σάρκα τοῦ κυρίου) (*HE* 3:11:1). That the qualification 'according to the flesh' (κατὰ σάρκα) was Jewish Christian terminology with reference to the family of Jesus is also suggested by the fact that Julius Africanus, in a passage dependent on Jewish Christian sources, refers to Jesus' 'relatives according to the flesh' (οἱ κατὰ σάρκα συγγενεῖς) (Eusebius, *HE* 1:7:11). James is also called

'our Lord's brother according to the flesh' in Didascalia 24, which probably preserves Jewish Christian tradition (cf. Ap. Const. 8:35:1: 'the brother of Christ according to the flesh'; and Joseph as Jesus' father 'according to the flesh' in Hist Jos;[223] cf also Rom 1:3; 9:5; 1 Clem 32:2 for Jesus' ancestry κατὰ σάρκα). In these phrases 'according to the flesh'[224] designates the realm of merely physical relationships, by contrast with relationships 'according to the Spirit' (cf. Rom 1:3–4; Gal 3:23, 29; Philem 16). So, whereas 'the Lord's brother' might indicate a special relationship with Jesus not shared by other Christian leaders, 'the Lord's brother *according to the flesh*' relativizes that relationship as *only* a natural relationship. It recognizes that to call a natural brother of Jesus *the Lord's* brother really is as inappropriate as to call the one who is David's Lord David's son (Mark 12:35–37: for the coherence of this passage with the christological attitude of the brothers of Jesus, see chapter 7 section IV).

(4) There is also evidence that the brothers of Jesus themselves[225] were responsible for this downplaying of their family relationship to the Lord. James begins his letter: 'James, a servant of God and of the Lord Jesus Christ' (Jas 1:1), while Jude begins his: 'Jude, a servant of Jesus Christ and brother of James' (Jude 1).[226] In this first part of the 'parties' formula' of a letter opening, the author needed both to identify himself and to indicate his authority for addressing his readers. James did not need to distinguish himself from other Christian leaders called James: his name is sufficient self-identification. Jude did need to identify himself and does so by reference to his well-known brother James. Neither uses the title 'brother of the Lord' either to identify himself (as Jude could have done) or to establish his authority. Neither establishes his authority by using the title 'apostle,' which was not generally

---

[223] For a claim that HistJos preserves some Jewish Christian traditions, see Manns (1977) 94–105.

[224] On the phrase, see Blinzler (1967) 108–110.

[225] For the authenticity of the letter of Jude, see chapter 3 section VII. The authenticity of the letter of James cannot be discussed here (see n. 233 below), but this paragraph is itself an argument in its favour.

[226] See Bauckham (1983A) 23–25.

used of them, though their authority was apostolic, but both avoid the title 'brother of the Lord,' which was commonly used of them in place of 'apostle.' Instead, both use a term ('servant') which was an honorific title of authority ('servant of God' designates Abraham [Ps 105:42], Moses [Neh 9:14; Rev 15:3], David [Ps 89:3], Daniel [Dan 6:20]) and could be used by an apostolic author in a letter-opening ('servant of God': Tit 1:1; 'servant of Jesus Christ': Rom 1:1; Phil 1:1; 2 Pet 1:1). But it indicates their authority as deriving from a call to serve the Lord Jesus Christ. They avoid, it seems, the term which might suggest that their claim to authority was based on their family relationship to Jesus ('brother of the Lord') and characterize themselves instead as servants of the Lord. This is not modesty, as some commentators suggest. It is recognition that natural relationship to Jesus is not a basis for authority in the church. 'Servant' goes better than 'brother' with 'Lord.'

(5) This relativizing of family relationship to Jesus may well have its roots in the Gospel tradition. As we have seen (section I above), sayings such as Mark 3:31–35; Luke 11:27–28 (cf. GThom 79, 99) should not be attributed to the evangelists' polemic against the authority of the family of Jesus. They reflect Jesus' own teaching that what counts in the kingdom of God is not natural relationship to himself, but doing the will of God. Such sayings are likely to have been current in the Gospel tradition as known in the circle of the relatives of Jesus.[227] They run directly counter to the instinctively dynastic attitude to authority which was current in Jewish, as in other ancient cultures. If the brothers of Jesus resisted this attitude and disclaimed the advantage which their kinship with Jesus gave them in popular estimation, it may well have been out of faithfulness to Jesus' own teaching.

(6) So we must conclude that there is unlikely to have been an explicit dynastic principle operative in favour of the *desposynoi*, and certainly not one which they themselves advocated and maintained. If anything, they played down the

---

[227] The suggestion of Stauffer (1952) 198, that James will have regarded the resurrection appearance of Jesus to him as annulling such sayings is scarcely plausible.

significance of their kinship with Jesus. But it is nevertheless likely that the dynastic thinking – and even more the dynastic feeling – current in the culture and deeply rooted in the religious traditions of the culture will have influenced, consciously or unconsciously, the continuing authority of the family of Jesus in Palestinian Jewish Christianity. After all, a kind of Christian dynastic succession could come about – doubtless without there being any question of a recognized dynastic *principle* – even where there was nothing remotely like kinship with Jesus at stake. Polycrates, bishop of Ephesus at the end of the second century, wrote: 'I live according to the tradition of my relatives, some of whom I have followed. For seven of my family were bishops and I am the eighth' (*ap*. Eusebius, *HE* 5:24:6).[228] So it is entirely probable that membership of the family of Jesus played a major, though not the only, part in the choice of Symeon as James' successor (section IV above), and in the authority exercised by other members of the family, such as the grandsons of Jude, in the half-century after the martyrdom of James.

(7) Finally, we should recall that the traditions refer not only to particular individuals of the family, but to the family group as a whole (Eusebius, *HE* 1:7:11, 14; 3:11). The spread of the Gospel and the leadership of the church were, so to speak, a family concern. The women of the family, such as Jesus' mother Mary, her sister (John 19:25), Mary the wife of Clopas, and perhaps the sisters of Jesus, will have played a part as well as the men, though no evidence survives as to what this was. But this involvement of the family as a group need not be attributed to some dynastic principle. In a society where family ties were strong, and farms and businesses would commonly involve whole families, it was a natural development. So long as allegiance to the Christian Gospel did not divide families and require the rejection of family ties, there must have been many prominent Christian families corporately involved in Christian ministry.

---

[228] The 'dynastic' character of this claim becomes striking when we compare it with Darius I's Behistun inscription: 'Eight in my family previously exercised kingship. I am the ninth' (quoted in Wilson [1977] 69).

IX. Conclusion

It is scarcely necessary to reiterate that the evidence assembled in this chapter establishes the very considerable importance of the relatives of Jesus in the mission and leadership of the churches of Palestine in the first century after the death and resurrection of Jesus. Insofar as the earliest years of Jewish Christianity in Palestine were the crucially formative years for Christianity as such, to which all the churches elsewhere were permanently indebted, the importance of the role of the relatives of Jesus was by no means limited to Palestine, even apart from the missionary activity which may have taken some of them outside Palestine and the continuing, if waning, influence of the Jerusalem church beyond Palestine after the initial period of the spread of Christianity.

Unfortunately, the evidence studied in this chapter has given hardly any hints of the kind of Christian belief and practice the *desposynoi* promoted or of the character of the Christian movement in which they were leaders. But it does allow one significant point to be made about this. We have seen that, alongside the role of James and Symeon in Jerusalem, others of the *desposynoi* were based in Galilee: in Nazareth, Kokhaba and later perhaps also in Sikhnin. In fact, the relatives of Jesus are the only early Christian leaders we can confidently locate in Galilee. It is quite possible – even probable – that other Galilean disciples of Jesus returned to Galilee and exercised an apostolic ministry there. Perhaps some members of the twelve returned to their homes around the northern shore of the lake and were active in that heartland of Jesus' own Galilean ministry, while the *desposynoi* were largely active in the southern hills of Galilee around and north of Nazareth. But this is speculation. What the leadership of the *desposynoi* in Galilee makes unlikely is the thesis of two very different kinds of Christianity in Galilee and Jerusalem. James' and Symeon's leadership of the Jerusalem church is not likely to have been seriously out of step with their relatives' leadership of the Galilean churches. That Symeon succeeded James in Jerusalem shows that the *desposynoi* outside Jerusalem maintained close links with the Jerusalem church. We can be confident that the traditional Galilean attachment to the Temple[229] will have continued among Galilean Christians in the form of pilgrimage to Jerusalem for the feasts and respect for the authority of the Jerusalem church leadership, even though, as we have seen, special messianic significance was probably also attributed to Nazareth and Kokhaba. If members of the twelve at first shared the leadership of the churches of Galilee with the *desposynoi*, other members of the twelve shared the leadership of the Jerusalem church with James, even after his rise to a unique position there, if our interpretation of the Jerusalem bishops list (section III above) is correct. These indications of leadership in Galilee and Jerusalem by the same circles of *desposynoi* and apostles are a firmer basis for considering the character of Galilean Christianity than are attempts to read the Gospels as reflecting the nature of early Christianity in Galilee after Easter.[230] Thus, for example, Elliott-Binns' attempt to distinguish early Galilean Christianity, including some of the twelve, from 'the narrower Judaistic Christianity which was growing up at Jerusalem under the leadership of St James,'[231] must be rejected, while his attribution of the letter of James to Galilee *rather than* to James the Lord's brother[232] proves unnecessary.

However, in order to give some real content to the leadership role of the relatives of Jesus in the early church, we have to turn from the information about them surveyed in this chapter to the surviving evidence of their teaching. Apart from what can be gathered from Paul and Acts as to James' attitude to the law and the Gentile mission, we have two primary sources: the letters of James[233] and Jude. Were we to continue our investigation by focussing on the teaching attributed to James, we should have to discuss the question of

---

[229] Freyne (1980).

[230] Against such attempts, see Stemberger (1974); Freyne (1980) 356–380. Freyne shows that conclusions about Galilean Christianity drawn from the accounts of Galilee in the Synoptic Gospels are largely unfounded, but his own thesis about Galilee in the Fourth Gospel seems to me as speculative as those he rejects with reference to the Synoptic Gospels.

[231] Elliott-Binns (1956) 11, cf. 62.

[232] Elliott-Binns (1956) 45–52.

the law, faith and works, James' 'theology of the poor,' the use of the tradition of Jesus' sayings in James, and his debt to the wisdom tradition. But instead, in the rest of this book, we shall follow the less well-trodden path represented by the letter of Jude, which will open up for us other aspects of the Christianity of the *desposynoi* and their contribution to the developing theology of earliest Christianity.

The letter of Jude has not usually in recent scholarship been regarded as important evidence for the early Palestinian Christianity in which the relatives of Jesus were leaders. In order to provide background and justification for our use of it in this way the next chapter surveys the history of research on Jude.

[233] Of course, the authorship, date and provenance of James are very far from agreed: see the useful survey of recent scholarship in Davids (1988). In my view, the case for its origin in pre-70 Palestinian Jewish Christianity is a very good one. It should be treated as authentic at least in the sense of embodying James' teaching and being sent out with his authorization. Against the thesis of pseudepigraphy as applied to James, see Bauckham (1988D).

3

The Letter of Jude: A Survey of Research[1]

An article on Jude published in 1975 was entitled, 'The Most Neglected Book in the New Testament',[2] and it would be difficult to dispute the aptness of this description. This neglect is partly due to the way in which, because Jude and 2 Peter clearly have material in common, the two have been treated as very closely related works. The widely accepted view that 2 Peter is a very late work and theologically one of the least valuable in the New Testament has led to rather similar judgments about Jude. In fact, the close association of Jude with 2 Peter has promoted an even greater neglect of Jude than of 2 Peter. To many older scholars, from Luther onwards,[3] Jude seemed nothing more than an excerpt from 2 Peter, and although most modern scholars have recognized the priority of Jude, they have still treated the two works as very similar in background, character and message, so that Jude has attracted little attention in its own right. It has often featured in recent scholarship as no more than an illustration of one feature of 'early Catholicism' (see section IV below). The tradition of scholarly contempt (this is scarcely too strong a word) for

---

[1] This chapter is a revised and updated version of Bauckham (1988B), with the addition of section II.4, which first appeared in Bauckham (1988A).

[2] Rowston (1975).

[3] For Luther as the precursor of modern neglect of Jude, see Albin (1962) 713.

Jude has led to scholarly neglect of Jude and hence to ignorance of Jude.[4] The usual scholarly judgments about Jude are little more than clichés which have simply been repeated for a century or more without re-examination.

In recent years there have been a few, though only a few, examples of willingness to take a fresh look at Jude and to break fresh ground in research on Jude.[5] This chapter aims to show that if these are followed up there are grounds for expecting a radical reassessment of Jude and its place in the history of early Christianity.

I. Textual criticism

Considering the brevity of Jude, the textual critical problems are remarkably numerous and difficult. Mayor judges that 'the text is in a less satisfactory condition than that of any other portion of the New Testament',[6] while, according to Osburn, Jude 22–23a is 'undoubtedly one of the most corrupt passages in New Testament literature'.[7] In recent years, especially since the discovery of P[72], which provides important new evidence of the early textual history of Jude,[8] there have been several special studies of the text of verse 5,[9] of verse 12,[10] and of verses 22–23.[11] In these cases broad exegetical questions are intimately connected with the textual problems. Albin provides an exhaustive discussion of the text of Jude.[12]

[4] Cf. Albin (1962) 713–714.
[5] See Albin (1962); Eybers (1975); Ellis (1978); Busto Saiz (1981); Bauckham (1983A).
[6] Mayor (1907) clxxxi.
[7] Osburn (1972) 139.
[8] For the text of P[72] see Grunewald (1986) 159–171.
[9] Black (1964) 44–45; Wikgren (1967); Mees (1968) 554–556; Osburn (1981). See also Mayor (1907) clxxxiii–clxxxv; Zahn (1909) 260–262; Schelkle (1963) 410–411.
[10] Whallon (1988).
[11] Bieder (1950); Birdsall (1963); Mees (1968) 557–558; Osburn (1972); Kubo (1981). See also Mayor (1907) clxxxviii–cxci; Bauckham (1983A) 108–111.
[12] Albin (1962).

II. Literary Relationships

1. Old Testament

The more closely Jude is studied, the more pervasive its allusions to the Old Testament are found to be.[13] Though it is true that some of these are mediated through later Jewish literature and paraenetic traditions,[14] it is also clear that such allusions belong to Jude's literary technique (see section III below) and are largely deliberate. Many scholars repeat the assertion that Jude knew the Old Testament in the Septuagint version,[15] but this piece of scholarly tradition needs to be treated with suspicion. Those writers who provide evidence for it do not in fact claim that Jude alludes to specific Old Testament passages in the Septuagint translation, but only argue that certain terms (such as ἐκπορνεύειν, ἐνυπνιάζεσθαι, θαυμάζειν πρόσωπα)[16] have been drawn from Septuagint usage.[17] Jude's use of these terms really only proves his familiarity with Jewish Greek, in which there were common Greek renderings, used both in the Septuagint and in other Jewish Greek literature, for certain Old Testament Hebrew expressions. It is rather stretching the evidence to say that he was 'steeped in the language of the Septuagint',[18] while there is in fact more significant evidence for his familiarity with the Hebrew Bible. Chase[19] and Chaine[20] long ago pointed out, without sufficiently stressing its significance, the fact that

---

[13] Rowston (1971) 37–45; Bauckham (1983A) passim, especially 25–26, 87–89, 114–117, 122.

[14] Cf. Chaine (1939) 277; Windisch (1951) 41; Rowston (1971) 44–45; Cantinat (1973) 270; Busto Saiz (1981) 84–85, 97–102; Bauckham (1983A) 46–47, 77–84.

[15] Chase (1899) 800; Wand (1934) 192; Chaine (1939) 277; Kelly (1969) 272.

[16] Chase (1899) 800; Chaine (1939) 277, list ἐμπαίκτης as a word derived from the LXX, but in fact Jude's use of ἐμπαίκτης does not follow LXX usage. He uses it as equivalent to לץ, whereas in the LXX ἐμπαίκτης and its cognates never translate לץ.

[17] Chase (1899) 800; Chaine (1939) 277. Cf. Bigg's hesitations about this argument: Bigg (1901) 311.

[18] Chase (1899) 800; Wand (1934) 192.

[19] Chase (1899) 801.

[20] Chaine (1939) 277, 317. So also Kelly (1969) 271–272.

one of Jude's Old Testament allusions cannot be dependent on the Septuagint because it does not even give the meaning he adopts (Jude 12: Prov 25:14),[21] while another is closer to the Hebrew than to the Septuagint (Jude 12: Ezek 34:2).[22] Others have noticed a third, even more decisive, case where the Hebrew text, not the Septuagint, must be the basis for Jude's allusion (Jude 13: Isa 57:20).[23] Chase again plausibly suggested that in Jude 23 there is an allusion to the associations of the word צואים in Zechariah 3:3–4.[24] Moreover, it has not been generally observed that in no case where Jude alludes to specific verses of the Old Testament does he echo the language of the Septuagint.[25] In my judgment, these neglected facts refute the usual assumption that Jude's knowledge of the Old Testament was dependent on the Septuagint and indicate on the contrary that it was with the Hebrew Bible that he was really familiar. When he wanted to allude to it he did not stop to find the Septuagint translation, but made his own translation, in terms appropriate to the style and context of his work.[26]

2. 1 Enoch

Jude's explicit quotation from Enoch (vv 14–15) was a problem for the Fathers, who knew that the quotation derived from the book of Enoch (1 Enoch 1:9). For Tertullian this was an argument for the authenticity of 1 Enoch (*De cult. fem.* 1:3),[27] but others used it to dispute the canonicity of Jude (Jerome, *De vir. illustr.* 4). Nineteenth-century scholars, who knew the Ethiopic version of 1 Enoch and after 1892 the Akhmim Greek fragment (which includes 1:9), realised that the case for Jude's dependence on 1 Enoch rests not only on

[21] See Bauckham (1983A) 87.
[22] See Bauckham (1983A) 87.
[23] Kelly (1969) 274; Bauckham (1983A) 88. It is noteworthy that Jude has paraphrased the Old Testament verse in good literary Greek.
[24] Chase (1899) 801; Bauckham (1983A) 116.
[25] Bauckham (1983A) 7. Note especially Jude 11: Num 26:9; Jude 22: Amos 4:11; Zech 3:3.
[26] Bauckham (1983A) 7.
[27] See Schelkle (1963) 415.

the one explicit quotation (vv 14–15) but on many other more or less probable allusions to 1 Enoch.[28] However, many nineteenth-century scholars, especially Roman Catholics, still found it difficult to accept that a canonical writer could quote an apocryphal book, apparently attributing its words to Enoch himself, and so various other explanations of the resemblances were offered.[29] Some held that Jude was dependent on a reliable historical tradition of Enoch's prophecy, which was also incorporated into 1 Enoch.[30] Philippi[31] and Hofmann[32] argued that 1 Enoch is a Jewish Christian book dependent on Jude, while Keil and others held the passages resembling Jude to be Christian interpolations in 1 Enoch.[33]

Since 1900, however, Jude's dependence on 1 Enoch has scarcely ever been disputed,[34] and this is normally no longer felt to be a problem, though some commentators have still found it necessary to explain how it can be reconciled with the canonicity of Jude.[35] Since the discovery in 1892 of the Greek fragment which includes 1 Enoch 1:9 it has been widely held that the resemblances are sufficiently close to require the conclusion that Jude used the Greek version of 1 Enoch.[36]

[28] For lists of allusions, see Farrar (1882) 241 n. 3; Salmon (1894) 480 n.; Chase (1899) 801–802; Zahn (1909) 288.

[29] To some extent these explanations were also a response to Volkmar's view that 1 Enoch is a second-century work and that therefore Jude, being dependent on it, must be dated in the late second century A.D.

[30] E. Murray (1838), according to Farrar (1882) 240.

[31] Philippi (1868) 138–152.

[32] Hofmann (1875) 187, 205–211. The views of Philippi and Hofmann are countered by Zahn (1909) 287–288; cf. also Gloag (1887) 386–408; Salmon (1894) 479–480.

[33] Keil (1883) 322–323; others who took this view are listed in Farrar (1882) 241 n. 3. Alford (1880) 194–198, thought Jude's dependence on 1 Enoch not proved.

[34] Ellis (1957) 36 n. 10, still leaves some doubt, but in (1978) 224, no longer leaves the question open.

[35] Mayor (1907) clvi–clvii; Chaine (1939) 279–280; Green (1968) 49; Guthrie (1970) 918–919; Ellis (1978) 224; Kugelman (1980) 77–79.

[36] Chaine (1939) 322, makes a quite detailed comparison of the texts and thinks Jude probably dependent on the Greek version. Dependence on the Greek Enoch is also asserted, e.g., by Mayor (1907) 45; Grundmann (1974) 42; Cantinat (1973) 268; Green (1968) 45; Kümmel (1975) 428. Kelly (1969) 276, is cautious.

However, Zahn already argued that some features of the quotation in Jude 14–15 are only explicable if Jude used the Semitic original of 1 Enoch. He admitted that the verbal agreement with the Greek version is 'closer than is usually found in two independent translators', but suggested that the Greek Enoch was translated by a Christian who knew Jude's letter.[37] The original Aramaic text of 1 Enoch 1:9 is now partly available in the Qumran fragment (4QEn[c] 1:1:15–17),[38] which unfortunately lacks the crucial opening words of the verse, but to a very limited extent supports the view that Jude knew 1 Enoch in Aramaic.[39] The case for this view, briefly suggested by Black,[40] has now been argued in detail by Osburn[41] and myself.[42] The resemblances to the Greek version remain difficult to attribute to mere coincidence, though this may not be impossible. It is possible that Jude knew the Greek version but made his own translation from the Aramaic,[43] or that Zahn's view is correct. I have argued that a Christian hand can be detected at least in the extant form of the Greek text of 1 Enoch 1:9.[44] However, Dehandschutter prefers to think that Jude followed a Greek version significantly different from the extant Greek text.[45]

Judgments on the extent of Jude's dependence on 1 Enoch outside verses 14–15 have varied, though it is widely agreed to be considerable.[46] Dependence on 1 Enoch in verse 6 is universally admitted,[47] and can be shown to be very

[37] Zahn (1909) 287.

[38] Milik (1976) 184, and Plate IX.

[39] Also Jude 6, in using μεγάλης, agrees with 4QEn[b] 1:4:11 (Milik [1976] 175) against the Greek and Ethiopic versions of 1 Enoch 10:12. But this cannot carry much weight.

[40] Black (1971) 10–11; idem (1973) 195–196.

[41] Osburn (1977) 335–338.

[42] Bauckham (1983A) 94–96.

[43] Cf. Bauckham (1983A) 96.

[44] Bauckham (1981).

[45] Dehandschutter (1986).

[46] Recent studies of Jude's use of Enoch include Black (1973); Osburn (1977); idem (1985); Rubinkiewicz (1984); Dehandschutter (1986); Wolthius (1987).

[47] Even by Dubarle (1950), who nevertheless argues that v 6 refers primarily to the Israelite spies in Canaan.

precise.[48] Following a suggestion by Spitta,[49] I have argued that the set of four images from nature in verses 12b–13 was inspired by reflection on 1 Enoch 2:1–5; 80:2–8.[50] Thus, of the major sections of 1 Enoch, Jude certainly knew the Book of Watchers (1 Enoch 1–16) and the Astronomical Book (1 Enoch 72–82). To the Dream-Visions (1 Enoch 83–90) there is one quite probable allusion (Jude 13: 1 Enoch 88:1: see below, chapter 4 section II.2). Allusions to the other major parts of our 1 Enoch (the Journeys of Enoch [1 Enoch 17–36]; the Parables of Enoch [1 Enoch 37–71]; and the Epistle of Enoch [1 Enoch 91–107]) are much less certain (possibilities which have been suggested are Jude 13: 1 Enoch 18:15–16; Jude 4: 1 Enoch 48:10[51] or 1 Enoch 67:10;[52] Jude 13: 1 Enoch 67:5–7;[53] Jude 14: 1 Enoch 60:8; Jude 8: 1 Enoch 99:8; Jude 11: the woes in 1 Enoch 94:6 etc.; Jude 16: 1 Enoch 101:3). However, it is unquestionable that Jude displays detailed familiarity with parts of the Enoch literature.[54] Arguably 1 Enoch 1–5 was Jude's most fundamental source in constructing the exegetical section of his letter (vv 4–19: see chapter 4 below).

The influence of 1 Enoch on the New Testament in general has sometimes been exaggerated.[55] In reality, Jude's dependence on 1 Enoch is rather unusual among the New Testament writers. Otherwise, it is only in the Christian literature of the end of the first century and the second century that use of 1 Enoch becomes widespread. Two conclusions seem possible: either Jude derives from apocalyptic Palestinian Christian circles, in which we may suppose the Enoch literature to

[48] Bauckham (1983A) 51–53.

[49] Spitta (1885) 361.

[50] Bauckham (1983A) 90–91. For 1 Enoch 80:2–8, see also Osburn (1985).

[51] Cf. Kelly (1969) 252.

[52] Osburn (1985) 300–302.

[53] Osburn (1985) 302.

[54] There are also resemblances between Jude 6 and 2 Enoch 7:2; 18:4, 6 (Bauckham [1983A] 53), but these may reflect only common dependence on 1 Enoch.

[55] E.g. by Barker (1988).

have been popular but from which little other literature survives,[56] or Jude must be placed in a second-century context when the Enoch literature had become popular in hellenistic Christianity. Especially if Jude did use 1 Enoch in Aramaic, the former conclusion would be much the more probable.

3. The Testament of Moses

According to the Alexandrian Fathers (Clement, *Fragm. in Ep. Jud.*; Didymus the Blind, *In Ep. Jud. Narr.*; Origen, *De Princ.* 3:2:1), the story of the dispute over the body of Moses, to which Jude 9 refers, was contained in an apocryphal work called the Assumption of Moses.[57] Attitudes to this apparent borrowing from an apocryphal work have paralleled those to the quotation of 1 Enoch. According to Didymus, it was a reason why some in his day disputed the authority of Jude's letter. Some nineteenth-century scholars took the account in Jude 9 to be a factual one (Philippi suggested that the information was revealed by Jesus to the disciples after the transfiguration, to account for Moses' appearance there), and denied any dependence on the Assumption of Moses, which Philippi argued was a second-century Christian work based on Jude.[58]

The source of Jude's reference in verse 9 is a more difficult problem than that of the quotation in verses 14–15, since the source is no longer extant. Since 1864 an incomplete Latin version of a work which has often been called the Assumption of Moses has been known, but its relationship with the work known to the Fathers by that title is open to question and the

---

[56] Some scholars suggest that Jude's use of apocryphal apocalyptic literature is an indication of authenticity: such literature would have been popular in the circles in which the Lord's brothers moved: Wand (1934) 189. Others take it as an indication only of Palestinian Jewish-Christian origin: Grundmann (1974) 15–16; Eybers (1975) 115.

[57] In the Latin translations of Clement and Didymus it is called the *Assumptio Moysi* or *Moyseos*; in the Latin translation of Origen the *Adscensio Mosis*. The Greek title is preserved by Gelasius Cyzicenus, *Hist. Eccl.* 2:17:17 (ἐν βίβλῳ ἀναλήψεως Μωσέως).

[58] Philippi (1868) 153–191.

recent tendency, following R. H. Charles, to call it the Testament of Moses is probably justified (the Stichometry of Nicephorus lists both a Testament of Moses and an Assumption of Moses). The manuscript breaks off before Moses' death, but the work must have gone on to record Moses' death. This Testament of Moses certainly existed when Jude wrote, and its lost ending could have been his source. However, the problem is complicated by the existence of a large number of accounts in Christian sources of a dispute between Michael and the devil at the death of Moses, some of them quoting the Assumption of Moses by name, some of them claiming to record the story to which Jude refers.[59] Some scholars have held that these accounts derive from the lost ending of the Latin Testament;[60] Charles thought they derived from an Assumption of Moses originally separate from the Testament, but later combined with it;[61] Laperrousaz denies that the Assumption of Moses from which they derive had any connection with the Latin Testament.[62] The claim that the Latin Testament is the work Jude knew, in a form which included an account of the dispute over Moses' body, has often been supported by parallels between the extant Latin text and other parts of Jude, indicating Jude's dependence on this work.[63] Laperrousaz, however, has disputed these alleged instances of dependence on the Testament,[64] and it may be doubted whether the parallels are sufficient to demonstrate a relationship. Another difficulty which has not usually been noticed is that the various extant accounts and fragments of a dispute between Michael and the devil cannot easily be regarded as all deriving from the same source. The attempts

---

[59] Collected in Charles (1897) 106–110; James (1920) 42–51; Denis (1970) 63–67; Bauckham (1983A) 67–76; and chapter 5 below (these last two are the fullest collections).

[60] Burkitt (1900) 450; James (1920) 49–50.

[61] Charles (1897) xlvi–l.

[62] Laperrousaz (1970) 29–62.

[63] Charles (1897) lxii–lxiii; Chase (1899) 802; Bigg (1901) 336–337; Moffatt (1918) 32, 347; Rowston (1971) 54–55, 59. The most plausible parallels are in v 16 (cf. TMos 7:7, 9; 9:5); cf. also v 3 (cf. TMos 4:8).

[64] Laperrousaz (1970) 51–58.

of James,[65] Charles[66] and Loewenstamm[67] to reconstruct a composite account from these divergent testimonies apparently convinced them, but do not really produce a coherent and consistent narrative. They suggest that the evidence requires a more careful and critical investigation.

Fresh interest in the background of Jude 9 was stimulated by the publication of 4QVisions of Amram, in which Amram in a dream sees the two chief angels, the Prince of Light and the Prince of Darkness, engaged in a dispute over him. Milik thought that the Assumption of Moses, which was Jude's source in Jude 9, was actually inspired by 4QAmram,[68] but despite a striking coincidence of language (cf. 1:10–11 with Jude 9) the similarities are best explained by placing both 4QAmram and Jude 9 within a broader tradition of contests between the devil and the chief of the angels. Berger[69] sought to link both 4QAmram and Jude 9 to a tradition in which two angels, or two groups of angels, contend for the possession of the departed soul at death, for which he provided a wealth of evidence from later Christian apocalyptic texts. It is doubtful, however, whether Jude 9, which is not about the fate of Moses' soul, really belongs in this tradition. I have argued that we should identify a general tradition of contests (originally courtroom disputes) between the devil and the angel (beginning with Zech 3:1–5, and evidenced by Jub 17:15–18:16; 48:2–5, 9–18; CD 5:17–18), of which 4QAmram and Jude 9 are specific instances, while in Berger's texts about the fate of the soul the general tradition has taken a special form.[70]

As for the source of Jude 9, I have tried to show that the extant accounts of a dispute over the body of Moses can be divided into two groups, deriving from two different versions of the story.[71] One version probably derives from the lost

[65] James (1920) 48–49.
[66] Charles (1897) 105–107.
[67] Loewenstamm (1976) 209–210.
[68] Milik (1972) 95.
[69] Berger (1973) 1–18.
[70] Bauckham (1983A) 65–67.
[71] Bauckham (1983A) 67–76.

ending of the Testament of Moses and was Jude's source in verse 9. The story in this version can be reconstructed with some confidence, and my reconstruction has some significant consequences for the exegesis of Jude 9 and its role in Jude's argument.[72] The second version of the story was probably composed as a revision of the first, in the second century A.D. in the interests of anti-Gnostic polemic, and this was the version which the Alexandrian Fathers knew in the Assumption of Moses. (See chapter 5 below for this argument in detail.)

4. 2 Peter

All scholars have admitted that some kind of close relationship exists between 2 Peter and Jude, and almost all have held that the degree of verbal correspondence between the two works is such as to require a literary relationship.[73] Five different kinds of relationship have been proposed:[74]

(a) The view that Jude is dependent on 2 Peter was the normal opinion before the nineteenth century,[75] and was still defended in the later nineteenth century and early twentieth century,[76] especially by Spitta,[77] Zahn,[78] and Bigg.[79] However, since 1925 this view has received almost no support,[80]

---

[72] Bauckham (1983A) 59–62.

[73] Reicke (1964) 190, thinks an *oral* common source possible.

[74] A good summary of the main arguments for (a), (b) and (d) is Guthrie (1970) 919–927. Gloag (1887) 236–255, surveys the main arguments for (a) and (b) and finds them equally balanced.

[75] Pseudo-Oecumenius (PG 119:708, 712, 720); Luther, Grotius, Bengel, Semler, J. D. Michaelis (see Zahn [1909] 285).

[76] Hofmann (1875); Mansel (1875) 69–70; Alford (1880) 145–148; Wordsworth (1882) 136; Plummer (1884) 506–507; Spitta (1885) 381–470; Bigg (1901) 216–224; Falconer (1902) 218–224; Lumby (1908) xv–xvi; Zahn (1909) 250–251, 265–267, 285; Wohlenberg (1923) XLI–XLIII.

[77] Spitta (1885) 381–470.

[78] Zahn (1909) 250–251, 265–267, 285.

[79] Bigg (1901) 216–224.

[80] Lenski (1966) 241, is a very rare exception. Tricot (1933) 1779–1780, is undecided whether Jude or 2 Peter is prior. Guthrie (1970) 926, thinks there is something to be said for the priority of 2 Peter, but leaves the question open.

even from those who defend the Petrine authorship of 2 Peter.[81]

(b) The view that 2 Peter is dependent on Jude has, since the late nineteenth century, become by far the most widely accepted solution.[82]

(c) A few scholars, while admitting that in its present form 2 Peter is dependent on Jude, regard the passages which show dependence on Jude as interpolations into the original 2 Peter.[83]

(d) The view that both letters are dependent on a common source has occasionally been suggested.[84] Lumby[85] argues that both were translating from a Hebrew or Aramaic source. Robson[86] thinks that one of the sources of 2 Peter was a 'prophetic discourse' (1:20–2:19), which both Jude and the compiler of 2 Peter used. Spicq,[87] Green,[88] Michaels[89] and

[81] Dependence of 2 Peter on Jude is regarded as quite consistent with Petrine authorship of 2 Peter by Weiss (1866) 256–264, 300–301; Plumptre (1879) 79–81; Keil (1883) 203–204; Gloag (1887) 220–221; Salmon (1894) 493; Chase (1900) 814; Henkel (1904) 38–44; Maier (1905); Lumby (1908) xv; James (1912) xvii; Wohlenberg (1923); Charue (1946); Green (1968) 22–23; Guthrie (1970) 925–926.

[82] For early advocates of this view, see Zahn (1909) 284–285; Moffatt (1918) 351. Later nineteenth-century advocates of it include Weiss (1866) 256–264; Huther (1881) 254–260; Abbott (1882) 139–153; Salmon (1894) 492–494; Davidson (1894) 523–529; Soden (1899); Chase (1899) 802–803. Major arguments for this view are Maier (1905); Mayor (1907) i–xxv; idem (1910) 303–317; James (1912) x–xvi; Moffatt (1918) 348–352; Chaine (1939) 18–24; Sidebottom (1967) 65–69; Schmidt (1972) 75–81; Grundmann (1974) 75–83.

[83] Kühl (1897); Bartlet (1900) 518–521; Benoît (1941); and for earlier suggestions on these lines, see McNamara (1960) 14; Zahn (1909) 284; Guthrie (1970) 851.

[84] For older views along these lines, see Moffatt (1918) 350–351. A common source seems to have been first proposed in the eighteenth century by Thomas Sherlock, who argued that both authors were dependent on a Jewish writing in Hebrew and also on a set of precepts agreed by a meeting of the apostles: Sherlock (1812) 132–149.

[85] Lumby (1876) 446, 449, 452 n. 1, 461.

[86] Robson (1915) 6, 44–48, 58–59.

[87] Spicq (1966) 197 n. 1.

[88] Green (1968) 50–55.

[89] Michaels (1969) 355, who thinks the tract might have been written by Peter.

White[90] suggest that an anti-heretical tract lies behind the two letters, while Reicke[91] proposes a 'sermonic pattern,' perhaps oral, on which both writers drew. Selwyn supposes that the two authors had been 'companion prophets, using the same plan of teaching and preaching.'[92]

(e) Common authorship has rarely been suggested, but Robinson[93] has argued that Jude wrote both works, while Smith[94] also regards common authorship as a plausible hypothesis.

In recent work, especially by Fornberg, Neyrey and myself,[95] the insights of redaction criticism have been brought to the study of the relationship between Jude and 2 Peter. Previous attempts to investigate the details of the parallel passages, in order to determine priority, have always, as least in a rudimentary way, involved considerations of redaction, but usually without sufficient awareness of the possibility that an author may be adapting earlier material for a new purpose. The vast majority of scholars have assumed that, because of the parallel material, the two letters must have been written to combat similar or identical heresies and must reflect a common background, but our redaction-critical studies of the differences between the two letters in the parallel passages have led Fornberg, Neyrey and me to the common conclusion that Jude and 2 Peter derive from very different historical situations and oppose different adversaries. We have all assumed the priority of Jude as a working hypothesis, and sought to explain 2 Peter's redactional treatment of Jude as an

[90] White (1975) 731: 'a common core of apologetic literature.' Cf. also Loisy (1935) 135–136; idem (1950) 281: 2 Peter may be dependent on a 'diatribe' of which Jude is an expansion.

[91] Reicke (1964) 148, 189–190.

[92] Selwyn (1901) 230, cf. 112. According to Selwyn, Silas (=Luke) wrote 2 Peter and Judas Barsabbas wrote Jude.

[93] Robinson (1976) 192–195. His view was anticipated by Leaney (1970) 319.

[94] Smith (1985) 74–78. Like Robinson, he takes 2 Peter 3:1 to be a reference to the letter of Jude.

[95] Fornberg (1977) chapter 3; Neyrey (1977) chapter 3; Bauckham (1983A). Redaction criticism is also applied by Danker (1977) 89–90; Cavallin (1979); Carr (1981) 132–135.

adaptation of the material to new circumstances.[96] While we may not thereby have solved the problem of literary relationship conclusively,[97] we have strengthened the case for 2 Peter's dependence on Jude by providing plausible redaction-critical accounts of 2 Peter's use of Jude. Probably more importantly, we have refuted the assumption that Jude and 2 Peter are similar works, with similar backgrounds and similar theological outlooks. The reuse of some of the material in one work by the writer of another no more proves that in this case than it does in the case of Kings and Chronicles or Mark and Luke. The habit of classing 2 Peter and Jude together has for too long been a serious hindrance to research. In this respect, the recent attempt by Soards[98] to include Jude with 1 Peter and 2 Peter in a 'Petrine school' is a retrograde and misleading step, taken in ignorance of the best recent work on Jude and 2 Peter.[99]

5. Other early Christian writings

Many scholars have thought it clear that Jude shows acquaintance with Pauline terminology and ideas,[100] and most of these scholars have assumed that he derived these from the Pauline literature.[101] Chase, for example, writes: 'There can be no doubt that the writer was acquainted with and influenced in language and thought by St Paul's epistles';[102] Sidebottom speaks of 'definite acquaintance with Pauline

[96] For recognition that 2 Peter adapts the material from Jude to a new situation, see also Leconte (1961) 126–127; Schmidt (1972) 100.

[97] Fornberg (1977) 58, thinks that his redaction-critical study has 'refuted' the theory of the priority of 2 Peter, but this is too confident a conclusion. He has shown that 2 Peter's redaction of Jude is a plausible hypothesis, but not that Jude's redaction of 2 Peter is relatively less plausible, because he has not tested the latter hypothesis.

[98] Soards (1988).

[99] The 'Addenda' to Soards' article by V. A. Ward (Soards [1988] 3844–3849) is a rather incompetent attempt to maintain Soards' argument in the light of my arguments in Bauckham (1988A) and (1988B), which she seriously misrepresents.

[100] For lists of parallels, see Chase (1899) 802; Chaine (1939) 278; Cantinat (1973) 271–272; Rowston (1971) 60–61.

[101] Bigg (1901) 312, thought the author must have been a friend of Paul.

[102] Chase (1899) 802.

terminology'.[103] Some scholars are more cautious. Rowston admits that no single parallel to Paul can be said to be certainly influenced by Paul, but thinks the cumulative impression of the parallels carries much more weight.[104] Moffatt thinks there is not much evidence of Jude's use of the genuine Pauline letters.[105] Chaine thought the parallels need not indicate Jude's use of the Pauline letters, but could derive from catechesis influenced by Paul.[106] However, as Wand[107] and I[108] have pointed out, the idea that Jude is in any way indebted to Paul is too dependent on the facile assumption that ideas and terminology which Paul uses are distinctively Pauline. The realisation, in modern Pauline scholarship, that Paul took over a great deal from the common traditions of primitive Christianity requires that Jude's parallels with Paul be assessed in a much more discriminating fashion. In my judgment all of Jude's contacts with 'Pauline' language belong to the common vocabulary of the early church.

In the past some scholars have argued that Jude is dependent on the Pastorals,[109] and seen this as an indication of a late date, but the case for specific literary dependence on the Pastorals has now been generally abandoned. At most the parallels indicate a similar background and situation.[110]

Remarkably, the author of Jude has been credited with the authorship of three other early Christian writings. Dubarle argued that the intended letter to which Jude refers in Jude 3 was Hebrews, of which Jude was the redactor, while the 'word of exhortation' mentioned in Hebrews 13:22 is the letter of Jude.[111] Robinson has suggested that the intended

---

[103] Sidebottom (1967) 72.

[104] Rowston (1971) 65.

[105] Moffatt (1918) 348.

[106] Chaine (1939) 278.

[107] Wand (1934) 192.

[108] Bauckham (1983A) 8; cf. also Guthrie (1970) 928.

[109] Cone (1901) 2630; Pfleiderer (1911) 254; Moffatt (1918) 348.

[110] Wand (1934) 192–193; McNeile (1953) 242–243; cf. Robinson (1976) 171.

[111] Dubarle (1939). This theory has also been argued by P. J. Deshpande in an as yet unpublished monograph.

letter was 2 Peter, which Jude wrote as Peter's secretary.[112] Chase suggested, on the basis of resemblances between the letter of Jude and the Didache, that Jude may have been the ultimate author of parts of the Didache.[113] However, the most striking resemblances (in Did 2:7 and Jude 22–23) could easily result from common use of catechetical tradition.[114]

6. Classical Greek literature

Glasson[115] thought Jude 6 dependent on the Greek myth of the Titans, which is recounted in Hesiod. Some Jewish writers identified the fallen angels with the Titans, but Jude's use of δεσμοῖς and ὑπὸ ζόφον (used of the Titans chained in Tartarus: Hesiod, *Theog.* 718; 729) is insufficient to show that he made this identification or knew Hesiod.[116] Oleson's argument for further allusions to Hesiod (*Theog.* 190–192) and to Euripides (*Hercules furens* 850–852) in Jude 13 depends on very tenuous connections.[117]

III. Literary form and structure

Until recently the literary form of Jude has been discussed only cursorily. The obvious formal characteristics of the letter-opening (vv 1–2) and the doxology (vv 24–25) have been noted, and the rest of the work has often been classified as a homily: 'close to Jewish homiletics, of a form strongly tinged with hellenism.'[118] Salmon commented on its remark-

---

[112] Robinson (1976) 193–194.

[113] Chase (1899) 795; cf. Moffatt (1918) 352; Rowston (1971) 142–143.

[114] Sidebottom (1967) 73; Bauckham (1983A) 110–111. The readings of C and A, which have ἐλέγχετε in Jude 22, may show scribal assimilation to Did 2:7 or the tradition it records.

[115] Glasson (1961) 62–63.

[116] The phrase ὑπὸ ζόφον (Jude 6) is commonly used in Greek poetry for the underworld, but not necessarily with reference to the Titans: Homer, *Il.* 21.56; *Od.* 11.57, 155; 20.356; Aeschylus, *Pers.* 839; SibOr 4:43.

[117] Oleson (1979); cf. Bauckham (1983A) 88–89; Osborn (1985) 298–299, 302.

[118] Cantinat (1965) 594; cf. Chase (1899) 801 ('resumé of words spoken by an elder in the assembly'); Rowston (1971) 120; Cantinat (1973) 270; McDonald (1980) 61.

able conciseness: 'Many of the phrases packed together in Jude's Epistle might each be the text of a discourse; so that I could easily believe that we had in this Epistle heads of topics enlarged on, either in a longer document, or by the Apostle himself in *viva voce* address.'[119] Loisy classified the body of the work as part of a diatribe, and thought the epistolary opening and doxology might have been added later.[120] It has quite often been thought that the epistolary opening is only a literary device and that Jude is not a real letter,[121] but there is no real basis for this view, since precisely the opening was the really essential part of the ancient letter form and since there cannot be formal grounds for distinguishing between real and fictional examples of the letter form.[122]

Attempts to go beyond a general description of the form of Jude to a detailed structural analysis have included Cladder's elaborate analysis into strophes,[123] which Rowston follows;[124] Selwyn's analysis into six sections corresponding to six characteristics of the opponents;[125] and Albin's attempt to determine a fourfold or a fivefold division of the work on formal as well as material grounds.[126] But Perrin holds that the letter 'defies structural analysis'.[127]

Of pioneering significance for the literary analysis of Jude is an article by Ellis,[128] who regards Jude 5–19 as a 'midrash' (using the word in the loose sense of 'commentary' on Scripture, not with strict reference to the rabbinic midrashim) with characteristics found both in the Qumran pesharim and in early Christian expositions of Scripture. He identifies a series of 'citations' (vv 5–7; 9; 11; 14–15; 18), each of which is followed by a commentary-section (vv 8; 10; 12–13; 16; 19).

[119] Salmon (1894) 477 n.
[120] Loisy (1935) 138; idem (1950) 280.
[121] E.g. Jülicher (1904) 229; Fuller (1971) 160; Vielhauer (1975) 590.
[122] Bauckham (1988D).
[123] Cladder (1904).
[124] Rowston (1971) 120–122.
[125] Selwyn (1901) 231–235.
[126] Albin (1962) 741–743.
[127] Perrin (1974) 261.
[128] Ellis (1978), especially 220–226.

The 'citations' are not all actual quotations of Scripture, but include a summary of Old Testament passages (vv 5–7), two apocryphal quotations (vv 9; 14–15), an apostolic prophecy (v 18), and perhaps a Christian prophetic oracle (v 11). Although this variation from strict quotation goes beyond anything to be found in the Qumran pesharim and might be thought to throw doubt on Ellis's analysis, his case is sufficiently established by the fact that the transition from 'citation' to commentary is in each case formally marked by a shift of tense and by the use of a phrase including οὗτοι, usually οὗτοί εἰσιν, to introduce the comment. This formula resembles similar formulae used at Qumran, where, as in Jude, 'they signal the application of the preceding citation to the current eschatological situation'.[129] A further stylistic characteristic of Jude's exegetical method is 'the extraordinarily abundant catchword connections'.[130] This feature of the work has been noticed before,[131] but Ellis sees that it has a formal exegetical function: the catchwords link text to interpretation, and one text to another.

In my own work on Jude[132] I have taken over Ellis's analysis and exploited it as an invaluable aid to the exegesis of the work. One refinement of Ellis's analysis is required: it is best to regard the whole of verses 8–10 as the commentary on verses 5–7, with the 'citation' in verse 9 introduced as a secondary text to aid the interpretation of verses 5–7 (this practice can be paralleled in Qumran pesher exegesis). Other passages of commentary (vv 12–13; 16) also include less explicit allusions to additional scriptural texts.

There are differences between Jude and the Qumran pesharim: his use of various substitutes for Old Testament texts as citations, and his interpretation of Old Testament material as typology (vv 5–7, 11) as well as prophecy, have no real parallels in the Qumran texts, while his use of the οὗτοί εἰσιν formula is similar but not precisely parallel to Qumran

[129] Ellis (1978) 225.
[130] Ellis (1978) 225.
[131] Rowston (1971) 94–98; idem (1975) 558–559.
[132] Bauckham (1983A); see especially 3–6.

usage.[133] But it is still true that Jude 5–19 bears a close resemblance to the 'thematic pesharim' (4QFlor, 11QMelch, 4Q176, 177, 182, 183) in which the Qumran exegetes expound a collection of texts on one theme. With the formal resemblances there goes also a common attitude to exegesis: the conviction that the ancient texts are eschatological prophecy which the interpreter applies to the events of his own time, understood as the time of eschatological fulfilment.

The identification of Jude's commentary structure is perhaps the most important advance in recent studies on Jude, with many implications for introductory and exegetical questions. In particular, it reveals that Jude 5–19 is not, as so many earlier scholars have thought, a mere stream of undisciplined denunciation. On the contrary, this section of the letter is a very careful piece of scriptural exegesis designed not merely to denounce but to argue that Jude's opponents are people whose behaviour is condemned and whose judgment is prophesied in Scripture and in apostolic prophecy. The skilful use of catchwords and scriptural allusions reveals Jude as a highly accomplished practitioner of pesher exegesis, who achieves almost poetic economy of expression in what must be considered, in literary terms, a very fine example of the genre of 'thematic pesher.' This understanding of Jude's exegesis will be further developed in chapter 4 below.

Working independently of Ellis's work and my own, Busto Saiz, developing Cantinat's remarks on the structure of Jude,[134] has also noticed the structural significance of the οὗτοί εἰσιν formula (and equivalents) which in each case (vv 8, 10, 12, 16, 19) introduces an explanation of the Old Testament example given in the preceding verse.[135] He does not connect the formula with pesher exegesis, but derives it rather from the interpretation of visions in apocalyptic (a parallel which has often been noticed before). Busto Saiz regards ἀγαπητοί (vv 3, 17, 20) as another structural term which creates three sections: verses 3–16 on the opponents; verses 20–

[133] Bauckham (1983A) 45.
[134] Cantinat (1973) 267–268.
[135] Busto Saiz (1981) 86–87.

23 exhorting the readers; and verses 17–19 as a transitional passage.[136] Finally, he finds the description of the opponents in verse 4 to be a structural key to the passage verses 5–16. In verse 4 there is a triple characterization of the opponents: (a) their judgment was prophesied long ago; (b) they turn the grace of God into libertinism; (c) they deny the only Master and Lord Jesus Christ. These three characteristics are then unfolded in reverse order: (c) verses 5–10; (b) verses 11–13; (a) verses 14–16.[137] In criticism of this proposal, it may be noted that these links with verse 4 are not, as might have been expected, indicated precisely by the catchword connections.

In my commentary on Jude[138] I have developed a further, very important structural consideration concerning the relation between the statement of the theme of the letter (vv 3–4)[139] and the body of the letter (vv 4–23). The statement of theme is a version of the 'petition' form common in ancient letters,[140] and in accordance with this form contains two major parts: an appeal to the readers ('to carry on the fight for the faith') and the background to the appeal, which explains why the author is making it (v 4: the false teachers, their character and judgment). To this twofold division of the statement of theme correspond the two parts of the body of the letter (vv 5–19, 20–23), i.e. verse 4, the background, is the statement of theme for the exegetical section (vv 5–19), while verse 3, the appeal, is the statement of theme for the exhortatory section (vv 20–23). These relationships are reinforced by the catchword connections between verse 3 and verse 20, and between verse 4 and verses 5–19. (As far as the connection between verse 3 and verses 20–23 goes, the importance of this has also been seen by Albin.[141])

---

[136] Busto Saiz (1981) 86. For this structural significance of the threefold ἀγαπητοί, see also Albin (1962) 742–743.

[137] Busto Saiz (1981) 88–104.

[138] Bauckham (1983A) 4, 28–29, 111.

[139] For vv 3–4 as the statement of theme, cf. also McDonald (1980) 61.

[140] Mullins (1962), who does not, however, discuss Jude 3–4.

[141] Albin (1962) 741–742. But he confuses the formal analysis by grouping vv 1–3 together as 'introduction'.

This formal analysis indicates (as Cantinat sees[142] but few other commentators have recognized) that the real substance of Jude's appeal to his readers 'to carry on the fight for the faith' (v 3) is contained not in verses 5–19 but in verses 20–23. The exegetical section on the wickedness and judgment of the opponents (vv 5–19) constitutes essential background, but only background, to the appeal. This has two important implications. In the first place, it means that Jude's conception of 'fighting for the faith' does not, as many commentators have thought, consist mainly in condemnation and denunciation of the opponents, but in the positive exhortations of verses 20–23. Secondly, it means that verses 20–23 are not, as they have often been regarded, a kind of postscript or 'closing exhortation',[143] but the climax of the letter to which all the rest leads up. This is a vital key to the understanding of the work as a whole. As Albin points out, the merely quantitative dominance of the polemical part of Jude (vv 4–19) has all too often led to an unjustified stress on this part of the work in scholarly assessments of the character of the letter.[144] If the formal analysis suggested above is correct, it follows that the polemic must be assessed as subordinate to Jude's main purpose in writing, which is contained in verses 20–23.

Ellis's discovery of the pesher structure of verses 5–19 and my own analysis of the structural relationships between verses 3–4 and verses 5–23, should, if accepted, revolutionize the understanding and evaluation of Jude. The importance of formal analysis in New Testament studies is strikingly illustrated in this instance.

Finally, Deichgräber's important study of the form of Jude's doxology (vv 24–25)[145] should be mentioned, though his conclusions that the New Testament doxologies derive exclusively from the hellenistic synagogues of the diaspora and that several formal characteristics of Jude's doxology are indicative of a later date, can be questioned.[146]

---

[142] Cantinat (1973) 267, 279.
[143] E.g. Ellis (1978) 225.
[144] Albin (1962) 742.
[145] Deichgräber (1967) 25–40, 99–101.
[146] Bauckham (1983A) 120–121.

IV. Theological character

Jude is not only 'the most neglected book in the New Testament',[147] but also, in regard to its theological character, perhaps the most misunderstood New Testament work. In Protestant scholarship, at least, a long tradition of theological denigration of Jude[148] has led to the widespread acceptance of a largely negative evaluation of the letter which is based on highly questionable but usually unexamined assumptions. In addition, Jude has suffered considerably as a result of its obvious literary relationship with 2 Peter, which has led, quite unjustifiably, to the general assumption that Jude and 2 Peter belong to broadly the same theological milieu. Probably it has been this (really quite superficial) similarity to 2 Peter which has brought Jude under the comprehensive umbrella of 'early Catholicism' in much recent New Testament scholarship.[149] In reality, it is only because it is first assumed that Jude is 'early Catholic' that it is read in an 'early Catholic' sense. The 'early Catholic' reading of Jude is a reading-between-the-lines which the text of Jude itself does not require. It has blinded scholars to the evidence that Jude really belongs to a quite different theological milieu: that of Palestinian apocalyptic Christianity.

Two judgments on Jude predominate in the literature and are closely connected with the classification of Jude as 'early Catholic'. The first is the complaint that Jude's letter is violently polemical, and that instead of arguing with his opponents' theological position Jude merely denounces and threatens.[150] Krodel describes the letter as 'a highly polemical

---

[147] Rowston (1975).

[148] See Albin (1962) 713–714.

[149] For Jude as 'early Catholic', see especially Schelkle (1963A) (synthetic treatment of Jude and 2 Peter as 'early Catholic'); Rowston (1971) 150–153 (with reservations); Schrage (1973); Perrin (1974) 260; Hahn (1981). The survey of scholarship in Heiligenthal (1986) shows how the classification of Jude as 'early Catholic' has dominated especially German scholarship since 1960.

[150] Jülicher (1904) 230; Fuller (1971) 161; Wisse (1972) 134; Kümmel (1975) 426.

writing with a low kerygmatic profile'.[151] Jude's 'mere de-nunciation'[152] is frequently contrasted with Paul's more reasoned approach to combatting false teaching.[153] Writers who do not wish to condemn Jude for this merely offer excuses: Moffatt calls him 'a plain, honest leader of the church, who knows when round indignation is more telling than argument';[154] according to Wand, 'It is perhaps the hurried and spontaneous character of the message that has left no room for argument';[155] while Krodel speculates that Jude may have 'become tired of trying to persuade' his opponents.[156] Nearer the mark is Grundmann's observation that, in abandoning reasoned discussion and concentrating on attacking his opponent's moral character, Jude is typically Jewish Christian.[157] Even if the judgment that Jude's polemic is 'mere denunciation' were justified, it would still not follow that it should be placed in a period of 'early Catholic' decline from the Pauline standard. To suppose that such an approach to the problem of false teaching could not have occurred in the earliest period of the church is historical romanticism.[158]

However, the usual view of Jude's polemical approach is mistaken on four counts:

(a) It exaggerates the relative importance of the polemical section (vv 4–19) in the letter. The formal considerations discussed in Section III above show that verses 4–19 contain only the background to Jude's main purpose in writing, which is fulfilled in verses 20–23. Due weight should also be given to the positive theological material in verses 1–2, 24–25.[159] That 'the letter does not contain any real message of

---

[151] Krodel (1977) 92.

[152] Taylor (1934) 439; cf. Kelly (1969) 223; Krodel (1977) 94.

[153] E.g. Taylor (1934) 439; Fuller (1971) 161; Grundmann (1974) 18; Kümmel (1975) 426; Hahn (1981) 213.

[154] Moffatt (1918) 353.

[155] Wand (1934) 191.

[156] Krodel (1977) 95.

[157] Grundmann (1974) 19.

[158] For a different attempt to deflect this kind of denigration of Jude, see Seethalter (1987): Jude displays the oriental characteristic of thinking in pictures.

[159] Cf. Albin (1962) 742.

Christ at all'[160] is much less apparent when the polemical material is placed in its proper context and not treated as the main point of the letter. Cantinat[161] and Grundmann[162] are among the commentators who show appreciation of the non-polemical material in Jude. Cantinat notes that in verses 1–3, 20–25, the brevity of the text contrasts with the richness of the doctrine it contains.[163]

(b) The polemical section (vv 4–19) is not in fact 'mere denunciation,' but, as Ellis has shown (see Section III above) a carefully composed pesher exegesis, in which Jude argues that the ethical libertinism of his opponents identifies them as the sinners of the last days whose judgment was prophesied in Scripture and in the apostolic preaching.[164] This is not the kind of theological argument in which Paul usually engaged, but it is a style of argument which was at home in apocalyptic Jewish Christian circles. It needs to be understood according to its own presuppositions and context, not dismissed as 'mere denunciation.'

(c) Jude's polemical argument in verses 4–19 hinges entirely on the ethical libertinism of his opponents, which he shows from prophecy to be behaviour which incurs God's judgment. This attack on his opponent's morals is not a polemical device for slandering people with whom he disagreed on purely doctrinal grounds. On the contrary, it is precisely their ethical libertinism to which he objects. The controversy is about the moral implications of the Christian Gospel. In that case, given his hermeneutical assumptions, Jude's exegetical argument in verses 4–19 is not inappropriate.

(d) The polemical section (vv 4–19) is not addressed to Jude's opponents, but is intended to persuade his readers of the danger they face if they succumb to the libertine teaching

---

[160] Kümmel (1975) 426. This particular judgment shows how German Protestant denigration of Jude is heir to Luther's principle of canon-criticism; cf. Albin (1962) 713.

[161] Cantinat (1973) 278–279.

[162] Grundmann (1974) 21–23.

[163] Cantinat (1973) 278.

[164] In substance this point is recognized by Wisse (1972), but he retains the prejudice that this kind of argument must represent a late development by which the earlier Christian approach to opponents was superseded.

and example of the false teachers. When Jude advises his readers how to treat these people, in verses 22–23, his awareness of the danger is combined with a genuinely Christian pastoral concern for the reclamation of even the most obstinate.[165]

A second negative judgment on Jude, which contributes even more decisively to the classification of the work as 'early Catholic', concerns Jude's language about 'the faith' in verses 3 and 20. This is said to evince a 'formalized view of the Church's message as a clearly defined and authoritatively transmitted deposit';[166] 'the life of those who are led by the Spirit of God ... has been codified and hardened into a rule of faith, an orthodoxy',[167] 'the fixed and final Christian tradition'.[168] In contrast to the normal early Christian understanding of faith,[169] here 'faith is the acceptance of authoritative tradition'.[170] Faith for Jude is *fides quae*, 'the tradition which is to be believed', 'the infallible and immutable divine tradition',[171] 'a system of doctrine or a fixed confession',[172] 'the orthodox creed'.[173] In this Jude shows a 'post-apostolic consciousness', which is aware of the distance from the apostolic age and the need to preserve the authoritative apostolic tradition in a permanent doctrinal form.[174] This authoritative tradition is then the standard according to which Jude so sharply condemns those who deviate from it.[175] This interpretation of Jude's view of faith and tradition recurs throughout the literature on Jude from the nineteenth century to the present day. Sometimes it is expounded with more or less sympathy, as by Schelkle,[176] Grundmann[177] and Hahn,[178]

---

[165] See Bauckham (1983A) 114–117.
[166] Kelly (1969) 248.
[167] Sidebottom (1967) 78.
[168] Moffatt (1918) 346.
[169] Kümmel (1975) 427.
[170] Perrin (1974) 260.
[171] Krodel (1977) 95.
[172] Cone (1901) 2631.
[173] Jülicher (1904) 231.
[174] Hahn (1981) 209–211; cf. Moffatt (1918) 346.
[175] Hahn (1981) 213.
[176] Schelkle (1963A) 226.
[177] Grundmann (1974) 1–2, 27.
[178] Hahn (1981) 209–211.

but it remains essentially the same interpretation. It is the real basis for the classification of Jude as 'early Catholic'.

When the language about credal orthodoxy and immutable tradition, which writers on Jude so often use, is set beside the words it is intended to interpret in verses 3 and 20, it is not at all clear that this interpretation arises out of the text itself. The reason so many scholars have found it plausible is that they have assumed an 'early Catholic' context for Jude and then read Jude in a way which confirms this assumption. Supported by the weight of scholarly tradition, this reading of Jude has seemed simply obvious, and few voices have been raised to challenge it. It has quite often, however, been noticed that Jude's view of tradition in verse 3 can be paralleled in Paul,[179] as can the objective use of πίστις.[180] If it is then objected that, unlike Jude, Paul does not think of the tradition of the Gospel in terms of a fixed body of formal doctrine or confessional formulae, then it must be emphasized that it is precisely these overtones which are being read into Jude's language. If they are not required by Paul's language, then no more are they required by Jude's language. There is no need to take 'the faith' in Jude as meaning anything more or less than 'the Gospel.'[181] In fact, the 'early Catholic' interpretation of Jude 3 in terms of a body of orthodox doctrine is peculiarly inappropriate since the dispute between Jude and his opponents was not concerned with orthodoxy and heresy in belief, but with the relationship between the Gospel and moral obligation. Whether or not a set form of Christian belief existed in Jude's churches, he had no occasion to refer to it, since his concern was with the moral implications of the Gospel, which certainly featured in Christian catechesis from the beginning.[182]

If the appeal to Jude's view of faith and tradition cannot

---

[179] Chase (1899) 803; Mayor (1907) 61–62; Chaine (1939) 295; Cantinat (1973) 279, 296; Ellis (1978) 233; Robinson (1976) 171.

[180] Chase (1899) 803; Cantinat (1973) 294; Ellis (1978) 233.

[181] Bauckham (1983A) 32–34.

[182] Bauckham (1983A) 9.

establish the 'early Catholic' interpretation of Jude, two other considerations specifically refute it. As well as the development of credal orthodoxy, 'early Catholicism' is usually connected with the fading of the imminent eschatological expectation and with the growth of institutionalized offices in the church. In Jude, the parousia hope is lively and pervades the letter (vv 1, 14, 21, 24). The whole argument of the exegetical section (vv 5–19) hinges on the belief that Jude's opponents are to be judged by the Lord at the parousia and so presupposes an imminent parousia.[183] As for ecclesiastical officials, they are not so much as mentioned in Jude,[184] so that Krodel is obliged to speculate that 'the bishops in Jude's situation had failed to eliminate the heretics from the Christian love feasts, a possibility which Ignatius had apparently not foreseen'.[185] Jude's opponents were evidently charismatics who claimed prophetic revelations, but his response is not the 'early Catholic' one of insisting that charismatic activity must be subject to properly constituted officials or stressing that it is the officials who are endowed with the Spirit.[186] He addresses not the officials, but the whole community, who all enjoy the inspiration of the Spirit in charismatic prayer (v 20)[187] and are all responsible for upholding the Gospel (v 3).

The strongly Jewish character of the letter of Jude has been recognized in some older[188] and some recent scholarship,[189] and the apocalyptic features of its thought and background

---

[183] Bauckham (1983A) 8–9; similarly Wisse (1972) 142.

[184] The 'glories' of v 8 are angels, most certainly not church leaders, as Desjardins (1987) 91, 93–94, merely asserts without any evidence to counter the well-established case that the term was widely used of angels.

[185] Krodel (1977) 95.

[186] Fuller (1971) 161.

[187] Cf. Dunn (1977) 363: Jude 'probably qualifies (as early Catholic) if only because for it too "the faith" has already become fixed and established – though there is also evidence in Jude of a livelier and less formalized experience of the Spirit than would be typical of early Catholicism'.

[188] E.g. Farrar (1882) 236–241; Wand (1934) 191; McNeile (1953) 242–242.

[189] E.g. Green (1968) 43, 46; Grundmann (1974) 15–16; Eybers (1975); Ellis (1978).

are too obvious to be missed even by scholars who stress its 'early Catholic' character.[190] Thus, for Perrin, Jude 'shows that apocalyptic is still a living force in the period of emergent Catholicism'.[191] However, once Jude has been disentangled from the 'early Catholic' interpretation, it is possible to recognize that the letter belongs simply within the milieu of apocalyptic Jewish Christianity. All the evidence points in this direction: the use of 1 Enoch and the Testament of Moses (section II, 2, 3, above), the use of the Hebrew Bible and the probable use of 1 Enoch in Aramaic (section II, 1, 2 above), the pesher exegesis of vv 5–19 (section III above), the emphasis on ethics rather than doctrine in the controversy with the opponents, the prominence of angelology.[192] Moreover, insofar as a distinction between Palestinian and diaspora Judaism is valid, some of these features point more in the direction of Palestinian Jewish Christianity.

The dominance of the apocalyptic outlook in Jude has been given a special interpretation by Rowston, who locates the letter within that Palestinian 'dynastic Christianity' which in the post-apostolic period looked to the relatives of Jesus as authorities.[193] He argues that the author used apocalyptic in a deliberate attempt to counter a developing antinomian Gnosticism. Gnosticism developed out of Paulinism and apocalyptic, but away from the apocalyptic sources of Paul's theology. The author of Jude attempted to reverse this trend, to revive the apocalypticism of Paul and the apostolic church against the post-apostolic drift towards Gnosticism. The author's choice of pseudonym, his dependence on Paul, and his use of Jewish religious literature all belong to a deliberate strategy of returning to the apocalyptic sources of Christianity.[194] However, this is surely too subtle a view of Jude's work, which bears no indications of such a self-conscious choice of approach. Unlike Paul in 1 Corinthians 15 and the

---

[190] Perrin (1974) 261–262; Hahn (1981) 213–214.
[191] Perrin (1974) 262.
[192] Stressed by Eybers (1975) 116–117.
[193] Rowston (1971) 76–79; idem (1975) 559–560.
[194] Rowston (1971) 100–119; idem (1975) 561–562.

author of 2 Peter 3, Jude does not assert apocalyptic eschatology against denials of it. He takes it for granted and assumes his readers will. It is the world-view within which he naturally thinks.

V. The opponents

Throughout the history of scholarship the opponents in Jude have normally been regarded as in some sense Gnostics, and as either identical with or very similar to the opponents in 2 Peter. Thus, according to Zahn, 'There is no essential difference between the descriptions of 2 Peter and Jude,'[195] and the same point was still being made in 1987 by Desjardins.[196] The opponents in both letters were treated synthetically as one subject in Werdermann's monograph on the subject,[197] and in many commentaries.[198] Until recently there have been only occasional reservations about this procedure.[199] It has probably distorted the picture of Jude's opponents rather less than that of 2 Peter's, because it is in Jude's references to the opponents that the most plausible evidence for their Gnostic character has usually been found.

Clement of Alexandria thought that Jude wrote prophetically of the Carpocratians,[200] but modern writers who have accepted this identification have used is as evidence of a second-century date for Jude.[201] Other specific Gnostic groups

---

[195] Zahn (1909) 279.

[196] Desjardins (1987).

[197] Werdermann (1913).

[198] E.g. Windisch (1951) 98–99; Schelkle (1961) 230–234; Green (1968) 37–40.

[199] E.g. Salmond (1907) viii. The redactional-critical approach to 2 Peter's relationship to Jude taken recently by Fornberg (1977), Neyrey (1977) and Bauckham (1983A) enables these scholars to distinguish between 2 Peter's opponents and those of Jude.

[200] *Strom.* 3.2.10–11.

[201] Cone (1901) 2631; Pfleiderer (1911) 251–253; Gunther (1984) 554–555; and for older representatives of this view, see Spitta (1885) 503 n. 1. Against this view, see Spitta (1885) 503–504; Bigg (1901) 313; Zahn (1909) 292–293; Colon (1925) 1676.

which have been suggested are the Docetists[202] and the Marcosians.[203] However, in this century the attempt to identify a particular second-century Gnostic sect has been largely abandoned, and many scholars are content to classify Jude's opponents as Gnostics or as antinomian Gnostics without further specification.[204] As in the case of 2 Peter, many scholars refer in this connection to the beginnings of Gnosticism,[205] 'incipient Gnosticism',[206] 'embryonic Gnosticism',[207] the 'germs' of Gnosticism,[208] or Gnostic 'tendencies',[209] and it is not always clear whether these scholars differ in more than terminology from others who deny that Jude's opponents should properly be called Gnostics at all.[210] Those who argue that Jude's opponents can easily be dated within the first century often adduce Paul's opponents in 1 Corinthians[211] and the Nicolaitans in Revelation[212] as groups with similar characteristics to those which Jude attacks in his opponents. In general it may be said that whether the opponents are regarded as Gnostics or only as some kind of precursors of the real Gnostics, there is nowadays little support for the view that they display clearly

---

[202] Goodspeed (1937) 345, 347.

[203] Barns (1905) 399–411, answered by Mayor (1905).

[204] Jülicher (1904) 230–231; Werdermann (1913); Loisy (1935) 138; Leconte (1949) 1285–1286; Beker (1962) 1010; Schrage (1973) 218–219; Grundmann (1974) 18; Vielhauer (1975) 591; Krodel (1977) 92–94.

[205] Leconte (1961) 70; Hahn (1981) 211.

[206] Sidebottom (1967) 75; Bruce (1980) 832; cf. Eybers (1975) 118; Moffatt (1918) 355: 'the incipient phases of some local, possibly syncretistic, development of libertinism upon gnostic lines.'

[207] Wikenhauser (1958) 489.

[208] Farrar (1882) 242.

[209] Ermoni (1910) 1808; cf. Cantinat (1965) 597–598: 'the initial tendency out of which Gnosis will develop.'

[210] Cf. Eybers (1975) 118: not 'gnosticism in the strict sense'; Bartlet (1900) 346–347; Cantinat (1973) 282.

[211] Salmon (1894) 476–477; Chase (1899) 805; Selwyn (1901) 259–265; Zahn (1909) 280–282; Sidebottom (1967) 70; Ellis (1978) 231–232; Fuchs (1980) 143.

[212] Mansel (1875) 70–71; Huther (1881) 383–384; Gloag (1887) 367–368; Bartlet (1900) 346–347; Zahn (1909) 282–283; Ermoni (1910) 1808; Moffatt (1918) 354 n.; Robinson (1976) 172.

second-century Gnostic features, such as to require a late date.[213]

The following are the main characteristics of the opponents in Jude in which clearly and specifically Gnostic teaching has been detected:

(a) Their denial of God (if v 4 is interpreted in this sense) is said to represent the Gnostic degradation of the Old Testament Creator God to the status of demonic Demiurge.[214]

(b) Their denial of Christ (v 4) is said to consist in docetic Christology.[215]

(c) Their rejection of 'lordship' (v 8) is said to reflect the Gnostic view that the world is under the rule of the archons, not the highest God;[216] while their blaspheming of angels (v 8) can be taken as a further reference to the Gnostic archons.[217]

(d) Verse 19 is interpreted in terms of the Gnostic division of mankind into psychics and spirituals.[218]

(e) The reference to 'the only God' (v 25; cf. v 4: 'the only Master') is understood as directed against Gnostic ideas of the Demiurge and the archons.[219] However, all these interpretations have been contested exegetically,[220] even by many who regard the opponents as in some sense Gnostics, and are scarcely necessary interpretations. It seems unlikely that Jude should oppose such extensive deviations from common Christian belief with such obscure hints of disapproval.

---

[213] But Sidebottom (1967) 76, still thinks the Gnostic character of the opponents requires a second-century date.

[214] Pfleiderer (1911) 251; cf. Grundmann (1974) 30.

[215] Mayor (1907) 27; Pfleiderer (1911) 251; Wand (1934) 200, 208; Green (1968) 162.

[216] Pfleiderer (1911) 251; Windisch (1951) 48.

[217] Sidebottom (1967) 88; Seethalter (1987) 262.

[218] Pfleiderer (1911) 252; Moffatt (1918) 355; Kelly (1969) 284–285; Rowston (1971) 355; Grundmann (1974) 46; Seethalter (1987) 262.

[219] Moffatt (1918) 353; idem (1928) 221; Wand (1934) 221; Gunther (1984) 554.

[220] Against all these points, see Chase (1899) 804; and for examples of scholars who reject each of them see (1) Chaine (1939) 283; (2) Werdermann (1913) 92; Cantinat (1973) 299; (3) Chaine (1939) 283; Bauckham (1983A) 56–59; Sellin (1986) 214; (4) Bigg (1901) 339; Bauckham (1983A) 106–107; Desjardins (1987) 94–95; (5) Werdermann (1913) 91; Chaine (1939) 335; Robinson (1976) 171–172.

Once the attempt to read such clearly Gnostic ideas into Jude is given up, we are left with a picture of the opponents as charismatics who, on the basis of their understanding of grace, rejected all moral constraint and authority. Everything Jude says about them can be directly related to their anti-nomianism, which is the target of his attack.[221] The most puzzling feature, their attitude to angels (vv 8–10), is probably to be understood with reference to angels as guardians of the Law and of the moral order of the world.[222] Such an attitude to the angels of the Law does resemble the views of many later Gnostics, but there is no evidence that Jude's opponents went any further in the direction of Gnostic dualism. In the absence of cosmological dualism it is probably misleading to speak of Gnosticism at all. At most the antinomianism of Jude's opponents was one of the streams which flowed into later Gnosticism.

Of special interest is the relationship which many scholars, especially on the basis of verse 4, have postulated with Paulinism. The Tübingen school regarded Jude as a late second-century Jewish Christian tract against Paulinist Christians, while Renan, taking Balaam (v 11) to be a nickname for Paul (see Rev 2:14–15), thought Jude was actually written against Paul himself at the time of the Antioch incident.[223] Sellin has recently considered the opponents of Jude antinomians in the Pauline tradition, who can be closely connected with the theology of Colossians.[224] The moderate view that the opponents of Jude were taking to an extreme and misinterpreting in a libertinistic way Paul's teaching about grace and the Law has frequently been suggested,[225] and remains quite plausible.[226] According to Rowston, Jude opposed misunderstandings of Paul in a

---

[221] For a sketch of the opponents on these lines, see Bauckham (1983A) 11–12.

[222] Chaine (1939) 308; Cantinat (1973) 309; Bauckham (1983A) 11–12.

[223] Renan (1869) 300–303. Against this view: Salmon (1894) 24–25.

[224] Sellin (1986) 210–212, 221–224.

[225] Weiss (1888) 122; Wand (1934) 194, 210; Taylor (1934) 439; Chaine (1939) 283–284; Leconte (1949) 1286.

[226] Bauckham (1983A) 12.

Gnostic sense which perhaps appeared when the Pauline corpus was published.[227]

Among those who dissent from the general view that Jude's opponents were more or less Gnostic, are those who identify them as Essenes,[228] and Reicke, who finds in Jude the political agitators he finds throughout the Catholic epistles.[229] Remarkably, Ellis regards the opponents as Judaizers, the same as those encountered by Paul.[230] Carr finds similarities with Edessan Christianity.[231] However, these interpretations neglect the one clear characteristic of the opponents, against which all Jude's argument is directed: their antinomianism and rejection of moral constraints.

A series of scholars have denied that the opponents in Jude were teachers with a specific religious message at all: Jude's 'language is fully satisfied if we suppose them to be private members of the Church who lived ungodly lives, and who were insubordinate and contumelious when rebuked by their spiritual superiors'.[232] However, the implication of verses 11–13, including the implied description of them as shepherds in verse 12, is that the opponents were teachers,[233] and verse 8 (ἐνυπνιαζόμενοι) suggests that they claimed prophetic revelations as authority for their teaching.[234]

Finally, Wisse proposes a radical hypothesis which dispenses with any identification of the opponents at all. Jude's letter (which he regards as a genuinely 'catholic' letter, i.e. 'addressed to Christendom in general'[235]) has no specific heretics in mind, but is 'an eschatological tract' about the false prophets of the last days. The characteristics of the opponents are not

[227] Rowston (1971) 31; idem (1975) 556–557.
[228] Daniel (1968); idem (1969) 68; Szewc (1976).
[229] Reicke (1951); idem (1964).
[230] Ellis (1968) 235.
[231] Carr (1981) 131–132.
[232] Salmon (1894) 477; so also Hofmann (1875); Chase (1899) 804–805; other nineteenth-century representatives of this view mentioned by Weiss (1888) 121. Weiss himself regarded the opponents as 'libertines on principle': Weiss (1888) 122.
[233] Bauckham (1983A) 79–92.
[234] Bauckham (1983A) 55–56.
[235] Wisse (1972) 135.

drawn from the historical situation, but are mostly 'stock phrases taken from the description of the eschatological false prophets in Jewish and early-Christian literature'.[236] Against Wisse, it may be said that Jude is trying to demonstrate to his readers that the false teachers in their churches actually are the false prophets of the last days. He would have failed in his purpose if the characteristics he attributes to them were not actually to be found in the false teachers known to his readers. Moreover, not all of Jude's accusations are stock charges: the blaspheming of angels (v 8) is a highly unusual feature.

From the exegetical work in my commentary on Jude, I developed the following sketch of the opponents. They were evidently itinerant charismatics who had arrived in the church or churches to which Jude writes (v 4). They were libertines by principle, rejecting all moral authority, whether that of the law of Moses (vv 8–10) or that of Christ himself (vv 4, 8). Their denial of Christ as Master and Lord (v 4) is not to be understood as a doctrinal error, but as rejection of his moral demands: by their immoral practice they in effect disowned him as Master and repudiated his authority as Lord. Evidently they understood the grace of God in Christ (v 4) as a deliverance from all external moral constraint, so that the person who possesses the Spirit (v 19 is Jude's response to this claim) becomes the only judge of his or her own actions, subject to no other authority. Like the Corinthians, whose slogan was 'All things are lawful for me' (1 Cor 6:12; 10:23), they took Christian freedom to mean that the really spiritual person is free from the constraints of conventional morality. For their authority they appealed to their charismatic inspiration, manifested in prophetic visions ('dreaming,' v 8, is a pejorative reference to these), in which perhaps they received revelations of the heavenly world and their own exalted status in it. Their attitude to angels (vv 8–10) should be related to the role of angels as guardians of the moral order. When accused of sin by the standard of the Law of Moses or of the order of creation, they spoke disparagingly of the angels who gave the

[236] Wisse (1972) 142.

Law and administered the moral order, alleging that these angels were motivated by ill-will towards humanity.

Jude's opponents were not simply members of the church, but teachers (vv 11–13 portray them, with appropriate Old Testament types, as people who lead others astray, and, notably, as shepherds who feed themselves instead of the flock). They were present at the church's fellowship meals (v 12), where no doubt they imparted their prophecies and teachings to the church. They gathered their own faction of followers, who considered themselves truly in possession of the Spirit (v 19).

Whether Pauline teaching had had some influence on them must remain uncertain. They could have been taking to an extreme and misinterpreting Paul's teaching about grace and the Law. Not only did Paul himself recognize and oppose the danger of an antinomian distortion of his teaching on Christian freedom (Rom 3:8; 6:1, 15; Gal 5:13), but also the blaspheming of angels, so distinctive of Jude's opponents (vv 8–10), is not too distant from some of Paul's treatment of the angels of the Law and 'the elemental spirits of the world' (Gal 3:20; 4:3, 8–9; Col 2:8–23; Rom 8:33–39).

VI. Date

In the scholarship of the past century Jude has been assigned to an extraordinarily wide range of dates, from the 50s to the late second century.[237] Recent writers show little inclination

[237] The following dates are suggested in the literature:

c. 54	Renan (1869)
55–65	Ellis (1978)
58–69	Selwyn (1901)
60–65	Weiss (1888); Bigg (1901)
60–70	Gloag (1887); Salmond (1907)
60–80	Wikenhauser (1958); Payne (1969)
61	Robinson (1976)
62–67	Vrede (1916); Willmering (1953)
62–70	Charue (1946)
62–80	Keil (1883)
63–69	Wandel (1898)

to date the work very far into the second century, but otherwise the range of date remains very wide, and there seems no sign of any convergence of scholarly opinion on this issue. This situation partly reflects the fact that Jude offers few indications of date, and partly corresponds to the fact that the interpretation of aspects of the work which could be relevant to its date is very much debated. Thus, we have already considered the question of 'early Catholicism' in Jude (section IV above) and the identity of the opponents (section V above), both of which have had considerable influence on estimates of the date of Jude. The argument that Jude presupposes a developed Gnosticism of a second-century kind has

65–80	Kühl (1897); Chase (1899); Green (1968); Guthrie (1970)
c. 68	Symes (1921)
68–80	Eybers (1975)
c. 70	Cantinat (1965)
70–75	Wohlenberg (1923)
70–80	Bartlet (1900); Mayor (1907); Chaine (1939)
70–100	Leconte (1961)
70–130	Danker (1982)
c. 75	Zahn (1909)
c. 80	Hofmann (1875); Spitta (1885); Werdermann (1913); Dalton (1969)
80–90	Soden (1899)
80–100	Knopf (1912); Kelly (1969); Fuchs (1980)
c. 90	Reicke (1964)
90–100	Windisch (1951)
90–110	Kugelman (1980)
90–120	Hahn (1981)
c. 100	Moffatt (1928); Leaney (1967); Schrage (1973); Kümmel (1975); Vielhauer (1975)
100–110	Beker (1962)
100–120	Hollmann (1907); Sidebottom (1967)
100–125	Taylor (1934); Fuller (1971)
100–130	Harnack (1897)
100–140	Perrin (1974)
100–180	Jülicher (1904)
120–130	Gunther (1984)
c. 125	Goodspeed (1937)
c. 140	Davidson (1894)
140–150	Loisy (1935)
after 160	Pfleiderer (1911)
c. 160	Barns (1905)

declined in popularity in recent scholarship, and this may account for the fact that very late dates (after c. 120) are now rarely suggested, but the assumption that Jude belongs to the 'early Catholic' period, and is therefore post-apostolic, is still very influential. However (as section IV has indicated) it is also very questionable. The alternative characterization of Jude, as deriving from Palestinian apocalyptic Christianity, opens up the possibility of a relatively early date but cannot rule out a relatively late date.

Only three other considerations have had any significant influence on views of the date of Jude. In the first place, the literary relationship with 2 Peter provides either a *terminus a quo* (if 2 Peter is prior) or a *terminus ad quem* (if Jude is prior), but in either case this only relates Jude to the equally wide range of dates which scholars have proposed for 2 Peter. Secondly, some older scholars argued that Jude 5b refers to the fall of Jerusalem in A.D. 70, and therefore provides a *terminus a quo*.[238] Others denied such a reference, but argued that Jude would have referred to the fall of Jerusalem if it had occurred when he wrote, so that A.D. 70 is a *terminus ad quem*.[239] Surprisingly, Robinson, whose thesis about the dating of the New Testament documents hinges on lack of reference to the fall of Jerusalem, makes little of this point in relation to Jude.[240] In this he belongs to the general consensus of scholarship, which interprets Jude 5b without reference to the fall of Jerusalem but also without relevance to the date of the letter.[241]

Modern scholarship has been much more impressed by the chronological implications of Jude 17, which has often been said to represent the age of the apostles as belonging to the past.[242] However, serious exegetical objections to this view have also been made sufficiently often to merit serious consideration.[243]

---

[238] Vrede (1916) 94; and others listed in Moffatt (1918) 346; cf. Maier (1904) 397.

[239] Zahn (1909) 252–255; and others listed in Maier (1904) 395.

[240] Robinson (1976) 172.

[241] Moffatt (1918) 346–347; Leconte (1949) 1287; Cantinat (1973) 287; Grundmann (1974) 17.

[242] Moffatt (1918) 346; Sidebottom (1967) 78; Kelly (1969) 233, 281; Grundmann (1974) 16; Kümmel (1975) 428.

(1) The verse does not represent the apostles themselves, but only their predictions, as belonging to the past.[244] It need not follow that the apostles are no longer making such predictions, and so must be dead or dispersed,[245] because verse 17 should be interpreted in line with verses 3 and 5, which indicate that Jude is recalling his readers to the instruction they received at their conversion, from the apostles who founded their churches.[246] Understood in this way, Jude's statement is exactly parallel to many of Paul's in which he refers his readers back to the teaching he gave them when he founded their churches (1 Cor 15:1–3; Gal 1:9; 1 Thess 4:1–2), with the one difference that, since Jude was evidently not one of the founding missionaries of the churches to which he writes, he speaks of the apostles' teaching rather than his own (but cf. Rom 6:7; 16:17). As in the case of Jude 3, there has been a tendency to give similar language in Paul and Jude one sense in Paul and another sense in Jude.

(2) The most natural meaning of verse 18 is that Jude's readers themselves heard the apostles' preaching.[247] In that case, the verse implies that most of the original converts were still living, and thus puts not a lower but an upper limit on the date, though since we do not know when the churches Jude addresses were founded the indication of date is still very vague.

VII. Authorship

The identity of the Judas to whom the letter is attributed is a

---

[243] See, generally, Robinson (1976) 172–173; Ellis (1978) 253–254; Bauckham (1983A) 103.

[244] Wand (1934) 188.

[245] For the view that the dispersal of the apostles would satisfy the requirements of the verse, see Chase (1899) 803; Bigg (1901) 314.

[246] The imperfect ἔλεγον cannot be pressed against this interpretation, because Paul uses similar imperfects to refer to his teaching during his one, initial visit to Thessalonica (1 Thess 3:4; 2 Thess 2:5; 3:10). 1 Thess 3:4 provides a good parallel to the prediction in Jude 17, already fulfilled at the time of writing.

[247] Chase (1899) 803; Wand (1934) 190; Grundmann (1974) 44–45; Eybers (1975) 115; Robinson (1976) 173; Ellis (1978) 254. Against this view: Kelly (1969) 282.

distinct question from whether the name is used authentically or pseudonymously, though inevitably the two questions have been somewhat interconnected. The following identifications of Jude have been made:

(a) The overwhelming majority of scholars have understood this Judas to be the brother of Jesus (Matt 13:55; Mark 6:3; Hegesippus, *ap*. Eusebius, *HE* 3:19:1–3:20:6). This view is strongly supported by the phrase, 'brother of James,' which distinguishes this Judas from others of the same name by mentioning his relationship to the only man in the primitive church who could be called simply 'James' without risk of ambiguity.

(b) The traditional view, before the nineteenth century, was that the author was Judas the apostle, one of the Twelve (Luke 6:16; Acts 1:13: Ἰούδας Ἰακώβου used to be translated, as in the AV, 'Judas the brother of James,' on the strength of the analogy with Jude 1). This is not really an alternative to (a), since most writers who took this view held the apostle 'Judas of James' to be the same person as the relative of Jesus mentioned in Mark 6:3. A number of nineteenth-century scholars still attributed the letter to the apostle Judas,[248] and since the Council of Trent had taken this view it was still found in Roman Catholic scholarship until recently.[249] Jessein in 1821[250] was the first to argue in detail against it, distinguishing the brother of Jesus and author of Jude from the apostle Judas, and it has now been generally abandoned, even in Roman Catholic scholarship.[251]

(c) A few scholars have thought that the Judas intended is the apostle Thomas, who in Syrian Christian tradition was known as Judas Thomas.[252] Since this tradition interpreted the name Thomas as meaning that this apostle was the 'twin'

---

[248] Hofmann (1875); Wordsworth (1882) 137–139; Keil (1883) 295–296; others listed in Moffatt (1918) 356; Gloag (1887) 358–359.

[249] E.g. Vrede (1916) 91–92; Willmering (1953) 1191

[250] According to Weiss (1888) 127.

[251] E.g. Chaine (1939) 269–271; Wikenhauser (1958) 490–491; Cantinat (1965) 595; Grundmann (1974) 14. Cantinat (1973) 284, however, still leaves open a possiblity that Jude might be the apostle.

[252] Koester (1965) 297; Sidebottom (1967) 69, 79; Carr (1981) 130–132.

of Jesus, the phrase 'brother of James' (Jude 1) is explained as identifying Judas Thomas with Judas the brother of Jesus. However, the usual understanding of 'twin' was that Thomas bore a close physical resemblance to Jesus or that he was a kind of spiritual twin of Jesus. His identification as a blood-brother of Jesus and therefore with Jude the brother of Jesus appears to be a later development. (For fuller discussion of this issue, see chapter 1 section III above.)

(d) Several scholars have identified Jude with Judas Barsabbas (Acts 15:22, 27, 32).[253] Barns takes 'brother of James' to be a gloss;[254] Plessis interprets it of spiritual fraternity;[255] and Ellis argues for the meaning 'co-worker'.[256] A weighty argument against both (c) and (d) is that the obvious way to distinguish these figures from others of the same name would have been to use their surnames Thomas and Barsabbas, not 'brother of James'.

(e) In order to be able to date the letter in the early second century without regarding it as pseudepigraphal, a few scholars have identified Jude with an early second-century bishop of Jerusalem called Judas.[257] But in chapter 2 section III above, we have argued that in fact there was no such bishop of this name.

(f) Harnack[258] and Moffatt[259] thought the author an otherwise unknown Judas. This cannot explain 'brother of James', but Harnack considered this phrase a later gloss intended to give the letter authority.[260]

---

[253] Plumptre (1879) 85–86; Selwyn (1900) 148; idem (1901) 112, 230; Barns (1905) 393; Plessis (1966), developing an earlier argument by W. J. Fournier; Ellis (1987) 226–236; others listed in Gloag (1887) 359–360; Moffatt (1918) 356.

[254] Barns (1905) 393.

[255] Plessis (1966) 197.

[256] Ellis (1978) 227.

[257] Grotius (see Chase [1899] 804 n.) (he thought 'brother of James' an episcopal title at Jerusalem); Streeter (1929) 178–180 (he thought 'brother' a gloss in Jude 1); Adam (1957) 46; Klein (1961) 100.

[258] Harnack (1897) 467–468.

[259] Moffatt (1918) 357–358; idem (1928) 244–246.

[260] Harnack's view was also taken by Taylor (1934) 438; and others listed in Guthrie (1970) 907 n. 3; Kümmel (1975) 428 n. 5. It is considered

The vast majority of scholars hold the letter to be attributed to Judas the brother of Jesus, but the authenticity of this attribution is disputed.[261] Until c. 1960 a considerable majority of scholars maintained the authenticity of Jude against an important minority who regarded the letter as pseudepigraphal. During the last two decades the pseudepigraphal hypothesis seems to have gained ground, and has been adopted in most of the important commentaries of this period. Those who defend authenticity remain, however, a significant minority.[262] The pattern is thus rather different from the history of opinion on the authenticity of 2 Peter, where the case for

at least possible by Beker (1962) 1010; Boobyer (1962); Danker (1982) 1154.

[261] Authors since 1880 who hold Jude to be authentic, by the brother of Jesus (whether or not they also identify him with the apostle): Alford (1880); Huther (1881); Farrar (1882); Wordsworth (1882); Keil (1883); Plummer (1884); Gloag (1887); Weiss (1888); Plummer (1891); Salmon (1894); Kühl (1897); Wandel (1898); Chase (1899); Bartlet (1900); Bigg (1901); Maier (1906A); idem (1906B); Salmond (1907); Mayor (1907); Zahn (1909); Mayor (1910); Ermoni (1910); James (1912); Vrede (1916); Wohlenberg (1923); Colon (1925); Holtzmann (1926); Wand (1934); Chaine (1939); Charue (1946); Leconte (1949); Willmering (1953); Wikenhauser (1958); Cranfield (1960); Leconte (1961); Schlatter (1964); Cantinat (1965); Lenski (1966); Green (1968); Payne (1969); Dalton (1969); Guthrie (1970); Lawlor (1976); Robinson (1976); Bruce (1980); Bauckham (1983A). For earlier advocates of authenticity, see Gloag (1887) 355.

Authors since 1880 who hold Jude to be pseudepigraphal: Davidson (1894); Cone (1901); Jülicher (1904); Barns (1905); Hollmann (1907); Pfleiderer (1911); Knopf (1912); Loisy (1935); Goodspeed (1937); Hauck (1937); Loisy (1950); Windisch (1951); Barnett (1957); Schelkle (1961); Reicke (1964); Leaney (1967); Sidebottom (1967); Michl (1968); Kelly (1969); Rowston (1971); Fuller (1971); Wisse (1972); Cantinat (1973); Schrage (1973); Grundmann (1974); Perrin (1974); Kümmel (1975); Rowston (1975); Vielhauer (1975); Krodel (1977); Kugelman (1980); Fuchs (1980); Hahn (1981); Gunther (1984); Sellin (1986). For early advocates of pseudonymity, see Gloag (1887) 355.

Writers who leave the question open are McNeile (1953); Schneider (1961); Danker (1982). The only writer who seems to have suggested that Jude is only partially authentic ('slightly modified by a second-century editor') is Symes (1921) 189.

[262] Heiligenthal (1986) 120, is quite inaccurate in stating that the pseudepigraphal character of Jude is no longer disputed: several recent works in his own bibliography dispute it!

pseudepigraphy has been much more generally accepted for a much longer period. This difference indicates that in the case of Jude the arguments for and against authenticity have been more evenly balanced and much less decisive.

Very often the matter has been decided largely in terms of the considerations relevant to the date of Jude (identity of the opponents, 'early Catholicism', interpretation of v 17). Hegesippus' story about the grandsons of Jude in the reign of Domitian (Eusebius, *HE* 3:19:1–3:20:6) has normally been thought to imply that Jude was then dead, but it is still possible to regard the letter as authentic and to date it as late as c. 80. Thus the interpretation of verse 17 in terms of a post-apostolic situation has not been a decisive argument against authenticity.[263] The 'early Catholic' reading of Jude and the view that the opponents represent a relatively developed Gnosticism have been more prejudicial to authenticity. However, not only our arguments against these views (sections IV and V above), but also the recognition that in fact nothing in the letter requires a late date (section VI) should clear the way for recognizing the authenticity of Jude.

A favourite argument against the hypothesis of pseudepigraphy has been that Jude was too obscure a figure to be adopted as a pseudonym.[264] To answer this point, a few scholars who favour pseudepigraphy postulate some real connection with Jude: that the author was a disciple, friend or relative of Jude,[265] or belonged to circles influenced by Jude.[266] Others point to the authority of James in the early church, especially in Jewish-Christian circles, and think the choice of the pseudonym Jude was a way of claiming the authority of James.[267] Some have thought that Jude was

---

[263] Scholars who regard Jude as authentic and date it in the period 70–85 include Mayor (1907); Zahn (1909); Wohlenberg (1923); Chaine (1939); Dalton (1969); cf. Grundmann (1974) 16.

[264] Farrar (1882) 220–221; Weiss (1888) 127–128; Zahn (1909) 268; Moffatt (1918) 357; Wohlenberg (1923) XLVIII; Cranfield (1960) 148; Green (1968) 46; Guthrie (1970) 907.

[265] Reicke (1964); Michl (1968); Grundmann (1974) 15–16.

[266] Hollmann (1907) 572.

[267] Schrage (1973) 220; Fuchs (1980) 147.

considered a more suitable pseudonym than James for a writer conscious of his post-apostolic situation because Jude outlived James.[268] Some have thought a relatively obscure pseudonym (but one connected with James and with Jesus himself) suited the author's purpose.[269] The most plausible defence of the pseudonymous use of the name Jude is that which argues that Jude was not in fact an obscure figure in the Jewish Christian circles from which the letter must come.[270] Thus, Rowston finds the choice of pseudonym natural, within the Palestinian 'dynastic Christianity' which revered the Lord's family, by an author who wished to follow up the previously published pseudepigraphal letter of James.[271] The major difficulty for all attempts to explain the pseudonym from Jewish Christian reverence for the family of Jesus is that the letter does not call Jude 'the brother of the Lord,' the title by which he would have been known in such circles and by which his authority, in Jewish Christian eyes, was indicated. The lack of reference to Jude's relationship to Jesus is much more easily explicable on the assumption of authenticity than on the assumption of pseudepigraphy.[272]

Apart from considerations of date, the only major objection to authorship by the brother of Jesus has been the language of the letter, which has often been said to be Greek too good to be plausibly attributed to a Galilean Jew of peasant stock.[273] To this a number of replies can be made. In the first place, the excellence of the Greek can be overestimated. The author's wide vocabulary is more impressive than his skill in literary style: a feature which could 'stamp him as a man whose knowledge of Greek was acquired in later rather than in earlier life'.[274] Farrar judged the style to be 'exactly such as we should expect from one to whom Greek was not so

[268] Jülicher (1904) 232; Hahn (1981) 216–217.
[269] Danker (1982) 1154.
[270] Cantinat (1973) 286–287.
[271] Rowston (1971) 76–79, 83–85; idem (1975) 559–561.
[272] Cf. Farrar (1882) 223–224; Bigg (1901) 318–319; Green (1968) 44; Bauckham (1983A) 21–23.
[273] Kelly (1969) 233; Kugelman (1980) 81.
[274] Chase (1899) 802; cf. Bauckham (1983A) 6.

familiar as his native Aramaic ... It is the language of an Oriental who knows Greek, partly by reading and partly by moving among Hellenistic communities, but whose vocabulary is far richer and more powerful than his grammar'.[275] However, the Semitic features of the style should not be overstressed,[276] and certainly cannot support Maier's conjecture that Jude wrote the letter in Aramaic.[277]

Secondly, it is difficult to estimate how competent in Greek a Galilean Jew could have been.[278] Recent studies have tended to stress the extent to which Greek as well as Aramaic was spoken in first-century Palestine, including Galilee,[279] as well as the impact of hellenistic culture in Palestine. Moreover, we know so little about Jude that it is impossible to set limits to the extent to which, in a long career as a Christian missionary, he could have acquired a rhetorical skill in Greek.[280] Finally, the hypothesis of a Greek-speaking secretary is always available[281] but, in the case of a work such as this, in which the thought is inseparable from the carefully studied expression, should be avoided if possible.

In the context of the fresh look at Jude which has begun to emerge in this chapter (and will be carried further in the next three chapters) authenticity appears not only possible but very probable. The work has all the marks of a fairly early work of Palestinian Jewish Christian provenance – in its use of the Hebrew Bible, haggadic traditions and apocryphal works of Palestinian origin, its strongly apocalyptic character, its skilful pesher-type exegesis, its imminent eschatological expectation and strong orientation towards the parousia, its concern with a controversy about antinomian teaching rather than about doctrine. Resemblances to other Christian literature (apart from 2 Peter, which actually borrows from Jude) are easily

---

[275] Farrar (1882) 236.
[276] Cantinat (1973) 268; Bauckham (1983A) 6.
[277] Maier (1906) 171.
[278] Cantinat (1973) 286; Grundmann (1974) 15; Leconte (1949) 1288.
[279] Sevenster (1968); Fitzmyer (1979) 29–56; Argyle (1973–74); Freyne (1980) 139–141.
[280] Bauckham (1983A) 15–16.
[281] Chaine (1939) 281; Cantinat (1973) 286.

explicable in terms of the debt which all early Christian thought owed to the Palestinian Jewish Christianity of the first two decades. Jude, the Lord's brother, a prominent missionary leader in the Palestinian churches of the earliest period, is entirely plausibly the author of this letter. It could easily be among the earliest of the New Testament documents, as well as being rare and valuable firsthand evidence of the character of the Christian devotion and developing theology of those original Palestinian circles in which Jesus' own relatives were leaders. Further study of it (in chapters 4 and 6 below) will throw significant light on the contribution of those circles to the development of Christian thought in the earliest period.

4

Jude's Exegesis

Though it has been rarely recognized, Jude's letter contains a peculiarly elaborate and interesting example of formal exegesis of Scripture in the style of the Qumran pesharim. Study of this aspect of Jude will illuminate both the letter itself and the tradition of early Christian exegesis to which it belongs.

I. The structure of Jude's commentary

Before analysing the commentary section itself (vv 4–19), we must first ascertain its role within the letter as a whole, whose structure can be analysed as follows:

ANALYSIS OF THE LETTER

1–2	Address and Greeting
3–4	Occasion and Theme
3	A. The Appeal to Contend for the Faith
4	B. The Background to the Appeal: the False Teachers, their Character and Judgment (forming Introductory Statement of Theme for B¹)
5–23	Body of the Letter
5–19	B¹. The Background: A Commentary on Four Prophecies of the Doom of the Ungodly
20–23	A¹. The Appeal
24–25	Concluding Doxology.

In form Jude is a letter, with a formal letter structure, as this analysis shows, but containing (in vv 4–19) a section of formal scriptural exegesis. In the structure of the whole letter it is especially important to notice that the initial statement of theme of the letter (vv 3–4) contains two parts (here labelled A and B) which correspond, in reverse order – a chiastic arrangement – to the two parts of the body of the letter (labelled B¹ and A¹). The main purpose of the letter is the appeal 'to contend for the faith' which is announced in v 3 and spelled out in verses 20–23.[1] But verse 4 explains that this appeal is necessary because the readers are in danger of being misled by false teachers. The claim in verse 4 that these teachers are people whose ungodly behaviour has already been condemned by God is then substantiated by the exegetical section[2] (vv 5–19) which argues that these are the ungodly people of the last days to whom the scriptural types and prophecies of judgment refer. Thus we should not be misled by the length and central position of the discussion of the false teachers (vv 4–19) into considering it the main object of the letter. This section establishes the danger in which the readers are placed by the influence of the false teachers and so performs an essential role as background to the appeal, but the real climax of the letter is only reached in the exhortations of verses 20–23. In verses 4–19 Jude establishes the need for his readers to 'contend for the faith', but only in verses 20–23 does he explain what 'contending for the faith' involves. Thus his negative polemic against the false teachers is subordinate to the positive Christian teaching of verses 20–23, which is what 'contending for the faith' consists in.

This analysis shows that B and B¹ form together a section which crosses the main divisions of the letter: B (v 4) forms

[1] See, in more detail, Bauckham (1983A) 4, 29, 111.
[2] In other works (e.g. Bauckham [1983], [1988E]), I have used the term 'midrash', but this has developed such potential for misunderstanding, being used both very strictly (of the rabbinic midrashim only) and very loosely (of any kind of Jewish scriptural interpretation, even where there is no explicit quotation of or reference to Scripture), that it seems best avoided. So I use the English terms 'exegesis' and 'commentary'.

an introductory statement of theme for the commentary in verses 5–19. The commentary provides the exegetical argument to support the claim made in verse 4: that the false teachers are people whose ungodly behaviour has already been condemned and whose judgment has long ago been prophesied. Thus, the exegetical section (vv 5–19) is not, as it has so often seemed to modern readers, mere undisciplined denunciation, but a very carefully composed piece of scriptural commentary which *argues* for the statement made in verse 4. Though strange to modern readers, the argument is one whose hermeneutical presuppositions and exegetical methods were widely accepted in contemporary Judaism and can be paralleled especially from the Qumran pesharim. Its aim is to demonstrate the danger posed by the false teachers to the readers by showing how their practice and advocacy of libertine behaviour corresponds to the character of those ungodly people whose appearance in the last days and whose judgment at the imminent parousia has been prophesied.

The structure of the exegetical section (B + B¹) itself is as follows:[3]

ANALYSIS OF THE COMMENTARY SECTION

4	Introductory statement of theme
5–7	*'Text' 1: Three Old Testament types*
8–10	+ interpretation
9	including secondary 'text' 1a: Michael and the devil
11	*'Text' 2: Three more Old Testament types*
12–13	+ interpretation
12–13	including secondary allusions (Ezek 34:2; Prov 25:14; Isa 57:20; 1 Enoch 80:6)
14–15	*'Text' 3: A very ancient prophecy* (1 Enoch 1:9)
16	+ interpretation

[3] This is a modified version of the analysis offered by Ellis (1978) 221–226.

17–18   '*Text*' *4: A very modern prophecy* (a prophecy of the
         apostles)
19   + interpretation.

The basic structure is of four main 'texts,' each followed by
a section of commentary identifying the false teachers as
those to whom the 'text' refers. The four main 'texts' are
grouped in two pairs. However, the term 'texts' (with
inverted commas) has to be used because, although they
function as texts in the commentary, they are not all actual
scriptural quotations: in fact, none of them is an actual quotation from our canonical Old Testament. This may seem
to throw initial doubt on the plausibility of classifying this
passage as a piece of scriptural exegesis, but the structure of
text and commentary is in every other respect too clear for
the anomalous character of the actual 'texts' to outweigh
it. We must accept that Jude intended to write a piece of
exegetical argument, but chose to use 'texts' which are not
strictly speaking scriptural quotations.

The first pair, 'texts' 1 and 2, are summaries of
Scripture.[4] 'Text' 1 refers to three groups of people: Israel
in the wilderness (Num 14), the Watchers or fallen angels
(1 Enoch 6–19), and the cities of the Plain (Gen 19). 'Text'
2 refers to three individuals: Cain (Gen 4:8), Balaam (Num
22; 31:16; cf. Deut 23:5; Neh 13:2) and Korah (Num 16).
Both the groups and the individuals were well-known scriptural examples of judgment, who here function as types. So
in these 'texts' we have not verbal prophecies but historical
types, to which Jude refers in summary form rather than
by quoting Scripture. In verses 5–6, however, there are
some more or less precise verbal allusions to the actual texts
of Scripture:

v 5   μὴ πιστεύσαντας: cf. Num 14:11 (cf. Deut 1:32; 9:23;
       Ps 106:24);
v 6   ἀπολιπόντας τὸ ἴδιον οἰκητήριον: cf. 1 Enoch 12:4;

---

[4] Wright (1967) 108, considers this an acceptable way of citing the text
of a midrash, and compares 1 Cor 10:1–5; Heb 7:1–3.

15:3, 7; εἰς κρίσιν μεγάλης ἡμέρας: 1 Enoch 10:12 (text as in 4QEnᵇ 1:4:11); δεσμοῖς ἀϊδίοις ὑπὸ ζόφον τετήρηκεν: cf. 1 Enoch 10:4–6; τετήρηκεν: perhaps cf. 2 Enoch 7:2; 18:4–6.

It should also be noticed that the references to Cain, Balaam and Korah are not merely to the Old Testament texts as such, but to the haggadic traditions about these figures which had grown up around the Old Testament texts.[5]

It is possible that these two 'texts' (vv 5–7 and v 11) were already known to Jude in something like the form in which he quotes them. There is good evidence that verses 5–7 are an adaptation of a traditional schema of well-known examples of divine judgment: other examples of the schema (Sir 16:7–10; CD 2:17–3:12; 3 Macc 2:4–7; TNapht 3:4–5; m. Sanh. 10:3; 2 Pet 2:4–8) offer close parallels, both material and stylistic, to Jude 5–7.[6] Moreover, the introduction to verse 5 ('Now I should like to remind you, though you have been informed of all things once and for all') indicates that the material in verses 5–7 was part of the paraenetic tradition which had been communicated to these churches when they were founded.[7] So it may be that Jude's 'text' is here an already traditional summary of scriptural material, though it is likely that Jude himself is responsible for the actual wording and for the precise allusions to 1 Enoch. As for 'text' 2 (v 11), it is in the form of a prophetic woe-oracle, which might indicate that Jude already knew it in that form, as the oracle of a Christian prophet, though of course it is entirely possible that Jude composed it in that form himself.[8] The possibility that verse 11 already existed as a prophetic oracle could explain the formal difference between 'texts' 1 and 2. In any case, 'texts' 1 and 2 can function as scriptural texts because they summarize material in Scripture and traditional interpretation of Scripture.

[5] See Bauckham (1983A) 79–84.
[6] Details in Bauckham (1983A) 46–47.
[7] Bauckham (1983A) 48–49.
[8] Bauckham (1983A) 77–78; cf. Ellis (1978) 224.

'Texts' 1 and 2 are already a pair, being each a set of three types, and 'texts' 3 and 4 form a second pair, this time of verbal prophecies of the false teachers, one very ancient and one very modern. Enoch's was no doubt (ostensibly) the oldest prophecy available to Jude. Writing during the lifetime of the apostles, he looks back in verses 17–18 not, as commonly thought, to the time of the apostles as such, but simply to the time when apostles founded the churches to which he is writing,[9] so that the prophecy of the apostles is a very modern one. The effect therefore of pairing these two particular prophecies is to demonstrate that the false teachers and their judgment have been prophesied from the very earliest times, before the Flood, up to the most recent times, at the actual inauguration of the last days. Both prophecies are actual quotations, but the difference between the introductory formulae in each case (vv 14a, 17–18a) indicates the difference between quotations from a written and an oral source. Of course, the quotation from the apostles may well be simply Jude's own summary of the kind of thing that was part of the common apocalyptic teaching of the apostles. The written source is 1 Enoch, a work with which (or with parts of which) Jude shows himself to be very familiar.

Despite the anomalous nature of Jude's texts, the exegetical *structure* of 'text' followed by interpretation is plain, because the transition from 'text' to interpretation is in each case clearly marked in two ways.[10] (1) It is marked by a change of tense, from verbs in the past or future in the 'texts' to present tenses in the interpretation. 'Text' 1 is in the past tense, referring to the types in past history; 'texts' 2 and 3 are both in prophetic past tenses (i.e. aorists which, in imitation of the Semitic 'prophetic perfect,' in fact refer to the future); while 'text' 4 has a real future tense. Thus the types and prophecies are in the past and the future; the interpretations in each case use present tenses, referring to the fulfilment of the types and prophecies in the present, in the form of Jude's opponents. (2) The transition from 'text' to interpretation is

---

[9] Bauckham (1983A) 103–104.
[10] First pointed out by Ellis (1978) 225.

also marked by phrases with οὗτοι used in a formulaic way at the beginning of each section of interpretation. These phrases, which will be discussed in more detail in section III below, resemble exegetical formulae used in other texts to introduce an interpretation. They serve to identify the false teachers as the people to whom the prophecies refer, and so make the transition from the prophecy to its application to the false teachers. The interpretation in each case describes the false teachers in a way which conforms to the prophecy. (3) A further indicator of the division of the passage into 'texts' and commentary is found only in the cases of 'texts' 3 and 4, which, as we have already noticed, have introductory formulae (vv 14a, 17–18a), marking them off from the interpretation of the preceding text. 'Text' 2 does not have such a formula, but is sufficiently clearly marked out by its form as a prophetic woe-oracle.

As well as the four main 'texts,' there is a secondary 'text' (1a), which is introduced in verse 9 to help the interpretation of 'text' 1. This kind of use of a secondary text in the course of the interpretation of another text is a phenomenon which can be paralleled in the Qumran pesharim,[11] with which as we shall see Jude's exegesis has considerable affinity. In this case the 'text' is a summary, with considerable close verbal allusion, of an apocryphal account of the death of Moses. Jude's source in verse 9 (probably the lost ending of the Testament of Moses), though not extant as such, will be reconstructed from surviving references to it in chapter 5 below. That reconstruction will show that Jude 9 is quite close to being a quotation (the following are verbal allusions to the source: Μιχαὴλ ὁ ἀρχάγγελος ... τῷ διαβόλῳ διακρινόμενος διελέγετο περὶ τοῦ Μωϋσέως σώματος ... βλασφημίας ... Ἐπιτιμήσαι σοι Κύριος). Again this 'text' is marked off by a change of tense and by οὗτοι at the beginning of verse 10. But what marks out verse 9 as a *secondary* 'text,' rather than a 'text' in its own right alongside the other four, is the fact that verse 10 also continues the interpretation of 'text' 1 begun in verse 8. Moreover, verse 9 is not, like the

[11] Horgan (1979) 95; Brooke (1985) 130–133, 145–147, 304–305.

other 'texts,' a type or prophecy of the false teachers, but an example with which they are contrasted. It should therefore be seen as part of the commentary on 'text' 1.

The Qumran pesharim not only attest this practice of introducing a secondary text, more or less formally quoted, in the course of an interpretation; they also, to the same effect, incorporate implicit allusions to other texts in the interpretation of a given text.[12] Jude adopts the latter practice in verses 12–13, where a series of scriptural allusions are worked into the commentary on 'text' 2. The rather intricate composition of this commentary on 'text' 2 will be explained in the next section.

II. Exegesis of Jude's exegesis

Before analysing the formal characteristics of Jude's exegesis, it is necessary to see it in practice. In this section, therefore, we shall examine, comparatively briefly, 'texts' 1 and 2 and their respective interpretations (vv 5–13), in order to appreciate how the structure and the sometimes highly compressed and allusive content of these sections serve Jude's purpose of demonstrating exegetically the danger his opponents constitute for the church.

1. 'Text' 1 and its interpretation
'Texts' 1 and 2 refer to the opponents as guilty of flagrant disobedience to divine commandments (text 1) and furthermore as false prophets who corrupt others (text 2). The two sets of types are carefully selected to make these two rather different points.

'Text' 1 cites three classic examples of sin which incurred divine judgment: the whole generation of unbelieving Israel exterminated in the wilderness (Num 14), the angels who left their heavenly position of authority in order to mate with women (Gen 6:1–4, as interpreted in the Enochic book of Watchers), and the Sodomites (although Jude refers to the cities of the Plain, the sin he specifies was that only of the

---

[12] Horgan (1979) 95; Brooke (1985) 130.

Sodomites according to Gen 19:4–11). The sin for which the last of these three groups is condemned is not here homosexual rape, but the attempt at sexual relations with angels (as τὸν ὅμοιον τρόπον τούτοις as well as σαρκὸς ἑτέρας in v 7 make clear).[13] In each case the form of judgment is definitive and memorable: the utter destruction of the wilderness generation, the chaining of the fallen angels in the darkness of the underworld, and the eternal fire which makes the cities of the Plain an enduring witness to the fact of divine judgment. This last reference is explained by the fact that in antiquity the smoking, sulphurous waste south of the Dead Sea was believed to be the aftermath of the destruction of Sodom and Gomorrah, and so regarded as visible evidence of the reality of divine judgment.[14]

In using these three examples, Jude follows a standard pattern of Jewish paraenetic tradition, which listed anything from two to seven prime examples of judgment from the Old Testament (cf. Sir 16:7–10; CD 2:17–3:12; 3 Macc 2:4–7; TNapht 3:4–5; m. Sanh. 10:3; 2 Pet 2:4–8).[15] But he has used this pattern in a distinctive way. Not only has he selected the three examples which best suit his purpose, but he has treated them not merely as examples, but as *eschatological types*. That

[13] Cf. Wolthius (1987) 28–29. For comparison of the two cases – the angels desiring sexual relations with women, the Sodomites desiring sexual relations with angels – cf. TNapht 3:4–5. Klijn (1984) claims that, because the sexual transgression of the angels is not explicitly mentioned by Jude, the point of comparison is rather that 'both abandoned a particular position' (p. 243). He therefore denies any implication that Jude's opponents were sexual libertines. He is followed by Sellin (1986) 216–217, who also denies that 'defile the flesh' (Jude 8) has a sexual reference. But against both, the only natural sense of v 7 (ἐκπορνεύσασαι καὶ ἀπελθοῦσαι ὀπίσω σαρκὸς ἑτέρας) with reference to the Sodomites is sexual and therefore the beginning of v 7 must imply also the sexual element in the angels' sin. It is true, however, that in both cases the stress is not on the sexual transgression as such, but on the violation of the natural order which it involved. From vv 6–7, therefore, it would not necessarily follow that Jude's opponents were guilty specifically of sexual immorality. But parallels to the expression 'to defile the flesh' (σάρκα μιαίνουσιν) in v 8 leave no doubt that it refers to sexual immorality (Bauckham [1983A] 56).

[14] Wis 10:7; Josephus, BJ 4:483; Philo, Mos. 2:56; Abr. 141.

[15] Details in Bauckham (1983A) 46–47.

is, in his eyes they are events which prefigure the final judgment of the wicked at the parousia. The three different forms of judgment specified contribute to a typology of the final condemnation of the wicked, which is most commonly described by the three images of destruction, darkness and fire. The three sins which incur judgment are also appropriate to the typological function Jude gives them. In the first case, highlighted by being placed first, out of chronological order, the point is that the Lord's own people, who had experienced salvation, were not immune from judgment when they repudiated his lordship. The second case is also one of apostasy, but equally strikingly both it and the third are cases of outrageous transgression of the moral order of creation. No more flagrant flouting of the created order of things could be imagined than the desire for sexual union between human beings and angels (cf. 1 Enoch 15:3–10).

The interpretation (vv 8–10) of these three types aims to show how Jude's opponents identify themselves as the sinners of the last days to whom these types prophetically point. Jude's opponents sin 'in the same way' (v 8) as the types, and therefore they will incur the judgment at the parousia which the judgments of the past prefigure. Three sins of the opponents are specified in verse 8: they 'defile the flesh,' i.e. indulge in sexual immorality (like the angels and the Sodomites), they 'reject the authority of the Lord' (like Israel in the wilderness), and they 'slander the glorious ones,' i.e. treat angels insultingly (like the Sodomites). The last of the three charges is further expounded in verse 9 (with the help of the secondary 'text' 1a) and verse 10a. (This charge and the function of 'text' 1a in relation to it will be discussed in chapter 5 below). Finally, verse 10b makes clear that, because the opponents correspond to the types in sin, they will correspond to them in judgment.

2. 'Text' 2 and its interpretation
If 'text' 1 and its interpretation show the opponents to be apostates who flagrantly flout the moral order, 'text' 2 and its interpretation show their guilt to be even greater in that they are false *teachers* who lead others into sin. This comes

especially into focus when it is realized that the images of the three Old Testament figures of verse 11 are refracted through haggadic tradition. According to such tradition, Cain was not only the first murderer, but the great corrupter of humanity, who enticed others into sin (Josephus, *Ant.* 1:61; Philo, *Post.* 38–39).[16] Balaam is here not the rather ambiguous figure of the Old Testament so much as the villainous false prophet of Jewish tradition, who could not resist Balak's offer of reward. Although he failed to curse Israel, he eventually made up for the failure by giving the advice which enticed Israel into apostasy. Ironically, he met his end when he returned to collect his reward.[17] So Balaam's 'error' (πλάνη) should be taken in an active sense (as in Matt 27:64; 2 Thess 2:11), referring not just to his going astray himself, but to his leading others astray. Finally, Korah was the classic example of the antinomian heretic. He complained that the law of the fringes (Num 15:37–41) was an intolerable law, and led a rebellion against the authority of God's law as represented by Moses (LAB 16:1; Tg. Ps-Jon. Num 16:1–2). His sin was to teach others his antinomian opinions.[18] His spectacular fate, when the earth opened to swallow him up, was frequently cited as a prime example of judgment (Num 16:10; Ps 106:17; Sir 45:19; Josephus, *BJ* 5:566; LAB 57:2; 1 Clem 4:12; 51:4; Prot Jas 9:2; cf. also 1 Enoch 90:18; 99:2): Jude's climactic ἀπώλοντο refers to it as the type of the judgment which hangs over his opponents. It was probably because Korah's fate provided the most striking example of judgment that Jude placed him last, out of chronological order.

The interpretation (vv 12–13) aims to show that the false teachers conform to these types by being false *teachers* who lead others into sin, but in doing so it rapidly moves into a series of secondary allusions to further scriptural texts. The first of the series of six metaphors used in these verses to characterize the false teachers is not a scriptural allusion. It

---

[16] For other sources and detail, see Bauckham (1983A) 79–81.

[17] For sources and detail, see Bauckham (1983A) 81–83; Wolthius (1987) 33–36.

[18] For other sources and detail, see Bauckham (1983A) 83–84.

portrays them as dangerous reefs (σπιλάδες) on which the readers may be shipwrecked.[19] The point is that the opponents deliver their prophetic oracles at the church's fellowship meals (οἱ ἐν ταῖς ἀγάπαις ὑμῶν . . . συνευωχούμενοι ἀφόβως: 'who feast with you at your fellowship meals, without reverence'), and so expose the church to the dangerous influence of their teaching. The second metaphor (ἑαυτοὺς ποιμαίνοντες: literally, 'shepherding themselves') portrays them as people who claim to be shepherds, i.e. Christian leaders, but who, instead of tending the flock, care only for themselves. In suggesting that they are really only interested in making a good living out of their role in the church, this part of the interpretation takes up especially the reference to Balaam in the 'text' (v 11), which characterizes Balaam specifically as the prophet who hired out his services for reward. But it is also a scriptural allusion itself – to Ezekiel's prophecy of the false shepherds of Israel (34:2 RSV: 'shepherds of Israel who have been feeding yourselves! Should not shepherds feed the sheep?'; cf. also 38:4).[20] The allusion will be meant to suggest the whole of Ezekiel's condemnation of the shepherds who, instead of looking after the flock, exploit it for their own benefit.

The four metaphors from nature which follow in verses 12b–13 constitute a highly skilful composition.[21] All four characterize the opponents as false teachers. In the cases of the clouds which fail to give rain and the trees which fail to produce fruit, the point is that a benefit is promised and expected, but fails to materialize. The false teachers make great claims for their teaching, but in reality it provides no

[19] For this and other interpretations of σπιλάδες, see Bauckham (1983A) 85–86.

[20] See Bauckham (1983A) 87. The allusion to Ezek 34:2 is closer to the Hebrew than to the LXX. It is also possible that Jude connected Ezekiel's prophecy about the shepherds with the allegory of the shepherds who rule Israel and are to be judged at the last judgment in 1 Enoch 89:59–90:25 (cf. especially Ezek 34:5b–8 with 1 Enoch 89:65–66, 68; 90:2–4, 11; Ezek 34:5a, 6 with 1 Enoch 89:75; Ezek 34:3, 10 with 1 Enoch 89:74).

[21] On these verses see Osburn (1985); Bauckham (1983A) 87–91 (but I have now very considerably developed my earlier analysis of this passage).

benefit for the church. In fact, it is positively harmful, corrupting people, like the sea which throws up its filth on the shore. The opponents are like stars which go astray from their divinely ordained courses, as the planets did in the old astrological myths, misleading those who look to them for guidance. The traditional judgment of such stars is to be extinguished in the eternal darkness of the underworld. Thus the judgment of the opponents, incorporated already in the second image, of the fruitless trees uprooted, is climactically portrayed in the fourth, so that (as with 'text' 1 and its interpretation) this passage of interpretation ends on the same note as the 'text' it interprets (v 11). The last of the metaphors in the passage of interpretation is also linked back to the 'text' it is interpreting by means of the wordplay πλανῆται/πλάνη (vv 13, 11).

The four images relate to the four regions of the universe: clouds in the air, trees on the earth, waves in the sea, stars in the heavens. Thus they represent, with an example from each part of the universe, nature failing to follow the laws laid down for her by God in creation. Once this pattern is recognized, two passages from the Enoch literature can be seen to lie behind it. Immediately following the passage which Jude quotes in verses 14–15 (1 Enoch 1:9) is a passage (1 Enoch 2:1–5:4) which portrays nature as law-abiding, keeping to the created order laid down for her by God, by *contrast* with the wicked, lawless people who transgress the moral order.[22] The examples given in this passage of lawabiding nature include the opposites of Jude's four examples of lawless nature: clouds which give rain (1 Enoch 2:3),[23] trees which bear fruit (5:1), seas which keep to their tasks (5:3), and stars which do not change their courses (2:1). The special significance of this passage of 1 Enoch for Jude lies in the way it is connected with the key text in his commentary: 1 Enoch 1:9. The close

[22] The relevance of this passage of 1 Enoch was first noted by Spitta (1885) 396. Osburn (1985) 297, appears to discount it in favour of 1 Enoch 80:2–8. I agree that the latter is Jude's more immediate source, but that he read it in connexion with 1 Enoch 2:1–5:4 seems to me very probable.

[23] For this verse, cf. the fragmentary Aramaic in 4QEnᵃ 1:2:4 (Milik [1976] 146–147).

connection is indicated by the fact that the last words of that verse (as Jude quotes them: 'to convict all the ungodly of all the ungodly deeds which they have committed in their ungodliness, and of all the hard things which ungodly sinners have spoken against him' [Jude 15]; but note that the Aramaic fragment in 4QEn^c 1:1:17 has '*great and* hard things') are echoed in 1 Enoch 5:4 ('you have spoken great and hard words with your unclean mouth against his majesty'), forming an *inclusio*. As Hartman has shown, the intervening passage (1 Enoch 2:1–5:4) is the *indictment* of God against the wicked, by which he will 'convict' or 'denounce' them (1:9) at his eschatological coming to judgment.[24] Hartman places it within a biblical and post-biblical *rib*-pattern, in which God's charges against the wicked are presented in the presence of heaven and earth.[25] In one tradition the call to heaven and earth to witness against the wicked (Deut 30:19; 32:1; LAB 19:4; 2 Bar 19:1; 84:2) is interpreted as referring to the way God's natural creation keeps to the laws he has given it, thus highlighting by contrast the guilt of the wicked who stray from God's laws (Jer 5:22–23; 1 Enoch 101:6–7; TNapht 3:2–5; 1Q34^bis 2:1–4; LAE 29:12; Sifre Deut 306; implicitly 1 Clem 20:1–21:1[26]). 1 Enoch 2:1–5:4 sets out a sequence of works of God observing the order he has laid down for them in all three regions of the universe – heavens, earth, waters.[27] (The clouds and the rain belong here to the description of the works of the earth.) The same threefold reference occurs in other closely related texts (TNapht 3:4; Sifre Deut 306; cf. 1 Enoch 101:6–8): it corresponds to the most common form of division of the world into regions. Jude has a similar pattern, but follows a less usual division of the world into four regions: air, earth, sea, heavens.

However, Jude does not contrast the wicked with law-abiding nature. Instead, he uses examples of lawless nature as

---

[24] Hartman (1979) 26.

[25] Hartman (1979) 49–95.

[26] Milik (1976) 148, considers this passage to be closely related to 1 Enoch 2:1–5:4.

[27] See the analysis of the structure of the passage in Hartman (1979) 17.

metaphors for the wicked. It is unlikely that he will have been inspired to do this simply by 1 Enoch 2:1–5:4. But consideration of that passage seems to have led him to another part of the Enoch literature. The description of the regular courses and times of the heavenly bodies in 1 Enoch 2:1 is a summary statement of what Enoch is shown in enormous detail in the 'Astronomical Book' (1 Enoch 72–82). Following his conducted tour of the secrets of the heavens, Enoch is then told by his guide Uriel that these regularities will fail in the last days, 'the days of the sinners' (80:2), when nature will go astray into lawlessness, resulting in some of the familiar apocalyptic features of the last days (80:2–8). The passage has links, which Jude will have observed, with 1 Enoch 2:1–5:4.[28] In particular, the phrase 'at its proper time,' used in 2:1 to emphasize how the heavenly bodies observe their God-given laws, is repeatedly used in 80:2–6 to show how, when the heavenly bodies go astray in the last days nothing will happen at the proper time: the seasons will not occur when they should (80:2), crops and fruits will be late (80:3), the moon (80:4) and the stars (80:6) will not appear at their proper times. The result is that sinners will be misled (80:7), and will be judged: 'punishment will come upon them to destroy them all' (80:8)[29] – recalling the universal judgment of the wicked in 1:9.

The examples of the lawlessness of nature given in 1 Enoch 80:2–7 include three of Jude's four metaphors, in the same order as in Jude 12–13: rain withheld from the earth (80:2), fruits of the trees withheld (80:3), and, as the climax of the passage, the stars straying from their proper times and orbits, leading sinners on earth astray (80:6–7). Jude's reference to the wandering stars (v 13: ἀστέρες πλανῆται) seems to be an actual allusion to 1 Enoch 80:6 ('many heads of *the stars* in

---

[28] Milik (1976) 148, considers 1 Enoch 2:1–5:4 to be dependent on the Astronomical Book of Enoch and in particular points to the close relationship between 1 Enoch 3 and 4QEnastr^d 1:1, which appears to belong to a part of the Astronomical Book not represented in the Ethiopic version (Milik [1976] 269–270; cf. Black [1985] 418–419).

[29] Translation from Knibb (1978) 186.

command *will go astray*'³⁰), and alerts us to the fact that two
of his other three images from nature also correspond to
1 Enoch 80. Jude seems to have associated the two passages
from 1 Enoch (2:1–5:4; 80:2–8). Just as lawabiding nature
(1 Enoch 2:1–5:4) provides a contrast to the sinners of the last
days, so lawless nature (1 Enoch 80:2–7) can provide an image
of the wicked who go astray from their created order in the
last days.

Jude was not the first to associate these two passages of
1 Enoch. It seems to have been done within the Enoch literature itself, in 1 Enoch 101:

(101:1) Contemplate, therefore, children of men, the works of the Most High, and fear to do evil before him.	(2:1) Consider all his works and the works (of creation) in heaven . . .³¹
(101:2) If he closes the windows of heaven, and withholds the rain and the dew from descending on the earth because of you, what then will you do?	(80:2) . . . And the rain will be withheld, and heaven will retain (it).³²
(101:3) And if he sends his anger upon you because of all your deeds, will you not be the ones who plead with him? (But) because you uttered with your mouths proud and harsh words against his majesty, you will have no peace.³³	(5:4) . . . But you have transgressed, and have spoken proud and hard words with your unclean mouth against his majesty. You hard of heart! You will not have peace.³⁴

---

³⁰ Translation from Knibb (1978) 186; but on the translation of this verse, see Black (1985) 253.

³¹ Translation from Black (1985) 26, from the Aramaic in 4QEnᶜ 1:1:18 (Milik [1976] 185–186).

³² Translation from Knibb (1978) 185.

³³ Translation from Black (1985) 95.

³⁴ Translation from Knibb (1978) 65. Cf. also 100:11 with 2:3; 80:2.

1 Enoch 80 does not include reference to the sea. But we should notice a close parallel to 1 Enoch 80 in the *Divine Institutes* of Lactantius, written at the beginning of the fourth century A.D., but drawing on older apocalyptic sources:

Div. Inst. 7:16   1 Enoch 80

The air will be poisoned and be corrupt and pestilential, at one time from unseasonable rains or unusual dryness, at another from excessive cold or hot spells.

The earth will not give her fruit to men. Neither grain nor tree nor vine will bear; but rather, after they have given the greatest hope in the blossom, they will cheat at harvest.

Springs and rivers will dry up, so that they will not provide a drink; waters will be changed to blood and bitterness.

Because of this animals will desert the earth, as will birds the air and the fishes the sea.

Wondrous portents in heaven, as well as comets' tails, eclipses of the sun, the moon's colour, and falling stars will confuse the minds of men with the greatest fear. These things will not happen in the usual way, but unknown and unseen stars will suddenly shine forth.

(2) . . . And the rain will be withheld, and heaven will retain (it).
(3) And in those times the fruits of the earth will be late and will not grow at their proper time, and the fruits of the trees will be withheld at their proper time.

(4) And the moon will change its customary practice, and will not appear at its proper time. (5) But in those days it will appear in heaven, and come . . . on top of a large chariot in the west, and shine with more than normal brightness. (6) And many heads of the stars in

The sun will be perpetually darkened so that one can scarcely distinguish between night and day. The moon will fail, and not just for three hours; constantly covered with blood, it will complete unusual orbits so that men will not be able to know either the courses of the stars or the calculation of times. Summer will come in winter or vice versa. Then the year will be shortened, the month diminished, the day compressed to a brief moment . . .[35]

command will go astray, and these will change their courses and their activities, and will not appear at the times which have been prescribed for them. (7) And the entire law of the stars will be closed to sinners, and the thoughts of those who dwell upon the earth will go astray over them . . .
(2) But in the days of the sinners the years will become shorter, and their seed will be late on their land and on their fields, and all things on the earth will change, and will not appear at their proper time . . .[36]

Lactantius, of course, does not reproduce his sources slavishly. If we knew only these two passages in Lactantius and 1 Enoch, we should suppose Lactantius to be simply dependent on 1 Enoch 80, as we know it, and the differences to result from his creative rewriting of his source.[37] However, the coincidence between Lactantius and Jude is striking. Not only does Lactantius have a reference to disorder in the seas (waters), though it is not very close to Jude's reference to the sea. More significantly, Lactantius has the *four* regions of creation in the same order as Jude: air, earth, sea and heavens. That

[35] Translation from McGinn (1980) 60–61.
[36] Translation from Knibb (1978) 185–186.
[37] Lactantius is here much closer to 1 Enoch 80 than to SibOr 8:178–181, 214–215. Thus, although it is true that in book 7 Lactantius is frequently dependent on the Sibylline Oracles (Ogilvie [1978] 31) and immediately after the passage quoted in the text explicitly quotes SibOr 8:239, it is nevertheless easier to assume that in the passage quoted he is directly dependent on Enoch, than to posit a Sibylline text as intermediary, as Milik (1976) 21, does.

Jude and Lactantius knew a longer text of 1 Enoch 80 than ours[38] seems a plausible hypothesis, especially as we know from the Qumran Aramaic fragments of the Astronomical Book of Enoch that our Ethiopic version of that book (in which alone chapter 80 is extant) has been in general very considerably abbreviated.[39]

So Jude's sequence of images is modelled on 1 Enoch 80, carefully selected to represent the four regions of creation. But if 1 Enoch 80 provides the structure of Jude's four metaphors from nature, it does not provide the detail of each image. Jude, it seems, was not content simply to model his four images on 1 Enoch 80, because he required a scriptural source for each image precisely as a characterization of the false *teachers*. So we must look more closely at each of the four images.

In relation to the first image, 1 Enoch 80:2 (cf. 100:11; 101:2) indicates only the absence of rain, not Jude's specific image of *clouds* which fail to provide rain. The latter is essential to his purpose, because it portrays the opponents as false teachers who promise a benefit they cannot in fact provide. For this specific image Jude has turned to Proverbs 25:14 (RSV: '*Like clouds and wind without rain* is a man who boasts of a gift he does not have'[40] — literally, 'boasts in gifts of deception'). Jude's words (νεφέλαι ἄνυδροι ὑπὸ ἀνέμων παραφερόμεναι: 'clouds blown along by the wind without giving rain') are simply a good translation of the opening (italicized) words of Proverbs 25:14. Perhaps in rendering רוח (which could have been translated 'Spirit') by ὑπὸ ἀνέμων παραφερόμεναι (literally, 'carried away by the winds') Jude intended a sarcastic reference to the opponents' claim to be moved by the prophetic Spirit. The verb can be used of

---

[38] 1 Enoch 80 (or 80:2–8) has often been thought an interpolation into the Astronomical Book: Charles (1893) 187–188; Black (1985) 252; Neugebauer in Black (1985) 411. Its terminology and ideas, however, contain clear links with other material in the Astronomical Book. Milik (1976) 11–14 regards it as an integral part of the Astronomical Book.

[39] Milik (1976) 7–8, 19; Black (1985) 10.

[40] This sense is completely obscured in the LXX. Jude, as usual, follows the Hebrew.

being led astray by false teaching (Heb 13:9: 'do not be led away [παραφέρεσθε] by diverse and strange teachings'; cf. also Eph 4:14: 'carried about with every wind [περιφερόμενοι παντὶ ἀνέμῳ] of doctrine').

In the case of Jude's second image, 1 Enoch 80:3 ('the fruits of the trees will be withheld at their proper time') itself provided the basic metaphor Jude needed: trees which fail to provide fruit at the time when it would be expected[41] (δένδρα φθινοπωρινὰ ἄκαρπα, 'autumnal trees bearing no fruit'), but he has taken advantage of the potentiality of this image to express also the judgment awaiting the false teachers (δὶς ἀποθανόντα ἐκριζωθέντα, 'dead twice over, uprooted'). In this extension of the metaphor, it is hard to give 'twice dead' a precise botanical meaning: the phrase has probably been influenced by the notion of 'the second death' (Rev 2:11; 20:6, 14; 21:8). But the image of the uprooting of a tree as a metaphor of the judgment of the wicked was traditional (Deut 29:28; Ps 52:5; Prov 2:22; Zeph 2:4; Wis 4:4; Matt 15:13): Jude may not be dependent on a specific source for it. But he may have had in mind the parable of the fig tree, which failed to bear fruit. Although in the Lukan version of this parable the tree's threatened fate is to be cut down (Luke 13:7, 9), in the probably independent version in the Apocalypse of Peter (E2) the tree is to be uprooted.[42]

Jude's third image (κύματα ἄγρια θαλάσσης ἐπαφρίζοντα τὰς ἑαυτῶν αἰσχύνας: 'wild waves of the sea casting up the foam of their abominations') is based on Isaiah 57:20 (RSV: 'the wicked are like the tossing sea; for it cannot rest, and its waters toss up mire and dirt';[43] cf. allusions to this verse in 1QH 2:12–13; 8:15). But the allusion to Isaiah 57:20 is more than a choice of an appropriate image. This text, following a reference to the peace which God promises the righteous (Isa 57:19), describes the wicked for whom there is no peace

---

[41] Lactantius (quoted above) makes explicit the idea of disappointed expectation.

[42] See Bauckham (1985).

[43] Since the last clause does not appear in the LXX, Jude is, as usual, dependent on the Hebrew text.

(57:21). It can therefore be linked by the exegetical technique of catchwords (*gĕzērâ šāwâ*) with Jude's key passage 1 Enoch 1–5:

1 Enoch	Isaiah 57 (RSV)
(1:8) But with the righteous he will make *peace* . . . and he will make *peace* with them.	(19) *Peace, peace*, to the far and to the near, says the Lord; and I will heal him.
(1:9) . . . he will destroy all *the wicked* and convict all flesh of all the works of their wickedness which they have wickedly committed, and of all the great and hard words which wicked sinners have spoken against him.	(20) But *the wicked* are like the tossing sea; for it cannot rest, and its waters toss up mire and dirt.
(5:4) . . . have spoken great and hard words with your unclean mouth against his majesty. You hard of heart! You will have *no peace*.[44]	(21) There is *no peace*, says my God, for *the wicked*.

These catchword links establish, for the kind of Jewish exegesis Jude practises, that the wicked of whom Isaiah 57:20 speaks are precisely those who are condemned in 1 Enoch 2:1–5:4 for their failure to follow God's laws, by contrast with lawabiding nature, and are therefore to be judged at the parousia (1 Enoch 1:9).[45] (It is worth noticing, also, that

---

[44] My translation.

[45] Osburn (1985) 298, objects that in Isa 57:20 'the imagery of the violent sea . . . has to do with tumult rather than licentiousness.' But this misses the point that Jude is not here concerned with the false teachers' licentiousness as such, but with their corrupting influence on others. There is no reason why he should not have read the last clause of Isa 57:20 in this sense. Wis 14:1, however, is not a true parallel: see Bauckham (1983A) 88–89. Osburn (1985) 299, 302, further suggests 1 Enoch 67:5–7 as a source for Jude's image of the waves, but this is unlikely, and is not supported by Osburn's claim that Jude, from 1 Enoch 80, 'had only to turn back his Enochic scroll a few turns to chapter 67' (p. 299). Chapter 80 belongs to the Astronomical Book (1 Enoch 72–82), while

the phrase 'no peace', from Isaiah 57:21, frequently in
1 Enoch describes the final fate of the wicked [5:4, 5; 94:6;
98:16; 99:13; 102:3; 103:8] or of the Watchers [12:5, 6; 13:1;
16:4; 4QEnGiants^a 13], whom 1 Enoch, like Jude, regards
as prototypical of all the wicked.)

The fourth image (ἀστέρες πλανῆται, 'wandering stars')
is already in 1 Enoch 80:6–7 peculiarly appropriate as an image
of the false teachers: stars which stray from their courses and
in so doing lead people astray. But as with the second image,
Jude was not content with the metaphor as he found in it in
1 Enoch 80: he extended it into an image of judgment. He
has probably done so by linking 1 Enoch 80:6 with other
passages in the Enoch literature which portray the fallen Watchers as stars which have gone astray and are punished by
being chained in the underworld (see page 201).

These connexions establish a link again with the comparison
of the false teachers with the Watchers in Jude 6, and the link
is reinforced by the verbal connexion between the two verses
(v 13: ὁ ζόφος . . . τετήρηται; v 6: ὑπὸ ζόφον τετήρηκεν).

Thus the four metaphors from nature reveal themselves
to be the result of some highly studied and elaborate exegetical work. We should finally note that, although they
are primarily interpretation of 'text' 2 (v 11), they are also,
as we have seen, Jude's version of the indictment of the
wicked in 1 Enoch 2:1–5:4, on the basis of which they will
be judged at the Lord's coming to judgment (1 Enoch 1:9).
The link with 'text' 3 (1 Enoch 1:9) which follows is therefore even more precise than we might otherwise have
supposed: 'it was also about these people that Enoch the
seventh from Adam prophesied, saying . . .' (v 14a). Accordingly, the quotation itself is abbreviated in such a way as
to emphasize the element of legal conviction of the wicked
of the last days: where the original text probably read, 'and
to destroy all the ungodly and to convict all flesh' (cf. the
Greek and Ethiopic versions), Jude has simply, 'and to

chapter 67 belongs to the Parables (1 Enoch 37–71), which is extant only
in the Ethiopic version. We cannot assume these two distinct Enochic
works both occurred, in the same order as in the Ethiopic version, in
Jude's 'Enochic scroll'.

1 Enoch 80:6	1 Enoch 18:15–16	1 Enoch 88:1
And many of the heads of the stars in command will go astray, and these change their courses and their activities, and will not appear at the times which have been prescribed for them.[47]	And the stars which roll over the fire, these are the ones which transgressed the command of the Lord from the beginning of their rising because they did not come out at their proper times. (16) And he was angry with them and bound them . . .[48]	. . . he took hold of that first star which had fallen from heaven, and bound it by its hands and its feet, and threw it into an abyss; and that abyss was narrow, and deep, and horrible, and dark.[46]

convict all the ungodly' (καὶ ἐλέγξαι πάντας τοὺς ἀσεβεῖς).

III. Exegetical formulae

Although section II has dealt with only two of Jude's four main 'texts', it will have demonstrated that the exegetical section of Jude's letter is much more complex than the casual modern reader is likely to imagine. If we look for analogies to Jude's exegesis in contemporary Judaism, the best analogies are provided by the Qumran pesharim. Though the comparison cannot be pressed in every detail, it is an illuminating one, especially if we think of Jude's

[46] Translation from Knibb (1978) 198. Note also the account of the final judgment of the stars (i.e. the Watchers) in 1 Enoch 90:24, where the shepherds are judged and punished with them (90:25). However, in this passage the abyss is fire, not darkness. In general, Enoch distinguishes the temporary prison of the fallen angels, a place of subterranean darkness, from their final judgment in the abyss of fire. Jude 13 describes their final judgment in terms darkness rather than fire, but in so doing keeps more appropriately to his image of wandering stars: it is a more appropriate punishment for *stars* to be extinguished in eternal darkness than to be plunged into eternal fire.

[47] Translation from Knibb (1978) 186.

[48] Translation from Knibb (1978) 106.

commentary as comparable with the 'thematic pesharim' (4QFlor, 11QMelch, 4Q176, 4Q177, 4Q182, 4Q183), which are commentaries on a collection of texts on a common theme, rather than with the 'continuous pesharim', which comment on every verse in order of a biblical book or lengthy section of a book.[49] In order to pursue the comparison with Qumran exegesis in particular, as well as with other examples of Jewish and early Christian exegesis, we shall consider in turn Jude's exegetical *formulae*, his exegetical *principles and techniques*, and his hermeneutical *presuppositions*.[50]

The most important exegetical formulae used by Jude are those which introduce each section of interpretation. As we have noted already, each section of interpretation is introduced by a phrase with οὗτοι:

v 8   ὁμοίως μέντοι καὶ οὗτοι . . .
v 10   οὗτοι δὲ . . .
v 12   οὗτοί εἰσιν οἱ . . .
v 16   οὗτοί εἰσιν . . .
v 19   οὗτοί εἰσιν οἱ

The last three instances in particular have often[51] been compared to the standard formula ('This is . . .,' 'These are . . .') used in the interpretation of apocalyptic dreams and visions (Zech 1:10, 19, 21; 4:14; Rev 7:14; 11:4; 14:4; 1 Enoch 18:14, 15; 21:6; 22:4 [4QEn[e] 1:22]; 46:3; 64:2; 4 Ezra 10:44; 12:10, 30, 32; 13:26, 40; 3 Bar 2:7; 3:5; 6:3, 16; 12:3; 2 Enoch 7:3; 18:3; and frequently in other apocalypses). The formula refers to something or people seen in the vision ('this', 'these') and interprets it/them. Frequently, it is used by the interpreting angel or by God in response to the seer's request for an explanation of what he sees. Thus, for example, Zechariah asks, 'What are these two olive trees . . .?' (meaning, 'What do they symbolize?'), and eventually gets the explanation, 'These (אלה) are the two anointed ones who stand by the Lord of the whole earth' (Zech

---

[49] The terms were first used by Carmignac (1969–71) 360–361; cf. also Horgan (1979) 3.

[50] For the importance of a distinction between hermeneutical presuppositions and exegetical techniques, see Brooke (1985) 283.

[51] E.g. Krodel (1977) 97.

4:11, 14). Himmelfarb, who has studied these formulae especially in the apocalyptic tours of hell, has called them 'demonstrative explanations'.[52] It is worth noting that the fullest of the formulae in Jude (οὗτοί εἰσιν οἱ + participle: 'these are the ones who . . .') has precise verbal parallels in the apocalypses (1 Enoch 8:15 Greek; Rev 17:14).

But the same formula is also sometimes used in the Qumran pesharim to introduce the interpretation of a text: e.g.

4QpIsa[b] 2:6–7: 'these (אלה) [the people to whom the text refers] are the scoffers who are in Jerusalem'
4QpIsa[b] 2:10: 'this (היא) [to which the text refers] is the congregation of scoffers, who are in Jerusalem'
4QFlor 1:17: 'they (המה) [the people to whom the text refers] are the sons of Zadok and the men of their council who . . .'

(See also 4QpIsa[a] 3:7, 9, 10, 12; 4QFlor 1:2, 3, 11, 12.) This formula is not as common in the pesharim as the more usual formulae including the word pesher (פשר)[53] but it is perhaps significant that it is used rather frequently in the 'thematic pesher' 4QFlorilegium, which resembles Jude's commentary more than do the 'continuous pesharim'. There are also cases where the formula with 'pesher' and the formula with the personal or demonstrative pronoun are used together (1QpHab 10:3; 4QpNah 2:2; 4:1; 4QpPs[a] [4Q171] 2:5; 3:12; 4:1, 23; CD 4:14).

The parallels between the formulae as used in apocalyptic visions and those used in Qumran exegesis are probably not accidental, but result from a common background in the interpretation of dreams and oracles in the ancient Near East.[54] The pesharim treat Scripture as an oracle requiring inspired interpretation, just as the symbolic visions of the apocalyptic seers needed authoritative explanation. The fact that a background in the interpretation of dreams and oracles is plausible both for the 'demonstrative explanations', which are our particular concern here, and for the 'pesher'

[52] Himmelfarb (1983) 45–67.
[53] Cf. Horgan (1979) 239–242, for the various formulae including פשר.
[54] Cf. Finkel (1963–64); Patte (1971) 301–302; Horgan (1979) 252–259; Himmelfarb (1983) 58–59.

formulae, to which much more attention has been given in study of the Qumran literature, shows that both types of formula belong to the same tradition of exegetical terminology, as is clear also from the occasional use of both types of formula together. That Jude uses only the demonstrative explanations and not the 'pesher' formulae may be accidental. In any case, despite his familiarity with apocalyptic literature such as the Enoch literature, the fact that he is writing commentary rather than vision virtually requires that his use of the οὗτοι formulae must derive from a tradition of scriptural commentary similar to that of the Qumran sect.

In the demonstrative explanations, as they are used both in apocalyptic literature and in Qumran exegesis, the demonstrative pronoun refers to that which is to be interpreted, a figure in the vision which is being explained or a term in the text which is being interpreted. In the two instances where Jude uses the fullest formula (οὗτοί εἰσιν οἱ + participle: vv 12, 19) he conforms to this usage. In verse 12 οὗτοι refers to the people mentioned in the woe-oracle of verse 11; in verse 19 οὗτοι are the scoffers of whom the apostles prophesied (v 18). But Jude's use of the formula is flexible, and in the other cases οὗτοι does not refer to that which is to be interpreted, but to those people to whom the interpretation applies, the contemporary fulfilment of the text (vv 8, 10, 16): it means 'these people we are talking about, the people who are infiltrating your churches'. In these cases the formula is used to introduce a statement about the false teachers which demonstrates that they are the fulfilment of the type or the prophecy, but it does not state the identification directly in the way that the more usual use of the formula does. Perhaps this variation results from Jude's desire, not simply to *assert* that these types and prophecies refer to the false teachers, but to show that the false teachers' behaviour corresponds to them.

There are two interesting parallels to Jude's use of οὗτοι formulae elsewhere in the New Testament:[55]

---

[55] Note also οὗτοί εἰσιν (Mark 4:15, 16, 18; Luke 8:14, 15) and οὗτός

Gal 4:24: αὗται γάρ εἰσιν δύο διαθῆκαι ...: 'These women [Hagar and Sarah] are two covenants ...'

2 Tim 3:8: ὃν τρόπον δὲ 'Ιαννῆς καὶ 'Ιαμβρῆς ... οὕτως καὶ οὗτοι ...: 'Just as Jannes and Jambres ..., so also these people ...'

Galatians 4:24 conforms to the Qumran usage: αὗται refers to the two women in the scriptural story, who are then interpreted (decoded, as it were) as allegorically representing two covenants. 2 Timothy 3:8 rather strikingly resembles Jude 8 (ὁμοίως μέντοι καὶ οὗτοι ...: 'but in the same way also these people ...'). In both cases the comparison is typological, between Old Testament figures, as known through haggadic tradition, and false teachers in the church. In both cases also οὗτοί refers not to the types, but to the antitypes. This suggests that Jude's usage is in both respects not idiosyncratic but traditional.

That the material about false teachers in 2 Timothy is indebted to an *exegetical* tradition similar to that which is much more explicit in Jude can be inferred also from 2 Timothy 2:19. The quotation there from Numbers 16:5 ('The Lord knows those who are his': cf. Num 16:5 LXX) serves to identify faithful Christians, who are not swayed by the false teachers, with those who did not join the revolt of Korah.[56] Implicitly, Korah is treated as a type of the false teachers, as Jude treats him in Jude 11. But the exegetical work lies entirely behind the text, whereas in Jude it is explicit. Jude gives us formal exegesis in full, 2 Timothy only fragments from an exegetical tradition (cf. also Rev 2:19 with Jude 11).

In addition to the οὗτοι formulae for introducing interpretation, Jude uses one formula for the formal citation of a text, in verse 14:

ἐστιν (Matt 13:19, 20, 22, 23) in the interpretation of the parable of the Sower. But they should probably be related to the formulae as used in the interpretation of apocalyptic visions, rather than as used in scriptural exegesis. Ellis (1978) 160–161, offers some less strict New Testament parallels.

[56] Cf. Hanson (1968) 35.

Ἐπροφήτευσεν δὲ καὶ τούτοις ἕβδομος ἀπὸ ᾿Αδάμ Ἐνὼχ λέγων . . .: 'It was also about these that Enoch, the seventh from Adam, prophesied, saying . . .'

This use of the demonstrative pronoun in an introductory formula can be quite closely paralleled from the pesharim:[57]

> 4QFlor 1:16: 'and they (והמה) are those concerning whom (עליהמה) it is written in the book of Ezekiel the prophet . . .'
> 11QMelch 2:9–10: 'as it has been written concerning him/it (עליו) in the Songs of David, who said . . .'
> 11QMelch 2:10: 'and concerning him/it (ועליו), he [God or David?] said . . .'
> 4QpIsa[b] 2:7: 'they (המ) are the ones who . . .'
> CD 1:13: 'this was the time concerning which it was written . . .'

If this kind of formula is not very common, it is because it suits a circumstance which is not very common in the pesharim: where the contemporary reality to which the text is understood to refer has already been mentioned and the text is introduced as referring to it. The Qumran examples show that Jude's rather odd use of the dative τούτοις represents על (which is regularly used in Qumran exegetical formulae to indicate what the text refers to). Other New Testament parallels to this type of introductory formula are

> Acts 2:16: τοῦτό ἐστιν τὸ εἰρημένον διὰ τοῦ προφήτου Ἰωήλ . . .: 'this is what was spoken by the prophet Joel . . .'
> Matt 11:10 ‖ Luke 7:27: οὗτός ἐστιν περὶ οὗ γέγραπται . . .: 'this is he of whom it is written . . .'

IV. Exegetical techniques

Among the formal exegetical techniques which Jude uses the most important is the abundant use of catchword connections,

[57] Cf. Fitzmyer (1971) 9–10.

which in fact perform several distinct functions.[58] In the first place they are used to link one 'text' with another (roughly what the rabbis called *gĕzērâ šāwâ*):[59]

'texts' 1 and 2:   ἀπωλ-   (vv 5, 11)
'texts' 3 and 4:   ἀσεβ-   (vv 15, 18)
'texts' 1, 1a, 3:   κύριος, κρίσιν (vv 5–6, 9, 14–15).
'text' 2 and the secondary allusion in the interpretation: πλάνῃ (v 11), πλανῆται (v 13).

As well as these evident examples of *gĕzērâ šāwâ*, there are others, of which we have noticed some in section II, which are hidden from view. In other words, the links are between parts of the text not explicitly quoted. They functioned to bring the texts together in Jude's mind but have not been made explicit in the commentary. (There are parallels to this kind of implicit *gĕzērâ šāwâ* in the Qumran commentaries.) Thus we noted, in section II, how Isaiah 57:20 (to which Jude 13 alludes) is linked to 1 Enoch 1:9 (Jude 14–15) by catchword connexions between Isaiah 57:19 and 1 Enoch 1:8 and between Isaiah 57:21 and 1 Enoch 5:4. Some other examples will be suggested in section V below.

Secondly, catchword connections are used to link a 'text' and the interpretation of that 'text'. Horgan's account of the exegetical techniques used in the Qumran pesharim calls this the 'use of the same roots as in the lemma, appearing in the same or different grammatical forms',[60] and considers it 'the most frequent technique of interpretation found in the pesharim'.[61] The examples in Jude's commentary are:

'text' 1:   σαρκός (v 7), κύριος (v 5)
         interpretation: σάρκα, κυριότητα (v 8)

---

[58] Briefly noticed by Ellis (1978) 225. For the use of catchwords in other New Testament examples of scriptural commentary, see Ellis (1978) 155–159.

[59] For *gĕzērâ šāwâ* in the Qumran texts, see Slomovic (1969–71) 5–10; Brooke (1985) 166, 320; and for *gĕzērâ šāwâ* in Philo, see Brooke (1985) 22–24.

[60] Horgan (1979) 245.

[61] Horgan (1979) 245 n. 66.

'text' 1a: βλασφημίας, κύριος (v 9)
    interpretation: βλασφημοῦσιν (vv 8, 10), κυριότητα (v 8)
'text' 2:   πλάνη (v 11)
    interpretation: πλανῆται (v 13)
'text' 3:   ἐλάλησαν (v 15).
    interpretation λαλεῖ (v 16)

Thirdly, catchwords can link a 'text' and the interpretation not of that 'text' but of another 'text',[62] thus helping (along with *gĕzērâ šāwâ*) to bind the whole commentary together as a commentary on a series of closely related texts:

'text' 1:   ζόφον τετήρηκεν (v 6), αἰωνίου (v 7)
    interpretation of 'text' 2: ζόφος . . . αἰῶνα τετήρηται (v 13)
'text' 2:   ἐπορεύθησαν (v 11)
    interpretation of 'text' 3: πορευόμενοι (v 16)
'text' 4:   κατὰ τὰς ἑαυτῶν ἐπιθυμίας πορευόμενοι (v 18)
    interpretation of 'text' 3: κατὰ τὰς ἐπιθυμίας αὐτῶν
    πορευόμενοι (v 16).

All three of these techniques can be paralleled in the Qumran pesharim, though they are by no means unique to Qumran.[63] The final use of catchword connections in Jude – to link the opening statement of theme for the commentary (v 4) to the 'texts' – is not paralleled at Qumran, because we have no opening statement of theme for a 'thematic pesher' from Qumran. (We have, of course, the beginning of neither 4QFlorilegium nor 11QMelchizedek: it is quite possible that they began with an opening statement of theme like Jude's.) The links are as follows:

κρίμα   (v 4):   κρίσιν in 'texts' 1, 1a, 3 (vv 6, 9, 15)
ἀσεβ-   (v 4):   4 times in 'text' 3 (v 15), once in text 4 (v 18)
κύριον   (v 4):   κύριος in 'texts' 1, 1a, 3 (vv 5, 9, 14).

These links show that verse 4 is intended to be an anticipatory, summarizing interpretation of all four main 'texts', stating, as

---

[62] For this technique in the pesharim, see Horgan (1979) 245–246 n. 70.

[63] The exegetical techniques of the Qumran pesharim are not peculiar to them: Brooke (1985) 43, 283–287.

it were, the thesis of the commentary before it is demonstrated by exegesis of the texts.[64] The especially clear
catchword connections between this introductory statement
and 'text' 3 reinforce the impression, which is in any case
given by πάλαι in verse 4 ('who were *long ago* designated for
this condemnation'), that the prophecy of Enoch is actually
the key text in Jude's commentary. It is the key text because
of its clear statement of the judgment which is coming on the
ungodly (emphasized by its fourfold repetition of words from
the ἀσεβ- root) at the Lord's parousia. Verse 4 picks up its
two main points – the *condemnation* of the *ungodly* – and
makes ἀσεβεῖς Jude's definitive characterization of what is
damnable in the opponents.

One of the catchword connections which has been listed
above could be considered an example of a technique which
Horgan classifies separately, while noting that it is closely
related to the use of catchwords: the use of word-play.[65]
This is the link between πλάνη (v 11) and πλανῆται (v 13).
We noted in section II how the former is used actively, to
refer to Balaam's leading others astray. The latter, in the
standard phrase ἀστέρες πλανῆται, refers to the planets as
wandering stars, but the association with πλάνη in verse 11
can give it the added nuance that wandering stars lead astray
those who look to them for guidance – a thought which in
fact is present in the source of Jude's allusion to the wandering
stars (1 Enoch 80:6–7).

Another exegetical technique listed by Horgan is the use,
in the interpretation, of synonyms for words in the lemma.[66]
This rather obvious technique is used in Jude's interpretation
of 'text' 1 (v 5: ἀπώλεσεν; v 10 φθείρονται), and probably in
the interpretations of 'texts' 3 and 4.

Finally, the quotation of the text in a form modified to
suit or embody the interpretation of it which is proposed is

[64] Jude 4 has sometimes been thought to be based on 1 Enoch 48:10, but
against this see Osburn (1985) 301–302. Osburn himself (pp. 300–303)
argues that Jude 4 alludes to 1 Enoch 67:10, but I think this unlikely. Clear
evidence that Jude knew the Parables of Enoch (1 Enoch 37–71) is lacking.

[65] Horgan (1979) 245 n. 67.

[66] Horgan (1979) 245.

an exegetical technique found both in the New Testament[67] and in the Qumran literature.[68] Only one of Jude's 'texts' is a formal quotation from an extant source (vv 14–15). Since Jude is not following the extant (Akhmim) Greek text of 1 Enoch 1:9, but, most probably, translating from the Aramaic[69] or, perhaps, following a different Greek version,[70] and since the Aramaic of this verse of 1 Enoch is extant only in a very fragmentary form (4QEn^c 1:1:15–17), it is not easy to tell precisely how far Jude has modified the text he knew. But two modifications seem very probable: (1) In other versions of 1 Enoch 1:9 the subject is not explicit, but is God according to 1:4. κύριος has therefore probably been supplied by Jude, by analogy with other theophany texts which were applied to the parousia in early Christianity and which have verbal links with 1 Enoch 1:9 (Deut 33:2; Ps 68:17; Isa 40:10; 66:15; Zech 14:5; cf. 1 Enoch 91:7). It is therefore an *exegetical* modification of the text by reference to other analogous texts.[71] It is also a *christological* interpretation, which makes clear Jude's understanding of 1 Enoch 1:9 as referring to the parousia of Jesus Christ.[72] (2) The words καὶ ἐλέγξαι πάντας τοὺς ἀσεβεῖς ('and to convict all the ungodly') are an abbreviation of the text evidenced by the other versions, in which there are two verbs ('to destroy all the ungodly and to convict all flesh'). By his abbreviation Jude has omitted the idea of the destruction of the ungodly, which one might have expected him to retain (cf. vv 5, 10), but he has also omitted 'all flesh'. This omission has the effect of applying the text exclusively to the ἀσεβεῖς, whom Jude identifies as the false teachers, and of focussing attention on their legal condemnation. As we have seen in section II.2, the latter is appropriate

---

[67] Ellis (1957) 139–147; (1978) 152, 177–180; Dunn (1977) 92–93.

[68] Cf. Brooke (1985) 111–112. In the pesharim, this is most often achieved by selection of variant readings: Horgan (1979) 245 n. 69; Ellis (1978) 175–176; Brooke (1985) 288–289.

[69] Bauckham (1983A) 94–96.

[70] Dehandshutter (1986) 120.

[71] Cf. Wilcox (1988) 200–201, for the comparable case of Matt 21:5.

[72] Black (1973) 195; Osburn (1976–77) 337; *contra* Dehandshutter (1986) 118–119.

in view of the fact that the preceding verses (12–13) form a kind of version of the indictment of the wicked in 1 Enoch 2:1–5:4.

Jude shows no evidence of some of the more artificial exegetical techniques to be found occasionally in the pesharim, such as the rearrangement of the letters in a word in the lemma to form another word (the rabbinic technique of *hillûf*) or interpretation through the division of a word into two parts (the rabbinic *nôtārîqôn*), but such techniques would be much more difficult to use in Greek than in Hebrew and so we should probably not expect them. In any case, the brevity of Jude's exegetical section scarcely allows scope for the use of all available exegetical techniques.

V. Jude's Exegetical Links

This section offers a somewhat speculative reconstruction of Jude's exegetical procedure. We have already noticed that 1 Enoch 1:9 (Jude 14–15) is the key text for Jude's commentary. We have also noticed how some of his texts are linked together by implicit *gĕzērâ šawâ*. It seems possible that the whole of Jude's exegetical work has 1 Enoch 1–5 as its base, and all other texts to which he alludes can be seen to be reached by association with 1 Enoch 1–5. Possible relationships can be summarized by the following diagrams:

1 Enoch 1–5   Jude

1:5: Watchers → 1 Enoch 6–10 → traditional
                                schema of
                                examples of
                                judgment
                                (Watchers,
                                Sodom,
                                wilderness   → vv 5–7
                                generation: cf.
                                TNapht 3:4–5;
                                CD 2:17–3:12
                                etc)[73]

---

[73] For the traditional schema, see Bauckham (1983A) 46–47.

1:9: 'hard
things'
5:4: 'hard-
hearted'   → Ps 95:8
                 ↓
              Ps 95:10–11 →   Num 14   → v 5
                               Ps 106: 24–25

1:4: Sinai
1:9: 'he comes → Deut 33:2
with 10,000s of   ↓
holy ones'   Deut 34 → →   apocryphal
                  (burial of   account of   → v 9
                  Moses)   burial of Moses

2:1 → → → → →   1 Enoch 80:1
                     ↓
                  1 Enoch   →   Balaam (goes
                  80:6–7   astray and leads
                  (stars go astray   astray:
                  and lead astray)   Num.R.20:9)
                  (Jude 11: ἀστέ-   (Jude 13:
                  ρες πλανῆται)   πλάνῃ)
                                        ↓
                                  traditional
                                  schema of 3
                                  sinners who   → v 11
                                  led others astray
                                  (cf. t. Soṭa 4:9)

1:9: 'hard
things'
5:4:
'hardhearted' → Ps 95:8 → → →   Exod 17:3
                                 'murmuring'
                                     ↓
                                 Num 16:11   → v 11
                                 (Korah   (Korah)
                                 murmuring)

1:9: 'to destroy all the wicked → and to convict all flesh'

Jer 25:31: 'he is entering into judgment with all flesh, and the wicked he will put to the sword'

↓

Jer 25:34–37 → Ezek 34:1-10
(judgment of   (judgment of
the shepherds)   the shepherds)

↓

Ezek 34:2 → → v 12
(ἑαυτοὺς
ποιμαί-
νοντες)

2:1 → → → → → 1 Enoch 80:2

↓

2:3 (clouds & → 1 Enoch 80:2 → Prov 25:14 → → v 12
rain)   (rain withheld)   (νεφέλαι
                                                                              ἄνυδροι
                                                                              etc)

2:1 → → → → → 1 Enoch 80:2

↓

5:1: 'trees ... → 1 Enoch 80:3 → ?parable of
bear fruit'   ('fruit of the   barren figtree → ⎫ v 12
                          trees will be   ⎬ (δένδρα
                          withheld at → → → → → → → ⎭ etc)
                          their proper
                          time')

1:8: 'peace' → →   → → → → → → Isa 57:19
                                              ↓
2:1 → → → → → → 1 Enoch 80:1   ↓
                        ↓   ↓
5:3: 'seas' → → → ?reference to sea   ↓
                    in Jude's   → Isa 57:20 → → →   v 13
                    version of 1   ↑   (κύματα
                    Enoch 80?   ↑   etc)
                                            ↑
                                            ↑
5:4: 'no peace' → → → → → → Isa 57:21

2:1 → → → → → → 1 Enoch 80:1
                        ↓
                 1 Enoch 80:6 → → → → → → →   v 13
                                              (ἀστέρες
                            ↘   πλανῆται)

                           1 Enoch 18:15–
                           16
                                  ↓
                           1 Enoch 88:1 →   v 13 (ὁ
                                              ζοφος
                                              τοῦ
                                              σκότους)

1:9 →   vv 14–15

1:9: 'hard
things'
5:4:
'hardhearted' → Ps 95:8 → → → Exod 17:3 → →⌐
                     ↓   'murmuring' | v 16
                     ↓   at Massah/ | (γογγυσταὶ
                     ↓   Meribah   ⟩ μεμψί-
                 Ps 95:10–11 → Num 14:2, 27, | μοιροι)
                                 29, 36 |
                                 Ps 106:24–25 →⌐
                                 (murmuring at
                                 Kadesh)

1:9: 'hard
things'

↓

5:4: 'great and hard words with your unclean mouth'	→ → → → → →	Dan 7:8, 20 → ('a mouth speaking great things')	v 16 (τὸ στόμα αὐτῶν λαλεῖ ὑπέρογκα)

1:9: repeated ἀσεβ-	→ → → → → →	prophecy of → the apostles (ἀσεβειῶν)	v 18

There are also some scriptural allusions outside the exegetical section of Jude (vv 4–19) which could be similarly linked to 1 Enoch 1–5:

1 Enoch 1–5   Jude

1:8; 5:5–6: → → → → → → → → → → → → → → → → → → mercy	v 21 (ἔλεος)

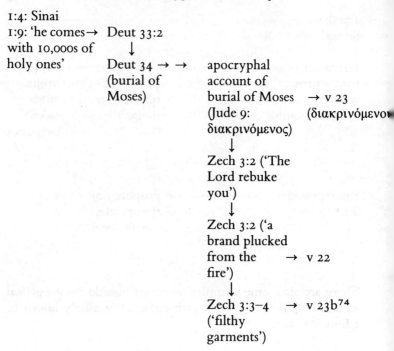

1:4: Sinai
1:9: 'he comes→ Deut 33:2
with 10,000s of   ↓
holy ones'   Deut 34 → →   apocryphal
                 (burial of   account of
                 Moses)   burial of Moses   → v 23
                                (Jude 9:   (διακρινόμενο⟩
                                διακρινόμενος)
                                       ↓
                                Zech 3:2 ('The
                                Lord rebuke
                                you')
                                       ↓
                                Zech 3:2 ('a
                                brand plucked
                                from the   → v 22
                                fire')
                                       ↓
                                Zech 3:3–4 → v 23b[74]
                                ('filthy
                                garments')

Some of these chains of connections seem somewhat contrived, and it is unlikely that they all represent Jude's exegetical
work accurately. However, they do show that Jude could have
reached many of his scriptural allusions by study of 1 Enoch 1–5.

VI. Hermeneutical presuppositions

Jude's exegesis shares one dominant hermeneutical presupposition with the Jewish apocalyptists, the Qumran community
and the early church. This is the assumption that the Old
Testament Scriptures are especially relevant to the last days,
the period in which God's purpose in history is reaching its
climax, when the final deliverance of his faithful people from
evil and the final judgment of the wicked will take place.
Those who read the Old Testament on this assumption also
believed that they themselves were living in the last days, so

[74] For the allusions in vv 22–23, see Bauckham (1983A) 114–117.

that the Old Testament referred, in a wide variety of ways, to their own religious community, its history and character-istics, and also to their enemies, to the coming salvation and vindication of the former and also to the imminent judgment of the latter. They themselves were living through the process of eschatological salvation and judgment to which all the Scriptures pointed forward, and they looked to the Scriptures for the understanding of this process in which they were involved and for hope and warnings relating to the comple-tion of the process in the future. Jude's sense of living in the last days before the imminent parousia of Jesus Christ is clear throughout his letter (cf. v 21), but emerges especially in the exegetical section (vv 4–19), whose purpose is to show that his opponents, by their immorality and their teaching of im-morality, identify themselves as the wicked of the last days, whose judgment is coming at the parousia. This is a warning to Jude's readers, not to be taken in by their teaching, lest they incur the same imminent danger, but to be those who can expect mercy and salvation rather than judgment at the parousia (vv 21, 24).

A number of explicit statements of this hermeneutical pre-supposition can be found in other New Testament writers (Rom 15:4; 1 Cor 10:11; 1 Pet 1:10–12): Jude simply takes it for granted. It leads him to treat scripture in two related, though broadly distinguishable ways: as *eschatological prophecy* and as *eschatological typology*. The former (for the explicit articulation of which, see 1QpHab 7:1–8; 1 Pet 1:10–12) is characteristic of the Qumran pesharim. It reads the inspired words of the prophets as predictive of the last days of history in which the interpreter is living, and so takes them to refer to people and events well known to the interpreter and his community. Thus Jude takes the very obviously eschato-logical prophecy of 1 Enoch 1:9 to refer to the imminent coming of Christ to judge the wicked, and those whose un-godliness is so stressed in that prophecy to be (or at least to include) his opponents, should they persevere in the ungodly behaviour they so deliberately flaunt and propagate (vv 14–16). He is taking seriously Enoch's own claim (1:2) to speak not for his own but for a remote generation: the last generation of world history, which the first generation of Christians believed themselves to be.[75] Prophets from the antediluvian times of Enoch to members of the last generation itself, the apostles (vv 17–18), spoke of those who would reject the grace of God and trouble the people of God in the period immediately before the end of history. So Jude can also take Isaiah 57:20 to refer to the same wicked people of the last days of whom Enoch prophesied. This interpretation of Isaiah was made, in fact, by the authors of the Enoch literature themselves (1 Enoch 5:4; 101:3, alluding to Isa 57:21). Although the comment on Isaiah 57:20 is not extant in the fragmentary Isaiah pesher from Qumran cave 4, we can be fairly sure that the Qumran community would have applied this text to their enemies, as Jude did. Indeed, allusions to Isaiah 57:20 in the Thanksgiving Hymns do apply it to the hymnist's enemies (1QH 2:12–13; 8:15).

Eschatological typology differs from eschatological prophecy in its concern with persons and events of the biblical narratives, rather than with verbal prophecies. Essentially, it takes the events of divine salvation and judgment in the biblical history, such as the Flood or the Exodus, to be prototypical of the final events of divine salvation and judgment at the end of history, which will correspond to, but also surpass God's earlier acts in history. It is not strictly accurate to say that it interprets events *rather than* texts, since it is a form of scriptural exegesis and interprets the *written record* of events in the texts of Scripture (cf. 1 Cor 10:11). It assumes that not simply the events, but also the way in which they have been recorded in inspired Scripture is instructive and of prophetic-typological significance (cf., e.g., Heb 7:1–3). For this reason the distinction between eschatological typology and eschatological prophecy is not absolute. But whereas the latter takes prophetic oracles to be predictive of the last days, the former takes biblical narrative as prefiguring the people and events of the last days.

Eschatological typology is not characteristic of the Qumran

[75] That Jude and the brothers of Jesus in particular believed they were the last generation of world history will be demonstrated in chapter 7 below.

pesharim, which are commentaries on prophetic oracles. Its prominence in Jude (vv 5–7, 11) is the most important formal difference between Jude and the pesharim. But it is found elsewhere in the Qumran literature. The War Scroll (1QM), for example, works with an implicit Exodus typology, in which the company of the sons of light corresponds to the camp of the Israelites in the wilderness, ready to conquer the promised land. Eschatological typology is especially characteristic of Jewish apocalyptic.[76] For example, the Apocalypse of Abraham (30:2–8) predicts ten eschatological plagues by which the Gentile enemies of the people of God will be judged, plainly modelled on the plagues of Egypt. The Enoch literature treats the Flood as prototypical of the eschatological judgment (note especially 1 Enoch 93:4), and when Jude treats the Watchers, the instigators of the evil which led to God's judgment in the Flood, as types of the wicked of the last days, he is following a typology implicit in the Enoch literature itself.

Later Christian use of typology came to be orientated to the past, i.e. it was largely concerned with the way Old Testament people and events prefigured Jesus and his history in the past. Much New Testament typology is also concerned with the events of the history of Jesus, but it would be a mistake to see it as orientated to the past. Rather, the events of Jesus' history were seen as the decisive beginning of the process of final salvation, which was under way and still to be completed at the parousia of Jesus. Exodus typology, for example, which is frequent in the New Testament, is applied to the (recent) past (the history of Jesus), to the present and to the (near) future (the parousia). As compared with Jewish apocalyptic, this is a shift of emphasis, but it did not prevent a very similar application of eschatological typology to the present and the immediate future.

Because of Jude's very limited purpose, we cannot expect to see the full range of early Christian eschatological typology in his letter. He is looking only for types of the wicked of

---

[76] Cf. Patte (1971) 159–164: but it is unfortunate that he uses Jubilees (not an apocalypse, though it has affinities with apocalyptic literature) as his example.

the last days and their judgment, and finds these in already classic cases: the faithless wilderness generation, the Watchers, the cities of the Plain, Cain, Balaam and Korah. His exegesis at this point belongs to a wider tradition in early Christianity (following Jewish precedent) of taking such figures as types of Christian apostates and false teachers (Luke 17:26–32; 2 Tim 2:19; 3:8; 1 John 3:12; Rev 2:14, 20). But, as it happens, his first type (v 5) incorporates a wider reference: to the Exodus from Egypt as a type of the salvation which Christians have already experienced through the saving act of God in Christ. Thus despite Jude's lack of reference, otherwise, to the saving work of Christ – which in such a short letter with a specific purpose should not be thought surprising – he certainly presupposes it.

In sections III, IV and VI we have seen that Jude's exegesis – in its formulae, techniques and presuppositions – resembles, often in strikingly detailed ways, the Qumran pesharim. Especially in the areas of formulae and techniques, this may be partly because the Qumran pesharim are almost the only extant examples of formal exegesis (lemma and commentary) from the Palestinian Judaism of New Testament times. It need not indicate that Jude or the Christian circles to which he belonged had specific links with the Qumran community; only that he practised a learned exegetical method which was common to the exegetes of the Qumran community and probably many other Jewish exegetes. Like the authors of the pesharim, he was skilled in the exegetical methods of his time and place. He also shared with them a hermeneutical presupposition that was common to apocalyptic Judaism (as also to early Christianity, a special variety of apocalyptic Judaism). In the case of his eschatological typology, his hermeneutical presupposition has more in common with apocalyptic works (including works such as 1 Enoch which were popular at Qumran) than with the pesharim, but the formulae and techniques he uses to expound it are again better paralleled in the pesharim, because the apocalypses do not provide us with formal exegesis of the kind Jude is practising.

Parallels with other early Christian literature which we have noted from time to time have shown that Jude's formulae and techniques became part of a Christian exegetical tradition to which other New Testament writers are also indebted, but also that the parallels are rather fragmentary and occasional. Although there are other passages of formal exegesis in the New Testament, Jude's is probably the most elaborate and complex early Christian example of commentary in the style of the Qumran pesharim. In the next section, however, we shall examine, for the sake of comparison, one rather close parallel, in structure and technique, to Jude's scriptural commentary.

VII. For comparison: 1 Peter 2:4–10[77]

1 Peter 2:4–10 is a carefully composed section of scriptural exegesis which resembles the 'thematic pesharim' of Qumran, much as Jude 4–19 does, though less extensively. The structure and meaning of this passage have been fully discussed by Elliott,[78] whose arguments seem to me largely to carry conviction, despite the criticisms of them by Best.[79] But if we compare the passage with Jude 4–19, the exact status of the introductory verses 4–5 in relation to the rest of the passage (a point in debate between Elliott and Best) can be clarified. These verses play a role analogous to that of Jude 4. In other words, verses 4–5 briefly state the theme which is then both supported and expanded by the Old Testament citations and their interpretation in verses 6–10. The introductory statement of the theme in verses 4–5 has been carefully composed to introduce verses 6–10, and so (like Jude 4) it already echoes the texts to be quoted and provides a basic framework for their interpretation. It divides into two parts, so that verse 4, on Christ the 'living stone', introduces the three texts and their interpretation in verses 6–8, while verse 5, on the readers as 'living stones', introduces the three texts in verses 9–10. The link between Christ and believers, established in verses

[77] Most of this section first appeared in Bauckham (1988E) 310–312.
[78] Elliott (1966).
[79] Best (1969); cf. Elliott (1982) 240–241; also the independent study of the use of the Old Testament in this passage by Danker (1967).

4–5, is also the link between the two parts of the commentary: verses 6–8 and verses 9–10.

Thus the structure of the passage 2:4–10 is:

4–5	Introductory statement of theme
4	A. Jesus the elect stone
5	B. The church the elect people of God

6–10	Commentary	
6a	Introductory formula	
6–8	A^1. The elect stone	
6b + 7a		Text 1 (Isa 28:16) + interpretation
7b + 7c		Interpretation + Text 2 (Ps 118:22)
8a + 8b		Text 3 (Isa 8:14) + interpretation
9–10	B^1. The elect people	
9		Text 4 (Isa 43:20–21) + Text 5 (Exod 19:5–6) conflated, with expansion of text 4
10		Text 6 (Hos 2:23) paraphrased (cf. Hos 1:6, 9; 2:1).

As in Jude 4–19, catchwords are used to link the texts together (*gĕzērâ šāwâ*), to link the introductory statement to the texts, and to link the interpretations to the texts. Thus, for example, in A (v 4) λίθον is the catchword which links together all three texts in A^1 (vv 6b, 7c, 8a), ἐκλεκτόν and ἔντιμον pick up the same words in text 1 (v 6b), and ἀποδεδοκιμασμένον picks up ἀπεδοκίμασαν in text 2 (v 7c). In the interpretation of text 1 (v 7a), τιμή and πιστεύουσιν echo ἔντιμον and πιστεύων in the text (v 6b). The words ἅγιον and ἱεράτευμα, the latter highly distinctive, link B (v 5) to B^1, while the three texts in B^1 are linked together by the catchword λαός.[80] This is true in spite of the fact that the word occurs only once in verse 9, because λαὸς εἰς περιποίησιν in verse 9 represents *both* λαόν μου ὃν περιεποιησάμην in Isaiah 43:21 LXX and λαὸς περιούσιος in Exodus 19:5 LXX. (In Malachi 3:17 LXX the phrase εἰς περιποίησιν translates *sĕgullâ*, which is translated λαὸς περιούσιος in

[80] *Contra* Elliott (1966) 138–141.

Exod 19:5 LXX.) It was this coincidence between Isaiah 43:20–21 and Exodus 19:5 which suggested and made possible the conflation of these two texts in verse 9.

This last point already indicates another pesher-type feature of the commentary: selection and adaptation of the text form to suit the interpretation. A striking example is the way in which ἐκλεκτόν is both the first adjectival description of the stone in A¹ (v 6b) and the first adjectival description of the people in B¹ (v 9). This has been achieved by the omission of πολυτελῆ from the quotation of Isaiah 28:16 in verse 6b, and by placing the phrase γένος ἐκλεκτόν from Isaiah 43:20 before the epithets from Exodus 19:6 in verse 9. This gives the idea of election the prominence which the introductory statement in verse 4 has already given it, and serves to link together the elect stone (Christ) in A¹ and the elect people in B¹. Hence the form in which the texts are quoted is governed by the intention of the whole commentary: to show how the election of Christ leads to the election of those who believe in him as the holy people of God.

The use of τίθημι in verse 6b, where Isaiah 28:16 LXX has ἐμβαλῶ, is probably an example of the selection of a text form. This form of the text was also known to Paul (Rom 9:33) and to the author of Barnabas 6:2–3, who in the manner of the pesharim in fact makes use of both text forms.[81] τίθημι is a natural word to use for laying a foundation, and so was probably simply a variant translation, not originally designed for any special interpretative purpose. But the author of 1 Peter has *selected* it for *his* purpose, because it can also mean 'appoint', and so again stresses the theme of elec- tion at the outset of his series of texts. The use of the same verb in this sense at the end of verse 8 (ἐτέθησαν) forms an *inclusio* with τίθημι in verse 6, and so marks the theme of election as the overarching theme of section A¹. The same theme is played up in B¹ by the interpretative expansion of Isaiah 43:21 in verse 9b (καλέσαντος).

The association and christological interpretation of 'stone' testimonia was already traditional in Christianity (cf. Luke

---

[81] Harris (1916) 31; cf. Kraft (1960) 344–345.

20:17–18; Rom 9:33; Barn 6:2–4),[82] following Jewish precedent.[83] The association of Hosea 2:23 with the 'stone' texts may also have been traditional (Rom 9:25–26, 33). But the exegetical skill of our author appears in the way he builds on the tradition in order to create an exegetical passage specifically designed for its context in 1 Peter. The passage 2:6–10 provides the scriptural grounding both for the previous part of the letter, in which the election of Christ (1:20) and the election of Christian believers (1:1–2) to be the holy people of God (1:15–16) are key themes, and also for the succeeding part of the letter, in which the relation of believers to unbelievers is the major topic. The priestly service, in both word and conduct, of a holy people, to the glory of God and as a witness to the world (2:5, 9), is the scriptural concept which undergirds all the paraenesis from 2:11 onwards. Thus 2:4–10 plays a key foundational and transitional role in the whole letter, for which its carefully studied composition is designed.

1 Peter 2:4–10 lacks the exegetical formulae which Jude uses, and is on a rather smaller scale than Jude's commentary, but in other respects forms a fairly close parallel to the structure and exegetical method of Jude 4–19. The parallel is particularly interesting in view of the fact that the circle of Christian leaders in Rome from which 1 Peter derives were in close touch with Palestinian Jewish Christianity. They included not only Peter himself (if the letter was written before his death), but also Silvanus and Mark (1 Pet 5:12–13), who had been members of the Jerusalem church.[84] By the same channels as the early Christian tradition of pesher-type exegesis moved from Palestine (Jude) to Rome (1 Peter), the letter of Jude itself must have travelled to Rome, where it

[82] Cf. Lindars (1961) 169–186.

[83] Black (1971) 11–14.

[84] For the origin of 1 Peter in a 'Petrine circle' in Rome, which was influenced by Palestinian traditions, see Elliott (1980). Elliott thinks of 1 Peter deriving from this group after Peter's death. For reasons given in Bauckham (1988D), I consider 1 Peter to have been written before Peter's death and sent out with his authorization, even if other members of the Petrine circle were responsible for its composition.

was available to another Roman church leader of a somewhat later date: the author of 2 Peter.[85]

VIII. Jude's use of apocryphal literature

Since the third century, readers of Jude have been puzzled or offended by his quotation from a non-canonical work (vv 14–15). This citation of 1 Enoch 1:9 is certainly not merely illustrative or *ad hominem*,[86] like the quotations from pagan literature in Acts 17:28; Titus 1:12. The introductory formula (v 14a) indicates that Jude regarded this text as inspired prophecy, while the description of Enoch as 'the seventh from Adam' (cf. 1 Enoch 60:8; 93:3; Jub 7:39) is intended to indicate not only Enoch's antiquity, but also his special authority by virtue of his position in the seventh generation of world history. It alludes to that very special role as prophet and visionary which the Enoch literature accords to Enoch, as the one to whom all manner of divine secrets were revealed for the benefit of succeeding generations of the elect and especially of the last generation, which in its proximity to the end of history and its living amidst the final outburst of evil in history corresponds typologically to Enoch's own position immediately before the Flood and amidst the evil unleashed by the apostasy of the Watchers. It seems that Jude took the attribution of 1 Enoch 1:9 to Enoch seriously, and deliberately parallels this prophecy from the seventh generation of world history with the prophecy of the apostles who belong to the last generation of world history (as we have seen in section I above, vv 14–15 and vv 17–18 form a pair of quotations).[87] Although it is true that 1 Enoch 1:9, like the whole theophany passage in which it occurs (1:3b–9), is very closely based on Old Testament texts describing the theophany of the divine Warrior (with 1:9, cf. Deut 33:2; Jer 25:31; Zech 14:5; Isa

[85] For the origin of 2 Peter in Rome in the late first century, see Bauckham (1983A) 157–161.

[86] As suggested by Beckwith (1985) 401–402.

[87] For the significance of the parallelism between Enoch and the apostles, see further chapter 7 section III.2 below.

66:15–16; Dan 7:10, 25–26)[88] and Jude may have found it a convenient and striking summary of such texts, he seems to value it as more than that, as an authoritative prophecy in its own right.

Moreover, we have seen that this particular quotation from Enoch, which is in fact the only formal citation of a written text which Jude gives in his commentary, occupies the key position in the commentary, being especially linked to the statement of theme for the commentary (v 4) and focussing especially clearly the message of all the 'texts'. We have also seen that it is far from being Jude's only use of 1 Enoch. As well as the clear allusions to 1 Enoch in v 6, other passages of 1 Enoch underlie vv 12b–13. There seems good reason to suppose that 1 Enoch 1–5 and related passages in the Enoch literature lie at the foundation of Jude's exegetical work. At least it must be said that the Enoch literature is as important to Jude in this commentary as canonical Scripture is, and when we remember that another apocryphal work, probably the Testament of Moses, provides a secondary 'text' in v 9, we are bound to ask what *status* the so-called pseudepigraphal literature (non-canonical Jewish works attributed to Old Testament figures) in general and the Enoch literature in particular had for Jude and his circle. Were the book(s) of Enoch and the Moses apocryphon Jude knew actually part of his canon of Scripture?

A comparison in the first place with the Qumran literature and secondly with other early Christian writers will put Jude's usage in perspective. From the surviving copies and fragments of apocryphal literature from Qumran, it is clear that the Qumran community read and valued a wide variety of apocryphal or pseudepigraphal works, including the Enoch literature. On the other hand, it is a notable fact that not only are the community's commentaries on Scripture, the pesharim, commentaries only on books which belong to the canon of the Hebrew Bible, but also formal citations of Scripture in these and other works of the community are confined to the books of the canon. There seem to be only two instances where apocryphal works are treated in the same way

---

[88] See Hartman (1966) 114–117; VanderKam (1973); Hartman (1979) 22–26.

as canonical Scripture.[89] One is 4QTestimonia (4Q175), a fragment of a catena of scriptural texts, without commentary. Here quotations from Deuteronomy and Numbers are followed by a quotation from the apocryphal Psalms of Joshua.[90] Another fragmentary work, known as 4Q Ages of Creation (4Q180),[91] appears to be a commentary (pesher) on an apocryphal work about the divinely ordained periods of world history. It uses the same exegetical formulae (including the word פשר) as the pesharim use in their interpretation of Scripture. These may be exceptions which prove the rule, but they provide at least distant parallels to Jude's use of apocryphal literature in a commentary resembling the thematic pesharim of Qumran.

The evidence of early Christian literature (including not only the New Testament, but also other early Christian works from the first century of Christian history) is not unlike that of Qumran. Of course, noncanonical Jewish literature influenced most early Christian writers, helping to form their religious outlook and influencing the way they read and interpreted Scripture. All kinds of parallels prove this in general, though it is often more difficult to be sure of the influence of any specific book on any specific Christian writer. We should also remember that most of the Jewish apocryphal and pseudepigraphal literature has been preserved only by Christians: it must have been read and valued by some Christians at least in the period when Christianity was still closely related to Jewish religious culture.

However, if we look for signs that such literature was treated in the same way as canonical Scripture, they are few. Even clear and deliberate allusions to such literature are not frequent, though they can certainly be found. Formal citations of these works, as authorities that can be cited in the way

[89] The allusion to the Testament of Levi in CD 4:15–19 need not imply a status for it equivalent to canonical Scripture.

[90] But Beckwith (1985) 74–75, suggests that it is the quotation from canonical Joshua contained in the quotation from the apocryphal Psalms of Joshua which is being placed alongside the Pentateuchal quotations.

[91] It may be the 'Book of the Divisions of the Times into their Jubilees and Weeks' to which CD 16:2–4 refers.

that Scripture is cited, are rare. Of the hundreds of formal quotations from Scripture to be found in early Christian literature, the overwhelming majority are from books which belong to the Hebrew canon. However, there are some that are not.[92] In some cases, because early Christian quotations from Scripture can take rather eccentric forms (variant text-forms, merged quotations of more than one Old Testament text, abbreviated, summarized, paraphrased and modified texts)[93] it is not always easy to be sure whether a quotation is intended to be an Old Testament quotation or derives from an apocryphal work which is no longer extant (debated cases in the New Testament are 1 Cor 2:9; 15:45; Jas 4:5; cf. also 1 Clem 29:3; 50:4; Barn 11:9–10). But it seems likely that some of these doubtful cases belong with others which are rather clearly from unknown apocryphal sources (1 Clem 23:3 ‖ 2 Clem 11:2; 1 Clem 46:2; Barn 12:1). There are some identifiable quotations from known apocryphal works (Barn 16:5, 6 seem to be from 1 Enoch 89:56–58, 66–67; 91:13, rather loosely quoted as is characteristic of Barnabas' quotations). Of course, it is possible that occasionally a writer might remember a quotation from a non-canonical source and mistakenly think it to be scriptural, but, to put the matter beyond doubt, there are some cases where a named apocryphal work is cited alongside or in the same way as canonical Scripture (Barn 16:6; Hermas, *Vis.* 2:3:4; AscIsa 4:21). There are enough cases where a non-canonical work is quoted with a formula normally indicating scriptural authority (γραφή: Jas 4:5?; Barn 16:5; 1 Clem 23:3; 46:2; γέγραπται: 1 Cor 2:9; Barn 4:3; 16:6; Hermas, *Vis.* 2:3:4; other formulae in Barn 12:1; 2 Clem 11:2) to make the way Jude refers to Enoch not unique in the broad context of early Christianity. Still such cases, though rather more common than the exceptions to the rule at Qumran, are marginal to the general pattern of scriptural citation in early Christianity.

Thus what needs explaining is why noncanonical works were not normally, but might occasionally be quoted as

---

[92] Rather underestimated by Beckwith (1985) 396–397.
[93] Ellis (1957) 33–36.

inspired and authoritative religious literature. This is not well explained by the argument of some recent scholars that in the New Testament period Judaism did not yet have a canon of Scripture in the sense of a closed collection of authoritative literature[94] – or that the only closed canon was the Torah, while all other Scripture constituted an undefined body of literature in which the writers of the pseudepigrapha intended their works to be included.[95] The most convincing interpretation of the evidence indicates on the contrary that the three divisions of the Hebrew canon – the Torah, the Prophets and the Writings – were by the first century A.D. already a defined body of literature, generally recognized by Jews as their authoritative Scriptures,[96] even if one or two of the books of the Writings (Esther, the Song of Songs) were still open to some debate.[97] The phenomena of scriptural quotation at Qumran and in early Christianity, which we have just noticed, support this view. If the canon really were still open – so that many Jews regarded many books which were later excluded from the canon as belonging to the same category as those which were later included in the canon – then we should expect much more quotation from such works than we find.

One of the pieces of evidence which has been held to support the open canon[98] is 4 Ezra 14: in fact it does not, but is nevertheless an illuminating passage. The chapter recounts the legend of Ezra's restoration of the Scriptures, which had all been burned (14:21). Under divine inspiration, he writes ninety-four books (14:44), twenty-four of which are to be made public for all to read, but seventy to be given only to

[94] E.g. Sundberg (1964).

[95] Barton (1986) 13–95.

[96] Beckwith (1985) provides the fullest presentation of the evidence.

[97] Five books (Ezekiel, Proverbs, Ecclesiastes, Song of Songs, Esther) were still the subject of some debate among the rabbis. But probably, as Beckwith (1985) 274–323, argues, these disputes (including those attributed to the academy of Jamnia at the end of the first century A.D.) should be seen as concerned not with books not yet included in the canon, but with books already generally accepted as canonical. The question is not whether for the first time they should be included, but whether after all they should be excluded.

[98] Barton (1986) 64–65.

the wise (14:45–46). The seventy books are evidently apocalyptic works such as 4 Ezra itself, which in circles such as his
own were regarded as even more valuable than the twenty-
four (14:47) but were not generally treated as Scripture in
Jewish religion (they were not, for example, read in synagogue). Quite clearly the twenty-four books are a defined
collection recognized by all Jews: they are the books of the
Hebrew canon, commonly reckoned as twenty-four.[99] The
number seventy probably indicates that the other books,
though in theological principle a defined collection (God
knows which they are), were in practice an undefined, open
collection (probably no one could have listed all seventy).
But the author does not add them to the twenty-four to
make a single collection; he places them alongside the
twenty-four as *another* collection. Thus he shows *both* that
there was (when he wrote, c. 100 A.D.) a closed canon,
which alone was recognized by all Jews, and that it was
possible for Jews to regard *other* works as also inspired, even,
in this case, as more valuable than the books of the canon.

In the New Testament period we should probably envisage
a situation in which the books of the Hebrew canon were
regarded as virtually a closed collection, which was generally
regarded as authoritative Scripture by Jews. Even if it might
still be debated whether Esther or the Song of Songs ought
really to be included in the Writings, nobody argued that
Jubilees or 1 Enoch or the Apocryphon of Ezekiel should be
included in the Prophets or the Writings. The collection was
virtually closed. This did not prevent anyone recognizing
other books as also inspired, but the status of such other,
noncanonical books was not agreed. Some circles valued some
of them, more or less highly. Some, like the writer of 4 Ezra,
might even value some of them above the generally recognized canon; others, like the Qumran community, it
seems, gave them a subordinate status. But the situation in
regard to such noncanonical works – both as to which of
them were regarded as inspired at all and as to how highly

[99] Beckwith (1985) 240. The alternative numeration of twenty-two was
also current.

they were valued – was entirely fluid. So it was not normally possible to quote them as authoritative in the way that the generally recognized canon of Scripture could be quoted. But any of them might occasionally be quoted as an inspired writing by a writer who recognized it as such and found something in it especially opposite to his theme, or who knew that within the limited circle for which he was writing it was generally valued. This hypothesis sufficiently explains the occasional citation of non-canonical Jewish writings by Christian authors.

Jude's use of Enoch remains striking by comparison with the Qumran pesharim, but we should remember that his commentary includes a 'text' which, by Qumran standards, is even more anomalous: the prophecy of the apostles (vv 17–18). That his quotation from Enoch is paired with this apostolic prophecy itself shows that there is no need to suppose that Jude included Enoch in the canon of Jewish Scriptures. Like all early Christians, for whom the tradition of the sayings of Jesus, the oracles of Christian prophets and the teaching of apostles were all inspired authorities, Jude would not in any case have limited inspiration to the Hebrew canon. There is no difficulty in supposing that he and presumably his circle valued the Enoch literature highly alongside the canon of Law, Prophets and Writings. Precisely what kind of authority it had by comparison with the canon we cannot tell; nor need he have done.

That Jewish apocalyptic works should have been popular among Palestinian Jewish Christians is not surprising. Those who believed themselves to live in the last generation before the end of history and looked for the imminent coming of Jesus Christ as eschatological Saviour and Judge would readily turn to such works and relate them to the Old Testament texts which they interpreted messianically and eschatologically. The Jewish apocalypses of Palestinian origin (including those of post-Christian date, such as 4 Ezra, 2 Baruch and the Apocalypse of Abraham) which the Christian church preserved were probably valued by Palestinian Jewish Christians in the first place and thence passed to other parts of the church. The opening section of 1 Enoch, from which Jude draws his key text, connects so closely with Old Testament texts early Christians interpreted with reference to the parousia and would itself have so obviously, in their eyes, described the parousia, that we can easily see why the circles in which Jude moved should have been attracted to the work.

So far as we can plot the use of 1 Enoch in early Christianity it was not widely used at first. We must be cautious about attributing to it the influence of the general world of ideas which it shares with other literature or the occurrence of traditions which it uses but may not have had a monopoly in. Clear traces of the influence of the book itself are rare in the New Testament. 1 Corinthians 11:10 is probably better explained than by reference to the story of the fall of the Watchers.[100] 1 Peter 3:19–20 may refer to the Watchers,[101] but if it locates their prison in the heavens it is closer to 2 Enoch 7 than to 1 Enoch. The relationship of parts of Luke's Gospel material to 1 Enoch 92–105, which has been claimed, seems dubious.[102] The influence of the Parables of Enoch on the Son of man sayings in the Gospels is now generally discounted,[103] though some still think their influence on Matthew 25:31–33 plausible.[104] Resemblances between Revelation and 1 Enoch are readily explicable by common apocalyptic traditions. It is noteworthy that the reference to Enoch in Hebrews 11:5 relies solely on Genesis 5:22–24 (LXX), with no hint of the rich extracanonical developments of the story of Enoch. The author of 2 Peter 2:4 may show knowledge of 1 Enoch independently of Jude 6, his source.[105] If so, he reflects a growing influence of the work at the end of the first century, if 1 Clement (whose chapter 20 is probably dependent on 1 Enoch 2–5)[106] and Barnabas (certainly depen-

---

[100] Fitzmyer (1971) 187–204.

[101] Dalton (1965); but see the recent argument against this view and for an alternative view in Grudem (1988) 203–239.

[102] Aalen (1966–67); Nickelsburg (1979); cf. chapter 7 n. 25 below.

[103] Cf. Rowland (1982) 264–266.

[104] Catchpole (1979) 378–383.

[105] Bauckham (1983) 249.

[106] Cf. n. 26 above.

dent on the Dream-Visions of Enoch in 16:5–6 and on some other Enochic prophecy in 4:3) are correctly dated at the end of the first century.[107] In any case, in the second century 1 Enoch became a very popular book in the Christian churches.[108]

This pattern may reflect the fact that 1 Enoch, though popular in some Jewish circles in Palestine, was not widely known in the western diaspora where most of the Christians addressed in the New Testament documents lived. Its use would have spread, not immediately from diaspora Jews to Christians outside Palestine, but slowly from Palestinian Jewish Christians to the rest of the church. This would be even more plausible if the translation of 1 Enoch into Greek occurred only towards the end of the first century.[109] This can be only an hypothesis. But in any case, especially since it is likely that Jude knew 1 Enoch (or the parts of it that he knew) in Aramaic, his use of the Enoch literature seems likely to reflect its popularity in some circles of apocalyptic Jewish Christianity in Palestine during the New Testament period, before it became popular in the church at large from the end of the first century onwards.

IX. Conclusion

The letter of Jude contains probably the most elaborate passage of formal exegesis in the manner of the Qumran pesharim to be found in the New Testament. There are many less elaborate examples in other New Testament works, and fragments of the results of such exegetical work can be detected frequently. Such exegesis must have flourished especially in the early Palestinian church, where Jewish Christian leaders, in order to justify, to explain and to develop their faith in Jesus the Messiah, studied and expounded the Scriptures with the exegetical techniques available to them in their

---

[107] For this date for Barnabas, see Richardson and Shukster (1983).

[108] Lawlor (1897); Charles (1912) lxxxi–xcv; Ruwet (1948) 242–243; Denis (1970) 20–24; Adler (1978); Schultz (1978).

[109] For this suggestion, see Bauckham (1981) 138.

religious culture. Such exegetical work and the skilled exegetes who produced it will have played a major part in the early development of Christian theology. Evidently Jude the Lord's brother was one such skilled exegete.

5

Jude and the Testament of Moses

One of the more distinctive characteristics of Jude's letter, among the New Testament documents, is its lavish use of apocryphal literature. The Enoch literature is Jude's particular favourite, but he also refers in verse 9 to a story which he must have known in some apocryphal source. This story and its source will be our concern in this chapter.[1]

I. Reconstructing the story Jude knew

Jude 9, in a translation which will be justified later, reads: 'When Michael the archangel, in debate with the devil, disputed about the body of Moses, he did not presume to condemn him for slander, but said, "May the Lord rebuke you!"' Clearly Jude is here referring to a story well-known to him and presumably also to his readers, but his source is no longer extant as such. There is, however, no lack of later sources which describe a debate between Michael and the devil over the body of Moses, some of which purport to recount the story which Jude knew. From these it should be possible to reconstruct Jude's source. Much of the evidence for the story of the dispute over the body of Moses has been

[1] The material in this chapter appeared in much more summary form in Bauckham (1983A) 65–76. A fuller form of it was read to the Pseudepigrapha Seminar of the Studiorum Novi Testamenti Societas in Canterbury in 1983: see the report in Charlesworth (1985) 139.

assembled before,[2] and attempts have been made to reconstruct the story from it, but it has not been subjected to the kind of critical investigation which is necessary if it is provide reliable access to the content of Jude's source.

The problem of reconstructing the story Jude knew is closely connected with two other dimensions of the question of Jude's source in this verse, which we shall therefore also have to consider: (1) The question of the identification of Jude's source. The ancient lists of apocryphal works[3] list two Moses apocrypha which could well have contained such a story: the Testament of Moses and the Assumption of Moses. We have also, in a sixth-century Milan manuscript first published by Ceriani in 1861, a Latin translation of a Moses apocryphon which is unfortunately incomplete, breaking off before the account of Moses' death which in all probability its lost ending contained. This work has been variously identified. Since Gelasius of Cyzicus, in the fifth century, quotes words which occur in the Milan manuscript at 1:14 and names their source as the Assumption of Moses,[4] the Latin fragment has often been thought to be from the work of that name. On the other hand, 'Testament of Moses' seems a more appropriate description of the contents of the work in the Milan manuscript,[5] and increasingly scholars have accepted the view that it should be identified as such.[6] In any case, it is universally agreed that this work predates Jude and could therefore have been the source of Jude 9. For many scholars this possibility has become a strong probability because they claim that other verses of Jude contain allusions to that part of the work which is extant in the Milan manuscript. Since these allusions are debated, we shall not rely on them as part of our

[2] Charles (1897) 106–110; James (1920) 42–51; Denis (1970A) 63–67; cf. Vegas Montaner (1987) 220–221.

[3] Collected in Denis (1970B) xiv–xv.

[4] Text J in section III below.

[5] On the genre of the work as a testament, see Vegas Montaner (1987) 232–237.

[6] Laperrousaz (1970); Nickelsburg (1973); Collins (1984A) 345; Vegas Montaner (1987) 218–224. Sparks (1984) 601–602, continues to call it the Assumption of Moses, but seems undecided as to the correct identification.

case for identifying Jude's source in verse 9, but reserve them for separate discussion later in this chapter (section V). The whole question is further complicated by the fact that the Alexandrian Fathers (Clement, Origen, Didymus) appear to indicate that Jude's source in verse 9 was the Assumption of Moses,[7] although strictly speaking, they say no more than that the debate between Moses and the devil to which Jude refers can be found in the Assumption of Moses.

Thus the question of identifying Jude's source is intimately connected with the problem of the relationship between the Testament of Moses and the Assumption of Moses and with the identification of the work in the Milan manuscript and the reconstruction of its lost ending. Our investigation may throw light not only on Jude 9 but also on the work in the Milan manuscript and the character of the two ancient Moses apocrypha.

(2) The discovery and partial publication of the Qumran text known as 4QVisions of Amram (or Testament of Amram), which was first published by Milik in 1972,[8] stimulated some fresh discussion of the background to Jude 9, first by Milik himself and then by Berger, in an important response to Milik.[9] Milik supposed Jude 9 to be ultimately dependent on 4QAmram, *via* the Assumption of Moses. Berger, by bringing a great many more related texts into the discussion, was able to contest this. He argued that both 4QAmram and Jude's source were dependent on a more general, oral tradition about the contest between the devil and the chief of the angels for possession of a person's soul at death. We shall see that neither Milik nor Berger was precisely correct, but they made clear that the task of reconstructing Jude's source in verse 9 must take account of the general background provided by other similar stories. The contest over the body of Moses is an instance of a whole genre of stories of contests between Satan and the chief of the angels. Awareness of this tradition is an important aid to critical investigation of the Moses story itself.

[7] Texts G, H, I in section III below.
[8] Milik (1972); published again by Kobelski (1981) 24–36.
[9] Berger (1973).

The rather complex discussion in this chapter will be easier to follow if we anticipate our major conclusions immediately. The hypothesis to be offered is that there were two different versions of the story of the debate over the body of Moses, one in the Testament of Moses and another in the Assumption of Moses. This hypothesis, which has not been proposed before, makes much better sense of the evidence than any other. It contrasts with the hitherto usual procedure, followed by Charles,[10] James[11] and Loewenstamm,[12] which was to assemble all the various details of a debate between Michael and the devil at the death of Moses which are given in a variety of texts, together with related information in these texts, and to combine them all in the reconstruction of a single story. Careful reading of such reconstructions shows the procedure to be implausible. It results in an improbably complicated, indeed incoherent story, whose purpose is impossible to grasp. It is also very difficult to see why certain of the texts which are supposed to be dependent on this comprehensive narrative have selected only the details they include and not others. Once the texts are examined to see whether there might not have been more than one story of the debate over Moses' body, they divide quite easily into two groups of texts, each of which provides a coherent account in its own terms but which cannot without confusion be combined with the other.

The first story, which is based on four texts (A–D below) and which can be assigned to the Testament of Moses, can be reconstructed as follows:

> Joshua accompanied Moses up Mount Nebo, where God showed Moses the land of promise. Moses then sent Joshua back, saying, 'Go down to the people and tell them that Moses is dead.' When Joshua had gone down to the people, Moses died. God sent the archangel Michael to remove the body of Moses to another place and to bury it there, but Samma'el, the devil, opposed him, disputing Moses' right to honourable burial. (The

[10] Charles (1897) 105–107.
[11] James (1920) 48–49.
[12] Loewenstamm (1976) 209–210.

text may also have said that the devil wished to take the body down to the people, so that they would make it an object of worship.) Michael and the devil engaged in a dispute over the body. The devil slandered Moses, charging him with murder, because he slew the Egyptian and hid his body in the sand [Exod 2:11–12]. But Michael, not tolerating the slander against Moses, said, 'May the Lord rebuke you, Satan!' At that the devil took flight, and Michael removed the body to the place commanded by God. Thus no one saw the burial-place of Moses.

The main point of this story is to highlight the supreme worthiness of Moses in the sight of God – a common theme in Jewish traditions about Moses. The biblical account provided at least one apparent blemish on Moses' record: his killing of the Egyptian. That this was a problem to Jewish exegetes we can see from Josephus, who omits to mention it when he explains Moses' flight from Egypt (*Ant.* 2:254), and from Philo, who justifies Moses' action (*Mos.* 1:44). In our story Satan, in his traditional role of malicious accuser, brings this incident forward as a charge of murder against Moses, which, if sustained, would have rendered Moses unworthy of honourable burial. But Moses' advocate, the archangel Michael, considers the charge slanderous and appeals to God's judgment to vindicate Moses from it. The devil, knowing the charge will not be upheld by God, departs. Thus Moses is deemed worthy of the unique honour of burial by God's archangel Michael.

Of course, according to Deuteronomy 34:6 (MT), it was God himself who buried Moses. Later rabbinic traditions lay great stress on this burial by God ('none other than God himself,' according to m. Soṭa 1:9) as testimony to Moses' supreme worthiness.[13] Our story, in ascribing the burial to Michael, is typical of the intertestamental (pre-rabbinic) Jewish literature which commonly introduces angels as God's agents in actions which the Old Testament attributes directly to God. (Deut 34:6 LXX ['they buried'] may already intend angelic agents of Moses' burial.[14]) Thus, although it is

---

[13] Haacker and Schäfer (1974) 165.

[14] For Moses' burial by angels, see also Tg. Ps-Jon. Deut 34:6 (God *and* his angels); Epiphanius, *Pan.* 9:4:13; Falasha *Death of Moses* in Leslau (1951) 111; Armenian *History of Moses* in Stone (1973) 120 (Michael).

preserved in late texts, our story arguably belongs to a pre-rabbinic stage of Jewish traditions about the death of Moses.

If, as is likely but not certain, the original story included the additional motif of Satan's wish to claim the body for himself so that he could make it an idol for the people of Israel, then the story also served the secondary function of explaining why, according to Deuteronomy 34:6, Moses' grave remained secret. Michael removed the body to a secret place of burial as a precaution against the kind of idolatrous reverence for the body which the devil wished to promote.

It should be noticed that in this story, although the burial of Moses is extraordinary, the death of Moses is entirely normal and raises no problem for the author. There is no trace of that resistance to the idea that Moses should have to submit to the common fate of sinful humanity, which is found in so many Jewish traditions about the death of Moses.[15] There is no trace of the idea of Moses' bodily assumption to heaven, which seems to have been current in some circles as early as the first century A.D.[16] There is no trace of the idea of Moses' own reluctance to die, or of the unwillingness of the angels and the inability of the angel of death to receive his soul, which were elaborated in rabbinic traditions (e.g. Sifre Deut. 305; Deut. R. 11:10; Midrash Peṭir-at Moshe).[17] There is not even any interest in the ascent of Moses' soul to heaven.[18] In this account the death of Moses is straightforwardedly related, and the interest focuses on the burial of his corpse. This may be another indication of an originally very early story, surviving now in late sources.

Since this story does not describe any kind of assumption of Moses, it is plainly not from the work called the Assumption of Moses, but it could well be from the Testament of

---

[15] See especially Loewenstamm (1976).

[16] This idea is reflected, though countered, in the accounts of Moses' death in Josephus, *Ant.* 4:326 and LAB 19:16; see Haacker and Schäfer (1974) 155–156; Loewenstamm (1976) 197–198; and rabbinic passages in Haacker and Schäfer (1974) 170–174; Strack and Billerbeck (1922) 754–755.

[17] That these traditions are very old is shown by Chazon (1985–86).

[18] As in texts O, P, Q, R in section III below.

Moses. A good case can also be made for identifying it as the lost conclusion to the work in the Milan manuscript:

(1) In the text of the Milan manuscript, Moses' imminent death and burial are prominent, so that we should expect it to have ended with an account of Moses' death and burial. Moreover, the work is plainly a testament in form,[19] and Jewish testaments commonly end with an account of the subject's death and burial.[20]

(2) The attitude to Moses' death in the text of the Milan manuscript is in keeping with that in our story. Moses expects his coming death (sleeping with his fathers) in a perfectly matter-of-fact way, accepting it without argument (1:15; 10:12, 14) and without implying that there should be anything out of the ordinary about it. In this respect, the Milan text and our story are not only in keeping with each other, but also (as we have seen) unusual among the various Jewish traditions about the death of Moses. (One feature of the Milan text which could suggest otherwise – the presence of the word *receptione*, which could mean 'assumption,' in 10:12 – will be discussed later.)

(3) Though the text of the Milan manuscript does not suggest anything remarkable about the death of Moses, it does suggest a unique form of burial. Joshua, lamenting the prospect of Moses' departure, asks: 'What place will receive you or where will be the marker of your sepulchre? Or who as a [mere] man will dare to move your body from place to place? For all who die according to their age there are sepulchres in their lands, but your sepulchre is from the rising to the setting of the sun, and from the south to the limits of the north: the whole world is your sepulchre' (11:5–8). Thus

---

[19] Vegas Montaner (1987) 232–237.

[20] Charlesworth (1985) 76, objects that some testaments (e.g. some of the Testaments of the Twelve Patriarchs) conclude with only a brief reference to the death and burial of the subject. But it is true that testaments nearly always end with some account, however brief, of the subject's death and burial (Testament of Solomon, which has no narrative framework, is an exception). In Moses' case, the nature of the biblical account of his death and burial (Deut 34:1–8) would have virtually demanded more than a bare reference to these events.

Moses' greatness suggests to Joshua that he cannot, like other people, be buried by human beings in a known grave. In particular, the suggestion that no human being will dare to move Moses' body from place to place (11:7) should be compared with the information in our story that the archangel Michael moved Moses' body to another place for burial. Though Moses' lack of a known grave is known from the Bible, the idea of the moving of his dead body is at any rate not explicit in the Bible, though it might be thought to be implied (Deut 34:5–6).

(4) The role of Joshua in our story coheres well with his role in the text of the Milan manuscript. In our story Joshua accompanies Moses up the mountain before Moses sends him down again. This feature does not derive from the Bible and is rare in the traditions about Moses' death,[21] but it follows on well from the text in the Milan manuscript, where it is Joshua whom Moses addresses throughout, who is commissioned to succeed Moses (10:15), who responds with consternation to the news that Moses must die (11) and has to be reassured by Moses (13).

(5) The roles of Michael and the devil in our story are at least consistent with the only mention of good and bad angels in the text of the Milan manuscript. In the eschatological section of Moses' prophecy, it is predicted that 'the devil will come to an end' (10:1), and that 'the angel who is in the highest place appointed . . . will at once avenge them of their enemies' (10:2). Most commentators identify this angel as Michael, as in Daniel 12:2. This final victory of the chief of the good angels over the chief of the evil angels presupposes an age-long conflict between the two, in which their contest over the body of Moses would be a significant episode.

Thus it seems probable that this first story of the dispute over the body of Moses derives from the lost ending of the work in the Milan manuscript, and that this work should be

---

[21] But cf. Josephus, *Ant.* 4:326: Eleazar and Joshua accompany Moses up the mountain, and a cloud removes him from their sight. Text O in section III below (and therefore probably the Assumption of Moses) presupposes that Joshua and Caleb had accompanied Moses up the mountain.

identified as the Testament of Moses. The second story, based on eleven texts (G–I, K–R below), can be reconstructed as follows:

> When Moses died on the mountain, God sent the archangel Michael to remove his body to another place and to bury it. But the devil resisted him, and, wishing to deceive, said, 'The body is mine, for I am the Master of matter'. Michael replied that God is the Master of matter, 'for from his holy spirit we were all created ... From the face of God his Spirit went forth, and the world was made' [cf. Ps 33(32):6; 104:30]. The devil is not the rightful lord of the material world, but a rebel who gained his power over humanity when he inspired the serpent to tempt Adam and Eve to sin. Finally, Michael said, 'May the Lord rebuke you!,' thereby appealing to the judgment of the Lord who is 'the Lord of the spirits and of all flesh' [cf. Num 16:22; 27:16 LXX], and therefore Lord of the devil himself and of the material world.
>
> [Probably the text went on to tell how] Joshua and Caleb, lifted up by the Spirit into the air, were able to witness the burial and assumption of Moses. Caleb, descending more quickly than Joshua, saw less of this. They saw the angels taking up Moses in two forms: the dead body was honourably buried in a mountain valley, while the spiritual Moses ascended to heaven accompanied by angels. [The text may have added that Joshua heard a new name, Melchi, being given to Moses upon his arrival in heaven.] Joshua then descended to earth again and told the people about the glory of Moses which he had witnessed.

Some of the material in the first paragraph of this account is explicitly ascribed to the Assumption of Moses by Origen and Gelasius (texts I and K below) and so we are in no doubt about the source of this story. The material in the second paragraph is given by Clement and Origen, who do not name their source, but since both knew the Assumption of Moses it is a fairly safe guess that it comes from the same source, especially as it actually describes an assumption of Moses.[22] Moreover, the kind of assumption it describes is not

---

[22] It is perhaps worth raising the possibility that the 'assumption' to which the title refers was not at or after death, but before death, a temporary visit of Moses to heaven, like that of Isaiah in the Ascension of Isaiah.

a bodily assumption, but an assumption of Moses' spirit, leaving his body to be buried. It is therefore a kind of assumption which is compatible with a story about a contest for Moses' dead body by Michael and the devil.

The debate over the body in this version has a quite different character and purpose from what it has in the version we have ascribed to the Testament of Moses. The devil here is no longer the accuser of sinners, attempting to establish Moses' guilt. Rather he claims to be the lord of the material world and to have a right to Moses' body for that reason. In other words, he is portrayed as a kind of Gnostic demiurge – or, rather, as claiming falsely to be a demiurge. Michael's refutation of this claim is the anti-Gnostic assertion that the one God, to whom the devil himself is subject, created the material world. The whole concern of this story is debate with Gnostic dualism.

The original ending of the work in the Milan manuscript cannot have contained this material, for the following reasons: (1) The text of the Milan manuscript does not, as we have seen, lead us to expect an assumption narrative of this kind. (2) The work in the Milan manuscript is generally agreed to be a Palestinian[23] Jewish work of the early first century A.D.[24] (Some think it was originally written in the Maccabean period and revised in the first century A.D.[25]) It is unlikely that a work of such a date should contain this kind

In extant traditions of Moses' ascent to heaven during his lifetime the ascension usually takes place at Sinai (see the traditions discussed in Schultz [1971]; also 3 Enoch 15B:2–5; 48:D4; while the ascension described in the Revelation of Moses translated in Gaster [1925] 125–141, takes place during the theophany at the burning bush). Some traditions (LAB 19:10) elaborate on the idea of Moses' sight of the land from Nebo, but they do not make it an ascension to heaven. (But see Ginzberg [1911] 446–448, for a medieval account of Moses' ascension to heaven before death on the day of his death.) In the absence of evidence for such a tradition in the patristic period, it is most likely that the Assumption of Moses known to the Fathers described an assumption at death.

[23] Denis (1970B) 135.

[24] For bibliography in favour of this date, see Denis (1970B) 135 n. 38; and add Priest (1983) 920–921; Vegas Montaner (1987) 228–231.

[25] Nickelsburg (1976); (1981) 80–83, 212–214.

of refutation of Gnostic dualism. (3) The account of the burial
of Moses' body and the assumption of his spirit to heaven is
quite closely paralleled in the Testament of Abraham, the
Testament of Job, and the Life of Adam and Eve. These
Jewish works are of uncertain date but are generally thought
to originate in the diaspora and to be more hellenistic in
character than the work in the Milan manuscript. Thus the
Assumption of Moses from which this second story comes
and which was known to the Alexandrian Fathers (its earliest
attestation is in Clement of Alexandria) seems best regarded
as a work of the second century A.D., perhaps originating in
Egypt.

It is not difficult, even apart from this conclusion about the
date of the second story, to tell which of the two stories Jude
knew. Only the first story refers to the devil's *slander*
(βλασφημία) against Moses, and it is that catchword βλασφημία
which Jude picks up (vv 8, 10) and which accounts for his
use of this story in verse 9. On the other hand, it is not
difficult to see why the Alexandrian Fathers, if the second
story were the only one they knew, should assume that this
was Jude's source. It includes a dispute between Michael and
the devil over Moses' body, along with the crucial words,
'May the Lord rebuke you!' as in Jude 9. But we need no
longer be mesmerized by the authority of the Alexandrian
Fathers in identifying Jude's source.

II. The evidence for the story Jude knew

So far no evidence has been given for our reconstruction
of Jude's source in verse 9. But before examining in detail the
four texts on which it is based, we need first to sketch the
general background to the story, in a genre of similar stories,
since this will aid the critical study of the texts.

The earliest example of this kind of contest between the
devil and the chief of the angels is the vision in Zechariah
3:1–5, from which Michael's words to the devil, 'May the
Lord rebuke you!,' in Jude's source derived. (In the MT of
Zech 3:5 these words are attributed, oddly, to Yahweh himself, but the author of Jude's source must have read 'the angel

of Yahweh' in his text of Zech 3:5.[26]) The vision is a courtroom scene, in which the accusing angel, the adversary (*sāṭān*),
and the angel of the Lord confront each other in a legal
dispute in which the defendant is the high priest Joshua.
Evidently Joshua's guilt, as representative of Israel, has placed
him in the power of Satan his accuser. When the angel of the
Lord, as the Lord's representative, silences Satan with the
words, 'May the Lord rebuke you, Satan,' he dismisses Satan's
case against Joshua by invoking the Lord's authority over
Satan. As Kee observes,[27] the translation 'rebuke' is somewhat
weak: גער here denotes more than a reprimand. It refers to
God's commanding word which asserts his authority over
Satan, delivering Joshua and his people from Satan's power
(cf. Pss 9:5; 68:30; Isa 17:13; Mal 3:11).[28]

The idea of a legal contest governs the subsequent tradition
in which the contest between Satan and the angel of the Lord
is applied to other episodes in the history of Israel. The book
of Jubilees provides several examples of this. Thus Jubilees
17:15–18:16 tells the story of the sacrifice of Isaac within the
framework of a heavenly trial of Abraham (cf. Job 1–2), in
which the prince Mastema (= משטמה, 'hostility'),[29] i.e.
Satan, again appears as accuser, arguing that Abraham's faithfulness should be tested. When Abraham proves faithful, it is
the angel of the presence who intervenes to save Isaac, while
'Prince Mastema was shamed' (Jub 18:12).[30]

In chapter 48 the idea of the contest between Satan and the
angel is used to illuminate the career of Moses and the exodus.
According to 48:2–3, it was the prince Mastema (not God, as
in Exod 4:24) who tried to kill Moses, and it was the angel of

---

[26] As in the Peshitta.

[27] Kee (1968) 239.

[28] See Kee's discussion of גער: (1968) 235–238.

[29] For the term, cf. 1QM 13:11; CD 16:5: מלאך משטמה: 'the angel of hostility.'

[30] Cf. also Gen. R. 56:4, where Samma'el tempts Abraham on his way
to sacrifice Isaac; and Yalqut Rubeni 43:3, quoted by Chaine (1939) 311:
'When Isaac was bound, there was a debate between Michael and Satan.
Michael brought a ram to free Isaac, but Satan wanted to keep him off so
that Isaac should be sacrificed.'

the presence who delivered Moses from his power (48:5). Though Satan's role as accuser is not explicit here, it is probably implicit, for it was Moses' failure to circumcise his son (Exod 4:25) which put him into Satan's power.

Then the prince Mastema opposed Moses in his confrontation with Pharaoh and aided the Egyptian magicians against him (48:9), while the angels of the presence assisted Moses by destroying them (48:11). This particular confrontation is also recalled by the Damascus Rule (CD 5:17–18): 'Moses and Aaron arose by the hand of the Prince of lights and Satan in his cunning raised up Jannes and his brother.'[31] However, according to Jubilees, the victory over the magicians did not yet result in the 'shaming' of Satan (48:12) because he took further action: the Egyptians' pursuit of Israel (48:12, 16–17). The angels then delivered Israel from him at the Red Sea (48:13). Again it should be noticed that in this account Satan's power against Israel seems to rest on his power to 'accuse them' (48:15, 18): as the leader of the forces of evil against the good angels he has not yet lost his legal function of accusation (cf. also Rev 12:10).

These stories provide the principal background for the story to which Jude 9 alludes. It fits readily into the same pattern.[32] At Moses' death, Satan makes a last attempt to assert his power over him, by accusing him of the murder of the Egyptian. Michael silences Satan by his appeal to God to assert his authority against Satan's malicious accusation ('May the Lord rebuke you!'), and thereby not only rescues Moses' body from Satan's power, but also vindicates Moses as the servant of God against Satan's attempt to claim him as a sinner.

Another text which clearly belongs in broadly the same

[31] Translated Vermes (1987) 87.

[32] My colleague George Brooke has argued that at Qumran the three works Jubilees, the Temple Scroll (11QT) and the Testament of Moses may have formed a single sequence, a kind of alternative Pentateuch, with a narrative extending from creation to the death of Moses and including the Mosaic law. Since later Christians were not interested in the legal material, they did not preserve the Temple Scroll, with the result that Jubilees and the Testament of Moses were separated.

tradition is 4QAmram, in which Moses' father Amram relates a dream in which he saw two angels engaged in a legal dispute over him.[33] The two angels are the two chief angels, the Prince of light and the Prince of darkness (though these titles do not survive in the extant text). One of the names of the latter is given as Melkireša' (4QAmr[b] 2:3); his counterpart was almost certainly called Melchizedek and one of his other names (since he is said to have had three: 3:2) may have been Michael.[34] The dispute is plainly over whether Amram is a 'son of light,' under the authority of the Prince of light, or a 'son of darkness,' under the authority of the Prince of darkness. Milik and Kobelski[35] both assume that it concerns Amram's fate at death, but the surviving text, as Noll also points out,[36] really gives no ground for thinking this. The vision took place during Amram's stay in Hebron, after which he returned to Egypt, and so some time before his death.[37]

At one point the text is strikingly close to Jude 9: 'behold, two of them were disputing about me . . . and they were holding a great contest [תגר – a legal dispute[38]] over me' (4QAmr 1:10–11; cf. Jude 9: διακρινόμενος διελέγετο). The similarity is not accidental, but we need not conclude, as Milik does,[39] that Jude's source was inspired by 4QAmram. The similarity can be adequately explained by the broader tradition of contests between the devil and the chief of the angels, in which the courtroom context of legal dispute, accusation and defence, gives rise to this kind of language.

Berger sought to link both 4QAmram and Jude 9 to a tradition in which two angels, or sometimes two groups of angels, contend for possession of the departed soul at death. For this tradition he marshalls a wealth of evidence from later Christian apocalyptic texts, though not from any text

[33] Cf. Milik (1972) 85.
[34] Milik (1972) 45; Kobelski (1981) 36, cf. 77–83.
[35] Kobelski (1981) 24, 77.
[36] Noll (1979) 85.
[37] Milik (1972) 85.
[38] See Milik (1972) 80; Kobelski (1981) 29, for the legal connotation of the word.
[39] Milik (1972) 95.

which is definitely as old as Jude. (TAsher 6:4–6 may be early evidence for his tradition, but the earliest indisputable evidence is Origen's quotation from an apocryphal text about the death of Abraham: *Hom. 35 on Luke.*) Clearly what he has identified is one specific form (a sub-tradition) which the tradition of contests between the devil and the angel took in relation to the fate of the soul at death. He recognizes that Jude 9, which is not about the fate of the soul at death, must represent an adaptation of the tradition for a specific purpose.[40] But it is better to see Jude 9 as a specific instance of the *general* tradition of contests between the devil and the angel, 4QAmram as another specific instance of this general tradition, and Berger's tradition of texts about the fate of the soul at death as a particular form which that tradition took, perhaps at a date later than the time of writing of Jude's source and certainly without any direct relation to Jude's source. Again the recurrence of the idea of dispute[41] (among Berger's texts, note especially: Origen, *Hom. 35: super Abrahae salute et interitu disceptantes;* Syriac ApPaul 11: 'a dispute between those good angels and those bad angels'[42]) derives from the common dependence on the general tradition, rather than from a dependence by Jude 9 on the specific tradition identified by Berger.

We turn to the four texts which preserve to some extent the content of Jude's source, the lost ending of the Testament of Moses:

A. *Palaea Historica.*

Περὶ τῆς τελευτῆς Μωϋσέως. Καὶ εἶπεν Μωϋσῆς πρὸς Ἰησοῦν τοῦ Ναυί· ἀνέλθωμεν ἐν τῷ ὄρει. καὶ ἀνελθόντων αὐτῶν εἶδεν Μωϋσῆς τὴν γῆν ἐπαγγελίας καὶ εἶπεν πρὸς αὐτόν· κάτελθε πρὸς τὸν λαὸν καὶ ἀνάγγειλον αὐτοῖς ὅτι Μωϋσῆς ἐτελεύτησεν. καὶ κατῆλθεν Ἰησοῦς πρὸς τὸν λαόν, ὁ δὲ Μωϋσῆς τὰ τέλη τοῦ βίου ἐκτήσατο. Καὶ ἐπειρᾶτο Σαμουὴλ ὡς ἂν καταβάσῃ τὸ σκύνωμα αὐτοῦ τῷ λαῷ ἵνα θεοποιηθῶσιν αὐτόν, Μιχαὴλ δὲ ὁ

---

[40] Berger (1973) 12–16, 18.
[41] Berger (1973) 16–17.
[42] Berger (1973) 7.

ἀρχιστράτηγος προστάξει θεοῦ ἦλθεν λαβειν αὐτό(ν) καὶ συνστεῖλαι, καὶ ἀνθίστατο αὐτῷ Σαμουὴλ καὶ διεμάχοντο. ἀγανακτήσας οὖν ὁ ἀρχιστράτηγος ἐμετίμησεν αὐτὸν εἰπών· ἐπιτιμᾷ σε Κύριος, διάβολε. καὶ οὕτως ἡττήθη ὁ ἀντικείμενος καὶ φυγὴν ἐχρήσατο, ὁ δὲ ἀρχάγγελος Μιχαὴλ συνέστειλεν τὸ σκύνωμα Μωϋσῆ ὅπου προσετάχθη παρὰ θεοῦ τοῦ Χριστοῦ ἡμῶν [καὶ οὐδεις εἶδεν τὴν ταφὴν Μωσέως].[43]

Of the death of Moses. And Moses said to Jesus the son of Nave, 'Let us go up into the mountain.' And when they had gone up, Moses saw the land of promise, and he said to Jesus, 'Go down to the people and tell them that Moses is dead.' And Jesus went down to the people, but Moses came to the end of his life. And Samuel (Σαμουήλ) tried to bring his body (σκύνωμα) down to the people, so that they might make him (it) a god. But Michael the chief captain by the command of God came to take him (it) and remove him (it), and Samuel resisted him, and they fought. So the chief captain was angry and rebuked him, saying, 'May the Lord rebuke you, devil!' And so the adversary was defeated and took flight, but the archangel Michael removed the body of Moses to the place where he was commanded by Christ our God, and no one saw the burial-place of Moses.[44]

The Palaea Historica is a Byzantine collection of biblical legends, which has received very little attention. Flusser's brief study at least shows that it preserves ancient Jewish traditions and that at least some of these derive from ancient apocryphal works.[45] What we know of the character of the work makes it quite plausible that its account of the contest over the body of Moses could derive from the Testament of Moses.

The text is almost certainly independent of Jude 9. The only vocabulary in common is the obvious words διαβόλος and ἀρχάγγελος, and Michael's words of rebuke, though even here the grammatical form is different, while the addition of διάβολε shows that the words derive directly from Zechariah 3:2 independently of Jude 9.[46] Moreover,

---

[43] Text in Vassiliev (1893) 257–258. My translation reflects the *v.l.* αὐτό in line 6.

[44] My translation.

[45] Flusser (1971).

[46] διάβολε is used in Zech 3:2 LXX to translate ‏השטן‎. However, the rest of the

whereas Jude's whole point is that Michael himself did *not* rebuke the devil, but appealed to the Lord to rebuke him, the Palaea Historica says that Michael *rebuked* the devil in these words.

Several features of this text should be noticed: (1) Features which have already been discussed in section I above are the unproblematic nature of Moses' death in this account, the role of Joshua and the burial by the archangel rather than by God himself. These distinguish the account from rabbinic traditions, with which there are nevertheless some contacts (2 and 3 below).

(2) The name Σαμουήλ is not really Samuel but Samma'el, a name by which the devil is known in the Ascension of Isaiah (where in 1:8 he is identified with Malkira, i.e. the Melkireša' of 4QAmram, and in 11:41 with Satan) and from rabbinic sources ('the chief of all the satans': Deut. R. 11:10). In rabbinic traditions of Moses' death he appears as the angel of death, commanded by God to take Moses' soul but unable to do so. A remnant of his dispute with Michael survives in these traditions, but transposed from the context of Moses' burial to that of his death (Midrash Peṭirat Moshe 11;[47] Deut. R. 11:10).

(3) The removal of Moses' body (συνστέλλειν must here mean 'remove,' despite the rarity of this meaning[48]) – to be buried elsewhere – corresponds to the tradition to be found in Targum Pseudo-Jonathan to Deuteronomy 34:6 and Sifre Deuteronomy 335, in which God and his angels carry the body four miles from the place of Moses' death to bury it.[49] This feature is intended to explain Deuteronomy 34:6.

(4) Alone among the texts to be considered in this section, this account represents the contest between Michael and the devil as a physical conflict rather than as a verbal dispute in which Satan brings accusations. Michael is portrayed in his military capacity as the chief captain of the angelic armies

words of rebuke in the Palaea Historica show that they are not dependent on LXX, but presumably on a Semitic source dependent on Zech 3:2.

[47] Abraham (1926) 99.
[48] Cf. Lampe (1961) 1350, *s.v.* B4.
[49] See Haacker and Schäfer (1974) 165–166.

(ἀρχιστράτηγος), and he and the devil fight (διεμάχοντο). This makes Michael's words, 'May the Lord rebuke you!,' taken from a context of legal dispute (Zech 3:2), less appropriate. Admittedly Michael's military role is a very ancient one (Dan 10:13, 21), while Revelation 12:7–11 shows that Satan's ancient role as prosecuting counsel could still be remembered in a context of military conflict between Michael and the devil. But since, in the Palaea Historica, the physical combat takes the place which our other texts (B–D below) give to Satan's accusation against Moses, and since the figure of Michael became increasingly militarized in Byzantine Christian tradition,[50] the military theme should probably be seen as a secondary intrusion into the tradition, replacing a legal dispute over Moses' guilt. The motif of the devil's resistance (which recurs in texts, E, M, and N) probably derives from Daniel 10:13.

(5) This text is alone in suggesting that Satan tried to take Moses' body to the people for them to worship it, but the idea that Moses' grave was unknown so that idolatrous use should not be made of it is a widespread feature of the traditions about Moses' burial.[51] Moreover, it is possible that Testament of Moses 11:7 already hints at the danger of the deification of Moses' body. However, it may be that this feature in our text A belongs with the secondary development of the military theme. It is hard to tell whether it is an original feature of the tradition.

B. *Slavonic Life of Moses 16*

But at the end of the same year in the twelfth month, on the seventh day (that is, in March), Moses the servant of God died and was buried on the fourth of the month September on a certain mountain by the Chief Captain (*Archistrategos*) Michael. For the devil contended with the angel, and would not permit his body to be buried, saying, 'Moses is a murderer. He slew a

---

[50] Rohland (1977).

[51] Midrash Leqaḥ Tov, cited by Loewenstamm (1976) 204; Origen, *Selecta in Num.* (PG 12:578B); Theodoret of Cyrus, *Quaest. in Deut.* 32 (PG 80:447C); Armenian *History of Moses* (Stone [1973] 120). Josephus, *Ant.* 4:326 hints at the danger of deification, though not in relation to the burial of the body.

man in Egypt and hid him in the sand.' Then Michael prayed to God and there was thunder and lightning and suddenly the devil disappeared; but Michael buried him with his (own) hands.[52]

Turdeanu has shown that the Slavonic *Life of Moses* is a fifteenth-century version of the medieval Hebrew *Chronicle of Moses*, similar to that in the *Chronicles of Jerahmeel*. The episode of the dispute over Moses' body is not found in *Jerahmeel*, and Turdeanu regards it as an interpolation in the original *Chronicle*, but an interpolation made in the Hebrew *Chronicle* before its translation.[53] Beyond this we know nothing about the transmission of the story and must consider it on its own merits.

This text, again independent of Jude 9[54] and also, it seems, of the account in the Palaea Historica, is of interest mainly because it preserves the devil's accusation against Moses. Whereas in text A the legal dispute has been largely transformed into a physical combat, in B the legal context is preserved through the retention of the devil's charge. The devil retains his ancient role of accuser. This must be an original feature of the tradition, not only on the general grounds that Satan retains his accusing role in the general background to Jude 9, as we have seen, but more specifically because the words of the archangel, 'May the Lord rebuke you!,' must originally have been a reply to Satan's accusation, as they are in Zech 3:1–2. It is an impressive indication of the complementary value of the divergent accounts A and B, that A preserves the archangel's words without the accusation, whereas B preserves the accusation without the archangel's reply. The accusation from B and the archangel's reply from A together form a coherent summary of the dispute. We may therefore be confident that the devil's charge of murder formed part of the lost ending of the Testament of Moses which Jude read.

---

[52] Translation in James (1920) 47–48, from the German translation in Bonwetsch (1908) 607, but I have corrected the opening words according to the suggestion of Turdeanu (1967) 55.

[53] Turdeanu (1967) 51.

[54] According to Turdeanu (1967) 61, the later revision of the Slavonic *Life of Moses*, the *Tolkovaja Paleja*, expands the account of the dispute by recourse to Jude 9.

The loss of Michael's words in B probably indicates that the tradition had lost sight of their significance as a way of ruling the devil's accusation out of court. In order to remove the devil, the tradition has had to introduce instead the thunder and lightning, which are therefore a secondary feature.[55] (Not only Zech 3:2, but also LAE 39:1 and b. Qidd. 81, show that the words 'May the Lord rebuke you!,' were alone sufficient to silence and dismiss the devil.[56])

C. *(Pseudo-) Oecumenius, In Jud. 9*[57]

Λέγεται τὸν Μιχαὴλ τὸν ἀρχάγγελον τῇ τοῦ Μωϋσέως ταφῇ δεδιηκονηκέται. τοῦ γὰρ διαβόλου τοῦτο μὴ καταδεχομένου, ἀλλ' ἐπιφέροντος ἔγκλημα διὰ τὸν τοῦ Αἰγυπτίου φόνου αἰτίου[58] ὄντος τοῦ Μωϋσέως, καὶ τοῦτο μὴ συγχωρεῖσθαι αὐτῷ τυχεῖν τῆς ἐντίμου ταφῆς.[59]

It is said that Michael the archangel served the burial of Moses. For the devil would not accept this, but brought an accusation because of the murder of the Egyptian, on the grounds that Moses was guilty of it, and because of this would not allow him to receive honourable burial.[60]

D. *From Cramer's Catena*

Τελευτήσαντος ἐν τῷ ὄρει Μωϋσέως, ὁ Μιχαὴλ ἀποστέλλεται μεταθήσων τὸ σῶμα, εἶτα τοῦ διαβόλου κατὰ τοῦ Μωϋσέως βλασφημοῦντος, καὶ φονέα ἀναγορεύοντος διὰ τὸ πατάξαι τὸν Αἰγύπτιον, οὐκ ἐνέγκων τὴν κατ' αὐτοῦ βλασφημίαν ὁ Ἄγγελος,

[55] James (1920) 48, says: 'The mention of the thunder and lightning does occur also in a Greek note which I have read in a recent German comment on Jude, but unfortunately cannot now trace.' Probably James was remembering this same passage from the Slavonic *Life of Moses*, given in German translation in Windisch's commentary (later edition: 1951).

[56] On these texts, see Bauckham (1983A) 62. Note also the frequent quotation of Zech 3:2 on Aramaic incantation bowls: Aune (1986) 217; Naveh and Shaked (1985) 40–41 (A1:5–6), 184–185 (B11:5–6).

[57] Whether this is an authentic work of Oecumenius is doubtful (see Denis [1970B] 129 n. 9) but unimportant for our purposes.

[58] MS αὐτοῦ, corrected following Hilgenfeld (1868) 299: the text as it stands is meaningless.

[59] Text in Denis (1970A) 67.

[60] My translation.

"ἐπιτιμήσαι σοι ὁ Θεὸς" πρὸς τὸν διάβολον ἔφη.[61]

When Moses died on the mountain, Michael was sent to remove the body. When the devil slandered Moses and proclaimed him a murderer because he smote the Egyptian, the angel, not tolerating the slander against him, said to the devil, 'May God rebuke you!'[62]

The material in these two comments on Jude 9 recurs in several scholia and anonymous comments in the catenae[63] (including texts M and N below). It represents the material in the Testament of Moses which was thought necessary for the understanding of Jude 9. The points of contact with A and B should be noticed: D agrees with A that Michael's mission was to remove the body (for burial elsewhere); both agree with B on the devil's accusation. It is also important for the exegesis of Jude 9 to notice that D refers to the devil's charge as βλασφημία against Moses.

These four texts are the only reliable sources of information about the content of the source of Jude 9. However, two further texts, which might at first sight seem to be related to them and which have been treated as evidence for the content of Jude's source, must be examined. They will prove to be no more than attempts to explain Jude 9 by authors who knew nothing more about the dispute over the body of Moses than they read in Jude 9.

E. *Severus of Antioch*

Here [in Deut 34] by means of a bodily image God set forth a mystery which occurs concerning the soul. For when the soul separates from the body, after its departure hence both good angelic powers and a very evil band of demons come to meet it, so that according to the quality of the deeds, evil and good, which it has done, either one group or the other may carry it off to the appropriate place, to be guarded until the last day, when

---

[61] Text in Cramer (1844) 163, lines 18–22; cf. also Charles (1897) 109–111; Denis (1970A) 67.

[62] My translation.

[63] See Denis (1970A) 67.

we shall all be presented for judgment, and led away either to eternal life or to the unending flame of fire. God, wishing to show this also to the children of Israel by means of a certain bodily image, ordained that at the burial of Moses, at the time of the dressing of the body and its customary depositing in the earth, there should appear before their eyes the evil demon as it were resisting and opposing, and that Michael, a good angel, should encounter and repel him, and should not rebuke him on his own authority, but retire from passing judgment against him in favour of the Lord of all, and say, 'May the Lord rebuke you!,' in order that by means of these things those who are being instructed might learn that there is a conflict over our souls after their departure hence and that it is necessary to prepare oneself by means of good deeds in order to secure the angels as allies, when the demons are gibbering jealously and bitterly against us. And when this divine image had appeared before their eyes, it seems that then some cloud or shining of light came upon that place, obscuring it and walling it off from the onlookers, so that they might not know his grave. Therefore also the holy Scripture says in Deuteronomy, 'And Moses the servant of the Lord died there in the land of Moab by the word of the Lord. And they buried him in the land of Moab near the house of Phogor. And no one saw his death (or, his grave) until this day' [Deut 34:5–6]. . . . These things, it is said, are found in an apocryphal book which contains the more detailed account (λεπτοτέραν ἀφήγηριν) of the genesis or creation.[64]

The following features of this passage should be noticed: (1) The explicit statement that Michael, in saying 'May the Lord rebuke you!,' was refraining from giving a judgment on his own authority, looks very much as though it depends on Jude's own interpretation of his source in Jude 9, rather than on the source itself. It was Jude's use of the source, rather than the source's own interest, which required this point to be made explicit.

(2) In explaining that the contest between Michael and the

---

[64] My translation from the Greek text in Cramer (1844) 161, line 20–162, line 17; and partly in James (1892) 17, whose text includes the last sentence, not in Cramer. With this text, cf. also Cramer (1844) 161, lines 9–18, attributed to Severus in James (1920) 46; and the further quotations from Severus in Cramer (1844) 162, lines 17–30; 162, line 31–163, line 10.

devil was shown to the people to teach them what happens to the soul at death, Severus draws on the tradition represented by the texts which Berger has assembled (discussed above). It is, however, an unsatisfactory use of the story of the contest, which was over Moses' body, not his soul. It must be regarded as a homiletical explanation of the story in Jude 9, rather than derived from the source of Jude 9.

(3) There is only one feature of the passage which derives neither from Jude 9 itself nor from the tradition of the angelic contest for the souls of the dead. This is the idea of the dazzling cloud which prevented the onlookers from seeing where Moses is buried. This is found in other accounts (Josephus, *Ant.* 4:326; *Memar Marqah* 5:3;[65] quotation from 'an apocryphal and mystical codex' in a catena[66]), and was evidently a fairly widespread tradition. In other accounts, however, the cloud hides Moses from view already *before* he dies. In Severus' account it has been transposed to follow the dispute between Michael and the devil, since the latter is represented as a public spectacle. The transposition is evident in the quotation from Deuteronomy 34:5–6, which is quoted in a form designed to show that no one saw Moses *die* (τελευτήν), but is then glossed according to the more usual form of the text, to convey the sense that no one saw his burial or grave (ταφήν).

(4) Severus apparently ascribes his account to the book of Jubilees (also known as *Leptogenesis*).[67] This must be a mistake, but Severus seems to have had his information at secondhand, at best. Moreover, the information which he claims to derive from an apocryphal book need not be the whole passage, but only the sentence about the cloud of light, together with the quotation from Deuteronomy. It may be Severus himself who has, first, made use of the tradition about the contest of good and bad angels for the soul at death in order to explain the purpose of the event he found narrated in Jude 9, and then added, from someone else's

[65] Edited Macdonald (1963) 202.
[66] Quoted in Charles (1897) xlviii.
[67] James (1920) 46.

report of an apocryphal narrative, the tradition about the cloud of light. If Severus is not simply misinformed, this apocryphal narrative might have been attached as a sequel to the book of Jubilees,[68] but in any case it was not Jude's source.

F. *From Cramer's Catena*

> Michael, since he lacked the authority, did not bring upon him (the devil) the punishment appropriate to blasphemy (βλασφημίας), but left him to the judgment of his Master. For when he brought Moses onto the mountain where the Lord was transfigured, then the devil said to Michael, 'God lied in bringing Moses into the land which he swore he should not enter.'[69]

This text is clearly no more than a Christian attempt to explain Jude 9 without any knowledge of its Jewish background. Assuming that the devil's βλασφημία, mentioned in Jude 9, was blasphemy *against God*, the writer tried to explain what such blasphemy, in connection with a dispute over the body of Moses, might have been. Not realising the Jude 9 refers to the time of Moses' burial, he placed the dispute at the time of the transfiguration of Jesus, when Moses' appearance on the mountain (in Palestine) apparently contradicted God's declaration that Moses should not enter the promised land.

Although James (relying on text N below) supposed these words to come from the lost ending of the Testament of Moses,[70] they cannot do so, because (1) they are incomprehensible apart from the Christian story of the transfiguration of Jesus, and (2) they do not constitute an accusation *against Moses*, but an accusation *against God*, which is out of keeping with the devil's role in the story of the dispute over the body of Moses.

---

[68] Cf. James (1920) 50: he thinks Severus' source was the Testament of Moses, which follows Jubilees in the Milan manuscript of the Latin version.

[69] My translation from the Greek text in Cramer (1844) 161, lines 4–8.

[70] James (1920) 47–48.

III. The Assumption of Moses

Before allowing our conclusions about the story Jude knew, probably in the lost ending of the Testament of Moses, to stand, we must consider texts which we have excluded from the reconstruction of that story and which it is suggested derive from a different version of the story of the contest over the body of Moses, which was contained in the Assumption of Moses. Here it will be convenient to give all the texts before discussing them. They include the texts on which our reconstruction of the ending of the Assumption of Moses in section I was based:

G. *Clement of Alexandria, Frag. in Ep. Jud.*

[On Jude 9:] *Hic confirmat Assumptionem Moysi.*[71]

This corroborates the Assumption of Moses.[72]

H. *Didymus the Blind, In Ep. Jud. Enarr.*

Adversarii hujus contemplationis praescribunt praesenti epistolae et Moyseos Assumptioni propter eum locum ubi significatur verbum Archangeli de corpore Moyseos ad diabolum factum.[73]

Those whose oppose this consideration object to the present epistle and to the Assumption of Moses, on account of that place where the archangel's word to the devil about the body of Moses is indicated.

I. *Origen, De Princ. 3:2:1*

Et primo quidem in Genesi serpens Evam seduxisse perscribitur: de quo in Ascensione Moysi, cujus libelli meminit in epistola sua apostolus Judas, Michahel archangelus cum diabolo disputans de corpore Moysi ait a diabolo inspiratum serpentem causam extitisse praevaricationis Adae et Evae.[74]

---

[71] Text in Charles (1897) 107.
[72] The translations of all texts in this section are my own.
[73] Text in Charles (1897) 108.
[74] Text in Koetschau (1913) 244; cf. Charles (1897) 108.

In the beginning in Genesis the serpent is recorded as having deceived Eve, and with regard to this, in the Ascension of Moses (a book which the apostle Jude mentions in his letter), Michael the archangel, disputing with the devil about the body of Moses, says that the serpent, inspired by the devil, was the cause of the transgression of Adam and Eve.

J. *Gelasius Cyzicenus, Hist. Eccl. 2:17:17*

...ὡς γέγραπται ἐν βίβλῳ ἀναλήψεως Μωσέως, προσκαλεσάμενος Ἰησοῦν υἱὸν Ναυῆ καὶ διαλεγόμενος πρὸς αὐτὸν ἔφη. "καὶ προεθεάσατό με ὁ θεὸς πρὸ καταβολῆς κόσμου εἶναί με τῆς διαθήκης αὐτοῦ μεσίτην."[75]

...as it is written in the book of the Assumption of Moses, Moses having summoned Jesus the son of Nave and disputing with him, said, 'And God foresaw me before the foundation of the world to be the mediator of his covenant.'

K. *Gelasius Cyzicenus, Hist. Eccl. 2:21:7*

ἐν βίβλῳ δὲ ἀναλήψεως Μωσέως Μιχαὴλ ὁ ἀρχάγγελος διαλεγόμενος τῷ διαβόλῳ λέγει "ἀπὸ γὰρ πνεύματος ἁγίου αὐτοῦ πάντες ἐκτίσθημεν" καὶ πάλιν λέγει "ἀπὸ προσώπου τοῦ θεοῦ ἐξῆλθε τὸ πνεῦμα αὐτοῦ, καὶ κόσμος ἐγένετο."[76]

And in the book of the Assumption of Moses, Michael the archangel, disputing with the devil, says, 'For from his holy Spirit we were all created' [cf. Ps 103(104):30?]. And again he says, 'From the face of God his Spirit went forth, and the world was made' [cf. Ps 32(33):6; Jdt 16:14?].

L. *From Cramer's Catena*

ὁ γὰρ διάβολος ἀντεῖχε θέλων ἀπατῆσαι, ὅτι ἐμὸν τὸ σῶμα ὡς τῆς ὕλης δεσπόζοντι· καὶ ἤκουσε παρὰ τοῦ Ἀγγέλου τὸ "ἐπιτιμήσαι σοι Κύριος." τουτέστι ὁ Κύριος τῶν πνευμάτων καὶ πάσης σαρκός.[77]

---

[75] Text in Denis (1970A) 63.
[76] Text in Denis (1970A) 64.
[77] Text in Cramer (1844) 160, line 29 – 161, line 1.

For the devil resisted, wishing to deceive, (saying) 'The body is mine, for I am the Master of matter,' and was answered by the angel, 'May the Lord rebuke you!,' that is, the Lord of the spirits and of all flesh [cf. Num 16:22; 27:16 LXX].

M. A scholion on Jude 9

τελευτήσαντος, φησίν, ἐν τῷ ὄρει Μωσέως ὁ ἀρχάγγελος ἀποστέλλεται μεταθήσων τὸ σῶμα. ὁ οὖν διάβολος ἀντεῖχε θέλων ἀπατῆσαι, λέγων ὅτι ἐμόν ἐστι τὸ σῶμα ὡς τῆς ὕλης δεσπόζων, ἤτοι διὰ τὸ πατάξαι τὸν Αἰγύπτιον βλασφημοῦντος κατὰ τοῦ ἁγίου καὶ φονέα ἀναγορεύσαντος· μὴ ἐνεγκὼν τὴν κατὰ τοῦ ἁγίου βλασφημίαν ὁ ἄγγελλος, "Ἐπιτιμήσαι σοι ὁ Θεός," πρὸς τὸν διάβολον ἔφη.[78]

When Moses died on the mountain, the archangel Michael was sent to remove the body. But the devil resisted, wishing to deceive, saying, 'The body is mine, for I am the Master of matter,' or slandering the holy man, because he smote the Egyptian, and proclaiming him a murderer. The angel, not tolerating the slander against the holy man, said to the devil, 'May God rebuke you!'

N. A scholion on Jude 9

ὁ γὰρ διάβολος ἀντεῖχεν θέλων ἀπατῆσαι, λέγων ὅτι Ἐμόν ἐστιν τὸ σῶμα, ὡς τῆς ὕλης δεσπόζων· καὶ ἤκουσεν τὸ Ἐπιτιμήσαι [κ.τ.λ.] τούτεστιν, ὁ κύριος ὁ πάντων τῶν πνευμάτων δεσπόζων. ἄλλοι δέ, ὅτι βουλόμενος ὁ θεὸς δεῖξαι ὅτι μετὰ τὴν ἔνθενδε ἀπαλλαγὴν, ταῖς ἡμετέραις ψυχαῖς, ἀνθιστάμενοι δαίμονες πορευομέναις τὴν ἐπὶ τὰ ἄνω πορείαν, τοῦτο οὖν συνεχώρησεν ὁρᾶσθαι ἐπὶ τῆς Μωσέως ταφῆς. ἐβλασφήμει γὰρ καὶ ὁ διάβολος κατὰ Μωσέως, φονέα τοῦτον καλῶν διὰ τὸ πατάξαι τὸν Αἰγύπτιον. ὁ Μιχαὴλ ὁ ἀρχάγγελος, μὴ ἐνεγκὼν τὴν αὐτοῦ βλασφημίαν, εἴρηκεν αὐτῷ ὅτι Ἐπιτιμήσαι σοι κύριος ὁ θεός, διάβολε. ἔλεγε δὲ καὶ τοῦτο, ὅτι ἐψεύσατο ὁ θεὸς εἰσαγαγὼν τὸν Μωσῆν ἔνθα ὤμοσεν αὐτὸν μὴ εἰσελθεῖν.[79]

For the devil resisted, wishing to deceive, saying, 'The body is

---

[78] Text in Denis (1970A) 67; cf. Charles (1897) 110.
[79] Text in James (1892) 18, from MS Bodl.Arch.E.5.9.

mine, for I am the Master of matter,' and was answered by, 'May the Lord rebuke you!,' that is, the Lord who is Master of all the spirits. Others say that God, wishing to show that after our departure hence demons oppose our souls on their upward course, permitted this to be seen at the burial of Moses. For the devil also slandered Moses, calling him a murderer because he smote the Egyptian. Michael the archangel, not tolerating his slander, said to him, 'May the Lord God rebuke you, devil!' He also said this, that God had lied in that he brought Moses into the land which he swore he should not enter.

O. *Clement of Alexandria, Strom. 6:15:2–3*

εἰκότως ἄρα καὶ τὸν Μωυσέα ἀναλαμβανόμενον διττὸν εἶδεν Ἰησοῦς ὁ τοῦ Ναυῆ, καὶ τὸν μὲν μετ' ἀγγέλων, τὸν δὲ ἐπὶ τὰ ὄρη περὶ τὰς φάραγγας κηδείας ἀξιούμενον. εἶδεν δὲ Ἰησοῦς τὴν θέαν ταύτην κάτω πνεύματι ἐπαρθεὶς σὺν καὶ τῷ Χαλέβ, ἀλλ' οὐχ ὁμοίως ἄμφω θεῶνται, ἀλλ' ὁ μέν καὶ θᾶττον κατῆλθεν, πολὺ τὸ βρῖθον ἐπαγόμενος, ὁ δὲ ἐπικατελθὼν ὕστερον τὴν δόξαν διηγεῖτο ἣν ἐθεᾶτο, διαθρῆσαι δυνηθεὶς μᾶλλον θατέρου, ἅτε καὶ καθαρώτερος γενόμενος.[80]

It is therefore reasonable that Jesus the son of Nave should have seen Moses being taken up in two forms, the one with angels, while the other was honoured with burial in the clefts on the mountains. Jesus saw this sight from above, when he was lifted up, with Caleb, by the Spirit. But they did not both see it in the same way, for one of them descended more quickly, since he bore much weight, while the other, descending after him, subsequently told of the glory he had seen, since, being purer than the other, he was able to perceive more.

P. *Origen, In lib. Jesu Nave Hom. 2:1*

... *in libello quodam in quo, licet in canone non habeatur, mysterii tamen hujus figura describitur, refertur quia duo Moyses videbantur: unus vivus in spiritu et alius mortuus in corpore.*[81]

... in a certain book in which, though it is not in the canon, a figure of this mystery is described, since it is related that two

---

[80] Text in Denis (1970A) 65; cf. Charles (1897) 107.
[81] Text in Denis (1970A) 65–66; cf. Charles (1897) 108.

Moses's were seen, one alive in the spirit, the other dead in the body.

Q. *Evodius of Uzala, Epist. ad Aug. 158:6*

...*in apocryphis et secretis ipsius Moysi, quae scriptura caret auctoritate, tunc cum ascenderet in montem ut moreretur, vi corporis efficitur ut aliud esset, quod terrae mandaretur, aliud quod angelo comitanti sociaretur.*[82]

...in the apocryphal and secret [words?] of Moses himself – a writing which lacks authority – [it is said that] when he went up the mountain to die, it came about through the power of the body that there was one body which was committed to the earth and another which was joined with angels as its companion.

R. *Clement of Alexandria, Strom. 1:23:1*

τῷ παιδίῳ οἱ γονεῖς ἔθεντο ὄνομά τι, ἐκαλεῖτο δὲ Ἰωακείμ. ἔσχεν δὲ καὶ τρίτον ὄνομα ἐν οὐρανῷ μετὰ τὴν ἀνάληψιν, ὥς φασιν οἱ μύσται, Μελχί.[83]

The parents gave the child a certain name, but he was called Joachim. He also had a third name in heaven after his assumption, so the initiates say: Melchi.

S. *Clement of Alexandria, Strom. 1:23:1*

φασὶ δὲ οἱ μύσται λόγῳ μόνῳ ἀνελεῖν τὸν Αἰγύπτιον.[84]

The initiates say that he slew the Egyptian with a word only.

T. *Gelasius Cyzicenus, Hist. Eccl. 2:17:18*

καὶ ἐν βίβλιῳ λόγων μυστικῶν Μωσέως αὐτὸς Μωσῆς προεῖπε περὶ τοῦ Δαυὶδ καὶ Σολομῶντος. περὶ οὗ Σολομῶντος οὕτω προεῖπε "καὶ διαδοχεύσει [ἐπ'] αὐτὸν ὁ θεὸς σοφίαν καὶ δικαιοσύνην καὶ ἐπιστήμην πλήρη, αὐτὸς οἰκοδομήσει τὸν οἶκον τοῦ θεοῦ."[85]

---

[82] Text in Denis (1970A) 65; cf. Charles (1897) 108.
[83] Text in Denis (1970A) 64.
[84] Text in Denis (1970A) 64.
[85] Text in Denis (1970A) 65.

And in the book of the mystical words of Moses, Moses himself prophesied about David and Solomon. About Solomon he prophesied thus: 'And God shall pour forth upon him wisdom and righteousness and full knowledge, and he shall build the house of God.'

Texts M and N have been included in this list because it is clear that they supply the words of the devil ('The body is mine, for I am the Master of matter') to which Michael replies in text K, and so must provide information from the same source as text K explicitly quotes. Texts M and N, however, are clearly conflated accounts. Text M combines the tradition represented by text D with the tradition represented by text L, while text N has brought together material from a whole series of divergent traditions, represented by texts D, E, F and L. These conflated versions are not, as previous studies have tended to treat them, evidence that all these elements were combined a single source, but represent the scholiasts' attempts to gather together the various versions of the story they found in their sources. The way they refer to the various items of information they give makes this quite clear, even apart from the evidence of the other texts. Thus the material in texts M and N which has already been discussed in section II can be discounted as evidence for the content of the Assumption of Moses.

Texts I, K, L, M and N provide an outline of Michael's dispute with the devil which is quite distinct from that of the texts in section II. Here the devil claims that the body of Moses belongs to him because he is the Master of matter. Michael evidently rejects this claim by means of scriptural quotations (which are not readily identifiable: they may be apocryphal), which show that the material world, including human bodies, was created by the Holy Spirit of God, and therefore belongs to God. The devil is not the rightful lord of the material world, but a rebel who, from the time of Adam and Eve, has tempted God's creatures to sin against God. Therefore when Michael, with the words 'May the Lord rebuke you!,' appeals to the judgment of God, he is appealing to the Creator of the world to whom Satan, like all other spiritual beings, is subject. This point is made by glossing 'Lord' in Michael's words of rebuke with the title 'Lord of the spirits and of all flesh,' derived from Num 16:22; 27:16 LXX. The title is taken to mean that all spiritual beings and all material beings are alike subject to the one God.

Attempts to combine this dispute with the dispute found in texts B, C and D[86] are mistaken. The two versions of the dispute exist in two distinct sets of texts, and are brought together only in the late *scholia* (M and N) which themselves indicate that they are found in distinct sources. Moreover, the role of the devil and the character of the dispute are quite different in the two versions. In texts B, C and D, the devil remains the malicious accuser of Jewish tradition, attempting to prove Moses' guilt. In the alternative version, the devil has become a kind of Gnostic demiurge, claiming to be the lord of the material world, and Michael's refutation of his claim is the kind of assertion of the one Creator-God which is so often found in anti-Gnostic argument of the second Christian century. Each version provides a coherent account in its own terms, but the attempt to combine them into one narrative can only produce incoherence.

This second version of the dispute is explicitly attributed to the Assumption of Moses by Origen (text I) and Gelasius (text K), while Clement and Didymus both claim that the Assumption of Moses contained the dispute to which Jude 9 refers. This link between the Assumption of Moses and Jude 9 is easy to understand, if the only version of the dispute which the Alexandrian Fathers knew was the one in the Assumption of Moses. After all, this version, like the one which we have argued was really Jude's source, contained the words, 'May the Lord rebuke you!,' which Jude quotes. Unlike the other version, it did not refer to the devil's slander (βλασφημία) against Moses, to which Jude 9 alludes, but in the absence of Jude's real source, the Alexandrian Fathers, like many modern commentators, would probably not have

---

[86] Charles (1897) 105–107; James (1920) 48–49; Loewenstamm (1976) 209–210.

read Jude 9 as referring to a slander by the devil against Moses.

Texts O, P and Q provide an account of the actual assumption of Moses.[87] That this derives from the Assumption of Moses is extremely likely, since Clement and Origen, who report it, certainly knew the Assumption of Moses (texts G, I). In distinguishing a spiritual Moses who is carried up to heaven accompanied by angels and the dead body of Moses which is buried in the earth, the account follows a pattern which is also found in the Testament of Job (52), the Testament of Abraham (rec. A 20:10–12; rec. B 14:7–8) and the Greek Life of Adam and Eve (ApMos 32–42).[88]

Whether the two statements (texts R and S) which Clement attributes to 'the initiates' (οἱ μύσται) also derive from the Assumption of Moses is rather less certain, though the reference to Moses' assumption in text R favours this. (The name Melchi for Moses is paralleled in LAB 9:16 [Melchiel], but as an earthly name given him by his mother.[89]) Clement's reference to οἱ μύσται could be related to Gelasius' reference (text T) to a 'book of the mystical words of Moses': either this was another Moses apocryphon or it was another way of describing the Assumption of Moses. That the latter possibility is correct would be confirmed by text Q ('in the apocryphal and secret [words] of Moses himself'), if this does derive from the Assumption of Moses. Perhaps Clement's 'initiates' were Joshua and Caleb, privileged to receive the secret revelations of Moses and to witness his assumption. Certainly, the links among texts O–S are such as to indicate that they all derive from the same work, which was either the Assumption of Moses or an unknown

---

[87] With this account, cf. Philo, *Mos.* 2:291; Purvis (1973) 113–114 (medieval Samaritan accounts); Denis (1970B) 132.

[88] That the assumption of Adam's soul and the burial of his body are distinguished in these chapters is now clear in Bertrand's edition: Bertrand (1987) 94–105; cf. his discussion on pp. 50–51, and more fully in Bertrand (1985). Previous editions and translations reflected the confusion of the two by both scribes and modern scholars.

[89] Cf. also the quotations from George Syncellus and George Cedrenus in Denis (1970A) 64.

Moses apocryphon. The fact that O, P and Q recount an assumption, as well as Ockham's razor, suggests that texts G–S are all evidence of the same work, the Assumption of Moses, with which the Alexandrian Fathers in particular were familiar.

In section I, on the basis of our reconstruction of its ending, we suggested that the Assumption of Moses was a work of the second century A.D., concerned, at least in part, with polemic against Gnostic dualism. It may well have been an Egyptian work, since before Gelasius and Evodius in the fifth century, it is only the Alexandrian Fathers who quote or refer to it. An Egyptian origin would also be supported by the affinities of the account of the assumption, since the Testament of Job, the Testament of Abraham and the Greek Life of Adam and Eve have all, though with more or less probability, been assigned to Egypt.[90]

The use of the title 'the Lord of the spirits and of all flesh' (ὁ Κύριος τῶν πνευμάτων καὶ πάσης σαρκός: text L) probably indicates that the work was dependent on the Septuagint and originated in Greek, since, whereas the MT has 'the God of the spirits of all flesh' in Num 16:22; 27:16, in both passages the Septuagint renders Θεὸς τῶν πνευμάτων καὶ πάσης σαρκός. The point of the use of this phrase in the Assumption of Moses – that Satan as a 'spirit' is subject to God – is dependent on the LXX rendering.[91]

We may discover a little more about the work if we ask why anyone should have thought of turning the contest between Michael and the devil over the body of Moses into a debate about Gnostic dualism. It is possible that Jude 9 was the inspiration for this. Jude's letter was not originally written against the kind of developed Gnosticism, including cosmological dualism, which the story as we have reconstructed

---

[90] Testament of Job: Nickelsburg (1981) 247; Spittler (1983) 833–834; Testament of Abraham: Delcor (1973) 67–69; Sanders (1983) 876; Greek Life of Adam and Eve (ApMos): Bertrand (1987) 32–35.

[91] For the LXX interpretation, cf. 2 Macc 3:24; Heb 12:9; 1 Clem 64; and Black (1984) 53–55. It is possible that 1QH 10:8 ('Lord of every spirit') is an allusion to Num 16:22; 27:16 and that the LXX translation of these verses therefore reflects an existing tradition of interpretation of the Hebrew text. But the correspondence is not exact.

it in the Assumption of Moses presupposes, although some modern interpreters of Jude have thought it was. However, there is no doubt that in Alexandria Jude was read and used as a tract against the developed Gnosticism of the second and third centuries.[92] Clement of Alexandria thought Jude wrote, with prophetic foresight, against the Carpocratians of his own day (*Str.* 3:2:10–11; *Letter to Theodorus* 1:3–6), while Didymus the Blind thought Jude's opponents were the disciples of Simon Magus. If Jude was understood as an anti-Gnostic tract, it could be that someone thought the puzzling reference in Jude 9 to a dispute over the body of Moses must have had an anti-Gnostic point, and therefore wrote an appropriate, anti-Gnostic form of the dispute.

This raises the possibility that the author of the Assumption of Moses knew no more about the dispute over the body of Moses than he read in Jude 9. Our two reconstructed versions of the debate have in common only what is also in Jude 9. There seems no reason, therefore, to suppose that the author of the Assumption of Moses knew Jude's source, the Testament of Moses, and rewrote its account of Moses' burial. He need only have been spinning a plausible story out of Jude 9, as the authors of texts E and F also did.

However, there is a problem about this theory, arising from text J, which we have not yet discussed. Texts J and K are both from Gelasius Cyzicenus' account of the Council of Nicaea. In text K he quotes from the Assumption of Moses material which we have concluded certainly belonged in its version of the dispute between Michael and the devil and which certainly could not belong to the other version, which we have attributed to the Testament of Moses. However, in text J, Gelasius attributes to the same work, the Assumption of Moses, a quotation which occurs in the Latin work in the Milan manuscript (which we have identified as the Testament of Moses) at 1:14. Laperrousaz, who denies that the Milan text has anything to do with the Assumption of Moses, simply dismisses Gelasius' evidence on the grounds that his account of the Council of Nicaea is generally admitted to be unreli-

[92] Schelkle (1963) 408; Smith (1973) 8, 11, 79.

able.[93] However, it does not follow from this that his quotations from the Assumption of Moses are unreliable.

It is possible that Gelasius made a mistake: that he found in his sources two quotations from Moses apocrypha and assumed that both came from the same work, the Assumption of Moses. This is perhaps the most plausible explanation. Alternatively, if we assume Gelasius' accuracy in text J, we should have to conclude that 1:14 of the Milan manuscript occurred *both* in the Testament of Moses and in the Assumption of Moses. In other words, the Assumption of Moses was a rewritten form of the Testament of Moses, in which at least this verse remained unchanged. This suggestion perhaps gains some plausibility from the relative lengths of the Testament and the Assumption, as given in the Stichometry of Nicephorus (1100 *stichoi* for the Assumption, 1400 *stichoi* for the Testament). This length for the Assumption seems too long if it were only, as Charles thought, an account of the death and assumption of Moses, whereas it is plausible for a rewritten version of the Testament.

There is a final, related question. The text of the Testament of Moses in the Milan manuscript has one possible reference to an *assumption* of Moses: the words *morte receptionem*, usually corrected to *morte receptione mea*, in 10:12. It has usually been thought that *receptio* here is a translation of ἀνάληψις ('assumption'), and that the original text read *morte mea*, on which *receptione* is a gloss,[94] presumably added by a scribe who knew the tradition of Moses' assumption. Laperrousaz argues at length that *receptio* need not mean 'assumption,' but could refer to a normal death (cf. TMos 11:5: 'What place will receive [*recipiet*] you?,' i.e. be your grave),[95] but still it remains a plausible translation of ἀνάληψις.[96] If it should be taken in that sense, then it is possible that the revision which transformed the Testament of Moses into the Assumption of Moses was almost entirely confined to the concluding

[93] Laperrousaz (1970) 60–61.
[94] See Charles (1897) xlix, 44, 89; Haacker and Schäfer (1974) 160.
[95] Laperrousaz (1970) 41–46.
[96] Cf. Laperrousaz (1970) 42 n. 3; 43.

part, leaving the part covered by the extant Latin fragment
untouched except by this gloss.[97] In that case, the Milan
manuscript would, after all, be a text of the Assumption of
Moses. But it seems unlikely that the reviser who wrote the
ending of the Assumption of Moses, as we have reconstructed
it, would have been so restrained in his treatment of most of
the work. Moreover, if the Assumption were a revised version
of the Testament and if text T comes from the Assumption,
it would surely belong in the section of the text of the Milan
manuscript in which Moses predicts the future history of
Israel (2–7). We conclude that it is not at all certain that the
Assumption had any literary relationship to the Testament,
except through the mediation of Jude 9.

This section has been a necessary detour in our argument,
required to account for material which other scholars have
supposed to have been in the source of Jude 9. We must now
return to Jude's source and his use of it in verse 9 of his letter.

IV. The exegesis of Jude 9

In chapter 4 we have argued that, within the structure of
Jude's pesher exegesis, verses 8–10 constitute the interpretation
of the three scriptural references in verses 5–7. The three Old
Testament types of divine judgment – Israel in the wilderness,
the Watchers and the Cities of the Plain – are applied to
Jude's opponents, the false teachers, in verses 8–10. In this
context, verse 9 is not one of Jude's main series of scriptural
references, but a secondary reference introduced in the course
of a passage of interpretation in order to help the interpretation. Its function is indicated by the catchword connexions:
βλασφημίας (v 9) picks up βλασφημοῦσιν at the end of verse
8 and is in turn picked by βλασφημοῦσιν in verse 10. This
indicates that the reference to the dispute over the body of
Moses (v 9) is intended to illustrate or to support the third
charge made against the opponents in v 8: that they 'slander
the glorious ones' (δόξας δὲ βλασφημοῦσιν), which is also
further specified in the first clause of v 10 ('but these people

---

[97] Cf. Charles (1897) xlix, 44, 89.

slander [βλασφημοῦσιν] whatever they do not understand'). But it is important to notice that the use of catchword connections is primarily a *literary* technique, creating a verbal link between the story in verse 9 and its context in verses 8, 10. It does not require too strict a conceptual parallel between the blasphemy of the false teachers (vv 8, 10) and the blasphemy to which verse 9 refers.

It is now widely recognized that the δόξας (literally 'glories') of verse 8 are angels.[98] The use of the term in this sense is quite widely attested in Jewish and early Christian literature (1QH 10:8; 2 Enoch 22:7, 10; AscIsa 9:32; OdesSol 36:4; Allogenes [CG XI,3] 50:19; 52:17–18, 34; 57:25; Codex Brucianus;[99] probably Exod 15:11 LXX). But it is not attested for evil angels,[100] and seems intrinsically unsuited for such a use.[101] So the view that Jude accuses his opponents of slandering *evil* angels can be rejected. It is in any case hardly likely that Jude should object so strongly to such a practice, and unthinkable that he should link rejecting the authority of the Lord (κυριότητα δὲ ἀθετοῦσιν) with disrespect for the forces of evil. While the angels in question may have been regarded as evil by the false teachers, Jude must have seen them as angels of God who deserve to be honoured. In fact, it is unlikely that the δόξας of verse 8 would ever have been thought to be evil angels, were it not for an interpretation of verse 9 as an example of respect for the devil which we shall see is unjustified.

Sellin has recently argued that the false teachers' contempt for angels was an expression of their superiority to angels, as ecstatic visionaries (v 8: ἐνυπιαζόμενοι, which refers to pretended visionary revelations[102]) who travelled through the heavenly realms into the immediate presence of God, exalted above all the angels.[103] That the opponents did have visions

[98] Desjardins (1987) 91, 93–94, merely asserts, without the slightest linguistic evidence, that they are church leaders.

[99] Schmidt and MacDermot (1978) 248–249, 266–269.

[100] Except in 2 Pet 2:10, as a (mis)interpretation of Jude 8.

[101] Sickenberger (1911) 626–629.

[102] For argument for this meaning, see Bauckham (1983A) 55–56.

[103] Sellin (1986) 214–222, 224.

of this kind is quite likely, but mystical exaltation in itself scarcely offers sufficient motive for slandering or insulting the angels and there are no convincing parallels to show that it could.[104] The opponents' attitude to the angels is more adequately explained if we connect it with their anti-nomianism, which is their best attested characteristic (cf. v 4). According to Jewish and Jewish Christian belief, angels were the guardians and administrators of the moral order of the world, who watched over the observance of the law (cf. Hermas, *Sim.* 8:3:3; and probably 1 Cor 11:10). Jude's opponents, who interpreted grace as liberation from all moral authority, rejected the moral order over which the angels presided. We can well imagine that, if reproached for immoral conduct which offended these angels as administrators of the law, they would justify themselves by proclaiming their liberation from subservience to these angels and speaking contemptuously of them. They understood Christian freedom to mean freedom from moral authority, and therefore from the authority of the angels. They would probably have emphasized the connection of the moral law with the angels precisely in order to be able to dissociate it from God and to reject it simply as an evil from which Christian redemption is deliverance. They may have accused the angels of imposing the law on humanity out of envy and malice. And they probably did claim visionary revelations of their superiority to the angels and their freedom from the moral authority of the angels. This would give added point to verse 10a: 'these people slander whatever they do not understand' – they do not *really* understand the angelic world which they claim to know all about. If they did, they would not speak contemptuously of the angels.

In this context verse 9 ought to function as a refutation of this contemptuous attitude to the angels who administer the moral law. But it is not immediately clear how it can be, and ignorance of the story to which it alludes has not aided the commentators. The interpretation of the verse really hinges

---

[104] The Prayer of Joseph and the Apocalypse of Abraham, adduced in Sellin (1986) 219–220, certainly do not show this.

on the phrase κρίσιν ἐπενεγκεῖν βλασφημίας. What was it that Michael did not dare or presume to do to the devil? The usual interpretation takes βλασφημίας to be a 'genitive of quality,' equivalent to a Semitic adjectival genitive, and the phrase is then translated 'a reviling judgment' (RSV) or 'a slanderous accusation' (NIV). In fact this interpretation is the earliest attested: it was adopted by the author of 2 Peter 2:11, who in adapting Jude's material to his own use replaced Jude's κρίσιν βλασφημίας by βλάσφημον κρίσιν ('a slanderous judgment'). But the author of 2 Peter probably did not know the story to which Jude alludes. This is why, not wishing to baffle his readers with Jude's obscure reference to a story they would not know, but wishing to retain what he took to be its significance, he substituted a general reference to the behaviour of angels, who treat even the demons with a healthy respect, when pronouncing God's judgment on them.[105] Similarly most modern commentators on Jude have taken the point of verse 9 to be that when Michael pronounced God's judgment on the devil, he refrained from using insulting or abusive language. If Michael treated even the devil with respect, how much more ought the false teachers to avoid insulting angels.

However, this seems a very odd way for Jude to have made his point. The idea that the devil should not be insulted seems a questionable principle, which it is not easy to imagine Jude advocating. Moreover, it is unparalleled in Jewish and early Christian literature (with the exception of 2 Pet 2:11), which evidences if anything the opposite attitude. At Qumran there were liturgies for the cursing of Belial and his angels (4Q280–282, 286–287).

In any case, our reconstruction of the story to which Jude alludes shows that the usual interpretation must be wrong. In that story the βλασφημία in question is not Michael's slander against the devil but the devil's slander against Moses (see especially text D). Jude's κρίσιν βλασφημίας must mean, not 'a slanderous judgment,' but 'a condemnation for slander.' Michael, Jude claims, 'did not presume to condemn [the devil]

[105] On 2 Pet 2:11, see Bauckham (1983A) 261–263.

for slander.' The point is that Michael was the advocate, not the judge. When the devil brought an accusation against Moses, Michael did not have the authority himself to dismiss it as malicious slander. Instead, he appealed to God's judgment ('he did not presume to condemn him for slander, but said, "May the Lord rebuke you!"'). God alone had the authority to dismiss the devil's accusation.

We recall that Jude's opponents claimed to be free of any moral authority, to be in fact their own autonomous moral authority. If it was pointed out to them that their immoral behaviour laid them open to the accusation of sin by the standards of the law, they rejected the accusation, saying that it was no more than a malicious slander by the angels responsible for the law. They were free people, not subject to the law or its angels, and they had the authority to reject any accusations brought against them under the law.

Well then, responds Jude, consider a case in which an accusation of sin was made against the most righteous of people, Moses himself, and in which Moses was defended by the most exalted of created beings, the archangel Michael himself. It was a charge of murder (i.e. sin by the standards of the law) brought by the devil, and so maliciously. Surely if anyone were entitled to reject such an accusation as slanderous, it was Michael, acting as advocate for Moses. But in fact Michael did not take it on himself to condemn the devil for malicious slander. He could not on his own authority dismiss the devil's accusations. He could only appeal to the Lord's judgment.

It is important to take account of the fact that in our reconstruction of the story the devil appears in his ancient role as a legal accuser trying to prove Moses' guilt. This means that Michael's behaviour is exemplary not in his treatment of the devil *himself* (in treating the devil with respect) but in his response to the *accusation* brought by the devil. Even though he recognized it as slanderous, he could not dismiss it because he was not the judge. Therefore the moral of the story is that no one except God is in this sense a judge, a moral authority. Even if it were true, as the false teachers alleged, that when the law accused them of sin it was only the malice of the angels that prompted these accusations, they would still not be justified in rejecting them on their own authority. Even if they were as righteous as Moses and had the authority of an archangel, they would not be above accusations of sin under the law. They remain subject to the moral authority of the Lord. We can finally see that verse 9 is linked not only to the third of the charges against the false teachers in verse 8 (they 'slander the glorious ones') but also to the second (they 'reject the authority of the Lord'). Michael's appeal to the Lord's authority is contrasted, by catchword connexion (κύριος – κυριότητα), with the opponents' rejection of the Lord's authority. This is what their attitude to the angels in the end amounts to: it reveals a resistance to moral authority which will not even submit to God.

This interpretation of Jude's point in verse 9 is rather more complex than the usual interpretation, but, given his readers' familiarity with the story to which he alludes, it makes a more cogent and significant point. Instead of the trivial and questionable notion that one should be polite even to the devil, it goes to the heart of the spiritual conceit of the false teachers, as Jude saw it: their claim to be free from all moral authority.

V. Other possible allusions to the Testament of Moses in Jude

Many scholars have thought that there are several allusions in Jude to the text of the Testament of Moses as we know it in the Milan manuscript. If this claim could be accepted, it would support our case that Jude alludes to the lost ending of this same Testament of Moses. The most impressive case can be made for Jude 16, because here Charles identified a cluster of three allusions to the Testament of Moses (7:7, 9; 5:5).[106] However, the case appears less impressive when it is examined in detail. We shall consider each of three claimed allusions in turn:

---

[106] Charles (1897) lxii.

(a) Jude 16 begins: οὗτοί εἰσιν γογγυσταὶ μεμψίμοιροι ('these people are discontented murmurers'). μεμψίμοιροι ('discontented, complaining') is a biblical *hapax legomena*, but Charles conjectured that it stood in the Greek text of Testament of Moses 7:7, in a passage describing the sinners of the last days, whom Jude might well have taken to be his opponents. All that can be read of one Latin word in 7:7 is *quaeru*[. . .]. Charles proposed the restoration *quaerulosi*, with which the Vulgate translates μεμψίμοιροι in Jude 16. However, this is only one possible restoration, which also involves emending the preceding words of the text to produce a plausible sense (*se et exterminatores quaeru*[. . .] becomes *sed ut exterminarent eos; quaerulosi*).[107] Laperrousaz offers a more economical emendation (*sint exterminatores quaerulorum:* 'they are banishers of those who complain'),[108] but in that case the *quaeruli* (rather than *quaerulosi*) would be not the wicked but their victims, and Jude could not be dependent on this text.

Jude's choice of words is readily explicable without the hypothesis of dependence on Testament of Moses 7:7. In verse 16 he is applying the quotation from Enoch (vv 14–15) to the false teachers. In particular, he is taking up Enoch's references to the 'hard words' (σκληρῶν) which the wicked speak against God. The connotations of the term σκληρῶν readily suggest the Israelites in the wilderness (cf. Ps 95:8),[109] who in their hardness of heart 'murmured' against God (normally in LXX and other Jewish Greek literature γογγύζειν and cognates). So Jude calls his opponents γογγυσταί ('murmurers'), and μεμψίμοιροι is a convenient synonym to strengthen the rhetorical impact. (Philo, *Mos* 1:181 uses μεμψιμοιρεῖν of Israel's murmuring in the wilderness.)

(b) Later in Jude 16 the words τὸ στόμα αὐτῶν λαλεῖ ὑπέρογκα (literally: 'their mouth speaks huge things,' i.e. 'they utter arrogant words') are exactly paralleled in Testament of Moses 7:9: *os eorum loquetur ingentia* ('their mouth will speak

---

[107] Charles (1897) 78–79.
[108] Laperrousaz (1970) 51–52.
[109] For Israel in the wilderness as the classic case of 'hardness of heart,' see Berger (1970).

huge things'). However, the phrase is a standard one in apocalyptic literature, deriving from Daniel 7:8, 20 ('a mouth speaking great things': LXX, Θ: στόμα λαλοῦν μεγάλα; cf. also Dan 11:36; Rev 13:5; 2 Bar 67:7). The Qumran Aramaic fragment of 1 Enoch 1:9 (4QEn^c1:1:17) says that the wicked spoke 'great and hard things' against God, where all the versions have simply 'hard things'. Jude in his quotation of this verse (Jude 15) also has simply 'hard things' (τῶν σκληρῶν). If he read 'great and hard things' in his text of 1 Enoch, he may have reserved the adjective 'great' for use in his interpretation of the Enoch quotation here in verse 16. But in any case, the phrase is repeated in 1 Enoch 5:4: 'you have spoken great and hard words (μεγάλους καὶ σκληροὺς λόγους) with your unclean mouth against his majesty,' and again in 1 Enoch 101:3: 'you speak with your mouth great and hard things (μεγάλα καὶ σκληρά) against his majesty' (cf. also 27:2). So it looks as though the coincidence between Jude and the Testament of Moses here results from common use of a standard phrase, used especially of sinners of the last days, which the Testament of Moses most probably took from Daniel 7, and Jude probably from 1 Enoch, perhaps with a reminiscence also of Daniel 7. Admittedly the coincidence is more striking than it might have been, since, whereas in the usual, literal Greek rendering of the phrase μεγάλα ('great things') is used, Jude has ὑπέρογκα and Testament of Moses 7:9 its Latin equivalent *ingentia* ('huge things'). However, ὑπέρογκα (which can be used in Greek of speech and of arrogance[110]) is the better Greek idiom, which Jude and the Testament of Moses could have hit upon independently, as Daniel 11:36 (Theodotion) also did (λαλήσει ὑπέρογκα).

(c) The third parallel adduced by Charles is between the words θαυμάζοντες πρόσωπα ὠφελείας χάριν ('showing partiality for the sake of gain') in Jude 16 and Testament of Moses 5:5: *erunt mirantes personas cupiditatum et acceptiones munerum*. The Latin text is corrupt, but must mean something like: 'they will be respecters of persons out of greed, and will

---

[110] See the quotations from Plutarch in Mayor (1907) 46.

receive gifts.' However, the only verbal link between the two passages is the very common standard expression θαυμάζοντες πρόσωπα/*mirantes personas* (from the Hebrew idiom נשׂא פנים). Without the support of the other claimed allusions to the Testament of Moses in Jude 16, this one becomes an insignificant coincidence.

The only other possible allusion worth mentioning[111] is in Jude 3: τῇ ἅπαξ παραδοθείσῃ τοῖς ἁγίοις πίστει ('the faith which was once and for all delivered to the saints'). According to Testament of Moses 4:8, the two tribes of Benjamin and Judah, returning to Judaea after the exile, 'will remain in the faith first laid down for them' (*permanebunt in praeposita fide sua*). While this is an interesting Jewish parallel to the objective use of 'faith' (meaning the content of belief)[112] in early Christianity, and it is possible that the phrase had stuck in Jude's mind, Jude's words are fully explicable on the basis of common early Christian usage.

We conclude, with Laperrousaz[113] against Charles, that the case for allusions in Jude to the extant text of the Testament of Moses is not proven. That Jude 9 is dependent on the lost ending of this work must rest on the argument offered earlier in this chapter, without such additional supporting evidence.

VI. Implications of Jude's use of the Testament of Moses

Neither the Testament of Moses nor the Assumption of Moses were ever at all widely used in the early church. No text of the Assumption of Moses survives. Of the Testament of Moses we have only the incomplete Milan text of a Latin version, while very few early church writers, attempting to explain Jude 9, seem to have had access to the story Jude actually knew (see sections II and III above). But of the two works, the Assumption was at least popular in Alexandria,

---

[111] Adduced not by Charles (1897), but by Chase (1899) 802.

[112] For πίστις in Jude 3, see Bauckham (1983A) 32–33.

[113] Laperrousaz (1970) 51–58.

whereas the Testament is never referred to by name in any document of the early church outside the lists of apocryphal books.

Charles thought some Gospel passages, Acts 7, and 2 Peter dependent on the Testament of Moses,[114] but Laperrousaz, after careful examination, rightly rejects these claims, with the exception of Acts 7:36 (cf. TMos 3:11).[115] Even that passage however, is easily explained as using a traditional formula in common with the Testament of Moses. The case of 2 Peter is in fact peculiarly interesting evidence of *ignorance* of the Testament of Moses in the early church. We have already noticed that when the author comes to rewrite Jude 9 in 2 Peter 2:11, he eliminates the story of the contest for the body of Moses and substitutes a generalized reference to the way angels behave towards evil angels. The suppression of Jude's story has nothing to do with an objection to apocryphal literature, as some commentators allege. 1 Enoch, for example, was consistently popular with Christian writers throughout the second century, who freely refer to it and quote it.[116] Objections to apocryphal works as such are not heard in Christian literature until long after even the latest dates assigned by some scholars to 2 Peter. Rather, this author's omission of Jude's reference to the story of the contest for the body of Moses must reflect his and his readers' ignorance of the story. His own ignorance of it is clear from the fact that he misunderstands Jude 9 in exactly the same way as some modern commentators, not knowing the story (and not always influenced by 2 Pet 2:11), have misunderstood it. He assumes that Jude's δόξας must be evil angels and that the moral of the story, which he presents in generalized form, concerns the need for respect for the powers of evil.

That Jude knows and can assume his readers' familiarity with the Testament of Moses suggests, therefore, a different milieu from those from which most extant early Christian literature comes. This Palestinian Jewish work would have

[114] Charles (1897) lxiii–lxv.
[115] Laperrousaz (1970) 63–76.
[116] Bauckham (1983A) 139.

been best known in the Palestinian Jewish Christian circles from which an authentic letter of Jude the Lord's brother would come.

6

Jude's Christology

To claim that the short letter of Jude provides very important evidence for the understanding of early christological development may risk sounding like exaggeration. But recent study of New Testament Christology has increasingly recognized that the crucial formative steps in christological development were taken within early Palestinian Jewish Christianity. Unfortunately, direct evidence of the christological beliefs and expressions of these Palestinian churches is very sparse. 'Would that we had some clear Semitic or Greek Palestinian texts used or composed by *Jewish Christian* Hellenists or Hebrews,'[1] sighs Joseph Fitzmyer in the course of his attempt to investigate the origins of the christological title 'Lord.' The contention of this book is that the letter of Jude is just such a text – a Greek Palestinian text by a Jewish Christian 'Hebrew' (i.e. Aramaic speaker), indeed by one of the leaders of early Palestinian Jewish Christianity. It could even date from within the first two decades of Christianity, the period in which Martin Hengel claims 'more happened in christology . . . than in the whole subsequent seven hundred years of church history.'[2] From such a source even a little christological evidence is of immense value. In this chapter we shall argue that the Christology of Jude's letter is in fact entirely consistent with what we can reasonably conclude from other indications about the Christology of early Jewish Christianity in

[1] Fitzmyer (1979) 123.
[2] Hengel (1983) 39–40.

Palestine. Though its evidence is not especially surprising, it is firsthand evidence of what have otherwise been only uncertain and highly debated inferences.

I. The christological titles

Even apart from the letter of Jude, the reliable evidence we have about the relatives of Jesus already tells us a remarkable amount, if not about their Christology, at least about the christological *titles* which were used in their circle. Four christological titles were certainly used: (1) 'Messiah' seems to have been the universal Christian designation of Jesus from the earliest period of the church.[3] Only if it goes back to the earliest Palestinian church can the fact that all the New Testament writers call Jesus Χριστός be explained. Moreover, in Jewish writings this designation is found most often in connection with the hope for the Davidic Messiah (e.g. PssSol 17:32; 18:5, 7; 4 Ezra 12:32). Since we know that the relatives of Jesus were well-known for their claim to Davidic ancestry (Eusebius, *HE* 3:20:1–2; 3:32:3), we may assume that they used the title Messiah to designate Jesus the royal Messiah of the house of David. (2) The brothers of Jesus were known in Palestinian Christian circles as 'the brothers of the Lord' (οἱ ἀδελφοὶ τοῦ κυρίου: 1 Cor 9:5; Gal 1:19; Hegesippus *ap.* Eusebius, *HE* 2:23:4; 3:20:1). So Jesus himself must have been known in their circle as 'the Lord' (Aramaic *mārê*' and Greek ὁ κύριος). (3) Most probably Jesus was known not only as 'the Lord,' but also as 'our Lord.' The Aramaic invocation preserved in Greek transliteration as μαραναθα (1 Cor 16:22; Did 10:6) should most probably be read as *māranā' 'āthā'*, 'Our Lord, come!'[4] This invocation must have been current in the circles in which Jesus' relatives moved. (4) The relatives of Jesus were also known in Palestinian Christian circles as οἱ δεσπόσυνοι (Julius Africanus, *ap.* Eusebius, *HE* 1:7:14). It follows that Jesus himself must have been called ὁ δεσπότης.

All four of these christological titles – and only these four

---

[3] Cf. Hengel (1983) 45.
[4] Fitzmyer (1981B) 226–228.

– occur in the letter of Jude. This is not especially remarkable in the case of the first three, but in the case of the last – δεσπότης – it is striking. If δεσπότης is used as a title for Christ (rather than for God[5]) in Jude 4, then this usage seems to be unique in extant early Christian literature before the late second century, with the sole exception of 2 Peter 2:1, which is dependent on Jude 4. But the term δεσπόσυνοι for the relatives of the Jesus is only explicable if ὁ δεσπότης was commonly used to refer to Jesus in Palestinian Jewish Christianity. Jude's use of this term is therefore an impressive, but neglected indication of his letter's origin in those Palestinian Christian circles in which the δεσπόσυνοι were leaders. The significance of the term will be discussed below in section III, but it is worth remarking at once on its implication for the *language* of Christology in the circle of the relatives of Jesus. The use of δεσπότης and δεσπόσυνοι, since in this use with reference to Jesus they are distinctive precisely as *Greek* words, shows that the Palestinian Christian circles in which the relatives of Jesus were leaders had its own *Greek* christological terminology. Therefore these circles must have been bilingual, not simply in the sense that they could speak Greek as well as Aramaic, but in the sense that they actually did use Greek as well as Aramaic *for religious purposes* (such as, presumably, missionary preaching to Greek-speaking Jews). This confirms the best interpretation of Acts 6:1, which takes the 'Hebrews' to be bilingual Jews who spoke Aramaic as well as Greek and the 'Hellenists' to be Jews of diaspora origin who spoke only Greek,[6] but goes beyond it in stressing the actual religious use of Greek by the former. It follows that interpretations of early Christology which make much of the linguistic transition from Aramaic to Greek must be suspect. Not only was this transition made already in Jerusalem among the 'Hellenists,' as Hengel has stressed.[7] It was made in Palestinian Christianity as such, probably from the very beginning: there was never a Christian com-

---

[5] For its christological reference, see section III below.
[6] Hengel (1983) 8–11.
[7] See especially Hengel (1983) 1–29.

munity which used only an Aramaic christological terminology without also developing a Greek christological terminology. We shall have to be appropriately cautious therefore about claiming that a particular christological development must derive from the Greek-speaking churches and cannot go back to the original Aramaic-speaking Christianity. There will have been much interchange and continuity between Aramaic-speaking (i.e. bilingual) and Greek-speaking Christians in the crucial period of christological development.[8] The latter (including Paul) will have taken over much from the former. But this is not to say that there was no distinction at all, as the term δεσπότης again shows. Whereas κύριος as a christological title was used in the Greek of native Palestinian ('Aramaic-speaking') Jewish Christians and of others, δεσπότης as a christological title was evidently confined to the former.

Thus the example of δεσπότης shows us that in the christological titles of Jude's letter we are dealing not merely with translations of the Aramaic terms used in the circle of the brothers of Jesus, but with the Greek christological terminology which had developed within that bilingual circle. The distribution of titles is as follows. The designation (perhaps better than 'title') Χριστός (never ὁ Χριστός) occurs six times, always following Ἰησοῦς. Only in two of these cases does Ἰησοῦς Χριστός stand alone (both in v 1). In three cases Ἰησοῦς Χριστός is combined with κύριος ἡμῶν:

v 17: τοῦ κυρίου ἡμῶν Ἰησοῦ Χριστοῦ
v 21: τοῦ κυρίου ἡμῶν Ἰησοῦ Χριστοῦ
v 25: Ἰησοῦ Χριστοῦ τοῦ κυρίου ἡμῶν.

Finally, Ἰησοῦς Χριστός occurs in v 4 in the full formula:

τὸν μόνον δεσπότην καὶ κύριον ἡμῶν Ἰησοῦν Χριστόν.

These (vv 4, 17, 21, 25) are also the only four occurrences of κύριος ἡμῶν. The absolute κύριος is used certainly once of Christ (v 14) in the quotation from Enoch. Its use in v 9 is probably of God, rather than of Christ. That it is the correct reading in the textually uncertain v 5 and there refers to God

[8] So also Hengel (1983) 40.

rather than to Christ will be argued in section IV below. Thus Jude shows a striking preference for the 'double name' Ἰησοῦς Χριστός (never Ἰησοῦς or Χριστός alone) and for the community-related title κύριος ἡμῶν, rather than for the absolute (ὁ) κύριος, which he uses christologically only when conforming to scriptural usage (v 14: see section II below).

The sheer frequency of Χριστός (six times in twenty-five verses) is noteworthy. Among other New Testament authors, this frequency (relative to length) is matched and sometimes surpassed only by Paul.[9] Perhaps this is an indication that Paul's christological terminology is closer than that of most New Testament authors to the Palestinian Christianity which Jude represents. We should not suppose that the use of Ἰησοῦς Χριστός as a 'double name' (with Χριστός virtually as a cognomen) arose in Gentile Christianity in which the meaning of Χριστός was not understood.[10] A sharp distinction between Χριστός as a title applied to Jesus and Χριστός as a name for Jesus cannot be drawn, because as soon as Jesus was regularly called *Yešūaʿ mešīḥā* the phrase would approximate to a double name serving to identify the Jesus in question. From the beginning Christians would have needed a way of distinguishing Jesus from others who bore this very common name, and *Yešūaʿ mešīḥā* or Ἰησοῦς Χριστός would soon have been preferred to 'Jesus of Nazareth' (Acts 2:22; 10:38 etc), precisely because it distinguished Jesus in the way which was theologically decisive for the early Christians. In such a development the meaning of 'Messiah' (the agent of God's eschatological salvation and judgment) would certainly not have been forgotten (and there is no reason to suppose that in the New Testament period Χριστός ever became, for Christians, a *mere* name without meaning). The use of the double name Ἰησοῦς Χριστός does not indicate that the eschatological significance of Jesus has been lost in some allegedly hellenistic development of Christology, but rather that it is assumed. The double name can be used because

[9] See the statistics in Hengel (1983) 65, who does not mention Jude.

[10] Against this, see Hengel's essay on Χριστός in Paul: Hengel (1983) 65–77.

Jesus' identity with the Messiah is taken for granted: the Jesus in question is Jesus the Messiah and for Christians there is no question of any Messiah except Jesus. The further development which enables Χριστός alone to be used as a name appears in Paul[11] but not yet in Jude. It would seem to be possible only as Christian linguistic usage developed for Christian purposes alone, independently of conversation and debate with non-Christian Jews, and is therefore perhaps unlikely in Palestine.

It is noteworthy that Jude uses the simple Ἰησοῦς Χριστός twice in his letter-opening (v 1), but once he moves into the subject-matter of his letter he refers to Christ exclusively by phrases including κύριος, the fullest of these being the first (v 4). This stress on the lordship of Christ is coherent with the theme of his letter. His opponents are people who claim to be above the moral law, free from its demands. In Jude's view they are therefore, by their disregard of the moral requirements of Christian obedience, disowning Christ as Lord (v 4) and rejecting κυριότης (v 8) – the moral authority of God, whose lordship is exercised by Christ. The understanding of Christ as κύριος – exercising the eschatological lordship of God – is orientated to the imminent parousia, when his lordship will be exercised in judgment on the wicked (vv 14–15) and in mercy to those who live in obedience to the Gospel (v 21).

There is much to suggest, as has often been pointed out, that the christological title Lord (mārē' and κύριος) in early Palestinian Christianity was especially associated with the parousia.[12] This is suggested by the invocation 'Maranatha' ('Our Lord, come!') and will be further discussed in section II below. But if the title was especially orientated to the parousia, when Christ's lordship would be manifested in universal judgment, to call him Lord was not to refer exclusively to the parousia.[13] 'Maranatha' itself shows this, for it shows that the coming

[11] Already three times in 1 Thessalonians (2:7; 3:2; 4:16), quite frequently in other letters.
[12] E.g. Fitzmyer (1979) 128–130.
[13] Cf. Marshall (1976) 101–104.

Lord can be already addressed as Lord in the present. Moreover, he is addressed as '*our* Lord.' In other words, he has already gathered a community who now acknowledge him as their Lord, while awaiting his coming to complete their salvation. It is doubtful whether there was ever a Christology in which the lordship of Christ did not evoke his constitution of the Christian community, through his ministry, death and outpouring of the Spirit, and his present status as Lord, through his resurrection and exaltation by God, as well as his future coming as eschatological Saviour and Judge. His past work of salvation and present status in heaven do not detract from the early community's strong orientation to the parousia. They are the necessary presuppositions of the prayer, 'Our Lord, come!'

Jude's use of κύριος ἡμῶν is entirely consistent with these implications of 'Maranatha.' The one who is coming in judgment at the parousia is already 'our Lord.'[14] Just as God made Israel his own people at the Exodus (v 5), so Christ has already made the church his people through a second Exodus (Jude has no occasion to specify the nature of the saving event, which would be well-known to his readers). And so just as those who had been saved by God from Egypt but repudiated his lordship in the wilderness were judged by him (v 5), so those who have confessed Christ as Lord but refuse to accept his lordship in practice will be judged by him at the parousia (v 14). But, because he is 'our Lord,' those who seek to live according to the Gospel in expectation of his coming, can expect mercy from him (v 21). Thus, while the orientation is to the future coming of Christ as Lord, his saving act in the past is presupposed and his present lordship over the church is stressed. The expression 'the apostles of our Lord Jesus Christ' (v 19)[15] presumably stresses their authority as

---

[14] Cf. Collins (1984c) 267–268, on Paul's use of 'our Lord Jesus Christ' in 1 Thessalonians.

[15] The argument in Kramer (1966) 59–63, that Paul was the first to link 'Christ' with 'apostle' in the phrase 'apostle of Christ' is entirely speculative. The Gospel tradition provides sufficient evidence that the apostles were already before Paul regarded as apostles of Christ, and so there is no reason why Jude, independently of Paul, should not have called them such.

missionaries of the Gospel sent out by the exalted and coming Lord.

This preliminary indication of Jude's understanding of Christ's lordship will be further developed in the following sections.

II. Jude 14

Jude's quotation from 1 Enoch 1:9 reads: 'Behold, the Lord came with his ten thousands of holy ones, to execute judgment on all, and to convict all the ungodly of all the ungodly deeds which they had committed in their ungodliness, and of all the hard things which ungodly sinners had spoken against him' (vv 14–15). We have already seen (in chapter 4 section IV) that Jude has modified the quotation in more than one respect. For our present purpose the significant modification is the specification of the subject as κύριος. In the extant versions of 1 Enoch 1:9 (and therefore most probably in the text Jude read) the subject is unstated, but must be taken from 1:3–4 to be 'the great holy One,' 'the eternal God.' Jude's addition of κύριος is certainly a christological interpretation of the text. He understands the eschatological coming of God to judgment to be the parousia of the Lord Jesus. We must examine further the precise significance of this christological interpretation.

In the first place, we should observe that 1 Enoch 1:3b–7, 9, which describes an eschatological judgment theophany, is a kind of anthology of phrases and themes from Old Testament 'day of the Lord' theophany passages.[16] (1 Enoch 1:8 is integral to the passage, describing the salvation of the righteous which accompanies the judgment of the wicked, but it is not based on Old Testament 'day of the Lord' texts.) Those to which the allusions are clearest are Deuteronomy 33:2; Isaiah 40:4, 10; Jeremiah 25:31; Micah 1:3–4; Habakkuk 3:3–9. 1 Enoch 1:3b–9 is evidence of the way in which such passages were associated and interpreted in pre-Christian apocalyptic Judaism as referring to the eschatological coming of God to

---

[16] Hartman (1966) 114–117; VanderKam (1973); Hartman (1979) 22–26.

judgment. (Further evidence of this is provided by Testament of Moses 10:3–7.) The same passages, or many of them, were similarly used in early Christianity, but were consistently understood to refer to the coming of the Lord Jesus.

Jude's addition of κύριος cannot come from the context of 1 Enoch 1:9 but it could be regarded as an interpretation of 1 Enoch 1:9 by reference to analogous texts, as can be seen by comparing some of those which either lie behind 1 Enoch 1:3b–9 or are closely related to it:[17]

Deuteronomy 33:2:	The LORD came from Sinai, and dawned from Seir upon us; he shone forth from Mount Paran, he came from[18] the ten thousands of holy ones, with flaming fire at his right hand.
Isaiah 40:10:	Behold, the Lord GOD comes with might, and his arm rules for him; behold, his reward is with him, and his recompense before him.
Isaiah 66:15–16:	For behold, the LORD will come in fire, and his chariots like the stormwind, to render his anger in fury, and his rebuke with flames of fire. For by fire the LORD will execute judgment, and by his sword, upon all flesh; and those slain by the LORD shall be many.
Micah 1:3–4:	For behold, the LORD is coming forth out of his place,

[17] Translations from RSV.

[18] See VanderKam (1973) 148–149, for the reconstruction by Cross and Freedman of an original text reading 'with him were the myriads of holy ones,' and for the understanding of the text in this sense in the Targums. The author of 1 Enoch 1:9 must have read it in this way.

and will come down and tread upon
the high places of the earth.
And the mountains will melt under
him
and the valleys will be cleft,
like wax before the fire,
like waters poured down a steep place.

Zechariah 14:5b: Then the LORD your God will come,
and all the holy ones with him.[19]

All these texts refer to the *coming* of *Yahweh*. (In Deuteronomy 33:2 modern readers usually take the coming to
be in the past, but the writer of 1 Enoch probably read it as
prophecy[20] and took the verbs in the perfect tense to be
prophetic perfects.[21] At the beginning of 1:9, modelled on
Deuteronomy 33:2, he probably used an Aramaic prophetic
perfect, which Jude has rendered literally as ἦλθεν.) It looks
as though Jude's κύριος, added to the text of 1 Enoch 1:9 by
analogy with these other texts, represents the tetragrammaton.

This is confirmed by other early Christian use of such
texts:
(a) Zechariah 14:5b (LXX: καὶ ἥξει κύριος θεός μου, καὶ
πάντες οἱ ἅγιοι μετ᾽ αὐτοῦ). The best evidence here is 1 Thessalonians 3:13: 'at the coming of our Lord Jesus with all his
holy ones.' The phrase was most probably already a traditional one which Paul took up.[22] The κύριος which represents the tetragrammaton in our texts of the Septuagint is

---

[19] The RSV here corrects the MT according to the versions. MT has:
'Then the LORD my God will come, and all the holy ones with you.'

[20] The Testament of Moses interprets Deut 31–33 as Moses' prophecy of
the future history of Israel: see Harrington (1973). TMos 10:8 echoes Deut
33:29, and probably 10:3 (the eschatological theophany) is meant to correspond to Deut 33:2. See also Betz (1967) 90–91, who sees a Sinai typology
in the dependence of 1 Enoch 1:9 on Deut 33:2.

[21] So Black (1973) 194. The prophetic perfect is rare in Aramaic (Black
[1973] 196), but is perhaps easier to accept if regarded as modelled on
Deut 33:2.

[22] Best (1972) 153.

interpreted, in spite of its clear reference to God, as τοῦ κυρίου ἡμῶν Ἰησοῦ. In 2 Thessalonians 1:7 (τοῦ κυρίου Ἰησοῦ ... μετ᾽ ἀγγέλων δυνάμεως αὐτοῦ) the basis in Zechariah 14:5b is not quite so obvious, but is very likely[23] (in the context of a passage where, as we shall see, other Old Testament theophany passages are echoed). Again (if 2 Thessalonians is authentic)[24] the formulation is probably pre-Pauline. Whereas in 1 Thessalonians 3:13 it is unclear whether 'holy ones' means angels (as originally in Zech 14:5b) or Christians (as usually in Paul), in 2 Thessalonians 1:7 it is interpreted explicitly as angels. But an interpretation of 'holy ones' in Zechariah 14:5b as Christians probably lies behind 1 Thessalonians 4:14[25] and is certainly attested in Didache 16:7, where Zechariah 14:5b is explicitly quoted with reference to the Christian dead. The Septuagint text is there adapted, by the omission of θεός μου, to the interpretation of it as referring to the parousia of the κύριος Jesus. The early and widespread Christian use of Zechariah 14:5b with reference to the parousia is further shown by the fact that it very probably lies behind other early Christian texts which speak of the coming of Christ with angels (Matt 16:27: μετὰ τῶν ἀγγέλων αὐτοῦ; Matt 25:31: πάντες οἱ ἄγγελοι μετ᾽ αὐτοῦ; Mark 8:38: μετὰ τῶν ἀγγέλων τῶν ἁγίων; Luke 9:26: καὶ τῶν ἁγίων ἀγγέλων; ApPet EI: 'with all my holy angels') or with Christians (Rev 19:14 where it seems, from 17:14, that the armies of heaven are composed of the Christian martyrs), though in none of these is he called κύριος. Ascension of Isaiah 4:14, which does use κύριος and clearly echoes Zechariah 14:5b, combines the two traditions of interpretation: 'the Lord will come with his angels and with the hosts of his holy ones' (from v 16 it is clear that the latter are the Christian dead).[26]

(b) Isaiah 66:15–16 (LXX: κύριος ... ἀποδοῦναι ... ἐκδίκησιν

---

[23] Kreitzer (1987) 118–119, is more doubtful.

[24] For the authenticity of 2 Thessalonians, see Best (1972) 50–58; Marshall (1982); Kreitzer (1987) 181–182.

[25] Kreitzer (1987) 118.

[26] For the two traditions of Christian interpretation of Zech 14:5b, see Bauckham (1981) 137–138.

... ἐν φλογὶ πυρός) is clearly echoed in 2 Thessalonians 1:7–8 (τοῦ κυρίου Ἰησοῦ ... ἐν πυρὶ φλογός, διδόντος ἐκδίκησιν). It also looks as though Isaiah 66:5 (LXX: ἵνα τὸ ὄνομα κυρίου δοξασθῇ) is echoed in 2 Thessalonians 1:12 (ὅπως ἐνδοξασθῇ τὸ ὄνομα τοῦ κυρίου ἡμῶν Ἰησοῦ), again involving an interpretation of the κύριος which in the Old Testament text represents the tetragrammaton as the Lord Jesus.[27] Kreitzer in his study of these Pauline passages calls the phenomenon a 'referential shift of "Lord" from God to Christ.'[28] Later evidence of the application of the same passage of Isaiah to the parousia of Jesus is found in the use of Isaiah 66:18 in 2 Clement 17:4–5.

(c) The phrase which recurs in Isaiah 2:10, 19, 21 (LXX: ἀπὸ προσώπου τοῦ φόβου κυρίου, καὶ ἀπὸ τῆς δόξης τῆς ἰσχύος αὐτοῦ), referring to the reaction of people to the theophany of Yahweh on the day of Yahweh, is taken over in 2 Thessalonians 1:9, modified only by the omission of φόβου, to refer to the relation of the wicked to the Lord Jesus at his parousia.[29]

(d) Joel 2:28–32: Although 'the Lord' in the conclusion to this explicitly 'day of the Lord' passage is understood in Acts 2:39 as 'the Lord our God' (alluding to Joel 2:32b), verse 32a is quoted in Romans 10:13 as the scriptural basis for the Christian confession of Jesus as Lord. It is probably also the source of the pre-Pauline description of Christians as those who 'call on the name of our Lord Jesus Christ' (1 Cor 1:2; cf. Acts 9:14, 21; 22:16; 2 Tim 2:22; Hermas, *Sim.* 9:14:3).[30]

(e) Isaiah 40:10 (LXX: ἰδοὺ κύριος ... ἔρχεται ... ὁ μισθὸς αὐτοῦ μετ' αὐτοῦ) is echoed in Revelation 22:12 (ἰδοὺ ἔρχομαι ... ὁ μισθός μου μετ' ἐμοῦ), in which the κύριος of Isaiah becomes the 'I' of Jesus, who at 22:20 is called Lord in a translation of the 'Maranatha' acclamation. For the application of Isaiah 40:10 to the parousia, see also 1 Clement 34:3; Barnabas 21:3.

[27] Kreitzer (1987) 119–120.
[28] Kreitzer (1987) 113.
[29] Kreitzer (1987) 121–122.
[30] Cerfaux (1954A) 181.

(f) Isaiah 45:23 does not belong to the same genre of theophany texts, but it was similarly interpreted in early Christianity with reference to the parousia of Jesus. Although in Romans 14:11 it is quoted with reference to God, its use in the pre-Pauline hymn in Philippians 2:10–11 makes very explicit reference to the confession of Jesus as Lord.

(g) We should also note that the Old Testament phrase 'the day of the Lord' is used of the parousia, with 'the Lord' understood as Jesus (1 Thess 5:2; 2 Thess 2:2; 2 Pet 3:10), expanded as 'the day of the Lord Jesus Christ' (1 Cor 5:5: but the text is uncertain) or 'the day of our Lord Jesus' (1 Cor 1:8; 2 Cor 1:14), and modified to 'the day of Christ Jesus' (Phil 1:6) or 'the day of Christ' (Phil 1:10; 2:16).[31]

These are the clear examples of Old Testament theophany texts applied to the parousia of the Lord Jesus. There are other possible, but less clear examples.[32] About the phenomenon of the application of these texts to Jesus, two important observations need to be made. In the first place, it is certainly not the case that Greek-speaking Christians have taken Old Testament texts about a κύριος to refer to Jesus without realising that κύριος in these texts refers to God. That the 'referential shift of "Lord" from God to Christ' (Kreitzer) was conscious and deliberate can be seen especially in the case of Zechariah 14:5b (LXX: κύριος θεός μου), which is the most widely used of these texts. Secondly, these examples should not be seen as part of an *indiscriminate* application to Jesus of *any* texts in the Greek Old Testament which use κύριος of God. In the vast majority of quotations and allusions to the Old Testament in the New Testament, κύριος is taken to be God,[33] even though in Christian usage the word κύριος designated Jesus much more frequently than God. Beside the theophany texts applied to the parousia, there are

---

[31] Kreitzer (1987) 112–113.

[32] E.g. Matt 13:41 (?Zeph 1:3): see France (1971) 156–157; 1 Thess 4:16 (?Mic 1:3): see Glasson (1947) 168–169; 2 Thess 1:10 (?Isa 24:23): see Glasson (1947) 168. See also the list (compiled from Glasson) in Kreitzer (1987) 101–102.

[33] So, for Paul, Cerfaux (1954A) 174–177.

some other examples[34] of the 'referential shift of "Lord" from God to Christ' in New Testament quotations from and allusions to the Old Testament (e.g. Matt 3:3; Mark 1:3; Luke 3:4; John 1:23 [Isa 40:3]; 1 Cor 1:31; 2 Cor 10:17 [Jer 9:24]; 1 Cor 2:16 [Isa 40:13]; Heb 1:10 [Ps 102:25]; 1 Cor 10:22 [Deut 32:21]: 1 Pet 2:3 [Ps 34:8]; 1 Pet 3:15 [Isa 8:13]), but they are occasional rather than consistent. It looks as though the practice began very deliberately with a quite specific class of Old Testament passages – 'day of the Lord' theophany texts which were interpreted of the parousia of Jesus – and later spread to some other passages. Why the practice began in this way will need discussion below, but it must have begun early. The examples given above (a–g) come from a number of different strands of early Christian tradition, which points to an early origin for the practice, and in particular the examples from Paul's earliest letters and from the Gospel tradition suggest, in combination, that the practice goes back to the Palestinian church. There is therefore no difficulty in supposing that in Jude 14 we have an example of the practice from the early Palestinian church.

Not only Jude 14, but also Jude 21 ('wait for the mercy of our Lord Jesus Christ') probably reflects the 'referential shift of "Lord" from God to Christ' in Old Testament passages applied to the parousia. It is unlikely to be an allusion to any specific text, but reflects the frequent use of 'wait' in prophetic texts which were interpreted eschatologically (Isa 30:18; 49:23; 51:5; 60:9; 64:4; Dan 12:12; Mic 7:7; Hab 2:3; Zeph 3:8)[35] and the traditional use of the term 'mercy' for the eschatological hope of the righteous (Isa 64:3 LXX; 2 Macc 2:7; PssSol 7:10; 8:27–28; 10:4, 7; 14:9; 17:45; 2 Bar 78:7; 82:2;

---

[34] The clear examples in Paul are listed and discussed in Cerfaux (1954A) 182–185.

[35] Hence also 'waiting' frequently expresses the eschatological expectation in early Christian literature: προσδέχεσθαι (as in Jude 21): Mark 15:43; Luke 2:25, 38; 12:36; 23:51; Acts 24:15; Titus 2:13; 2 Clem 11:2; προσδοκᾶσθαι: Matt 11:3; Luke 7:19–20; 2 Pet 3:12–14; 1 Clem 23:5; Ign. *Pol.* 3:2; ἐκδέχεσθαι: Heb 11:10; Barn 10:11; 2 Clem 12:1; ἀπεκδέχεσθαι: Rom 8:23; 1 Cor 1:7; Gal 5:5; Phil 3:20; Heb 9:28; ἀναμένειν: 1 Thess 1:10; 2 Clem 11:5.

4 Ezra 14:34; Matt 5:7). In most of these texts, however, it is the eschatological coming of *God* which is awaited, and *God's* mercy which the righteous will then receive. Jude can urge his readers to 'wait for the mercy of our Lord Jesus Christ' (cf. 2 Tim 1:18) because of his christological interpretation of God's coming to judgment. In fact, he may well have in mind the same passage of 1 Enoch as he quotes, with christological interpretation, in verses 14–15, for in 1 Enoch 1:8 the corollary of God's destructive judgment on the wicked is his eschatological mercy to the elect (cf. 5:5; 27:4).

However, there are two difficulties about the way we have so far traced the christological interpretation of Old Testament theophany texts to the early Palestinian church. In the first place, we have assumed that early Christians found κύριος as the substitute for the tetragrammaton in their Greek Bibles and so were easily able to shift its reference from God to Christ in quotations and allusions in Greek. Most of our manuscripts of the Septuagint do regularly use κύριος where the Hebrew text has the tetragrammaton, and this has generally been assumed to be the Jewish usage with which early Christians who read the Bible in Greek were familiar. Since New Testament (and other early Christian) quotations of and allusions to the Old Testament regularly use κύριος in place of the tetragrammaton this was a natural assumption. But it has been questioned on the grounds that the manuscripts of the Septuagint in question are all Christian, whereas the few fragments we have of Jewish copies of Greek versions of the Old Testament (including the Septuagint) do not use κύριος in this way.[36] They either reproduce the tetragrammaton in Hebrew letters (יהוה) or in a kind of Greek equivalent of the Hebrew letters (ΠΙΠΙ), or they give a kind of Greek transliteration (ΙΑΩ). However, this does not in itself settle the matter, since even if it shows that κύριος was not normally *written* in place of the tetragrammaton in Jewish Greek versions of the Old Testament, it does not tell us what Jews *pronounced* when they came to the tetragrammaton in

---

[36] See Conzelmann's summary of the evidence, quoted in Fitzmyer (1979) 120.

reading the Greek text aloud (and most reading in the ancient world was reading aloud). There is good evidence that by the New Testament period, the tetragrammaton was already considered too sacred to pronounce and Palestinian Jews reading the Hebrew text of the Bible were already substituting *'adōnāy* or some other alternative to the tetragrammaton.[37] Origen in the third century testifies that Greek-speaking Jews then used κύριος for this purpose,[38] and there is no reason why the consistent practice of the New Testament in its quotations from the Old Testament should not be regarded as good evidence that this use of κύριος was already common among Greek-speaking Jews in the first century.[39] It is inconceivable that this New Testament evidence could represent a distinctly Christian practice, especially since κύριος in most cases refers to God, whereas in Christian usage outside Old Testament quotations κύριος usually referred not to God but to Jesus. Moreover, there is some Jewish evidence, not only for the use of κύριος for God (frequently in the Wisdom of Solomon, for example), but also specifically for the use of κύριος as a substitute for the tetragrammaton.[40] This was apparently not the universal practice, since Josephus regularly uses δεσπότης as a substitute for the tetragrammaton and scarcely uses κύριος for God at all.[41] But that it was a quite common practice is plausible.[42]

The second difficulty concerns the possible background in Christian Aramaic to this Christian practice in Greek. If Jude's

[37] The Qumran evidence is summarized in Fitzmyer (1979) 126–127; cf. Schulz (1962) 133.

[38] Origen, *In Ps.* 2:2, quoted in Schulz (1962) 132.

[39] Cf. Fitzmyer (1979) 121.

[40] Fitzmyer (1979) 121–122; Moule (1977) 40–41; Schulz (1962) 131–132 (on Philo). There is almost certainly more evidence to be found through careful study of the Jewish apocryphal and pseudepigraphal literature written in Greek (not translated into Greek, where the translation may be Christian). Some of the occurrences of κύριος in the Wisdom of Solomon, for example, surely represent the tetragrammaton.

[41] Cf. Fitzmyer (1979) 121–122.

[42] Fitzmyer (1981B) 222, speaks rather cautiously of 'an incipient custom among both Semitic- and Greek-speaking Jews of Palestine to call Yahweh *'ādōn, mārê'*, or *kyrios*'; cf. Fitzmyer (1979) 126.

letter derives from the bilingual Palestinian Christian circles in which the relatives of Jesus were leaders, it is hard to believe that the kind of christological application of theophany texts which it attests in verse 14 took place only in Greek. The 'referential shift of "Lord" from God to Christ' could take place in Greek if κύριος was already used as a substitute for the tetragrammaton and was also a christological title. But was it also possible in Aramaic? If theophany texts such as Zechariah 14:5b and 1 Enoch 1:9 were already applied to the parousia of Jesus in Aramaic-speaking (bilingual) Christian circles, how was this done linguistically? This specific question cannot be entirely divorced from the much discussed issue of the relation between the invocation of Jesus as 'our Lord' in Aramaic (attested in 'Maranatha') and the Greek christological title κύριος. But it is peculiarly hampered by our lack of any clear evidence of what terms Aramaic-speaking Jews of the first century used as substitutes for the tetragrammaton.[43]

Aramaic-speaking Christians undoubtedly called Jesus *māranā'* ('our Lord'). Too much has frequently been made of the difference between this suffixal form ('*our* Lord') and the absolute usage of (ὁ) κύριος ('*the* Lord') in Greek.[44] The suffixal forms *mārî* ('my lord') and *māranā'* ('our lord') are Semitic idiom. Through the range of the word's use for respected persons, rulers and God, the suffixal forms are much more common than the absolute usage of *mārê'* or *māryā'*.[45] In Greek, however, although the possessive κύριος ἡμῶν can be used (for rulers, for example[46]), the absolute use is much more common. In view of this difference of usage between the two languages, (ὁ) κύριος could easily be used to translate *mārî* or *māranā'*. Thus, even if Aramaic-speaking Christians always called Jesus *māranā'* and never *mārê'* or *māryā'*, the predominantly absolute usage of (ὁ) κύριος by Greek-speaking Christians need not be attri-

---

[43] Cf. Fitzmyer (1981B) 223; but also Vermes (1976) 112 (on 1QGenApoc 21:2–3).

[44] This is true even of Fitzmyer's work: see (1981B) 220, 223.

[45] Dalman (1902) 324–326; Cerfaux (1954A) 34, 47; Vermes (1976) 120–121.

[46] Examples in Dalman (1902) 330; Cerfaux (1954A) 13, cf. 25.

buted to a quite different development, but could be completely continuous with the Aramaic practice. It used to be alleged that Palestinian Jews would never have used the unmodified 'Lord' or 'the Lord' of God: in Hebrew or Aramaic God would always be 'my Lord,' 'our Lord,' 'Lord of the ages,' 'Lord of the kings of the earth' or similar.[47] But again, even if this were true, it need not make the transition from Aramaic to Greek problematic. Just as the absolute κύριος, used as a Greek substitute for the tetragrammaton, could be regarded as equivalent to the special suffixal form 'adōnāy, used as a Hebrew substitute for the tetragrammaton, so it could have been regarded as equivalent to mārî or māranā', if either was used as an Aramaic substitute for the tetragrammaton. In fact, new Aramaic evidence from Qumran provides clear evidence of the absolute usage or mārê'/māryā' for God,[48] though in extant Aramaic literature of the relevant period it remains less common than the suffixal forms and genitival phrases.

That some form of mārê' could have been treated as a substitute for the tetragrammaton is likely. It is the only Aramaic word which would be equivalent to 'adōnāy in Hebrew or to κύριος or δεσπότης (as in Josephus) in Greek. Moreover, the evidence shows 'that "Lord" as a designation of God enjoyed universal familiarity among Jews'[49] of the period. In modified and unmodified forms, mārê' is used in the Genesis Apocryphon and the Qumran fragments of Enoch. That Jude uses κύριος rather than κύριος ἡμῶν in verse 14 might indicate that the Aramaic equivalent to which he was used in such a context was the absolute use of mārê', but on the other hand it may indicate no more than that he was familiar with the Greek use of κύριος rather than κύριος ἡμῶν as a substitute for the tetragrammaton. Whereas when he is not formally quoting Scripture he prefers the literal Greek translation of his usual māranā' (vv 17, 21, 25), in this case he follows the form he knew was used in Greek versions of Scripture.

[47] E.g. Bultmann (1952) 51.
[48] Fitzmyer (1979) 124–125; (1981B) 222.
[49] Vermes (1976) 120.

Thus we cannot tell which form of *mārê'* underlies or would be the equivalent for κύριος in Jude 14. But it is worth considering the possibility that here and in other theophany texts applied to the parousia Aramaic-speaking Christians were familiar with the use of *mārana'* ('our Lord') as the substitute for the tetragrammaton[50] whose reference they shifted to Jesus. It is noteworthy that in several of the other New Testament examples, given above, of christological interpretation of 'day of the Lord' texts, 'our Lord' is used (1 Thess 3:13; 2 Thess 1:12; 1 Cor 1:2; cf. 1 Cor 1:8; 2 Cor 1:14). This would bring the prayer 'Maranatha' ('our Lord, come!') even closer to these Old Testament texts than would otherwise be the case. The prayer would be a direct echo of prophecies (such as Zech 14:5b; Isa 40:10; 66:15) which announced that 'our Lord will come.' Matthew Black proposed that 'Maranatha' derived specifically from 1 Enoch 1:9 as quoted by Jude,[51] but this would require that Jude's addition of κύριος to this text was not his own *ad hoc* interpretation but followed a version of the text in Aramaic current among Palestinian Jewish Christians. It would be better to connect the invocation with the other texts, which already state the divine subject of the coming explicitly and whose early Christian use is also more widely attested.

In any case, 'Maranatha' should be quite closely connected with the christological interpretation of the prophecies of the eschatological coming of God. In early Christian literature κύριος ἡμῶν is quite often found in connection with the parousia (1 Thess 2:19; 3:13; 5:9, 23; 2 Thess 1:8, 12; 2:1, 14; 1 Cor 1:7, 8; 2 Cor 1:14; 2 Pet 1:16; Did 16:1; cf. Matt 24:42).[52] This may reflect the impact of stereotyped phrases translated literally from the Aramaic. More generally, in early Christian literature (New Testament and Apostolic Fathers)

[50] 1 Enoch 89:31 (where the Ethiopic has 'our Lord,' but the fragmentary Aramaic text in 4QEn^c 4:1–2 does not preserve the word) could perhaps be an example of this use (cf. Deut 5:24–26).

[51] Black (1973) 194–196.

[52] Matt 24:42 has ὁ κύριος ὑμῶν, but, addressed by Jesus to the disciples, this implies they would speak of ὁ κύριος ἡμῶν. Cf. also Luke 12:36: τὸν κύριον ἑαυτῶν.

outside the Pauline corpus 'our Lord' is rather infrequent, while both within and outside the Pauline corpus a majority of its occurrences are in stereotyped phrases.[53] Although the phenomena of usage cannot be completely fitted into any pattern, it may be that the influence of the Aramaic *māranā'* on the original Greek forms of standard Christian expressions accounts for many of its occurrences,[54] whereas the general trend of independent Greek usage was away from κύριος ἡμῶν in favour of the absolute κύριος.

If Jude 14 can be taken, along with other indications, as evidence that the 'referential shift of "Lord" from God to Christ' in the interpretation of eschatological theophany texts with reference to the parousia occurred within the earliest bilingual Christian churces of Palestine, it remains to consider the significance of this. Of course, *mārê'*, *mārî* and *māranā'* were not as such divine titles. They had a wide range of application: to religious teachers, to secular rulers, to God. When the first Jewish Christians called Jesus 'Lord,' it was probably with reference to his messiahship. God had anointed Jesus as the eschatological ruler and judge.[55] Psalm 110:1 may well have played an important part in the origin of 'Lord' as a christological title. In no sense did it *identify* Jesus the Messiah with God (in Ps 110:1 the distinction is clear between *'adōnāy* – Yahweh – and *'adōnî* – the one who is David's lord, the Messiah).[56] But it did indicate that Jesus exercised *God's*

---

[53] E.g. διὰ Ἰησοῦ Χριστοῦ τοῦ κυρίου ἡμῶν or διὰ τοῦ κυρίου ἡμῶν Ἰησοῦ Χριστοῦ (Rom 5:1, 11, 21; 7:25; 15:30; 1 Cor 15:57; 1 Thess 5:9; 1 Clem inscr; 20:11; 44:1; 50:7); ἐν Χριστῷ Ἰησοῦ τῷ κυρίῳ ἡμῶν (Rom 6:23; 8:39; 1 Cor 15:31; Eph 3:11; cf. Polyc. *Phil.* 1:1); ὁ θεὸς καὶ πατὴρ τοῦ κυρίου ἡμῶν Ἰησοῦ Χριστοῦ (2 Cor 1:3; Eph 1:3; 1 Pet 1:3; Polyc. *Phil.* 12:2; cf. Eph 1:17; Col 1:3); ἡ χάρις τοῦ κυρίου ἡμῶν Ἰησοῦ Χριστοῦ (Rom 16:20; Gal 6:18; 1 Thess 5:28; 2 Thess 3:18; 1 Clem 65:2); τὸ ὄνομα τοῦ κυρίου ἡμῶν Ἰησοῦ (Χριστοῦ) (1 Cor 1:2; Eph 5:20; 2 Thess 1:12; 3:6); ἡ παρουσία τοῦ κυρίου ἡμῶν Ἰησοῦ Χριστοῦ (1 Thess 3:13; 5:23; 2 Thess 2:1; 2 Pet 1:16; cf. 1 Thess 2:19).

[54] So Cerfaux (1954B) 350; Manns (1977) 37–38. The argument of Kramer (1966) 220, against this, depends on his own highly questionable reconstruction of the development of christological terms, criticized by Hengel (1983) 36–38.

[55] Cerfaux (1954A) 35–63; (1954B) 348–349.

[56] On Ps 110:1, see further chapter 7 section IV below.

royal and judicial authority. As God's anointed representative he was to carry out the divine *function* of eschatological judgment and salvation. Therefore it was
natural to transfer to him the Old Testament prophecies of
God's eschatological coming in judgment, and at this point
his title 'Lord' – indicating his royal and judicial authority
as God's anointed one – coaslesced with God's name 'Lord'
(the substitute for the tetragrammaton), which indicated
God's royal and judicial authority. As the one who exercises
God's authority at the last day, the divine name in prophecies of the last day can refer to him. This was not a
general identification of Jesus with God, but a functional
identification of him with God in his eschatological coming
to judge and to save. Nevertheless, its christological consequences were to be far-reaching.

Jewish messianic expectation could also attribute the divine
functions of eschatological judgment and salvation to the Messiah (4 Ezra 12:31–33; 13:26, 37–38; 2 Bar 40:1; 72:2; 1 Enoch
45:3; 46; 55:4; 69:27–29),[57] while 11Q Melchizekek is notable
for its application to Melchizedek of Old Testament passages
about 'God' (אלהים, אל) as the judge and bringer of salvation (Pss 82:1; 7:7–8; Isa 52:7), apparently taking the word to
mean 'judge' rather than as a reference to God. Kreitzer
speaks of 'a great deal of functional overlap between an intermediary agent and God himself' in Jewish apocalyptic texts
about the eschatological judgment.[58] We might also recall
the Jewish traditions about a principal angel who bears the
divine name (Yahoel in the Apocalypse of Abraham;[59] Metra-
tron as 'the lesser YHWH' in 3 Enoch). But precisely the direct
application of the eschatological theophany passages to a
messianic figure seems not to be exactly paralleled in Jewish
apocalyptic.[60] It is very important for the development of

---

[57] This may be one (not the only) reason why, as Hultgård (1985) 50–52,
observes, intertestamental Jewish works do not often describe an eschatological theophany of God, as 1 Enoch 1:3b–9 does.

[58] Kreitzer (1987) 90.

[59] On Yahoel see Hurtado (1988) 79–80.

[60] Cf. the contrast drawn, rather too sharply, by Glasson (1947) 171, and
the criticism of his view by Kreitzer (1987) 101–102.

Christology that early Christian expectation of the parousia owed less to Old Testament messianic texts than to the direct use of Old Testament texts about the coming of God. The rationale for such use we can see in the pre-Pauline Jewish Christian hymn in Philippians 2:6–11: in exalting Jesus to be his eschatological plenipotentiary God has bestowed on him his own name, the tetragrammaton ('the name which is above every name'), and in consequence Jesus receives the homage due from all creation to God. But he does so as the representative of God the Father, in God's name, and so 'to the glory of God the Father.' We can glimpse here also the consequence for the Christian religious attitude to Jesus. Since the figure in question is no mere figure of speculation, like Melchizedek or a still unidentified Messiah, but Jesus of Nazareth, a known human figure, now absent in heaven but present to the experience of his followers in the Spirit, a figure who could be addressed ('Our Lord, come!'), his divine function inevitably made him the object of divine worship.[61] Implicitly, in religious practice, he was already assimilated to God, and the way to his conceptual inclusion in the being of God was open.

III. Jude 4

Jude's first reference to the lordship of Christ (apart from the implied reference in calling himself Ἰησοῦ Χριστοῦ δοῦλος in v 1) is the emphatic phrase τὸν μόνον δεσπότην καὶ κύριον ἡμῶν Ἰησοῦν Χριστὸν in verse 4. Some commentators[62] have taken the phrase to refer to God and Jesus ('the only Master and our Lord Jesus Christ'), but it should probably be read as a reference entirely to Jesus ('our only Master and Lord Jesus Christ').[63] The absence of the article before κύριον would in similar cases tend to imply that both epithets apply to one person, but absence of the article before κύριος is so common that the point probably

---

[61] Cf. Hurtado (1988) 93–124; Bauckham (1992).
[62] E.g. Mayor (1907) 26–27; Kelly (1969) 252; Grundmann (1974) 30–31.
[63] Spitta (1885) 313–314; Chaine (1939) 298; Osburn (1985) 300–302.

cannot be pressed here. On the other hand, the fact that δεσπότης is sometimes in early Christian literature used of God but hardly ever of Christ (see below) cannot be decisive against its reference to Christ here, since at any rate the first reader of Jude whose understanding of the phrase is known to us took δεσπότης to refer to Christ (2 Pet 2:1), while the fact that the relatives of Jesus were known in Palestinian Jewish Christian circles as οἱ δεσπόσυνοι (Julius Africanus, *ap.* Eusebius, *HE* 1:7:14) shows that δεσπότης was used of Christ in precisely the circles from which Jude's letter comes. Finally, since δεσπότης and κύριος are virtually synonymous, it would seem very odd to combine a reference to 'the *only* Master' with one to another 'Lord.' Although on a theological level the lordship of Christ would not contradict the sole lordship of God, such a blatant contradiction on the linguistic surface seems unlikely.

We may therefore take it that τὸν μόνον δεσπότην καὶ κύριον ἡμῶν Ἰησοῦν Χριστὸν is a deliberately full reference to the lordship of Jesus Christ, strategically placed in the statement of theme (v 4) for the exegetical section of Jude's letter (vv 5–19), which is concerned with the coming judgment by Jesus the Lord on those who reject his lordship. He is called 'our *only* Master and Lord,' not because Jude's opponents are teaching some theological error (pagan or Gnostic) which infringes monotheism or the sole mediation of Christ, but because they are libertines, who deny Jesus Christ by deliberately ignoring his moral demands in practice and teach others to do so. To indulge in such behaviour is in fact to serve other masters, including their own misguided self-interest (cf. Matt 6:24; Rom 6:12–23; Gal 4:3, 8–9; 2 Pet 2:19). By thus subjecting themselves to other masters, they are disowning Christ, the only Master of Christians.[64]

The word δεσπότης, however, requires further attention. Though its use in Greek[65] is in many ways similar to that of κύριος, it has a rather narrower range. It normally refers either to the Master of a household, with absolute rights over

---

[64] Bauckham (1983A) 40.
[65] See Rengstorf (1964) 44–45.

his family and slaves, or to a ruler, whose unlimited power over a people is conceived by analogy with the Master of a household. Democratically minded Greeks and Romans therefore disliked the term, as suggesting the ruler's right to the service of his subjects as of slaves, and so degrading for free men. So, although it was popular in the East for oriental monarchs, it was declined by the emperors Augustus and Tiberius, but taken up enthusiastically by Domitian and commonly used of later Roman Emperors.[66] Jews had a rather different objection to the term, on occasion at least and especially when combined with suggestions of the divinity of the ruler: that the only δεσπότης they could serve was God.[67]

Jewish use of δεσπότης for God is not easily differentiated from the use of κύριος.[68] If we allow the Septuagint's use of κύριος as the substitute for the tetragrammaton as Jewish, then κύριος is much more frequently used of God in the Septuagint than δεσπότης is, but Josephus uses δεσπότης for God to the almost complete exclusion of κύριος, while Philo uses both frequently. It is significant that it occasionally occurs in the Septuagint in combination with κύριος, translating phrases which combine 'ādōn or 'adōnāy with the tetragrammaton (Gen 15:2, 8; Isa 1:24; 3:1; 10:33; Jer 1:6; 4:10; 14:13),[69] while in the other Greek translations of the Old Testament it is used more frequently to render 'ādōn or 'adōnāy and occasionally for the tetragrammaton.[70] While in some cases δεσπότης seems to have a stronger association with God's omnipotent sovereignty over the created world, on the whole it seems that δεσπότης and κύριος equally express the dominant Jewish perception of God as Lord in New Testament times.

Early Christianity took over the Jewish usage to some extent, especially in prayer and liturgical formulae, and extant Christian literature up to the mid-second century uses

[66] Mastin (1973) 354–355.
[67] Cerfaux (1954A) 27–31.
[68] Rengstorf (1964) 47, probably exaggerates the distinction.
[69] Rengstorf (1964) 46.
[70] Rengstorf (1964) 46 and n. 18.

δεσπότης almost exclusively of God the Father and sometimes, as in Jewish usage, with a stress on the Creator's sovereignty over his creation (Luke 2:29; Acts 4:14; Rev 6:10;
1 Clem 7:5; 8:2; 9:4; 11:1; 20: 8, 11; 24:1, 5; 33:1, 2; 36:2, 4;
40:1, 4; 48:1; 52:1, 55:6; 56:16; 59:4; 60:3; 61:1–2; 64; Did
10:3; Barn 1:7; 4:3; Hermas, *Vis.* 2:2:4–5; 3:3:5; *Sim.* 1:9;
Diogn 8:7 [cf. 3:2]; Justin, *1 Apol.* 12:9; 61:10; Melito, *Peri
Pascha* 76–77; Irenaeus, *Haer.* 2:26:1). Of δεσπότης referring
to Christ, Jude 4 and 2 Peter 2:1, which is dependent on Jude
4, are the only extant examples before the second half of the
second century (Melito, *Peri Pascha* 96–97; Mart. Justin [Rec.
B] 5:6; Clem. Alex., *Strom.* 4:7). But, as we have already
noted, Palestinian Jewish Christianity would seem, from the
evidence of the term δεσπόσυνοι, to have been peculiar in
this respect. Jude's use of δεσπότης for Christ, though exceptional by comparison with other extant Christian literature of
the first century of the church, probably reflects a usage
current in the circles in which the relatives of Jesus were
leaders.

What significance did δεσπότης have when applied to Jesus?
One possibility is that it evoked the image of the church as a
household and Jesus as the Master of his household slaves.[71]
This is how 2 Peter 2:1 uses it, in taking over the word from
Jude and combining it with a common image of Christian
salvation as redemption by Christ ('the Master who bought
them' – i.e. purchased them as slaves). The term οἰκοδεσπότης
(which, with the increasing political use of δεσπότης, had
come to be used as equivalent to δεσπότης in the domestic
sense) is used of Jesus in this way in figurative sayings and
parables in Matt 10:25; 13:27; Luke 13:25; Ign. *Eph.* 6:1 (cf.
also 2 Tim 2:21; GTruth 25:30–31). In parallels and other
Gospel parables and sayings about a master and his servants
which were interpreted christologically the Gospels use
κύριος (cf. Mark 13:35: ὁ κύριος τῆς οἰκίας) in the same sense,
but it would have been quite possible for a version of the
Gospel tradition to have used δεσπότης as the correlative
to δοῦλοι in sayings and parables of this kind. In fact, one

---

[71] I opted for this view in Bauckham (1983A) 39.

early manuscript (P⁷⁵) has δεσπότης in Luke 13:25; while Sibylline Oracle 2:180 describes the master in the parable of the Watching Servants (Luke 12:37) as ὁ δεσπόζων, and Epiphanius, *Pan.* 69:44:1, in a reference to the same parable which may reflect an independent tradition of it, has δεσπότης.⁷² Furthermore, Hermas, in his two parables of the Vineyard and the Tower (*Sim.* 5; 9), which are to some extent modelled on Gospel parables, uses δεσπότης (*Sim.* 5:2:2, 5, 8, 9, 10, 11; 5:4:1; 5:5:3; 9:5:7; 9:7:6; 9:9:4), interchangeably with κύριος (5:5:2; 9:5:2; 9:7:1; 9:10:4), for the master or owner, who in one case represents God, in the other Christ. (Note also the parabolic sayings in Hermas, *Mand.* 5:1:5; *Sim.* 9:26:4, where δεσπότης, meaning 'owner,' in the saying is interpreted as κύριος in the explanation.) The parousia parables about servants expecting (or not) their returning master (Matt 24:45–51; 25:14–30; Mark 13:34–36; Luke 12:35–38, 42–48; cf. Luke 13:25) as well as sayings which understand the mission of Jesus' disciples as that of servants sent by their master (Matt 10:24–25; John 13:16; 15:20; Ign. *Eph.* 6:1) would have been particularly relevant to the early Jewish Christian church's understanding of Christ's lordship. Of course, the image of Christians as slaves of their master Jesus is one way in which Paul uses the christological title κύριος (e.g. Rom 12:11; Eph 6:9), even though the title also has more exalted connotations.

However, although the image of Jesus as the Master of his household slaves may well have been a secondary nuance of δεσπότης in Jude's circle, just as it was of κύριος for Paul, it is rather unlikely to have been the primary meaning either in common usage or in Jude 4. The term δεσπόσυνοι for the relatives of Jesus is easier to understand if δεσπότης described Jesus as the messianic Ruler and δεσπόσυνοι therefore attributed to his relatives the dignity of a royal family. The close association of δεσπότης and κύριος in Jude 4 probably indicates not two distinct images, but one image, which the use of two terms reinforces. The most appropriate translation would be: 'our only Sovereign and Lord Jesus Christ.' The two terms

⁷²Cf. Bauckham (1983C) 130–132.

are probably alternative Greek renderings of the single Aramaic expression *mārana*ʾ. (In bilingual inscriptions from Palmyra, *māran* is translated as δεσπότης when it refers to the Roman emperor, but as κύριος when it refers to the local Palmyrene ruler.[73])

If we remember the interchangeability of δεσπότης and κύριος in Jewish use for God, the fact that either could represent the tetragrammaton, and the occasional use of both together with reference to God (cf. also Josephus, *Ant.* 20:90; TAbr [Rec.A] 4:6; 9:6), it becomes likely that the double expression δεσπότην καὶ κύριον ἡμῶν has the same kind of divine overtone as κύριος in verse 14: Jesus' lordship is the eschatological lordship of God. This is virtually necessitated by μόνον, which in a Jewish religious context could not fail to suggest the special Jewish insistence on the unique lordship of God. The closest parallels to Jude's phrase are in Josephus, when he reports the views of Jews who refused to submit to Roman rule on the grounds that God was their 'only Ruler and Sovereign' (*Ant.* 18:23: μόνον ἡγεμόνα καὶ δεσπότην; cf. *BJ* 7:323, 410). These parallels do not show that the issue in Jude 4 is political: there is no other indication that Jude's opponents were obeying Caesar rather than Christ. They do show that the phrase in Jude 4 evokes the exclusive lordship of God. A Jewish monotheist could use such a phrase only because he understood Christ's lordship to be God's. It is not that Christ is identical with God the Father, still less that his lordship is in competition with or replaces that of God the Father, but that the lordship he exercises is the exclusive lordship of the one God (cf. Phil 2:10–11).

IV. Jude 5

For the question of the relevance of verse 5 to Jude's Christology, the first, inescapable problem is that of the text. Besides other textual variations, the subject of the verse varies widely in the manuscripts. The majority of manuscripts have κύριος or ὁ κύριος (including ℵ C* K L Ψ), but there

[73] Cerfaux (1954A) 18, 53.

is important evidence for Ἰησοῦς (including A B lat cop⁽ˢᵃ⁾ᵇᵒ
eth Jerome Cyril), while a few manuscripts have θεός or ὁ
θεός, and P⁷² has θεός Χριστός.⁷⁴ It should be noted initially
that to some extent this textual situation is not unusual, since
there are many places, especially in the Pauline corpus, where
the text varies between two of the three words κύριος, θεός
and Χριστός, and in some cases between all three (e.g. 1 Cor
10:9; 2 Cor 11:17; Eph 5:17; Col 3:16; cf. Rom 15:32). There
may be a variety of reasons for such variation: misreadings of
the abbreviations for these words, attraction of more familiar
phrases, attempts to resolve the ambiguity of κύριος (God or
Christ?), and influence of patristic christological doctrinal
debates. What is exceptional in Jude 5 is the reading Ἰησοῦς,
which there seems to be no evidence of scribes deliberately
substituting for κύριος or θεός elsewhere. We should expect
a scribe who wished to make Christ the subject of the verse
to use Χριστός. This observation, together with the principle
of preferring the more difficult reading and the strength of
the early evidence, may seem initially to make a strong case
for the originality of the reading Ἰησοῦς.⁷⁵ The problem, in
that case, of accounting for the other readings is solved by
Osburn, who regards them as third-century doctrinal altera-
tions by Monarchians who rejected the personal pre-existence
of Christ (he accounts for the reading κύριος in 1 Cor 10:9 in
the same way).⁷⁶

However, although no conclusion on this issue is likely to
be very secure, the following reasons favour the reading
κύριος against Ἰησοῦς. (1) Jude never otherwise calls Christ
simply Ἰησοῦς, and it would seem odd for him to do so
at this point. Whether he is speaking, in verses 5–7, of God
or of the pre-existent Christ, his point is to stress the divine
authority to judge apostates (cf. vv 4, 8). The context seems
to require κύριος or a phrase including κύριος. The
uncharacteristic use of the simple personal name Ἰησοῦς

---

⁷⁴ A full *apparatus criticus* is given by Osburn (1981) 108.
⁷⁵ So Bruce (1968) 35–36; Osburn (1981).
⁷⁶ Osburn (1981) 114–115.

seems unlikely. (2) Ἰησοῦς certainly cannot refer to the Old Testament Joshua[77] or be prompted by a Joshua-Jesus typology, since, even if it could be said that Joshua saved the people from Egypt, he did not destroy them in the wilderness (v 5). Moreover, the subject of verse 5 is also, as the subject of verse 6, the one who has kept the fallen angels in chains, while the close connection with verse 7 virtually necessitates the implication that he also destroyed Sodom and Gomorrah. (3) That Jude should have attributed the action of verses 5–7 to the pre-existent Christ certainly cannot be ruled out, but the use of the name Jesus for the pre-existent Christ would be unparalleled in early Christian literature (2 Cor 8:9 and Phil 2:5 have the incarnation directly in view).[78] (4) The other readings can be explained as attempts to resolve the ambiguity of an original κύριος (perhaps P[72] combines two such attempts). This does not explain why Ἰησοῦς appears (rather than Χριστός), but this can be explained by means of the Joshua-Jesus typology which became popular in the second century (Barn 12:8; Justin, *Dial.* 24:2; 75:1–2; 113; 131–132; Clem. Alex., *Paed.* 1:60:3; Tertullian, *Adv. Marc.* 3:16:3–4). Probably owing to this typology, Justin can speak (to Trypho) of 'Jesus who also led your fathers out of Egypt' (*Dial.* 120:3). The point is that a scribe could be attracted to this typology by the beginning of Jude's statement (ὅτι ... λαὸν ἐκ γῆς Αἰγύπτου σώσας) and not notice, as an author would, the pitfalls it would encounter as the statement continues. (Alternatively, one might simply suppose a misreading of the abbreviation KC as IC.)

If the reading κύριος is preferred, we still need to ask whether Jude intended it to refer to God or to Christ. We have argued that κύριος in verse 14 is the divine title applied to Christ. The same could be true in verse 5: Jude could have chosen the term κύριος because it is used of God in the scriptural accounts he is summarizing in verses 5–7, but have intended it to refer to the pre-existent Christ exercising the

[77] Cf. Jerome, *In Jovin.* 1:21; Kellett (1903–4); Wikgren (1967) 148–149.
[78] Against Hanson (1965) 165–167, whose other examples are much more doubtful.

divine lordship. The strongest case for this interpretation has been made recently by Jarl Fossum, who prefers the reading Ἰησοῦς, but argues that even if κύριος was the original reading, Ἰησοῦς may have been a correct interpretation of κύριος.[79] He suggests that throughout verses 5–7 Jude 'is adapting certain Jewish traditions about a divinely delegated intermediary,'[80] i.e. the angel of the Lord or principal angel, who bore the divine name and acted as God's deputy. He assembles the evidence for attributing to such a figure the deliverance and destruction of Israel (v 5), the punishment of the fallen angels (v 6) and the destruction of Sodom and Gomorrah (v 7). This evidence certainly shows that it is far from impossible that Jude could have drawn on contemporary Jewish ideas in order to see Jesus as the principal agent of God's action not only in the last days but also in Israel's history. Some Jewish ideas about a principal angel are not too far from Jude's understanding of Christ as κύριος in verse 14.

However, there are difficulties in Fossum's case: (1) The weakest part of his evidence concerns verse 6, where for his evidence of Jewish traditions he can appeal only to the texts of 1 Enoch on which Jude is directly and closely dependent in this verse.[81] There the chaining of the Watchers is carried out, on the command of 'the Lord,' by Raphael (10:4–6) and Michael (10:11–12). Here there is not one, but two principal angels, and it is not obvious how Jude's κύριος (if we prefer that reading) could apply to Christ as a substitute for one or both of these angels, rather than to God. In appealing to 1 Enoch 10, as also to the later Jewish tradition which identifies the angel of the Lord at the Exodus with Michael,[82] Fossum neglects Jude 9, where Jude speaks of the archangel Michael without identifying him with or replacing him by Christ. From the background to the story in Jude 9 (see chapter 5) it is clear that Michael there plays the role precisely

---

[79] Fossum (1987) 237; similarly Hanson (1965) 137; cf. Bigg (1901) 328.
[80] Fossum (1987) 227.
[81] Fossum (1987) 232.
[82] Fossum (1987) 236.

of *the* principal angel, the angel of the Lord (cf. Zech 3:1–2). It looks as though Jude was familiar with the concept of the principal angel, but refrained from interpreting the idea christologically. (2) Verses 5–7 are closely dependent on a traditional schema which listed examples of divine judgment.[83] None of the other extant forms of this schema (Sir 16:7–10; CD 2:17–3:12; 3 Macc 2:4–7; TNapht 3:4–5; m. Sanh. 10:3; 2 Pet 2:4–8) refer to an intermediary agent of God. This does not preclude Jude's interpreting the schema with reference to other traditions which did, but makes it less likely.

Since we have already seen (section II) that Jude is close to traditions of christological exegesis which appear also in Paul, it is relevant to ask whether 1 Corinthians 10:1–22 could provide a parallel to Jude 5–7. The parallel will lie not so much in Paul's identification of the rock in the wilderness wanderings with Christ (10:4) as in his two subsequent references to 'the Lord' in phrases which echo the wilderness narratives (10:9: μηδὲ ἐκπειράζωμεν τὸν κύριον [*v. ll.* Χριστόν; θεόν], καθώς τινες αὐτῶν ἐπείρασαν; cf. LXX Pss 77:18; 94:9; Exod 17:2, 7; and 10:22: παραζηλοῦμεν τὸν κύριον: cf. LXX Deut 32:21). Whether Paul's identification of the rock with Christ is meant to indicate a 'real presence' of Christ in the wilderness in the Old Testament period[84] or means that, in a typological exegesis of the Exodus narratives as prefiguring the events of eschatological salvation through Christ, the rock *represents* Christ,[85] is disputed. The latter is more probable, but in any case it would not follow from the former that in verses 9 and 22 Paul must be identifying 'the Lord' in the wilderness narratives of the Old Testament as Christ. Verse 5 shows that at any rate Paul is not carrying through a consistent identification of this kind. It is probably true that the κύριος of verses 9 and 22 is Christ (since κύριος in v 21 must be Christ), but it is noteworthy that Paul refrains

---

[83] Bauckham (1983A) 46–47.

[84] So Hanson (1965) 10–25.

[85] Dunn (1980) 183–184; cf. his bold conclusion on p. 158: 'There is no evidence that any NT writer thought of Jesus as actively present in Israel's past, either as the angel of the Lord, or as "the Lord" himself.'

from saying specifically in either verse that Israel 'tested' or 'provoked to jealousy' the same κύριος as his readers are in danger of testing or provoking to jealousy. Thus his application of terms from Old Testament texts to Christ in these verses is best understood as typological.[86] Israel tempted and provoked the Lord God, but the corresponding behaviour by Paul's readers would be a tempting and provoking of the Lord Jesus, because the lordship of God is now exercised by him.

A rather similar understanding of Jude 5–7 seems the most plausible. The κύριος of verse 5 who judged Israel, the Watchers and the cities of the Plain is God, as is the κύριος of verse 9, to whose authority as judge Michael submitted the moral question raised by the devil about Moses. But the parallel to κύριος in verse 14 is intended, because the judgments of verses 5–7 are types of the judgment which Jude's opponents are in danger of incurring at the parousia. Jesus is κύριος in verse 14 because at the parousia he will be exercising *God's* authority to judge. The divine role and authority indicated by the title κύριος in verses 5, 9 and 14 are the same, but only in verse 14 does Jesus assume that role and exercise that authority. Similarly, the 'lordship' (κυριότητα) which the opponents reject (v 8) is the divine lordship (vv 5, 9) exercised now by Christ (v 14). The catchword connexions between κύριον, κύριος and κυριότητα (vv 4, 5, 8, 9, 14, 17) bind together the whole of Jude's exegetical section as concerned with the divine authority now – in the last days (v 18) – exercised by Jesus Christ. The variation of subject between God and Jesus is possible for Jude precisely because of his κύριος-Christology: the same divine authority is at stake throughout.

V. Conclusion

The central theme of Jude's Christology, as it becomes apparent in this short letter, is that Jesus is the eschatological agent of God's salvation and judgment. He is the Messiah (vv 1, 2, 4, 17, 21, 25), i.e. the one who has been anointed by God as

---

[86] Cf. Cerfaux (1954A) 182–183.

his viceroy. But as *God's* Messiah it is God's authority to save and to judge which he exercises. Therefore God's title κύριος (vv 5, 9) – or better, God's own divine *name* represented in Greek as κύριος – is his (v 14). This assimilates Jesus to God without simply identifying him with God. Certainly he acts as God towards the church and the world. The lordship of God is his lordship, and God is known now and in the future only with reference to Jesus. The roots of all later thinking about Jesus' divinity lie in this original Jewish Christian understanding of Jesus as the one through whom all God's eschatological action occurs and therefore as the one to whom Christians address their acknowledgement of the divine lordship.

As far as Jesus' relation to Christians is concerned, he is preeminently 'our Lord' (vv 4, 17, 21, 25) – where the 'our' is Semitic idiom, but an idiom expressing the fact that Lord is a relational term: someone is only Lord because he is Lord over a community. Jesus' lordship over the church is constituted by his eschatological saving action – the new Exodus, creating the eschatological Israel. This deliverance he has already accomplished (cf. v 5) but it has still to reach its goal at the imminent parousia (vv 21, 25). Christians are those who are 'kept for Jesus Christ' (v 1), i.e. kept safe by God until they are claimed by Jesus at his coming as those who belong to him. Because he is 'our Lord,' his faithful people can expect mercy at his coming to judgment (v 21), but for those who, having experienced his salvation, reject his lordship there can only be condemnation (vv 14–15).

We cannot expect that so short a letter, written in response to a specific need (vv 3–4), will give us a complete picture of the Christology current in the circles in which Jude was a leader. In particular, the salvation Christ has already accomplished for his people is presupposed but no more than hinted at in the typological form of verse 5. Behind this hint must lie a developed understanding of the cross and resurrection of Jesus. But insofar as an argument from silence can be allowed any weight, it is noteworthy that, in a letter so orientated to the role of Christ as judge at the imminent parousia, the term 'Son of man' goes unmentioned. This would seem to support the contention that there was never, as such, a 'Son-of-man Christology,' such as has so often been postulated for the early Palestinian church, but that the term 'Son of man' was confined to the tradition of the sayings of Jesus.[87]

Further light on the Christology of Jude's circle will be shed, from an unexpected quarter, in the next chapter.

[87] Cf. Lindars (1983).

7

The Lukan Genealogy of Jesus

The Lukan genealogy of Jesus is a more important historical document than has been generally appreciated. This chapter will demonstrate that it derives, in virtually the form that Luke has preserved, from the circle of the first generation of the *desposynoi*. Not only does it incorporate the family's own tradition of its ancestry. Like some other genealogies in the Old Testament and Jewish tradition, it is also a rather sophisticated theological construct, carefully designed to express the central messianic convictions of the brothers of Jesus and their circle. It deserves a significant place in any attempt to reconstruct the character of the Palestinian Jewish Christianity of the first few decades.

It is surprising that, despite the considerable amount of discussion the Lukan genealogy has received, the two major keys to its understanding have gone largely unnoticed, and certainly unused. One derives from the book of Enoch, the other concerns the proper understanding of the Old Testament expectation of a new Davidic ruler. These two keys will be used in turn to open up the secrets of the genealogy in the first two sections of the chapter. In the third section evidence will be offered for connecting the genealogy with the *desposynoi* in general and with Jude in particular.

I The Enochic Dimension

Discussion of the nature of the genealogy must begin with

Weeks	Luke 3:23–38	Apocalypse of Ten Weeks (1 Enoch 93:3–10; 91:11–17)	OT	
1	Ἀδάμ		Adam	
	Σήθ		Seth	
	Ἐνώς		Enosh	
	Καϊνάμ		Kenan	
	Μαλελεήλ		Mahalalel	
	Ἰάρετ		Jared	
	Ἐνώχ	Enoch	Enoch	
2	Μαθουσαλά		Methuselah	
	Λάμεχ		Lamech	
	Νῶε	Flood	Noah	
	Σήμ		Shem	
	Ἀρφαξάδ		Arpachshad	
	Καϊνάμ		Kenan (LXX/Jub)	
	Σαλά	Noah's law	Shelah	
3	Ἔβερ		Eber	
	Φάλεκ		Peleg	
	Ῥαγαύ		Reu	
	Σερούχ		Serug	
	Ναχώρ		Nahor	
	Θάρα		Terah	
	Ἀβραάμ	Abraham	Abraham	
4	Ἰσαάκ		Isaac	(Ezra 7:1–5)
	Ἰακώβ		Jacob	
	Ἰούδα		Judah	Levi
	Φάρες		Perez	Kohath
	Ἐσρώμ		Hezron	Amram
	Ἀρνί		Ram	Aaron
	Ἀδμίν	Sinai	Amminadab	Eleazar
5	Ἀμιναδάμ		Nahshon	Phinehas
	Ναασσών		Salmon	Abishua
	Σάλα		Boaz	Bukki
	Βόος		Obed	Uzzi
	Ἰωβήδ		Jesse	Zerahiah
	Ἰεσσαί		David	Meraioth
	Δαυίδ	Temple	Solomon	Azariah

6	Ναθάμ		Amariah
	Ματταθά		Ahitub
	Μεννά		Zadok
	Μελεά	Elijah	Shallum
	Ἐλιακίμ		Hilkiah
	Ἰωανάμ		Azariah
	Ἰωσήφ	Fall of Temple	Seraiah

7	Ἰούδα	
	Συμεών	
	Λευί	
	Μαθθάτ	
	Ἰωρίμ	
	Ἐλιέζερ	
	Ἰησοῦς	Revelation to elect

8	Ἤρ	
	Ἐλμαδάμ	
	Κωσάμ	
	Ἀδδί	
	Μελχί	
	Νηρί	
	Σαλαθιήλ	New Temple

9	Ζοροβαβέλ	
	Ῥησά	
	Ἰωανάν	
	Ἰωδά	
	Ἰωσήχ	
	Σεμεῖν	
	Ματταθίας	

10	Μάαθ	
	Ναγγαί	
	Ἐσλί	
	Ναούμ	
	Ἀμώς	
	Ματταθίας	
	Ἰωσήφ	Judgment of Watchers

11	Ἰανναί	New heaven
	Μελχί	Weeks without number
	Λευί	
	Ματθάτ	
	Ἠλί	
	Ἰωσήφ	
	Ἰησοῦς	

the observation that it consists of seventy-seven[1] human generations, from Adam to Jesus. (The final words of the genealogy
in its present form – τοῦ Θεοῦ – are unparalleled in a Jewish
genealogy. They are likely to be Luke's redaction of his
source, and will be discussed later in section V. For the time
being we treat the genealogy as ending with Adam.)

The number seventy-seven may already suggest that some
kind of numerical scheme, such as can be detected in other
Jewish genealogies, is present. Such schemes are not always
explicit, as in Matthew 1:1–17, but may be implicit, as in
1 Chronicles 6:1–15.[2] Most previous attempts to find a numerical scheme in the Lukan genealogy have observed that it
consists of eleven groups of seven generations and have
supposed that it must be connected with apocalyptic speculations which divide world history into twelve periods.[3] Jesus
would then conclude the eleventh and introduce the twelfth
and last period of history before the end. However, such
speculations elsewhere are concerned with periods measured
in years, not in generations.[4] Moreover, none of them attach
messianic or eschatological importance to the transition from
the eleventh to the twelfth period. The attempt to fit the
Lukan genealogy into a scheme of twelve periods is a false
track.

It is true that, to anyone familiar with biblical numerology,
eleven seems an unsatisfactory number of periods into which
to divide world history: it comes one short of twelve. But
whereas eleven suggests incompleteness, eleven times seven
(seventy-seven) suggests the opposite. If seven indicates fullness, seventy-seven implies ultimacy, a fullness beyond
measure, as in the song of Lamech, 'If Cain is avenged sevenfold, truly Lamech seventy-sevenfold' (Gen 4:24), and in Mat-

---

[1] This is the number of names according to modern editions of the
Greek New Testament. Some manuscripts have fewer names: see the Additional Note at the end of this chapter.

[2] Johnson (1969) 40–41.

[3] Bornhäuser (1930) 22; Kaplan (1930) 469–470; Ford (1984) 46.

[4] 4 Ezra 14:11–12; cf. 2 Bar 53–74 (where there are in fact thirteen periods
before the messianic age); ApAb 28–29 (where the twelve periods do not
cover the whole of world history); LadJac 5 (similarly).

thew 18:22, 'I do not say to you seven times, but seventy-seven times.'[5] These parallels to the symbolic use of the number seventy-seven encourage us to notice that seventh place in the Lukan genealogy is occupied by Enoch. Enoch was in fact well-known to be the seventh generation from Adam, which marked him out as a figure of special importance (1 Enoch 60:8; 93:3; Jub 7:39; Lev. R. 29:11; Jude 14). Enoch was probably the one person whose numerical place in a genealogy beginning from Adam was widely known and regarded as significant.[6] Thus, we may suspect some kind of relation between Enoch as the seventh generation and Jesus as the seventy-seventh. If Enoch as the seventh is special, Jesus as the seventy-seventh is the ultimate. The number seventy-seven designates Jesus as the furthest the generations of world history will go, both in number and in significance. Furthermore, we should remember that for a mind concerned with the symbolic significance of sevens special significance also attaches to *seven times seven* – the jubilee figure of forty-nine.[7] It cannot be accidental that in the Lukan genealogy the name Jesus occurs not only in seventy-seventh place, but also in forty-ninth place – where the only namesake of Jesus among his ancestors appears (Luke 3:29).

However, we do not have to depend on these general reflections alone for the conclusion that the genealogy designates Jesus as the climax and end of world history. The conclusion is confirmed by the text on which this genealogy of Jesus must have been based: 1 Enoch 10:12 (=4QEn[b]

---

[5] ἑβδομηκοντάκις ἑπτά should be translated 'seventy-seven times' (not 'seventy times seven'), as in Gen 4:24 (to which it probably alludes); TBenj 7:4.

[6] Significance was also attached to Moses' place as the seventh generation from Abraham: Philo, *Mos.* 1.17; Josephus, *Ant.* 2:229; Lev. R. 29:11. For the importance of the seventh generation see also the idea of the seventh king of Egypt as a messianic figure in SibOr 3:193, 318, 608.

[7] Cf. the use of jubilee periods of forty-nine years in chronological and apocalyptic calculations in Jubilees; Dan 9:24–27; 11QMelch; 4QPs-Ezek; 4Q180; 4Q181. On these see Wiesenberg (1961); Wacholder (1975), Beckwith (1980); (1981); Kobelski (1981) 49–51; Bacchiocchi (1986) 172–176. For the jubilee year as the forty-ninth (rather than the fiftieth, as in Lev 25:10), see Wacholder (1975) 204.

1:4:10).[8] The archangel Michael is there instructed to bind
the fallen angels, the Watchers, 'for seventy generations under
the hills of the earth until the [great] day of their
judgment.'[9] From v 14 it is clear that this day of the judgment
of the Watchers is *the* day of judgment at the end of world
history.[10] It is not easy to tell from the Enoch literature
exactly when the binding of the fallen angels occurred, but it
certainly happened after Enoch's translation and during the
lifetime of his son Methuselah. So a reader might easily suppose that it should be dated in the generation after Enoch's.
Thus from 1 Enoch 10:12 it appears that the whole of world
history from Adam to the Last Judgment comprises seventy-
seven generations, seven up to and including Enoch, followed
by a further seventy. For anyone familiar with 1 Enoch 10:12
the Lukan genealogy of Jesus would clearly designate Jesus
the last generation of history before the end.

The author of the Lukan genealogy must have been
inspired by 1 Enoch 10:12, but he will also have found elsewhere in the Enoch literature a model for a scheme of
periodizing world history in units of seven generations. The
Apocalypse of Weeks (1 Enoch 93:3–10; 91:11–17)[11] divides
the history of the world from Adam to the judgment of the
Watchers into ten 'weeks' of seven generations each. It has
sometimes been suggested that this scheme was based on
1 Enoch 10:12,[12] but unlike 1 Enoch 10:12 the Apocalypse of
Weeks includes the first seven generations up to Enoch in its
ten weeks or seventy generations. If it was inspired by
1 Enoch 10:12, it has reduced the eleven 'weeks' of world
history implied by that text to ten. The author of the Lukan

[8] Both Milik (1976) 257, and Brown (1977) 91, see the relevance of this
text to the Lukan genealogy, but fail to develop the point.
[9] Translation of the Ethiopic from Knibb (1978) 89, but with 'great'
supplied from the Aramaic in 4QEn^b 1:4:10.
[10] For the text of this verse, see Knibb (1978) 89–90 n.: Syncellus' Greek
seems preferable.
[11] This rearrangement of the text, long postulated by scholars, has been
shown to be the original form of the Apocalypse of Weeks by the Aramaic
fragments from Qumran: see Milik (1976) 247; Dexinger (1977) 102–109;
Black (1978); Knibb (1978) 14; Black (1985) 287–289, 291–292.
[12] Collins (1984B) 51; cf. Charles (1893) 261.

genealogy could easily have seen this as an inadequacy of the Apocalypse of Weeks. He has therefore not simply reproduced its scheme, which in any case would not easily coincide with his own understanding of world history in its later periods, but he has used it as a model for constructing his own scheme of eleven weeks of generations.

The Apocalypse of Weeks is the only extant apocalyptic scheme of world history (from Adam to the end) which makes use of generations as its unit of measurement.[13] It is therefore much the most suitable for comparison with a *genealogical* scheme such as the Lukan genealogy of Jesus. That the ten weeks of the Apocalypse of Weeks are weeks of *generations*[14] is made quite clear in the case of the first week, of which Enoch says, 'I was born the seventh in the first week' (1 Enoch 93:3). However, scholars have not generally accepted that the subsequent weeks are consistently intended to be measured in generations, because it is alleged that they cannot be made to fit into a scheme of generations.[15] The diagram is intended to show that they can.

Most important events noticed in the Apocalypse of Weeks happen at the end of each week, i.e. in the seventh generation, the sabbath of each week. Only the ninth week lacks a significant event at its end. From Adam to Abraham, we may suppose that the author followed the biblical genealogy, but, in view of the close relationship between the Enoch literature and Jubilees, he would have included in it the second Kenan,

---

[13] In SibOr 4:47–87, the ten generations cover only the period of the four kingdoms (Assyrians, Medes, Persians, Macedonians). In SibOr 1–2 the whole of world history is outlined in ten generations, but plainly these are not successive generations in the ordinary sense.

[14] They should therefore be distinguished from the more common apocalyptic reckoning in weeks and jubilees of *years*: on which see Wiesenberg (1961); Wacholder (1975); Milik (1976) 248–257; Beckwith (1980); (1981); Bacchiocchi (1986) 172–176.

[15] Cf. the discussion, with references to earlier literature, in Dexinger (1977) 119–120; also Beckwith (1980) 191–192. But Kaplan (1930) 467–468, rightly measures the weeks in generations. The most detailed alternative reckonings of the weeks are those of Beckwith (1980) and Koch (1983) 413–420: by comparison with a generational scheme both are very contrived.

the son of Arpachshad, who is not in the MT but appears in Jubilees 8:1–5, as well as in the Septuagint (Gen 10:24; 11:12). In that case there are twenty-one generations, placing Abraham exactly where the Apocalypse indicates (93:5): at the end of the third week. The law made for sinners by Noah, at the end of the second week, following the growth of iniquity after the Flood (93:4), should be identified not with the Noahic covenant of Genesis 9:1–17, but with the tradition, found in Jubilees 7:20–39, of Noah's instruction of his sons.[16] Although Jubilees dates this before the birth of Kenan, the author of the Apocalypse of Weeks could easily have supposed it to happen during the lifetime of Shelah, when, whichever of the divergent extant chronologies he followed, Noah was certainly still alive.[17]

The biblical genealogy from Isaac to Solomon would make Solomon the last generation of the fifth week, in which the Apocalypse of Weeks dates the building of the Temple (93:7). However, the giving of the Law at Sinai at the end of the fourth week (93:6) would then occur in the generation of Amminadab, whereas according to the biblical account the following generation, that of Nahshon, would be more appropriate (see Exod 6:23; Num 1:7; 1 Chron 2:10). But the main problem in following this line of descent would occur after Solomon. The Apocalypse of Weeks allows only one week for whole period of the divided monarchy, down to the destruction of the Temple and the exile. From Rehoboam to Jeconiah there were seventeen generations of the kings of Judah (1 Chron 3:10–16). We might expect the number to be adjusted to fit the artificial requirements of a numerical scheme, as it is by Matthew, who reduces it to fourteen generations or two 'weeks' (Matt 1:7–11), and by Josephus, who extends it to twenty-one generations or three 'weeks' (*Ant.* 5:336). But the reduction to a mere seven generations or one 'week' seems very drastic treatment. It is a mistake, however, to suppose that our author would count his genera-

---

[16] Dexinger (1977) 123–124; Black (1985) 289–290.
[17] Johnson (1969) 262–265, gives a handy conspectus of the chronological schemes in MT, LXX, Samaritan Pentateuch, Jubilees and Josephus.

tions according to the royal line, in which he shows no interest at all.[18] His interests are in the Law and the Temple, and he probably belonged to a dissident priestly group which did not recognize the second Temple (about which the account of the seventh week is eloquently silent).[19] He is likely to have followed a priestly genealogy, which we can confidently reconstruct as far as the end of the fourth week (cf. Exod 6:16–25). The generation of Eleazar the son of Aaron can be more plausibly than Amminadab's considered the generation of Sinai (see Exod 28:1; Num 3:2–4, 22).

From Phinehas to the exile the biblical literature supplies no standard priestly genealogy and we cannot tell what genealogy the author of the Apocalypse of Weeks might have known. The diagram provides the genealogy given (as that of Ezra) in Ezra 7:1–5 simply as an illustration (for variants of it see I Chron 6:4–14; 9:11; Neh 11:11). It does demonstrate that a priestly genealogy *could* fit the scheme of the Apocalypse of Weeks, since Azariah at the end of the fifth week could be considered contemporary with the building of the Temple (as in I Kings 4:2; I Chron 6:10)[20] and Seraiah at the end of the sixth week was high priest at the time of the fall of Jerusalem (2 Kings 25:18). Allowing both for the fact that a priestly genealogy known to the author could well, like this one, have far fewer generations than the line of the kings of Judah, and for the author's willingness to manipulate a genealogy to fit his numerical scheme, there is no difficulty in supposing that the sixth week is a week of seven generations like the previous weeks.

The scheme had in any case to cover the monarchical and post-exilic periods in no more than two weeks because the author clearly wanted to put his own generation – in which the secrets of Enoch's revelations (the 'sevenfold wisdom and knowledge' of 93:10) were given to his own religious group ('the chosen righteous' of Abraham's seed:

[18] Black's suggestion ([1985] 290) of an allusion to the house of David in 93:7 is quite unjustified.
[19] Cf. Hamerton-Kelly (1970) 1–4.
[20] On I Chron 6:10 (Hebrew 5:36) see Johnson (1969) 41.

93:10, cf. 93:5)[21] – in the key position of the whole scheme, i.e. the seventh generation of the seventh week, the 'jubilee' position.[22] This identifies the author's own generation as the turning-point of world history, after which the three remaining weeks of the ten contain several stages of eschatological fulfilment, culminating in the judgment of the Watchers in the last generation of all, the seventieth (91:15), before the new world of innumerable weeks (91:17).

The Lukan genealogy certainly does not conform to the details of this scheme, but the principle to be seen in the Apocalypse of Weeks, that the important generations are those at the end of each week is illuminating in relation to the genealogy. It cannot be applied throughout. But it should be noted that the name Joseph, in its two occurrences before the eleventh week, is found at the end of the sixth and tenth weeks respectively, just as the name Jesus is found in the 'jubilee' position at the end of the seventh week. It is as though the author wishes these key generations to point forward to the end of the whole genealogy. In themselves, according to the author's perspective on world history, they do not mark turning-points, but are significant only as pointing forward to the climax of history in Jesus the son of Joseph.

The principle of the significance of the end of the week also explains the genealogy's major divergence from the biblical number of generations. The three names 'Αρνί 'Αδμίν and 'Αμιναδάμ (Luke 3:33) correspond to only two biblical generations: Ram and Amminadab (Ruth 4:19; 1 Chron 2:9–10 – and so puzzled the scribes, resulting in the variant readings[23]). Even if the additional generation came about, in the history of the genealogy, by scribal error,[24] its presence now

[21] Cf. Dexinger (1977) 133–135; Vander Kam (1984) 147–149.

[22] An interesting parallel to the seven generations of the seventh week in the Apocalypse of Weeks is found in EpJer 3, which reckons seven generations from the beginning of the exile to its expected end. This is one of the many reinterpretations of Jeremiah's prophecy of seventy years of exile (Jer 25:11–12): cf. Knibb (1976).

[23] See the Additional Note at the end of this chapter.

[24] So Jeremias (1969) 293, who argues that Admin was originally an abbreviation of Amminadab, and that Amminadab was later added by a

performs an essential function. It serves to put David in the seventh, 'sabbath' generation of the fifth week, instead of merely in the sixth generation, where the biblical number of generations would leave him. Unlike the Apocalypse of Weeks, which is not interested in David but has the building of the Temple in this position, the Lukan genealogy highlights the position of David and therefore Jesus' descent from David. In order to understand this aspect of the genealogy more fully, we must turn from the Enoch literature to the other major key to interpretation of the genealogy.

Before doing so, however, it is worth stressing one conclusion which the Enochic structure of the genealogy entails. The genealogy must have been composed in this form during the generation of Jesus' contemporaries, for it conveys the apocalyptic message: Jesus belongs to the last generation of all, the seventy-seventh generation in which the last judgment will take place. Perhaps it cannot exactly have been intended to *prove* that point, since the number of generations has been artificially constructed, but on the other hand the number of generations is not at all implausible. To conclude that Jesus was the seventy-seventh generation from Adam was not difficult in relation to the chronological knowledge available in first-century Judaism. In any case, the genealogy is certainly constructed to *express* this belief – not simply the imminent eschatological expectation of early Christianity (which certainly survived into the second and subsequent generations), but the specific expectation of the parousia within the generation of Jesus' contemporaries. The genealogy is of a piece with the saying in Mark 13:30 (|| Matt 24:34; Luke 21:32): 'Truly, I say to you, this generation shall not pass away before all these things take place' (cf. Mark 9:1; 14:62). Luke's retention of this Markan saying of Jesus in Luke 21:32 suggests that he would not have objected to the apocalyptic meaning

---

copyist who did not understand this. But it should also be noticed that the only biblical authorities for Ram as the one generation between Hezron and Amminadab are Ruth 4:19; 1 Chron 2:9–10. The possibility of an alternative genealogical tradition cannot be ruled out (cf. 1 Chron 2:25, 27, where another [?] Ram is son of Jerahmeel and therefore *grandson* of Hezron).

of the genealogy, had he perceived it. But since the rest of his work provides no evidence that Luke knew or was interested in the Enoch literature, it is rather doubtful whether he even perceived the Enochic structure of the genealogy and very unlikely that he could himself have given it that structure.[25] That he nevertheless reproduced the list of seventy-seven names he found in his source may say something interesting about his sources and his faithfulness to them.

II The Davidic Dimension

The section of the genealogy between David and Jesus has two major peculiarities. In the first place the line of descent from David is traced not through Solomon and the kings of Judah, but through Nathan, a son of David by Bathsheba who is barely mentioned in the Old Testament (2 Sam 5:14; 1 Chron 3:5; 14:4; Zech 12:12). Secondly, although the rest of the names of Nathan's descendants in the genealogy are not drawn from any Old Testament genealogy, they include Zerubbabel and his father Shealtiel (Σαλαθιήλ). Zerubbabel is frequently called the son of Shealtiel in the Old Testament (Ezra 3:2, 8; 5:2; Neh 12:1; Hag 1:1, 12, 14; 2:2, 23). Only once, in the genealogy of the house of David in 1 Chronicles 3, is he given a fuller pedigree: as the grandson of king Jeconiah (1 Chron 3:16–19). (In fact, this genealogy in the MT makes Shealtiel, Jeconiah's eldest son, the uncle of Zerubbabel, whose father is said to be Jeconiah's third son Pedaiah. This discrepancy, corrected in the Septuagint (AB), has some-

---

[25] Similarly Bornhäuser (1930) 21. Aalen (1966–67) pointed out parallels between Luke's special material and 1 Enoch 92–105, and cautiously suggested that Luke was dependent on this section of 1 Enoch. However, Nickelsburg (1979) rightly rejects Aalen's case for specific dependence on the Greek text of 1 Enoch 92–105 by Luke, while showing that there are impressive parallels of thought between 1 Enoch 92–105 and (not only special Lukan) material on riches and the rich in Luke. His argument seems to me to show that these parallels belong to Luke's traditions rather than to Lukan redaction, while leaving it in any case doubtful whether it is a matter of dependence on 1 Enoch or of common traditions. Cf. the discussion of Nickelsburg's paper reported in Charlesworth (1985) 107.

times been explained by levirate marriage or adoption.[26])
Matthew's genealogy of Jesus follows Chronicles, making
Shealtiel the son of Jeconiah (Matt 1:12), but Luke's ignores
Chronicles and makes Shealtiel and Zerubbabel descendants
of David through Nathan. Clearly, a satisfactory understanding
of the line of Jesus' descent from David in the Lukan genealogy
must explain not only why the line is traced from Nathan
but also why it is traced from Nathan through Zerubbabel.

Two explanations of the descent from Nathan may be
rejected at the outset. (1) It has been claimed that in Jewish
messianic speculation Nathan the son of David was identified
with Nathan the prophet and made the ancestor of the
Davidic Messiah in order to give the Messiah a prophetic as well
as a royal pedigree.[27] As we shall see, the identification of the
two Nathans was a Jewish exegetical tradition, but it can
have nothing to do with ideas about the prophetic status
of the Messiah. Unlike royalty and priesthood, prophecy
is not inherited, and noone in Judaism ever supposed it was.
(2) A second suggestion is that the Messiah's descent from
Nathan was postulated because of the oracle of Jeremiah
which predicted that no descendant of king Jeconiah would
ever sit on the throne of David (Jer 22:30).[28] As we shall see,
there is a grain of truth in this view, but it is far from an
adequate explanation of the genealogy. In order to be exempt
from the curse on Jeconiah and his descendants, the Messiah
could be descended from any of the previous kings of Judah
except Jehoiakim, on whom a similar curse had been laid (Jer
36:30).[29] That the Messiah's genealogy has to bypass the
whole royal line from Solomon onwards cannot be explained
in this way. Moreover, neither of these suggestions explains
why the line from Nathan to Jesus should pass through Zerubbabel.

[26] Myers (1965) 21; Beyse (1972) 29; Williamson (1982) 57; (1985) 32;
[27] Johnson (1969) 240–252; Abel (1974) 206–210.
[28] Johnson (1969) 244–245, 247; Fitzmyer (1981A) 501.
[29] Later some rabbis considered Hezekiah the father of the Messiah: j.
Ber. 2:4; Lam. R. 1:14.

1. Zerubbabel the Head

We need first of all to establish that the pre-Lukan author of the genealogy, who gave it its Enochic sabbatical structure, did not invent the line from Nathan through Zerubbabel to Jesus, but took it over from an already existing genealogy. No doubt he adjusted it to fit his numerical scheme – adding, as we shall see later, a few names to make up the required number of generations, and securing, as we have noticed already, sabbatical and jubilee positions for the names Joseph and Jesus – but he did not invent the genealogy as such.[30] This is shown by two features of the genealogy which relate to Zerubbabel.

Since the suggestion was first made by Hervey in 1853,[31] it has been widely accepted that the name the genealogy now gives as the name of Zerubbabel's son (Rhesa) was not originally a name but the Aramaic word *rēˀšāˀ* meaning 'the head, the chief, the leader.'[32] It must originally have been a designation of Zerubbabel. At least, in a list which otherwise consisted only of names, it is easier to suppose that Zerubbabel himself was distinguished by this title than that his son was.[33] In that case, the genealogy must originally have been presented in the reverse order: not, as we have it in Luke, moving backwards from son to father, but forwards from father to son. Furthermore, if it was a simple list of names, not linked by 'son' or 'begat' (cf. 1 Chron 1:1–4), then the pre-Lukan author who took it over and adapted it could easily have taken the word after Zerubbabel to be, like all the other words in the list, the name of the preceding person's son, rather than Zerubbabel's title. There is no difficulty in supposing that an Aramaic speaker reading the list in Aramaic could make this mistake: it is comparable, for example, to the way in which the LXX translator of 1 Chronicles 3:17 took the

---

[30] Anthropological research shows that genealogies may be manipulated to suit the function that is given to them, but are not usually invented: Wilson (1977) 55.

[31] Hervey (1853) 111–114.

[32] Kuhn (1923) 212; Jeremias (1969) 296.

[33] As Brown (1977) 93, thinks. He incorrectly attributes this view to Jeremias; cf. Jeremias (1969) 296.

description of Jeconiah as a 'captive' (*'asir*) to be another name ('Aσίρ).[34] Of course, if the pre-Lukan author already had the genealogy in Greek, then the mistake had already been made by the translator, who transliterated the word as a name rather than translating it.[35] Or if the pre-Lukan author composed his genealogy in Aramaic, then the mistake was already made in Aramaic before the later translation of his work into Greek. But perhaps it is most likely that the pre-Lukan author himself used an Aramaic genealogy in constructing his own genealogy in Greek.

Thus a list of Nathan's descendants as it reached the pre-Lukan author already included Zerubbabel and singled him out, by the title 'head', as a specially important link in the genealogy. That it was not the pre-Lukan author himself who decided that Zerubbabel ought to be an ancestor of Jesus is confirmed by a second feature of the genealogy relating to Zerubbabel. The sabbatical position at the end of the eighth week is occupied by Zerubbabel's father Shealtiel (Σαλαθιήλ).[36] A very small adjustment of the genealogy could have put Zerubbabel himself in this position, but the author has not made this adjustment. Had he himself seen any importance in Zerubbabel's being an ancestor of Jesus he would surely have done so.[37] For him Zerubbabel was simply a name in the list he took over.

[34] Williamson (1982) 57.

[35] The mistake could not have been made in a Greek list of names, as Brown (1977) 93 n. 80, supposes. The word Rhesa could not have appeared in a Greek list unless it had first been misunderstood in Aramaic as a name rather than a title.

[36] The only possible reason why Shealtiel himself should be regarded as a key person in the genealogy could be his appearance as an apocalyptic seer, identified with Ezra, in 4 Ezra 3:1. But there is no evidence that he already had this reputation before the composition of 4 Ezra late in the first century.

[37] Kaplan (1930) 468, argues that the genealogy gives twenty-one generations from David to Zerubbabel and twenty-one from Zerubbabel to Jesus, but this is not accurate. There are twenty-two from David to Zerubbabel and twenty from Zerubbabel to Jesus. The scheme of weeks makes this inaccuracy intolerable if Zerubbabel were really intended to be midway between David and Jesus.

Thus it appears that in order to explain the place of Zerubbabel in the genealogy we have to go at least two stages back from Luke's text. The explanation will not be at the level of Lukan redaction nor in the intention of the pre-Lukan author who created the whole genealogy and gave it its sabbatical structure. Zerubbabel already belonged in a line of descent from Nathan the son of David which the pre-Lukan author used, and in this already existing genealogy Zerubbabel was marked out by the designation 'head.'

Analogies for this kind of designation in a genealogy might be found in 1 Chronicles 2:10, where Nahshon is singled out in the list of names as 'prince of the sons of Judah,' or Matthew 1:16, where David is called 'the king.' But what precisely would have been the significance of the title 'head' for Zerubbabel? It is unlikely to be equivalent to his official position as Persian 'governor' (*peḥâ:* Hag 1:1, 14; 2:2, 21), for which the same technical term was used in Aramaic as in Hebrew. Extant Palestinian Aramaic literature indicates that *rē'š* in the metaphorical sense of 'chief, leader' (11QTgJob 15:2 [=Job 29:25]; 4QEnastr^b 28:3 [=1 Enoch 82:11]; and two inscriptions;[38] cf. Ezra 5:10) has the same range of use as Hebrew *rō'š* in the Bible.[39] This permits two possible interpretations of it as applied to Zerubbabel in the genealogy.[40]

---

[38] Fitzmyer and Harrington (1978) texts A1, A53. The latter is also in Beyer (1984) 368 (yySU4).

[39] On *rō'š* = chief, see Bartlett (1969).

[40] Perhaps the possibility should be raised that the designation of Zerubbabel as 'head' was intended to identify him with the 'anointed one, a prince' (*māšíah nāgíd*) of Dan 9:25, who appears to be associated with the restoration of Jerusalem after the exile. However, this is unlikely. Modern scholars rightly prefer a reference to the high priest Joshua in this verse of Daniel (Montgomery [1927] 378–379; Charles [1929] 244; Hartman and Di Lella [1978] 251; Lacocque [1979] 178, 194–195). But, more importantly, ancient Jewish interpretation of Daniel's prophecy of the seventy weeks, as well as the LXX, Theodotion and other anicent versions, dated the coming of the 'messiah-prince' of v 25 after 7 + 62 weeks, i.e. during the last of the seventy weeks, so that he could be identified with the 'messiah' of v 26. An interpretation in accordance with the Massoretic punctuation of v 25, dating the 'messiah-prince' after the first seven of the seventy weeks, is first found in the early third century A.D., in Clement of Alexandria (*Strom.* 1:21 refers to a 'king of the Jews,' who might be Zerubbabel) and Hippolytus,

In the first place, it may designate Zerubbabel as the head of the house of David. In the post-exilic period 'head of a father's house' was an important status in the community, and this seems to have been in that period the most common meaning of *rō'š* in the metaphorical sense[41] (often in phrases, such as *rō'š bêt 'ābōt*, but also absolutely: e.g. 1 Chron 5:7, 12; 7:3; 8:28). That Zerubbabel was head of the house of David is probably implied in Ezra 4:3, and is the least that is required by the oracles of Haggai and Zechariah about him (Hag 2:23; Zech 3:8; 6:12–13). One of his descendants, Hattush, was certainly head of the house of David at a later date (Ezra 8:1–3; cf. 1 Chron 3:22).[42] This position was certainly significant enough to account for the designation of Zerubbabel as head in the genealogy, for to be head of the house of David was presumably to be heir apparent to the throne of David. In a genealogy of Zerubbabel's descent from Nathan the son of David, designating Zerubbabel as 'head' would indicate the point at which a previously non-royal Davidic line acquired the right of succession to the throne of David and would indicate that it was from the descendants of Zerubbabel that the promised restoration of Davidic rule over Israel could be expected.

However, there is also another intriguing possibility. Though most biblical uses of *rō'š* for 'leader' are in tribal or family contexts, there are a few occurrences in the sense of national leader, probably with military overtones (Num 14:4; 1 Sam 15:17; Sir 36:9; cf. Ps 18:43; Isa 7:8). Of special interest here is Hosea 1:11 (Hebrew 2:2), which prophesies the time when, after judgment, Yahweh will renew the covenant relationship with Israel:

And the people of Judah and the people of Israel shall be gathered

the latter of whom identifies the 'messiah-prince' as the high priest Joshua (Beckwith [1981]).

[41] Bartlett (1969) 7–8.

[42] For the text of Ezra 8:2–3, see Williamson (1985) 108. The text of 1 Chron 3:22 should probably be corrected, omitting 'the sons of Shemaiah,' so that Hattush is the second son of Shecaniah: see Williamson (1982) 58.

together, and they shall appoint for themselves one head (*rō'š 'eḥād*); and they shall go up from the land, for great shall be the day of Jezreel (RSV).

A post-exilic reader[43] of this text would certainly have taken the leader to be Davidic (cf. 3:5) and have noticed the close resemblance to Ezekiel 37:21–24 (cf. 34:23–24), where the 'one king' (v 22) or 'one shepherd' (v 24; cf. 34:23) of the restored and reunited nation is 'David my servant' (v 24).[44] Zerubbabel could well have been seen as the leader who brought the people of Israel from the land of exile. That the idealized view of the restoration under Zerubbabel as a restoration of the whole of the divided nation was held by some in the post-exilic community is shown by Nehemiah 7:7, where Zerubbabel heads a list of *twelve* leaders of the returning exiles, described as 'the people of Israel' (cf. Ezra 2:2; 1 Esd 5:8).[45] If to have called Zerubbabel 'king' or 'prince'[46] might have seemed too politically provocative or, after his death, simply inaccurate, the designation 'head', with allusion to Hosea 1:11, could have appeared an appropriate way to indicate his divinely ordained role in the restoration of the nation, while hinting that the restoration of the Davidic throne could be expected to come about through him, i.e. from his descendants.

Whichever of these explanations is preferred, it seems that the original genealogy, with its highlighting of the special significance of Zerubbabel, must derive from circles which kept alive the hopes for Davidic restoration as they had been focussed on the figure of Zerubbabel by the prophets Haggai

---

[43] The original intention may have been to indicate a military leader not of the royal house: see Mays (1969) 32–33.

[44] Cf. Tg. Hos 2:2: 'And the children of Judah and the children of Israel shall be gathered together as one, and they shall appoint for themselves one head, of the house of David, and they shall go up from the land of their Dispersion, for great shall be the day of their ingathering' (translation by Levey [1974] 88).

[45] Ezra 2:2 has only eleven names, but 1 Esd 5:8 has twelve.

[46] The latter (*nāśî'*) is the preferred designation of the future Davidic ruler in Ezekiel (34:24; 37:25; 44:3; 45:7, 16, 17, 22; 46:2, 4, 8, 10, 12, 16–18; 48:21–22).

and Zechariah. Most likely it is a traditional genealogy of the family of Zerubbabel.

This, however, invites comparison of the descendants of Zerubbabel in the Lukan genealogy with those listed, probably down to the Chronicler's own time, in 1 Chronicles 3:19–24. If Rhesa in the Lukan genealogy is taken to be a title for Zerubbabel, his son becomes Johanan ('Ιωανάν),[47] whom there is no difficulty in identifying with Hananiah in 1 Chronicles 3:19, 21. The names are equivalent in meaning, differing only in placing the divine element first or second, and parallels to the use of such equivalent names for the same individual can be found in the Old Testament (e.g. Jeconiah = Jehoiachin).[48] Further correspondence between the two genealogies can be obtained only if we suppose that Luke's skips at least three generations and identify Joda ('Ιωδά) in the Lukan genealogy with Hodaviah in 1 Chronicles 3:24.[49] Otherwise we must assume that the two genealogies diverge before the end of the line in Chronicles.[50] Since one of the names in Chronicles, Hattush the son of Shecaniah (1 Chron 3:22), appears as head of the house of David in Ezra 8:1–3, it seems that Chronicles gives the line of descent from which the official heads of the family – and therefore also presumably those with first claim to the throne of David – derived up to the time of the Chronicler. The Lukan genealogy must then represent a less prominent branch of the family, which nevertheless cherished the tradition of its descent from the Davidic head Zerubbabel. But we still have to explain its other divergence from 1 Chronicles 3: the

---

[47] So Hervey (1853) 115–118; Jeremias (1969) 296.

[48] Other examples are Eliam, the father of Bathsheba (2 Sam 11:3), called Ammiel in 1 Chron 3:5; and Jehoahaz (2 Chron 21:17) = Ahaziah (2 Chron 22:1).

[49] For the equivalence of the names, cf. Hervey (1853) 118–120 (he reads 'Ιούδα in Luke); Kuhn (1923) 212–213.

[50] So Jeremias (1969) 296. Kuhn (1923) 212–213, has an ingenious argument for identifying Luke's 'Ιωανάν, 'Ιωδά, 'Ιωσήχ and Σεμεΐν with names in 1 Chron 3:19–24 (Hananiah, Hodaviah, Shecaniah, Shemaiah), on the assumption that the text of the Lukan genealogy has been misread and disordered. The argument is possible but very speculative.

descent of Zerubbabel from Nathan rather than from Jeconiah and the kings of Judah.

2. *Zerubbabel the Branch*

In this section we shall argue that in the Old Testament prophetic tradition, which both condemned the kings of Judah and expected a renewal of the Davidic monarchy, under a righteous king in the future, the dominant expectation was for a new Davidic king who was not descended from David through the royal line of the kings of Judah. This expectation is classically embodied in Isaiah 11:1: 'There shall come forth a shoot (*ḥōṭer*) from the stump of Jesse, and a branch (*nēṣer*) shall grow out of his roots' (RSV). The image is of a tree chopped down to a stump.[51] A new shoot grows up from the roots (see Job 14:7–9 for the image). The natural meaning is that the tree of the royal house of David will be cut down in judgment, and the ideal king of the future will be derived, not from the royal line of the kings of Judah, but from the origins of the dynasty, indicated by the reference to Jesse. He will represent, as it were, a fresh start, taken, like David himself, from non-royal stock. If he is a descendant of David at all, then he will have to come of a line of David's descendants other than the royal line through Solomon and the kings of Judah.[52]

That this is the correct interpretation of Isaiah 11:1 is confirmed by the similar implication of Micah 5:2 (Hebrew 5:1):

> But you, O Bethlehem Ephrathah,
> who are little to be among the clans of Judah,
> from you shall come forth for me
> one who is to be ruler in Israel,
> whose origin is from of old, from ancient days (RSV).

The new king is to be born not in the royal palace in Jerusalem, but in insignificant Bethlehem, where David's line began. He will derive not from the royal line of the kings of

---

[51] Kaiser (1972) 156, connects 10:33–34 with 11:1–9 and finds in the former passage a prophecy of the destruction of the Davidic kingdom.

[52] So Coppens (1968) 85; Kellerman (1971) 24.

Judah, but from the ancient origins of the line, from the beginnings of David's dynasty. Again there is doubtless the intention of going back behind the corruption of the kings of Judah and making a fresh start, comparable with God's original choice of David himself.

This implication of a future king not descended from the kings of Judah has been recognized by some of the commentators on Isaiah 11:1 and Micah 5:2, but it seems not to have been recognized that the prophecy of the 'righteous branch' in Jeremiah 23:5–6 (cf. 33:15–16, a later prose version) should be read in continuity with the same tradition.[53] Yet this is quite clear at least for its meaning within the edited sequence of oracles[54] on the kings of Judah which extends from 21:11 to 23:8 (the beginning of 21:11 should be read as a heading – 'Concerning the house of the king of Judah' – parallel to 23:9: 'Concerning the prophets').[55] The various denunciations of the kings of Judah climax in the absolute finality of the doom pronounced on Jeconiah in 22:24–30. Not only is Jeconiah utterly rejected as king by Yahweh (v 24). Despite the debated text and interpretation of vv 28–30,[56] there is no doubt that it declares – not that Jeconiah would be literally childless[57] but that neither he nor any of

[53] Except, briefly and from a pre-critical perspective, Hervey (1853) 14–19.

[54] The question of how many of these oracles are authentically Jeremiah's is not important to our argument, nor is the date of the edited collection, so long as it was extant by the time of the restoration under Zerubbabel.

[55] For the extent of the collection, see Holladay (1986) 568; McKane (1986) 506.

[56] The LXX text of v 28 fails to mention Jeconiah's children, and its text of v 30 omits 'a man who shall not succeed in his days.' But if this shorter text is more original than the MT, it does not support the view that the oracle originally made no reference to Jeconiah's descendants. The end of v 30 is a necessary climax, and is supported by the parallel reference to Jehoiakim in 36:30. The LXX text of v 28 may be a deliberate adaptation in view of 2 Kings 24:12, which does not suggest that Jeconiah already had children who were taken with him into exile in 597. In fact, however, he may well have done, since the Babylonian tablets indicate that he already had five sons by 592, so that Jer 22:28 MT could be a historically accurate reference to his exile with children.

[57] Most scholars take the view that while '*ărîrî* means 'childless,' it should

his descendants would ever again occupy the throne of David.

It is true that, as an isolated oracle given in the reign of Zedekiah, this could have been taken to favour the supporters of Zedekiah against the supporters of the exiled Jeconiah who hoped for his restoration.[58] But it cannot bear that significance within the sequence of oracles, which continues by expecting a restoration of Davidic rule only after the exile and return of the nation (23:3, 7–8). In this context the judgment on Jeconiah becomes the final divine verdict on the whole dynasty, which is summed up in the woe against the shepherds in 23:1. Similarly, even if it were credible that the oracle of 23:5–6 originally referred to Zekekiah himself,[59] this cannot be its sense in the collection of oracles. From the perspective of the collection, Zedekiah can be seen only as belonging to the evil shepherds responsible for the exile (23:1–2), while the king of vv 5–6 is the first of the new line of good shepherds (v 4).[60] Indeed, the probability is that the sense of vv 5–6 was always to contrast, by means of a wordplay on Zedekiah's name,[61] the rightful heir to the throne with Zedekiah who never had any legitimate right to the throne.[62]

The phrase *ṣemaḥ ṣaddîq*, usually translated 'righteous branch', must mean primarily 'legitimate scion,' since it has this meaning, referring to the legitimate king of the Ptolemaic dynasty, in a Phoenician inscription of 273/272 B.C.[63] It was

not be taken literally but indicates that Jeconiah will be treated as childless because none of his heirs will inherit the throne: Carroll (1981) 147; (1986) 439; Holladay (1986) 611. But McKane (1986) 549–551, prefers the meaning 'stripped of rank.' Jeconiah's five sons are mentioned in the Babylonian tablets published by Weidner (1939) 925–926; English translation in Thomas (1958) 86.

[58] Carroll (1981) 147.

[59] Carroll (1981) 148; (1986) 446.

[60] Fishbane (1985) 472, points out that *Stichwörter* link vv 5–6 to v 4 and vv 7–8 to v 3 in a chiastic arangment, indicating a deliberate editorial composition of the series of oracles in 23:1–8.

[61] But McKane (1986) 564, denies any allusion to Zedekiah.

[62] Holladay (1986) 617–620; Unterman (1987) 130.

[63] Holladay (1986) 617–618; McKane (1986) 561; Swetnam (1965), with other supporting evidence.

probably therefore a standard phrase, which is used here in preference to *ḥōṭer* and *nēṣer*, used in Isaiah 11:1, because the emphasis is on the legitimacy of the expected king, by contrast with the discredited royal line.[64] But the claim that he is the righful king is, of course, connected with the righteousness of his rule. The prophecy corresponds in substance to Isaiah 11:1–9 and Micah 5:2–4 (3–5), but that it continues the expectation of a king who is, though a Davidide (v 5), not of the line of the kings of Judah, is required by its context. The explanation that vv 5–6 were framed deliberately to contradict and to counter the oracles against the royal dynasty in 21:11–22:30[65] fails to take into account the careful arrangement of 23:1–6, which accepts the irrevocable rejection of the line that ended in Jeconiah but expects its replacement by a new Davidic line in the future. This expectation is intelligible only if the 'rightful branch' descends from David by a line which bypasses at least the later kings of Judah. Such an understanding of the prophecy could be expected because it takes up a traditional expectation already established by Isaiah 11:1 and Micah 5:2.

Against this background we must consider Zechariah's designation of Zerubbabel as 'the branch' (3:8; 6:12). It is widely agreed, not only that the title did originally refer to Zerubbabel in these oracles,[66] but also that Zechariah, who alludes to Jeremianic prophecies elsewhere, took the term 'branch,' as a designation of a new Davidic ruler, from the oracle in Jeremiah 23:5–6[67] (and/or 33:15–16).[68] Zechariah's use of the term would scarcely be intelligible except as an allusion to a well-known oracle, while the standard phrase ('rightful branch') makes the use in Jeremiah 23:5 clearly the more

---

[64] Cf. the important connexion Balzer suggests between the origins of messianism and the issue of legitimacy: Balzer (1961) 41.

[65] Nicholson (1971) 90–91.

[66] Dissenters include Baldwin (1964) 95–97; (1972) 134–135; Smith (1984) 201, 218–219.

[67] Mowinckel (1956) 161, 164, thinks Jer 23:5–6 dependent on Zechariah.

[68] Fishbane (1985) 471–473, argues that 33:14–16 (which is not in LXX) is a later, post-exilic reformulation of 23:5–6.

original and Zechariah's use of 'branch' as a name secondary.[69] But Zechariah's allusions to Jeremiah 23:5-6 need to be seen in conjunction with Haggai's oracle to Zerubbabel. Yahweh's promise to Zerubbabel to 'make you like a signet ring; for I have chosen you' (Hag 2:23) is certainly to be connected with Yahweh's rejection of Jeconiah in Jeremiah 22:24: 'though Coniah the son of Jehoiakim, king of Judah, were the signet ring on my right hand, yet would I tear you off.'[70] It has often been thought that Haggai deliberately reverses Jeremiah's oracle,[71] since Zerubbabel, supposed to be a grandson of Jeconiah (1 Chron 3:17-19), comes under the ban pronounced on Jeconiah's descendants in Jeremiah 22:30. Only by reversing the oracle of Jeremiah could Haggai refer to Zerubbabel in terms which clearly designate him the restorer of Davidic rule. Recently Carroll has turned the argument on its head, giving priority to Haggai and ascribing Jeremiah 22:24-30 to an anti-Zerubbabel faction in the post-exilic period, who aimed this oracle specifically against Haggai's support for Zerubbabel.[72]

There is a simpler interpretation. Since Haggai 2:23 is connected with Jeremiah 22:24 and Zechariah 3:8; 6:12 allude, almost contemporaneously, to Jeremiah 23:5, we can assume that the collection of oracles in Jeremiah 21:11-23:8 was known to both the post-exilic prophets as a collection and that its outlook was in harmony with theirs. They understood Zerubbabel to be the man through whom the new line of Davidic rulers would be established. He was the 'rightful branch,' who was therefore also the Lord's signet ring, replacing Jeconiah, the rejected signet ring. He could be this, not because as grandson of Jeconiah he was descended from the rejected royal line, but precisely because he was not. Though

[69] There may well be a play on the meaning of Zerubbabel's own name ('offspring or shoot of Babylon') (Mowinckel [1956] 164), but this could not be sufficient to explain Zechariah's use of 'branch' (it is scarcely as a shoot of *Babylon* that he hails Zerubbabel).

[70] The connection seems to be made by Sir 49:11: Zerubbabel 'was like a signet ring on the right hand.'

[71] Balzer (1961) 38; Japhet (1982) 77; Smith (1984) 162.

[72] Carroll (1986) 441-442.

he could not have been called 'the branch' unless he was a Davidide (Jer 23:5), for his supposed descent from Jeconiah the sole authority is the genealogy in 1 Chronicles 3:17–19.[73] It seems that the Lukan genealogy of his descent from Nathan the son of David, by-passing the line of the kings of Judah, is historically more credible than the Chronicler's.

However, if the Chronicler's genealogy is to be judged inaccurate,[74] the judgment needs to be justified by explaining why it is so. A reason is not far to seek in the Chronicler's own theological attitude to the Davidic dynasty. As Hugh Williamson has shown in detail,[75] the Chronicler presents the promise of an eternal dynasty to David as established *through Solomon*. Although the promise that Solomon's kingdom should be for ever is made conditional on Solomon's obedience (1 Chron 28:7, 9; 2 Chron 6:16; 7:17–18), the Chronicler's idealized picture of a blameless Solomon portrays him as fulfilling the condition, so that the promise of an eternal Davidic dynasty is unconditionally inherited by the descendants of Solomon (cf. 2 Chron 13:5; 21:7; 23:3). Moreover, if 2 Chronicles 7:18 contains, as has been suggested,[76] a deliberate allusion to Micah 5:2 (Hebrew 5:1), it seems that the Chronicler attaches the prophetic promise firmly to the descendents of Solomon.

[73] Almost all Old Testament scholars have accepted the accuracy of the Chronicler's genealogy in regarding Zerubbabel as the grandson of Jeconiah. But Miller and Hayes (1986) 456, deny that Zerubbabel was a descendant of David at all, since it is 'almost unbelievable,' if he were, that Ezra, Nehemiah, Haggai and Zechariah should all fail to mention the fact. But Zechariah certainly implies Zerubbabel's Davidic descent in calling him 'the branch,' while the lack of reference to Zerubbabel's Davidic descent in Ezra-Nehemiah should be attributed to the redactional outlook of these books: see Japhet (1982–83). By contrast, the role of Zerubbabel is deliberately heightened in 1 Esdras (Japhet [1983] 219–225), but the explicit reference to Zerubbabel's descent from David in 1 Esd 5:5 notably fails to connect him with Jeconiah or the royal line through Solomon.

[74] Miller and Hayes (1986) 456, thinks the Chronicler has linked Zerubbabel to the house of David in order to ensure the continuity of leadership before and after the exile.

[75] Williamson (1977).

[76] Williamson (1982) 226.

It is reasonably clear, from 1 Chronicles 3:19–24, that in the Chronicler's time the Davidic house was represented primarily by the descendants of Zerubbabel and any realistic claim to the throne of David would have to be theirs. It is therefore natural that, in his genealogy of the house of David, the Chronicler should graft Zerubbabel and his family onto the royal line of the kings of Judah. (Precisely how he has done this it is impossible to say, but it may be, since Jeconiah is known from Babylonian sources to have had five sons,[77] that the Chronicler has added Shealtiel and Pedaiah). If the descendants of Zerubbabel were known to be in fact descended from Nathan rather than Solomon, the Chronicler will presumably not be attempting to contradict common knowledge. His genealogy is a theologico-political statement as much as a biological one. Modern anthropological research shows that genealogies are flexible and can be varied to perform different functions: apparently conflicting genealogies are acceptable if they function in different contexts for different purposes.[78] The Chronicler's genealogy of the family of Zerubbabel is designed to legitimate their claim to the throne of David. It does so by treating them as adopted into the royal line.

3. Zerubbabel's descent from Nathan

The view that the Lukan genealogy is historically credible in tracing Zerubbabel's descent from Nathan the son of David now needs further support and defence against objections.

(1) That Zerubbabel and his family were able to trace their line back to Nathan is not in the least improbable. The evidence of Ezra–Nehemiah is that genealogical consciousness was high among the returned exiles of the early post-exilic period, through a concern for racial purity and in order to reestablish continuity with the pre-exilic nation.[79] The census

---

[77] Weidner (1939) 925–926.
[78] Wilson (1975) 180–182; more fully (1977) 46–54; cf. also Mussies (1986) 43–44 for ancient Greek examples.
[79] Johnson (1969) 42–44; Williamson (1985) 36.

of returned exiles classified by families in Ezra 2 = Nehemiah 7 concludes with a group of families who 'could not prove their fathers' houses or their descent, whether they belonged to Israel' (Ezra 2:59 = Neh 7:61). The implication is that the other families could prove their descent, presumably by means of a genealogy, oral or written. Of the three priestly families who could not prove their descent, it is said that they 'sought their registration among those enrolled in the genealogies, but they were not found there' (Ezra 2:62 = Neh 7:64). This must be a reference to official genealogical records of priestly families,[80] but presumably lay families relied on their own family records. That a family descended from one of the sons of David had at least an oral genealogy must be considered certain. This does not, of course, mean that it would be a complete genealogy. Oral genealogies, like many of those in the Old Testament, regularly omit generations, since their function is not to preserve the memory of every name in the list but to link the family with an important ancestor who gives it its place in the community.[81] But that even families with less at stake than descent from king David could trace their line back to the time of David is shown from Ezra 2:61 = Nehemiah 7:63: a family suffered exclusion from the priesthood because of their descent from the daughter of David's contemporary Barzillai the Gileadite (2 Sam 17:27; 19:32; 1 Kings 2:7).[82]

(2) That the house of Nathan was in fact a prominent Davidic family in the post-exilic period is demonstrated by Zechariah 12:12. Unfortunately the prophecy to which this verse belongs (12:1–13:1) cannot be dated with even approximate accuracy. It consistently links 'the house of David' with 'the inhabitants of Jerusalem' (12:7–8, 10; 13:1), contrasted with 'the clans of Judah' (12:5–6). Clearly the house of David forms the natural leadership of the city of Jerusalem, though not, at least in the prophet's view, of the nation (12:7–8). The fact that 'the tents of Judah' are to win their victory without

[80] Johnson (1969) 43.
[81] Wilson (1975) 180; (1977) 32–36.
[82] Cf. Williamson (1985) 37.

Davidic leadership precisely so as not to emerge subordinate to the house of David and the inhabitants of Jerusalem (12:7) makes it difficult to suppose that the prophet is inspired by Davidic messianism.[83] His recognition of Davidic leadership in Jerusalem will therefore simply be a recognition of fact, and his mention of 'the house of Nathan' in 12:12 will have nothing to do with messianic speculation on his part, but a reflection of the situation in Jerusalem in his time. The oracle has been plausibly placed in the late Persian period,[84] when its evidence of the prominence of the house of David in the Jerusalem community can be linked with the Chronicler's record of the descendants of Zerubbabel at that time (1 Chron 3:21–24).

It has not always been recognized that the Nathan of 12:12 is the son of David.[85] But this is required by the parallel between, on the one hand, the house of David and the house of Nathan, and on the other hand, the house of Levi and the Shimeites (v 13). The latter are a subdivision of the tribe of Levi and so the house of Nathan must be a subdivision of the house of David. The passage (vv 12–14) describes how the mourning is to be organized. Each family assembles, divided into its sub-groups. Thus the family of David assembles, divided into its sub-groups, and the women of each sub-group segregated from the men. The house of Nathan is given as an example of a sub-group. Similarly the family of Levi assembles, divided into its sub-groups, the women forming their own groups. The family of Shimei is given as an example of a sub-group. Jerusalem is thus portrayed as dominated by the Davidic family and the priestly and levitical families. The remaining families of the inhabitants of Jerusalem are finally mentioned without being named (v 14).

The Shimeites might seem at first sight a surprising choice as the example of a levitical family. According to 1 Chronicles

---

[83] This is true even if we do not follow Hanson (1975) 365, in ascribing vv 8–9 to a later editor.

[84] Hanson (1975) 359–367; cf. pp. 349–350, where he hypothesizes that the governors for at least part of the fifth century were still of the house of David.

[85] Hanson (1975) 366–367, refers to 'the prophetic house of Nathan.'

23 they made up three of the twenty-four[86] divisions of the
Levites (vv 7–11), reckoned genealogically as the most senior
after the three families of the Libnites (vv 8–9: Ladanites, but
see Num 3:18, 21; 1 Chron 6:17). But perhaps more important is the fact that one of the main families of the Temple
musicians, the sons of Asaph, were reckoned to belong to the
chief of the three families of the Shimeites (1 Chron 6:39–43,
where in v 43 the names Shimei and Jahath should be
reversed, in accordance with 1 Chron 23:10).[87] The Temple
singers were the elite among the Levites,[88] and the sons of
Asaph were a prominent group in the post-exilic community
(Ezra 2:41 = Neh 7:44; Neh 11:17, 22; 12:8, 35).

The Shimeities were therefore among the most prominent
of levitical families. The parallel scarcely allows us to say
more than that the house of Nathan was among the most
prominent of Davidic families.

(3) Turning to the names between Nathan and Shealtiel in
the Lukan genealogy, four of them (Joseph, Judah, Simeon,
Levi) are certainly very suspicious, since the names of the
patriarchs do not seem to have been commonly used as
personal names in Israel until after the exile.[89] However, it
should be noted that these names occur together as a sequence
of four, and that the first of them, Joseph, occurs at the end
of the sixth week in the sabbatical scheme. We have already
suggested that this positioning of the name Joseph is

---

[86] In the text there are only twenty-two or twenty-three divisions. Since
there were later twenty-four (Jeremias [1969] 208) and 1 Chron 24:7–18
divides the priests into twenty-four courses, many have supposed there
should be twenty-four families of Levites in 1 Chron 23, but Williamson
(1982) 160–161, disagrees.

[87] The Temple musicians seem not to have been counted as Levites at
the time of the return from exile, but were by the time of Nehemiah:
Williamson (1982) 121. Presumably they were then grafted into the levitical
family of Jahath (1 Chron 23:10–11).

[88] Jeremias (1969) 208.

[89] Jeremias (1969) 296. It is not true that they were *never* so used, since
two clear cases are the prophet Gad (1 Sam 22:5; 2 Sam 24:11–14) and king
Manasseh (2 Kings 21:1–18) (cf. more dubious examples in 1 Chron 7:10;
25:2; 26:5). But the rarity of the patriarchal names before the exile makes
the sequence of four in the Lukan genealogy very implausible.

deliberate, on the part of the editor who gave the genealogy
its sabbatical structure, and corresponds to the positioning of
the name Jesus in the jubilee position at the end of the seventh
week. We can readily suppose that these two names Joseph
and Jesus were added to the traditional genealogy (though
the name Joshua was used in the monarchical period: 1 Sam
6:14; 2 Kings 23:8). Moreover, since the Lukan genealogy in
fact has rather more names than we might expect even in a
complete list of generations from Nathan to Zerubbabel[90]
and a traditional genealogy is not in fact likely to have been
complete, it is not difficult to suppose that more names also
needed to be added if the genealogy was to be made to fit
the scheme of seventy-seven generations.[91] Thus the editor
who gave the genealogy its sabbatical structure added Joseph
at the end of the sixth week and, needing to add some more
names to make up his numerical scheme, continued with
three more patriarchal names which were also among the
most common Jewish names of his own day.[92] Thus the four
patriarchal names by no means discredit the whole of the
monarchical period of the genealogy.[93] On the contrary, they
stand out as the sort of names which would be added. By
contrast, the rest of the names are quite credible for the
period, and the presence of several which are unparalleled
and may well be corrupt is exactly what we should expect in
a genealogy preserved over a long period in nothing more
secure than family memory or unofficial family records.

The claim sometimes made that the presence of the name

[90] Hervey (1853) 85–86.

[91] For the expansion of a genealogy in the interests of a numerical
scheme, cf. Johnson (1969) 40–41.

[92] Two of these names (Judah, Simeon) are names of brothers of Jesus.
However, if the intention were to continue with family names, we should
expect Jacob (James) rather than Levi. It is possible that the name following
Levi (Ματθάτ) is also an addition, copying the sequence Λευί, Ματθάτ
in the eleventh week of the genealogy. A point where the later part of the
genealogy may have been artificially expanded is the sequence Nahum,
Amos in the tenth week: the original presence of Nahum in the list may
have suggested another name from the twelve prophets to fill out the list.

[93] As Jeremias (1969) 296 thinks, followed by Johnson (1969) 229–230;
Brown (1977) 92.

Levi twice in the genealogy (in the seventh and eleventh weeks), along with perhaps others allegedly 'priestly' names, is an attempt to give the Messiah a priestly ancestry, so that he could be eschatological priest as well as Davidic king,[94] must be rejected. Tribal membership in Israel was exclusive: it was impossible to belong to more than one tribe. A member of the tribe of Judah, descended in the male line from David, could not also be a priest, since a levitical priest must be descended in the male line from Aaron. Thus, if Jesus' descent in the male line was from David, for Jewish genealogical understanding there was no way he could be a levitical priest, and no amount of levitical blood (still less levitical names!) in his ancestry would bring him any nearer to being a priest. The point was obvious to the author of Hebrews (7:14), who therefore made Jesus a *non-levitical* priest. In fact, it is unlikely that a first-century Jew would have seen any significance in the occurrence of the name Levi among Jesus' ancestors, since there is no evidence that the use of patriarchal names as personal names was linked to membership of the appropriate tribe.[95] The many Jews of New Testament times who were called Joseph or Simeon were certainly not claiming membership of those tribes, and there is no reason to think the name Levi was used differently.

(4) A second objection to the names in the genealogy may also be considered at this point, since it affects the section of the genealogy from Nathan to Zerubbabel as well as that from Zerubbabel to Jesus. It is said that the occurrence of five names which are variants of Matthat (Ματταθά, Μαθθάτ, Ματταθίας [twice], Ματθάτ)[96] is suspicious.[97] However, names of this type, from מתן or מתת ('gift') were very popular (Mattan, Mattaniah, Mattenai, Mattat, Mattattah, Mattithiah/Mattathias, Matthias), along with other names of

---

[94] E.g. Ford (1984) 48.

[95] Cf. Levites called Judah (Ezra 3:9; 10:23; Neh 12:8) and Issachar (1 Chron 26:5); a Benjaminite called Judah (Neh 11:9); and the brothers Simon and Judas Maccabaeus, who were priests.

[96] The name Μάαθ should not be included; it is a quite distinct name – Mahath (1 Chron 6:35; 2 Chron 29:12; 31:13).

[97] Bacon (1899) 140; Brown (1977) 92; cf. Johnson (1969) 229.

similar meaning from the same root נתן (Nathan, Neth-
anel/Nathanael, Nethaniah, Elnathan, Jehonathan, Jonathan).
The reason is obvious: they designate the child as a gift of
God and express the common feeling of parents, in a religious
culture, of thankfulness to God for the gift of a child.[98] The
recurrence of these names in the Lukan genealogy is no reason
for doubting its authenticity.[99] There is, however, a different
problem, not noticed by critics of the genealogy: the evidence
suggests that the forms used before the exile were Mattan
and Mattaniah,[100] while Mattat, Mattattah, and Mattithiah
came into use only after the exile.[101] So it may be that the
two pre-exilic examples in the Lukan genealogy (Ματταθά,
Μαθθάτ) have been conformed, in the later transmission of the
text, to the most common later forms of the name. Especially
if the genealogy were transmitted orally for part of its history,
this would easily have happened.

In conclusion, the Lukan genealogy's claim that Zerubbabel
was descended from David's son Nathan is historically plausible, and the actual genealogy it attributes to him probably
derives from authentic family tradition, though it has been

[98] Noth (1928) 168–169; Fowler (1988) 116. Brown's claim ([1977] 92)
that the name Mattat/Mattithiah is 'associated with the Maccabean or Hasmonean family of the House of Levi in the second century B.C. (1 Macc
2:1), rather than with the House of David, especially as we know it in the
monarchical period', is wholly inaccurate. The name was already popular
in the early post-exilic period, long before the father of the Maccabees
bore it (1 Chron 9:31; Ezra 10:33, 43; Neh 8:4), while the closely related
name Mattaniah was the original name of the Davidic king Zedekiah
(2 Kings 24:17).

[99] In the seven generations of his family given by Josephus (*Vita* 3–8),
Matthias occurs in four generations, but this is not a close parallel to the
Lukan genealogy. In Josephus' family Matthias was evidently regarded as a
family name. In the Lukan genealogy the names of the Matthat-type are
too far apart (as well as varying in form) for this to be likely.

[100] Mattan: 2 Kings 11:18; 2 Chron 23:17; Jer 38:1. Mattaniah: 2 Kings
24:17; 1 Chron 25:4, 16; 2 Chron 20:14; 29:13. References to extra-biblical
occurrences in the pre-exilic period in Fowler (1988) 116, 352. Mattaniah is
also found after the exile: 1 Chron 9:15; Ezra 10:26, 27, 30, 37; Neh 11:17;
12:25, 35; 13:13; cf. Mattenai: Ezra 10:33, 37; Neh 12:19.

[101] The only pre-exilic cases are the doubtful ones of 1 Chron 15:18, 21;
16:5; 25:3, 21.

somewhat manipulated to fit the requirements of the Enochic numerical scheme.

4. *The Messiah ben Nathan in Jewish tradition*

Johnson has presented evidence that there was a Jewish tradition in which the Messiah was expected to be descended from David through Nathan.[102] However, the four pieces of evidence he offers for this tradition need rather more careful critical evaluation:

(1) In one manuscript of the Targum to Zechariah 12:12 the reference to the house of Nathan is rendered: 'the descendants of the house of Nathan the prophet, son of David.'[103] Although this text cannot be dated, it is certainly evidence of a traditional identification of Nathan the son of David with Nathan the prophet (2 Sam 7:1–17; 12:1–15; 1 Chron 17:1–15; Sir 47:1). As we shall see, this identification does also appear in references to the descent of the Messiah from Nathan, but it would be a mistake to conclude that therefore it originated from speculation about the genealogy of the Messiah. It is an example of the common Jewish exegetical habit of identifying biblical characters with the same or similar names. For example, Job was identified with Jobab the king of Edom mentioned in Genesis 36:33–34 (Job 42:17c LXX; TJob 1:1, 6); Orpah (Ruth 1:4, 14) was identified with the mother of Goliath and his brothers (by reading *hārāpâ* 'the giant' in 2 Sam 21:22 as a name very similar to Orpah: LAB 61:6; Ruth R. 2:20).[104] The pervasive haggadic motive of finding connexions between biblical texts is at work in these examples and is sufficient motive for the identification of the two Nathans. When Pseudo-Jerome[105] identified the prophet Nathan with David's nephew Jonathan (2 Sam 21:21; 1 Chron 20:7; cf. 1 Chron 27:32) he was probably following

---

[102] Johnson (1969) 240–247; followed by Abel (1974).

[103] Johnson (1969) 241.

[104] Cf. Bauckham (1983B) 35, for examples of the identification of biblical characters with different names or of anonymous characters with named figures.

[105] Pseudo-Jerome, *Quaestiones Hebraicae in II Regum* qu. 95 (cf. also qu. 178, not in early MSS): Saltman (1975) 91 (cf. PG 23:1403, 1425).

an alternative Jewish exegetical tradition of the same type.[106] In neither case need we invoke the question of the ancestry of the Messiah to explain the tradition.

(2) Julius Africanus, in his *Letter to Aristides*, from the first half of the third century, discusses the two Gospel genealogies of Jesus. He apparently refers to a view (later found in a fragment ascribed to Gregory of Nazianzus)[107] that the Lukan genealogy of Jesus' descent from Nathan was meant to indicate that Jesus was a priest, just as the Matthean genealogy indicated his kingship. Quite how Nathan is associated with priesthood is unclear, but the assumption seems to be that his name is a characteristically priestly one[108] (a possible conclusion from occurrences of the related names Nethanel and Jonathan in Scripture). In any case, in rejecting this view, Africanus refers, without further explanation, to the possibility that Nathan was a prophet.[109] Since Africanus elsewhere in this letter draws on Jewish Christian traditions about the genealogy of Jesus (see section III.1 below) it is likely that the identification of Nathan the son of David with Nathan the prophet reached him from that source. No doubt it is ultimately the same Jewish tradition as found its way into the Targum on Zechariah. But the evidence of Africanus does not require the conclusion that as a (non-Christian) Jewish tradition it was connected with the genealogy of the Messiah. Such a connection need only have been made by Christians who knew the Lukan genealogy of Jesus.

(3) One of the extant fragments of the *Quaestiones Evangelicae ad Stephanum* of Eusebius (early fourth century) appears to refer to a Jewish tradition of the Messiah's descent from Nathan:

> For differing opinions concerning the Messiah prevail among the

---

[106] Saltman (1975) is generally dubious about Pseudo-Jerome's value as evidence of Jewish haggadah, but this case at least is thoroughly Jewish in character.

[107] Quoted in Reichardt (1909) 25.

[108] See the beginning of this fragment of Julius Africanus: Reichardt (1909) 53.

[109] Reichardt (1909) 55; cf. the translation in Johnson (1969) 242–243.

Jews, though all agree in leading [the pedigree] up to David, because of the promises of God to David. But yet some are persuaded that the Messiah will come from David and Solomon and the royal line while others eschew this opinion because serious accusation was levelled against the kings and because Jeconiah was denounced by the prophet Jeremiah and because it was said that no seed from him [Jeconiah] should arise to sit on the throne of David. For these reasons, therefore, they go another way, agreeing [with the descent] from David; not, however, through Solomon but rather through Nathan, who was a child of David (they say that Nathan also prophesied, according to what is said in the books of Kings). They are certain that the Messiah would come forth from the successors of Nathan and trace the ancestry of Joseph from that point. Therefore, Luke, necessarily taking account of their opinion – though it was not his own – added to his account the ὡς ἐνομίζετο ['as was supposed']. In doing this he allowed Matthew to relate [the matter], not on the basis of supposition but as having the truth in the matters of the genealogy. This, then, is the first reply.[110]

It is possible that Eusebius had this account from Julius Africanus. The second reply which follows is explicitly quoted from Africanus' *Letter to Aristides*,[111] and so it is possible that this first reply derives from an earlier point in the *Letter*, where it was a view Africanus reported and rejected. (This would explain Africanus' later passing reference to the identification of Nathan with the prophet.) If so, it could come from Jewish Christian sources. The account is puzzling because it begins by talking about the views of the future coming of the Messiah current among Jews, but ends by saying that they – the same people – trace *Joseph's* descent from Nathan. The latter can only be a Christian view. Abbreviation of a source might account for this confusion. The problem of Jeremiah's curse on Jeconiah is discussed, with reference to the perpetuity of the Davidic line, in rabbinic

[110] Eusebius, *Quaestiones Evangelicae ad Stephanum* 3:2: translation from Johnson (1969) 244, who also (243–244) prints the Greek text from PG 22:896.
[111] PG 22:900–901.

literature (e.g. Lev. R. 10:5; 19:6), but this solution is not mentioned there. If this were the only evidence of a Jewish tradition of the Messiah's descent from Nathan, it could be suspected of being no more than a Christian theory about Jewish views, invented to explain the divergent Gospel genealogies of Jesus. However, it receives support in just one, much later Jewish work.

(4) In the medieval Hebrew Book of Zerubbabel (Apocalypse of Zerubbabel)[112] the Davidic Messah is called Menaḥem ben Ammiel and his mother is called Hephzibah. The following three points are relevant here: (i) elsewhere in Jewish literature where the Messiah is called Menaḥem his patronymic is ben Hezekiah (Lam. R. 1:16; j. Ber. 2:4);[113] (ii) Hephzibah was the wife of Hezekiah (2 Kings 21:1: the only biblical occurrence of the name, except as a symbolic name

[112] Text (based on Bodleian MS 2797, with variants from other MSS) and French translation in Lévi (1914) 129–160; English translation (from three divergent texts) in Buchanan (1978) 338–382. I have also made use of an unpublished translation of Lévi's text by P. S. Alexander.

The date of the work cannot be established with certainty. Since the messianic redemption is expected 990 years after the destruction of the Temple (Lévi [1914] 150, 155, 157), the work has been dated in the eleventh century. But the figure could easily have been increased in the course of transmission by scribes who saw that the time originally indicated had passed without the fulfilment of the prophecy. On the basis of the reference to Shirsi, king of Persia (= Siroes, 628–629), Lévi dates the original work between 629 and 636 (Lévi [1919] 108–115, followed by Silver [1927] 49). That at least traditions incorporated in the work go back to the seventh century seems likely.

For reasons for the attribution of the work to Zerubbabel, see Lévi [1920] 57–58, but the most important reason is no doubt Zerubbabel's role as the leader of the return from exile. In the opening part and the closing sentences of the work, which is set in the exile under the Persian Empire before the return under Zerubbabel, the exile functions as a type of the diaspora situation at the time of writing. If the work was written in seventh-century Persia, this setting would be even more appropriate. That Zerubbabel is also given (for the first time in apocalyptic literature) a military role in the events of the last days is probably the result of, rather than a reason for the attribution of the work to him.

[113] Goldberg (1979) 10–11, 14–16, 21–24, 32–35. In one manuscript of the Apocalypse of Zerubbabel itself, the Messiah is called 'son of Hezekiah': Lévi [1914] 146 (cf. n. 4).

for the new Jersualem in Isa 62:4); (iii) Ammiel was the father of David's wife Bathsheba, the mother of Solomon (1 Chron 3:5).[114] This allows the following genealogy of the Messiah:

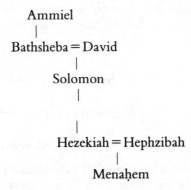

Ammiel
|
Bathsheba = David
|
Solomon
|

|
Hezekiah = Hephzibah
|
Menaḥem

The name Menaḥem ben Ammiel would then result from the deliberate choice of an obscure patronymic. Ammiel would be the most obscure name in the Messiah's genealogy. Such a name is required because in this apocalypse Zerubbabel meets the Messiah living in obscurity in Rome before his revelation to Israel at the end time.[115]

However, the matter is complicated by an additional piece of genealogical information: that Hephzibah is 'the wife of Nathan the prophet, the son of David,'[116] and 'the wife of Nathan the son of David, who was born in Hebron.'[117] (The last piece of information contradicts the biblical account, according to which Nathan the son of David was born in Jerusalem [2 Sam 5:14; 1 Chron 3:3], but perhaps it was necessary to correct the biblical account in order to make the identification with Nathan the prophet. A son born to David in Jerusalem could not have been old enough to appear in the biblical narrative as Nathan the prophet.) Accordingly in one

---

[114] For a few other references to the Messiah as Menaḥem ben Ammiel, see Goldberg (1979) 35–36; cf. Buchanan (1978) 243. Sometimes he is taken to be the Messiah of Joseph, which must be a misunderstanding.

[115] Lévi (1914) 145–146.

[116] Buchanan (1978) 351, 362; cf. Lévi (1914) 151 and n. 7.

[117] Buchanan (1978) 378; cf. Lévi (1914) 157.

text the Messiah is said to have been born in the time of David,[118] though another text gives the more usual tradition about Menaḥem, that he was born in the time of Nebuchadnezzar (at the time of the destruction of Jerusalem).[119] Since Bathsheba was the mother of Nathan as well as of Solomon, we deduce the following genealogy:

Ammiel
|
Bathsheba = David
|
Nathan the prophet = Hephizbah
|
Menaḥem

We have to assume that two traditions about the descent of the Messiah have been fused. Only our first genealogy explains the name Hephzibah for the mother of Menaḥem and so the more common tradition of descent from Hezekiah must lie behind the text. This tradition was associated with the idea of a Messiah born at the time of the fall of Jerusalem and living in obscurity in Rome.[120] But an alternative view of the Messiah's descent has been grafted onto this tradition: the Messiah as the son of Nathan.

The descent from Nathan cannot here be intended to enhance the Messiah's obscurity, since Nathan is identified with the prophet. More obscure sons of David and even grandsons of Ammiel could have been chosen (1 Chron 3:5). It is hard to resist the conclusion that here we have a unique survival, in later Jewish literature, of the view to which Eusebius referred. Certainly it is odd that, in the rather extensive rabbinic discussions of the names and patronymics of the Messiah,[121] descent from Nathan never appears. But it is probably easier to suppose that the Book of Zerubbabel

[118] Lévi (1914) 148.
[119] Lévi (1914) 148 n. 6.
[120] Lam. R. 1:16; j. Ber. 2:4; Num. R. 13:5; cf. also Buchanan (1978) 452–458, 505.
[121] Cf. Goldberg (1979).

contains an isolated survival of an old Jewish tradition than that it has been influenced by Christian views on this point.

Such a tradition is not attested before the fourth century or perhaps (if we postulate Julius Africanus as Eusebius' source) the third century. As to its origin there are two possibilities: (1) If, as we argued above, the descendants of Zerubbabel were of the house of Nathan and cherished the expectation that the Davidic Messiah would come from their line, then the later Jewish tradition could be simply a relic of that expectation. In that case the coincidence between the later tradition and the Lukan genealogy would also be explained. (2) The tradition could be a speculative solution to the problem posed by Jeremiah's oracle about Jeconiah, as Eusebius suggested. This in itself would not explain why Nathan was chosen as the Messiah's ancestor. It is very unlikely that the intention was to give the Messiah a prophetic ancestry, as Johnson suggests,[122] since prophethood is not inherited[123] and such a concern is nowhere evident in Jewish or Christian discussion of the ancestry of the Messiah. It may be, however, that, given a concern to derive the Messiah from a Davidic line other than Solomon's, the identification of Nathan the son of David with Nathan the prophet made him the most suitable of David's sons to be the ancestor of the Messiah. Perhaps it was thought appropriate that the prophet who gave David the divine promise of an eternal kingdom for his descendants (2 Sam 7:11–16) should be himself the ancestor of the Davidic Messiah who will finally fulfil the promise.

However, this second possibility raises the question: Could not the Lukan genealogy of Jesus be a purely artificial construction intended to give Jesus the ancestry required by one line of Jewish speculation about the Messiah's pedigree? In reply it must be insisted that such Jewish speculation cannot explain why the Lukan genealogy traces Jesus' descent from Nathan *through Zerubbabel*. Especially in the face of the genea-

---

[122] Johnson (1969) 240–252. Johnson attributes this intention to Luke, not explicitly to the Jewish tradition Luke follows.

[123] Only Mussies (1986) 43, seems to have seen this entirely obvious objection to Johnson's case.

logy of Zerubbabel in 1 Chronicles 3, it is inexplicable that a purely artificial construction should place Zerubbabel among Nathan's descendants. It should be remembered that Zechariah's prophecies of the Branch would not have been associated with Zerubbabel in later Jewish exegesis, which characteristically takes such passages as referring directly to the eschatological future (cf. Tg. Zech 3:8; 6:12; Num. R. 18:21).[124] Only very occasionally in later rabbinic literature is it explicitly assumed that the Messiah will be descended from Zerubbabel, because in these cases it is taken for granted that the Messiah will come from the royal line through Solomon and the kings of Judah, which according to 1 Chronicles 3 was perpetuated through Zerubbabel (Gen. R. 97; *Tanḥuma toldot* 14). Of a tradition which could provide the basis for a line of descent through Zerubbabel from Nathan there is no trace.

III. The genealogy and the relatives of Jesus

So far we have distinguished and established two pre-Lukan stages in the formation of the genealogy: (1) A traditional genealogy of a Davidic family descended from Zerubbabel. This genealogy traced the family's descent from David through Nathan and Zerubbabel, and by designating Zerubbabel 'the head' preserved longstanding expectations for the fulfilment, through the line of Zerubbabel, of the prophetic expectations of a restored Davidic monarchy. The key role of Zerubbabel has been forgotten in the second stage of the formation of the genealogy, though the descent from Nathan and with it the prophetic theme of a Davidic Messiah from a non-royal branch of the family is preserved. (2) In the second stage the genealogy is extended to Adam and ends with Jesus. It is adapted to an apocalyptic world-historical scheme of weeks of generations and so structured as to convey an understanding of Jesus, not only as the legitimate heir to the throne

---

[124]Tg. Zech 4:7 refers to both Zerubbabel and the Messiah. Levey (1974) 98, thinks Zerubbabel is taken to be the name of the Messiah, but this is not at all clear.

of David, but also as the climax and completion of world history. In this second stage the genealogy has become a quite sophisticated document of early Jewish Christian theology.

We have still to establish where the traditional genealogy came from and in what early Christian circles it was given the Enochic sabbatical structure of the pre-Lukan genealogy. We cannot jump to the conclusion, without further evidence, that the traditional genealogy was that of the family of Jesus. Jesus and Joseph might have been, at the second stage of the formation of the genealogy, artificially grafted onto the traditional genealogy of some other Davidic family. On the other hand, the tradition of Jesus' Davidic descent is an early one, already known to Paul (Rom 1:3), and we know from Hegesippus' stories about other members of the family (the grandsons of Jude and Symeon the son of Clopas) that the family itself believed in its Davidic descent (Eusebius, *HE* 3:20:1–2; 3:32:3).[125] So the possibility that the genealogy derives from the family of Jesus is a real one.

In this section two converging lines of evidence will connect the genealogy with the relatives of Jesus in such a way as to show, not only that it embodies the traditional genealogy of the family, but also that it was given its theological, Enochic shape also within the circle of Jesus' relatives in the early church.

1. The evidence of Julius Africanus

Julius Africanus' *Letter to Aristides*, most, though not all, of which is extant in two long passages,[126] was written some time in the first half of the third century and reports two traditions about the genealogy of Jesus which Africanus claims were handed down by the relatives of Jesus. Since he was born in Jerusalem (Aelia Capitolina) and lived part of his later life at Emmaus (Nicopolis), he would have had access to

---

[125] Against the view that the relatives of Jesus merely deduced their Davidic origin from their belief in Jesus' Messiahship, see Stauffer (1952) 199.

[126] Texts in Reichardt (1909).

Palestinian Jewish Christian traditions. Descendants of the family of Jesus were certainly still living in Nazareth in his lifetime,[127] but he cannot have had direct contact with them or he would surely have said so. In fact, at least in the case of the second tradition, it seems clear that he is following a written source. He must have known one or more written accounts of traditions which circulated in Jewish Christian circles in Palestine.

It is important to realise that the two traditions he reports are quite distinct, although both concern the genealogy of Jesus. His purpose in reporting the second is to corroborate the first, but it is clear that this was not the real point of the account he reproduces. The two traditions are really quite distinct and the connection Africanus makes between them is his own.[128]

The first tradition is an explanation of how the two divergent genealogies of Jesus in Matthew and Luke can be reconciled. The two alleged fathers of Joseph (Jacob in Matthew, Eli in Luke) are said to be half-brothers, with different fathers but the same mother. Eli died without children. Jacob his half-brother married Eli's widow in a levirate marriage which produced Joseph. Eli was therefore the legal father of Joseph, Jacob the physical father. This ingenious explanation, which modern readers unerringly feel to be much too good to be true,[129] seems to be a traditional one which Africanus attributes to the relatives of Jesus. This is clear, not only from the fact that he explicitly says that the name of Joseph's grandmother, Estha, was handed down by tradition (Eusebius, *HE* 1:7:8),[130] but also because he introduces the second tradition as *also* handed down by the family of Jesus (1:7:11).

The first tradition, of course, presupposes the existence of the two canonical genealogies, though it does not follow that the Jewish Christian circles from which it comes knew these

---

[127] *Martyrdom of Conon* 4:2: see chapter 2 section VII above.

[128] The distinctness of the two traditions is neglected, e.g., in the treatment of Africanus' evidence by Vogt (1907) 1–34.

[129] Mussies (1986) 40–41, offers other objections.

[130] Vogt (1907) 18, thinks the name derives from that of the mother of king Jeconiah (Nehushta: 2 Kings 24:8).

genealogies in our Gospels of Matthew and Luke. Not only Luke's but also Matthew's genealogy may well have circulated in Palestine before its incorporation into the Gospel. However, at least one of the Jewish Christian Gospels in Hebrew or Aramaic seems to have been based on Matthew's Gospel[131] and may have taken over the Matthean genealogy.[132] Whether Luke's Gospel was well known in Jewish Christian circles is more doubtful, but the Greek Gospel used by the Ebionites does appear to be dependent on Luke as well as Matthew.[133] So although this first tradition reported by Julius Africanus might reflect knowledge of the Lukan genealogy independently of Luke's Gospel, this is no more than a possibility. The tradition need be only a rather late attempt to reconcile the two genealogies derived from the canonical Gospels. But its lateness and its inherent historical improbability should not discredit the second, quite independent tradition, which Africanus reports as follows:

> When Idumaean brigands attacked the city of Ascalon in Palestine among their other spoils they took away captive from the temple of Apollo, which was built on the walls, Antipater the child of a certain Herod, a *heirodoulos* [temple slave], and since the priest was unable to pay ransom for his son, Antipater was brought up in the customs of the Idumaeans and later was befriended by Hyrcanus the high priest of Judaea. When sent on a mission to Pompey on behalf of Hyrcanus he won for him the freedom of the kingdom which had been taken away by his brother Aristobulus, and so was himself fortunate enough to gain the title of overseer of Palestine. Antipater was assassinated from envy of his great good fortune, and suc- ceeded by a son Herod, who later was appointed by Antony and by decree of the august Senate to be king of the Jews. His children were Herod [Antipas] and the other tetrarchs. So much is shared with the histories of the Greeks also.

---

[131] Vielhauer (1963) 146; Klijn (1988) 4032.

[132] Cf. Vogt (1907) 15–17. From Epiphanius, *Pan.* 29–30, it seems that the Gospel of the Ebionites did not contain a genealogy, but it is uncertain whether the Gospel of the Nazarenes did.

[133] Vielhauer (1963) 155; Howard (1988) 4037–4049.

But[134] since the Hebrew families and those traceable to proselytes, such as Achior the Ammonite [Jdt 14:10], and Ruth the
Moabitess, and the mixed families which had come out of Egypt,
had until then been enrolled (ἀναγράπτων) in the archives (ἐν
τοῖς ἀρχείοις), Herod, because the family of the Israelites contrib-
uted nothing to him, and because he was goaded by his own
consciousness of his base birth, burned the records (ἀναγραφάς)
of their families, thinking to appear noble if no one else was able
by public documents (ἐκ δημοσίου συγγραφῆς) to trace his
family to the patriarchs or proselytes, to the so-called gers
(γειώρας) of mixed descent.[135]

For the next section, which is the crucial one for our argument, I give the Greek text and my own translation:

ὀλίγοι δὲ τῶν ἐπιμελῶν ἰδιωτικὰς ἑαυτοῖς ἀπογραφὰς ἢ
μνημονεύσαντες τῶν ὀνομάτων ἢ ἄλλως ἔχοντες ἐξ ἀντιγράφων
ἐναβρύνονται σῳζομένης τῇ μνήμῃ τῆς εὐγενείας· ὧν ἐτύγχανον οἱ
προειρημένοι δεσπόσυνοι καλούμενοι διὰ τὴν πρὸς τὸ σωτήριον
γένος συνάφειαν, ἀπό τε Ναζάρων καὶ Κωχαβὰ κωμῶν Ἰουδαϊκῶν
τῇ λοιπῇ γῇ ἐπιφοιτήσαντες καὶ τὴν προκειμένην γενεαλογίαν ἔκ
τε τῆς βίβλου τῶν ἡμερῶν ἐς ὅσον ἐξικνοῦντο ἐξηγησάμενοι.[136]

But a few careful people have private records of their own,
either by remembering the names or in some other way securing
them from copies, and pride themselves on preserving the
memory of their noble birth. Among these are those already
mentioned, known as the *desposynoi* [those who belong to the
Master] because of their kinship with the family of the
Saviour.[137] From the Jewish villages of Nazareth and Kokhaba
they travelled around the rest of the land and interpreted

[134] On this paragraph, see Jeremias (1969) 281–283.
[135] Translation of Eusebius, HE 1:7:11–13 from Lake (1926) 61, 63.
[136] Text from Reichardt (1909) 61–62 (corresponding to Eusebius, HE
1:7:14), but I prefer the reading ἔκ τε τῆς βίβλου, which is found in the
manuscripts of Eusebius, whereas Reichardt follows the manuscripts of the
Catena of Nicetas in omitting τε. τε is the *lectio difficilior* and should be
preferred.
[137] The phrase σωτήριον γένος probably means no more than 'the
Saviour's family' (for parallels to this meaning of σωτήριον, see Lampe
[1961] 1369). It is Julius Africanus' own phrase, which he uses to explain
the term δεσπόσυνοι which was in his Jewish Christian source, and so it
is a mistake to find a Jewish Christian ideology in it, as Stauffer (1952)
199–200, does.

(ἐξηγησάμενοι) the genealogy they had [from the family tradition] and from the Book of the Days [i.e. Chronicles] as far as they could trace it [*or:* as far as they went on their travels].

This concludes the report of the tradition. Africanus continues:[138]

> Whether, then, it be so or otherwise [i.e. whether the explanation of the two genealogies given in the first tradition is the correct one or not], noone would be able to discover a more lucid explanation (ἐξήγησιν), in my opinion and that of all fairminded people. [So] let us pay attention to this one, even though it is unattested [in public records], since there is no better or truer one available. At any rate the Gospel speaks the truth in every respect [and so both genealogies must somehow be accurate].[139]

The account of Herod's descent from a temple slave is probably not historically accurate,[140] though Jeremias conjectures that when Africanus says it is confirmed by the Greek historians he is referring to Ptolemaeus of Ascalon,[141] who wrote an account of Herod's reign and certainly dealt with Herod's Idumaean origins in a frank way, unlike the court historians.[142] Moreover, Justin Martyr (*Dial.* 52) considered it a Jewish opinion that Herod was an Ascalonite. Whether true or not, Africanus' account is just the sort of story about Herod that would have circulated in Jewish circles. We know that Herod was sensitive about his Idumaean and therefore only half-Jewish origins, which many Jews regarded as disqualifying him from legitimate rule over Israel (Josephus, *Ant.* 14:403; cf. 15:370; 17:42; b. B.B. 3b),[143] that his court historian Nicolaus of Damascus gave him a pure Jewish ancestry (*Ant.* 14:9), presumably as part of an attempt by Herod himself to conceal his origins, and that his fear of

---

[138] This passage is misunderstood by Johnson (1969) 103–104.

[139] My translation from the text in Reichardt (1909) 62 (corresponding to Eusebius, *HE* 1:7:15).

[140] Cf. Schürer (1973) 234 n. 3; Vogt (1907) 13–14; Heer (1910) 21–23 (who defends the account).

[141] Jeremias (1969) 331–332.

[142] Schürer (1973) 27.

[143] Cf. Jeremias (1969) 332.

rivals to his throne led to decimation of the leading Jewish aristocratic families (*Ant.* 14:175; 15:6; *B.J.* 1:358). That he should have destroyed any public records of the genealogies of such families, especially Davidic families, is therefore entirely credible, even if the tradition reported by Julius Africanus exaggerates it.

Africanus' evidence is part of that used by Jeremias to support the view that there were official public records of non-priestly genealogies,[144] and it is doubted by Johnson as part of his questioning of that view.[145] I doubt if Johnson has successfully refuted Jeremias' case, but the issue is not decisive for our argument. In the tradition Africanus reports the story of Herod's destruction of the genealogies functions only to explain why there are no public records of Jesus' genealogy. It merely clears the way for the claim that the family of Jesus was one of those Jewish families which kept its own records, oral or written, of its ancestry. Both its relative modesty (since it would have been easy, after A.D. 70, to claim that the genealogy of Jesus had been publicly verified in records which only perished in the destruction of Jerusalem[146]) and its inherent probability recommend this claim as an early and reliable one. Whether or not there were ever public genealogical records of lay families and however common or uncommon it was for Jewish families to keep their own records, it is likely enough that a Davidic family would do so. Pride in their royal descent along with the traditional expectation of a Messiah ben David would be strong motives for doing so. A family of no social consequence, like Joseph's, would, for that reason, be just as proud of its Davidic ancestry as more prominent Davidides (and would no doubt delight in a story which contrasted their own noble birth with the base origins of the hated Herod). The opinion of some scholars that at this date there would no longer be any families which could plausibly claim descent from David is refuted not only by the

---

[144] Jeremias (1969) 281–283.

[145] Johnson (1969) 103–108.

[146] This counts against Johnson's view that the story of Herod's burning of the genealogies is purely apologetic: Johnson (1969) 103–104.

evidence of Hegesippus (*ap.* Eusebius, *HE* 3:12; 3:19:1–20:2; 3:32:3–4) and of rabbinic traditions, some, though not all of which, can be regarded as good evidence,[147] but also by an ossuary, discovered in Jerusalem and dating from some time in the century and a half before A.D. 70, which is inscribed: 'belonging to the house of David'.[148]

It is clear that in the passage of which the Greek text is quoted above Africanus is closely following a source,[149] at least from the mention of the *desposynoi* onwards. This term is not his own: he does not use it at the earlier point at which he mentions the relatives of Jesus, in introduction to the second tradition (*HE* 1:7:11) and he finds it necessary to explain its meaning. In fact, it is found in no other extant early Christian writer. It must have been the technical term for the family of Jesus which was current in the Greek usage of Palestinian Jewish Christian circles, but not elsewhere.

It is also clear that Africanus here quotes a tradition which he does not himself understand quite accurately. Because he wishes to use it to authenticate his first tradition (about the reconciliation of the two canonical genealogies), which is his real interest, he supposes that when it is said that the *desposynoi* 'interpreted' or 'explained' (ἐξηγησάμενοι) the genealogy, the meaning is that they gave the explanation of Jesus' two lines of descent which Africanus has reported in the first tradition. That he understood it in this way is clear from his subsequent comment (beginning, 'Whether, then, it be so . . .'), where he uses the term 'explanation' (ἐξήγησιν) in this sense. That he misunderstood it is clear from the phrase 'and from the Book of the Days': the Books of Chronicles would not have been any help in this attempt to reconcile the two genealogies. Africanus may not in fact have recognized in this phrase the

---

[147] Jeremias (1969) 226–228, 276–297. Note also the interpretation of Josephus, *Ant.* 15:260–266, offered by Flusser (1986) 38–39: he suggests that the 'Pharisees' in this story prophesied that the messianic king will be a descendant of the wife of Pheroras because she was known to be a Davidide.

[148] Flusser (1986).

[149] The view of Heer (1910) 19, that the source must have been oral, is based on a misunderstanding of ἀμάρτυρος in Eusebius, *HE* 1:7:15.

Hebrew title of Chronicles and may have supposed (as Rufinus in his Latin translation probably did[150]) that it referred to the family's genealogical records mentioned earlier. We can see that the tradition itself was not concerned with the issue of the two divergent genealogies, but assumes a single family genealogy.

In chapter 2 (section II) above, we have argued that the tradition refers to the missionary travels of the *desposynoi* of the first generation, to which Paul also alludes in 1 Corinthians 9:5. What is of the greatest interest now is the claim that the interpretation of the family genealogy had an important place in their missionary activity. What is meant by saying that they interpreted or explained 'the genealogy they had [literally, 'which was before them': though προκειμένην could mean 'aforesaid', the genealogy has not, strictly speaking, already been mentioned in this account] and from the Book of the Days, as far as they reached' is not obvious, and the awkward Greek may reflect Africanus' own misunderstanding of his source. However, it would make sense to suppose that the family genealogy itself extended no further back than David and the generations preceding David were supplied from Chronicles. If the phrase ἐς ὅσον ἐξικνοῦντο (literally, 'as far as they reached' or 'attained') refers, not to their travelling, but to their tracing of the genealogy, then it will mean, not that they traced it as accur- ately as they could or as far back as they could, but that they traced it forwards in Chronicles as far as they could, to the point where they could connect the line of David in Chron- icles with the family genealogy. All this would well suit the Lukan genealogy (in its complete pre-Lukan form, from Adam to Jesus), though it could also fit the Matthean genealogy.

That they explained or interpreted (ἐξηγέομαι can be used of expounding scripture) the genealogy suggests more than that it was used to prove Jesus' Davidic descent. It suggests a

---

[150] *ordinem supra dictae generationes partim memoriter partim etiam ex dierum libris*, quoted in Reichardt (1909) 62 n. The Syriac version explicitly explains 'the books of days' as 'the books of genealogies.'

genealogy with theological significance which could be explained as part of the exposition of the Christian message about Jesus. The genealogy, in other words, was a missionary theological document, in which the *desposynoi* had embodied something of the messianic significance of Jesus as they understood it. Whether it was the Matthean or the Lukan genealogy can be decided only by a second strand of evidence.

2. The evidence of the Letter of Jude

We recall that the theological structure of the Lukan genealogy was inspired by the Enoch literature and reflects, in fact, rather close study of parts of that literature. We recall also that it must date from the generation of Jesus' contemporaries. Only one other extant Christian writing from that period alludes indisputably to the Enoch literature: the letter of Jude. Moreover, Jude's letter shows its author to be intimately familiar with major parts of the Enoch literature, which he has studied with much the same attention and christological interest as other early Christian writers applied to the Old Testament scriptures.

However, the link between the letter of Jude and the Lukan genealogy is even more precise. We recall that the 'text' for the genealogy must have been 1 Enoch 10:12, which reckons the time from the binding of the fallen angels to the last judgment as seventy generations, and that the genealogy depends upon dating the binding of the angels after the first week of world history, i.e. the first seven generations from Adam to Enoch. 1 Enoch 10:12 is one of the verses of Enoch to which Jude makes precise verbal allusion. Jude 6: 'The angels, too, who did not keep their own position of authority, but abandoned their proper home [cf. 1 Enoch 12:4; 15:3, 7], he has kept in eternal chains in the nether darkness [cf. 1 Enoch 10:4–6] until the judgment of the great day.'[151] The last phrase, 'until the judgment of the great day', echoes 1 Enoch 10:12: 'for seventy generations . . . until the great day of their judgment.' (The adjective 'great', missing in the Greek and

[151] For the detailed correspondence of this verse to material in 1 Enoch, see Bauckham (1983A) 52–53.

Ethiopic versions of 1 Enoch, is found in the Aramaic in 4QEn^b 1:4:11: it reveals Jude's closeness to the text of 1 Enoch.) The context of Jude 6 does not call for an explicit reference to the seventy generations, but it is clear that Jude is familiar enough with that verse of 1 Enoch to know very well the length of the period to which he refers. Moreover, the other necessary datum for the theological arithmetic of the genealogy – Enoch's special position as the seventh generation of world history – is explicit in Jude 14, which calls Enoch 'the seventh from Adam'. It is rather remarkable that in the mere twenty-five verses of his letter Jude makes contact with the two most essential foundations of the sabbatical structure of the genealogy.

In the light of the genealogy, it is possible to see the precise significance of Jude's pairing of the two prophecies by 'Enoch the seventh from Adam' (v 14) and 'the apostles of our Lord Jesus Christ' (v 17). These are the two climactic texts in his exegetical argument. They correspond, not simply, as we suggested in chapter 4, as a very ancient prophecy and a very modern prophecy, but more precisely as deriving from the seventh and the seventy-seventh generations of world history, the end of the first week and the end of the last week of world history. Their prophecies of evildoers and their judgment come from a prophet who saw the first eruption of evil into history and its initial judgment in the binding of the Watchers, and from the prophets who will live to see the final judgment of all evil, of the Watchers themselves and all who have followed in their way.

The letter of Jude, as an authentic work of the brother of Jesus, provides uniquely the link we need to locate the origin of the Lukan genealogy in early Christianity. Jude links the family of Jesus, its Davidic descent and its traditional genealogy, with the learned inspiration from the Enoch literature which has shaped the traditional Davidic genealogy into an apocalyptic world-historical scheme. If the genealogy is not the work of Jude himself, it must certainly come from his circle.

IV. The genealogy and the *Davidssohnfrage* (Mark 12:35–37)

The genealogy embodies a Christology. It gives Jesus the place of ultimate significance in world history. It includes and highlights his descent from David by the non-royal line as the prophesied messianic Branch. However, he is more than just a second David. David has his sabbatical place of special significance at the end of the fifth week, but Jesus' position at the end of the eleventh week, in the seventy-seventh generation, surpasses that of every predecessor from Adam onwards. He is greater than Enoch and greater than David, the consummation of world history.

Since the genealogy in this highly theological form seems to derive from the circle of Jesus' closest relatives, it is relevant to compare it with the only possible indication we have of Jesus' own attitude to his Davidic descent. The interpretation, as well as the authenticity, of Mark 12:35–37 (‖ Matt 26:41–46; Luke 20:41–44) has been much debated, and all the details of the debate cannot be entered here.[152] But interpretations which understand Jesus to be denying the Davidic descent of the Messiah may be rejected at once: (1) The view that either Jesus himself[153] or a later Christian group[154] maintained in this way his messiahship in spite of his lack of Davidic ancestry is improbable. Belief in Jesus' Davidic descent was very widespread in early Christianity (Matt 1:6, 17, 20; Mark 10:47–48; Luke 1:27, 32; 3:31; Acts 2:30; 13:23; 15:16; Rom 1:3; 2 Tim 2:8; Heb 7:14; Rev 5:5; 22:16; Did 10:6; AscIsa 11:2; Ignatius, *Eph.* 18:2; 20:2; *Smyrn.* 1:1; *Trall.* 9:1), and we know of no group which denied it (Barn 12:10–11 is as ambiguous as Mark 12:35–37, which it probably reflects). So it is difficult to believe, not only that a dominical saying denying the Davidic descent of the Messiah could have been formulated in the early church, but also that an authentic saying of Jesus with this meaning could have been transmitted, with this understanding of its meaning, in the early

---

[152] For references to recent literature, see Chilton (1982).
[153] Klausner (1925) 320.
[154] Burger (1970) 52–59.

church. (2) Chilton has argued that Jesus accepted the designation 'son of David', on account both of his Davidic descent and of his Solomonic reputation as a skilled healer, but denied that this was a messianic claim. The effect of Jesus' argument in the pericope is that since the Messiah is not son of David but Jesus is, Jesus cannot be the Messiah.[155] But again, even if this were what Jesus meant, it cannot have been what the tradition meant to those who transmitted it after Easter, when the universal Christian confession was of Jesus as Messiah. It was one thing for the tradition to retain a memory of Jesus' reserve in relation to the term Messiah, another thing for it to contain a flat denial of his Messiahship. And if, in the earliest Christian tradition the saying was already understood quite differently from Jesus' intention, it is relevant to ask how we can expect to know the latter. If the saying's meaning in the earliest tradition seems unattributable to Jesus, it would be easier to deny its authenticity.

The clue to the significance of the saying, whether authentic or not, was suggested by Daube,[156] who is correctly followed by Jeremias[157] and Fitzmyer.[158] Jesus propounds an exegetical question concerning the interpretation of biblical passages which appear contradictory. Such questions, in rabbinic tradition, expect the answer that both passages are correct, but refer to different points. Jesus in this instance does not cite scripture for the view that the Messiah is the son of David, but refers to the unanimous view of contemporary exegetes that this is the teaching of scripture. He does not mean to reject this view of 'the scribes' (Mark 12:35), but to pose the question: in what sense is the Messiah son of David if he is also, as Psalm 110:1 shows, David's lord? The fact that the question is left as a question is probably more consistent with authenticity than otherwise. It coheres with Jesus' attested habit of referring only indirectly and allusively to his

[155] Chilton (1982).
[156] Daube (1956) 163.
[157] Jeremias (1958) 53.
[158] Fitzmyer (1971) 124.

messianic claim,[159] rather than with the explicit christological interests of the later Christian community. But the implied answer need not be that the Messiah's real origin, despite his appearance on earth among the human descendants of David, is heavenly and divine[160] (which seems to be the interpretation given in Barn 12:10–11). It need be only that the Messiah is not simply another king in succession to David, like Solomon and the kings of Judah, but a greater figure, through whom the kingdom of God will come. It suggests what is elsewhere quite evident in Jesus' teaching: that the kingdom he proclaimed as coming was more than a restoration of Jewish national sovereignty.

Had Jesus been seen as just another son of David in succession to Solomon and the kings of Judah, then of course the brothers of Jesus could have claimed the succession to the throne after him, and they would have expected not Jesus himself, returning in glory, but one of themselves or a descendant of theirs to restore the Davidic monarchy to power. But for them to have thought in this way would have been inconsistent with even the very earliest Christology of the Palestinian church. The Lukan genealogy, as well as the letter of Jude, shows that in fact they did not. Jesus, according to the genealogy, does not simply inherit the throne of David: he brings the Davidic monarchy to its climactic eschatological fulfilment. 'Great David's greater Son' aptly sums up the view of Jesus' Davidic descent which is expressed, in very different idiom, both in the Lukan genealogy and in Mark 12:35–37. It is not difficult to believe that both were current in the Palestinian Jewish Christian circles in which Jesus' relatives moved.

V. The genealogy in Luke

For the sake of completeness, we must finally turn to Luke's redaction of the genealogy, since an argument about an author's source is never complete without an account of his use of it. The discovery that the genealogy already had a

---

[159] Cf. Taylor (1952) 493.
[160] Cf. Cullmann (1963) 131.

traditional origin and a tight theological structure before Luke incorporated it into his Gospel frees us from the need to give every aspect of it a significance at the level of Lukan theology. We need not, for example, resort to Johnson's speculation that Luke knew the Jewish haggadic identification of David's son Nathan with the prophet Nathan and traced Jesus' descent from Nathan in order to emphasize the prophetic element in the Christology of his Gospel.[161] More plausibly, Luke may have found the descent from Nathan consistent with the humility and obscurity of Jesus' origins as he portrays them: a child born to a Davidic but poor family (2:24; cf. Lev 12:8), made known as the Davidic Messiah first to shepherds (2:8–20) – and the whole event of his birth the act of the God who favours the humble and the poor rather than the rich and the powerful (1:51–53). But we cannot be sure that Luke reflected on the line of descent from David that he found in his source.

The significance of the genealogy for Luke will have consisted mainly of two points, which also account for his placing of it where he does in his Gospel.[162] It sums up, at the outset of Jesus' ministry, the identity of Jesus as his narrative up to that point has revealed it: that Jesus is both son of David and son of God. Jesus' Davidic origin is prominent in Luke's infancy narrative (1:27, 69; 2:4, 11), and Gabriel's announcement to Mary makes clear that he fulfils the promise to David of an eternal kingdom (1:32–33). But his sonship to God is equally prominent in the annunciation story (1:32, 35) and is emphatically confirmed by the heavenly voice at the baptism (3:22), immediately preceding the genealogy.

Jesus' Davidic descent was clear in the genealogy as Luke found it in his source, but Jesus' sonship to God was not a theme of the pre-Lukan genealogy. Luke's redaction of the genealogy was therefore confined to adapting it to express this theme. Since the pre-Lukan genealogy did extend to

---

[161] Johnson (1969) 240–252; followed by Abel (1974); Ford (1984) 47–49.

[162] Against the rather popular view that the position of the genealogy is a relic of a 'proto-Luke' which lacked chapters 1–2.

Adam, Luke was able to adapt it to his purpose by making only two small additions to it. (Most likely he also turned a descending genealogy into an ascending one.) At one end of the genealogy he added the words ὡς ἐνομίζετο ('being *as was supposed* the son of Joseph') and at the other he added the words τοῦ Θεοῦ ('Adam *the son of God*'). Many commentators have suspected that the Lukan genealogy, with this highly unusual ending, must be connected with the theme of Jesus' sonship to God,[163] but at first sight it is difficult to see how. To trace Jesus' descent from Adam as the son of God seems an odd way of saying that Jesus is the son of God: in this sense he would be no more distinctively the son of God than any other (male) descendant of Adam.[164] Nor does it really seem plausible that the words ὡς ἐνομίζετο make the whole genealogy from Joseph to Adam an enormous parenthesis, leaving τοῦ Θεοῦ (v 38) to be connected immediately with υἱός (v 23).[165] The key to the matter is to recognize that the two Lukan redactional additions to the genealogy are closely connected.

The first, of course, indicates the virginal conception,[166] which Luke connects closely with Jesus' divine sonship (1:35).[167] The account of the virginal conception in terms of the creative overshadowing power of the Spirit (1:35) indicates the difference between Jesus' human origin and that of other human beings. Jesus' conception results from the direct creative action of God without human initiative in sexual activity. As has been recognized,[168] there is a kind of cumulative parallelism implicit in Luke's account of the conception of John the Baptist followed by that of Jesus. Implicitly there are three forms of conception: normal human

---

[163] Cf. Johnson (1969) 235–239; Fitzmyer (1981A) 504.

[164] The problem is correctly seen by Marshall (1978) 161.

[165] This view of B. Weiss is rejected by Plummer (1901) 105; Marshall (1978) 161.

[166] This view is contested by Johnson (1969) 230–231, but remains virtually self-evident.

[167] On Luke's understanding of the virginal conception and divine sonship, see Bauckham (1987B) 328–330.

[168] Brown (1977) 300–301; Fitzmyer (1981B) 61–62.

conception – miraculous conception (as in John's case) – virginal conception in Jesus' case. Every human child is a gift of God in that human activity is necessary but cannot guarantee conception. In John's case, as in similar Old Testament instances, the child is a gift of God in a special sense, since at Elizabeth's age conception would not normally have been possible at all. But the couple still have to act to produce the child. In Jesus' case, however, no human initiative is required at all. His conception results from sheer divine action, for which only Mary's willing acceptance is required. Thus Jesus' human origin is absolute gift of God.

It seems clear that it is in this sense primarily that Luke understands Jesus to be son of God. His humanity results from a direct creative act of God (1:35). In this sense, Jesus' origin is unparalleled in previous human history since Adam and Eve. But God's direct creation of Adam and Eve *is* a kind of parallel. Thus the Lukan additions at the beginning and end of the genealogy mark a parallel between Jesus and Adam. Jesus is not, like all the other generations since Adam, a product of human generation, but a generation that comes directly from God as the very first did. (This need not mean that Luke understood there to be no physical continuity between Jesus and his mother, though we cannot know which of the various ancient views of human procreation[169] Luke held. The parallel concerns not the origin of the material of Jesus' humanity but the originating *act*. Neither Jesus nor Adam result from the human act of procreation.)

Luke seems to have been aware that the title 'Son of God' had a traditional association with Davidic kingship (1:32–33). But by associating it with the virginal conception he gives it a broader and deeper significance which connects with the universalism of Lukan theology. Jesus is indeed the Davidic Messiah of Israel but he is also the Saviour of the world. The genealogy at the outset of the ministry announces this. It traces Jesus' descent from David. But it also indicates that

[169] Bauckham (1987B) 327. The Aristotelian view that the mother's contribution is the matter and the father's the form was probably the most common view at this time, but not the only one.

Jesus is a divine gift to humanity of unprecedented significance. Coming from God as no one since Adam had done,
his life and ministry are equally relevant to all the children of
Adam.

In this way Luke is at one with the intention of the pre-
Lukan genealogy: both are concerned to say that Jesus is both
son of David and also much more than son of David. But
whereas the pre-Lukan genealogy expressed this in terms of
an Enochic apocalyptic chronology, Luke expresses it and
adapts the genealogy to express it in terms of his own
Christology of divine sonship.

Additional Note on the Text of the Lukan Genealogy

It is not surprising that this list of names, many of which
would be unfamiliar to the scribes and which lack the numerical indications of Matthew 1:1–17, has suffered in transmission in some manuscripts. We are not here concerned
with variations in the forms of the names, but only with
variations in the number of names, since the argument of this
chapter has rested on the figure of seventy-seven names,
which is found in most but not all manuscripts. Some have
fewer names, ranging from seventy-two to seventy-six. In
justification of the seventy-seven printed in modern editions
of the Greek New Testament,[170] the following points may
be made:

(1) In general, it is easier for names to drop out of a list of
this kind than for names to be added. A name which is
lacking in a few manuscripts should therefore not be rejected
without very good reason.

(2) The sequence of three names Ἀμιναδάμ,[171] Ἀδμίν
and Ἀρνί (v 33) is a point of great confusion in the manuscript tradition, which is best explained if these three names

[170] Against the detailed argument for the originality of only seventy-
two names in Heer (1910) 58–81. He gives excessive weight to the witness
of Irenaeus.
[171] The reading Ἀμιναδάμ should be preferred to Ἀμιναδάβ, since
the latter can be explained as a correction and the former explains also the
reading Ἀδάμ, found in some manuscripts.

were original. The copyists detected a discrepancy with the Old Testament (Ruth 4:19; 1 Chron 2:9–10) and with Matthew 1:3–4, which have only two generations: Amminadab and Ram (LXX and Matt: 'Αράμ). Hence the omission of one of these names in some manuscripts and the substitution or addition of 'Αράμ, which is also found corrupted to 'Ιωράμ.

(3) A text with apparently only seventy-two names is already attested by Irenaeus, *Adv. Haer.* 3:22:3. However, the fact that Irenaeus gives a symbolic significance to the number, connecting it with the seventy-two nations of the world (according to Gen 10 LXX) – the seventy-two generations mean that Christ 'recapitulated in himself' all the nations of the world since Adam – make the precise number of names Irenaeus found in his text of Luke somewhat doubtful. For the sake of the symbolism he may have made approximately seventy-two into precisely seventy-two. Moreover, although it is usually said that Irenaeus knew only seventy-two names, it is not in fact possible to tell from his words whether he counted Adam and Jesus in the figure of seventy-two. What he says is compatible with seventy-three or seventy-four names. We should notice that, as Irenaeus illustrates, in the early period of the transmission of Luke's text seventy-two was a more obviously symbolic number than seventy-seven. This could have led to the deliberate reduction of the number of names in some manuscripts.

(4) Julius Africanus (*ap.* Eusebius, *HE* 1:7:5), reporting the explanation (which he attributes to the *desposynoi*) of the two divergent genealogies of Jesus, says that the grandfather of Joseph, 'the third name from the end according to Luke' is Melchi. Whatever form the tradition he received from Palestinian Jewish Christian sources took, it seems that at this point he reports what he found in his own text of Luke (cf. 1:7:10), which therefore lacked the names Ματθάτ and Λευί. That these two names also occur in v 29 (Μαθθάτ, Λευί) may have led to their omission in v 24.

(5) Finally, the fact that (as noted in section I above), if seventy-seven names are accepted, the name Jesus occurs in forth-ninth as well as seventy-seventh position (from Adam),

strongly favours the view that the seventy-seven name list was a deliberately composed one, not an accident of the transmission of the text.

Conclusion

It has been no part of the purpose of this book to create as complete a picture of early Palestinian Jewish Christianity as the evidence permits. For that purpose, much other evidence would have to be discussed and synthesized. Rather, the aim has been to shed new light on this subject by a concentrated focus on the role of the family of Jesus (excluding James) and on the evidence of the letter of Jude. When the scattered evidence about the relatives of Jesus is critically assessed and its implications considered, when the letter of Jude is restored to its true historical context and thoroughly examined, when the Lukan genealogy of Jesus is made to reveal its surprising secrets, and when all three of these areas of investigation are seen in relation to each other, valuable fresh insight into early Palestinian Jewish Christianity results.

Both in Jerusalem and in Galilee, until the Bar Kokhba war, the family of Jesus – the *desposynoi* – were the most influential and respected leaders of Jewish Christianity, at first along with members of the twelve, later more exclusively. Even the more hagiographical and apologetic features of the early second-century Palestinian traditions recorded by Hegesippus enable us to glimpse the veneration with which such men as Symeon the son of Clopas and the grandsons of Jude were regarded by the Palestinian churches and the important role they must have played. It may be, as we have suggested, that James the grandson of Jude even left his mark, exceptionally among Jewish Christians, in rabbinic tradition. What was true of the family at the beginning of the second century would seem to have been already true within the first two decades of Christianity. The brothers of Jesus other than James were already obvious examples for Paul to cite in the 50s, even when writing to Corinth, of travelling missionaries of whose work everyone knew and whose apostolic credentials were unquestionable.

There was no gulf between different types of Christianity in Jerusalem and Galilee. James and Symeon in Jerusalem were the acknowledged heads of the churches founded and supervised by their relatives based at Nazareth and Kokhaba in Galilee. These Galilean homes of the *desposynoi* were given special messianic-theological significance along with the central eschatological role inevitably attributed to Jerusalem. From the beginning the Jewish Christian mission was not only to pilgrims in Jerusalem, but also extended throughout Palestine through the travels of missionaries among whom the younger brothers of Jesus and other members of the family were prominent. It is as missionaries engaged in preaching Jesus the Messiah to their fellow-Jews that the relatives of Jesus are primarily to be envisaged. Their mission was far from unsuccessful. It should not be judged by historical hindsight from the eventual fate of Palestinian Jewish Christianity. At least until the revolt of A.D. 66, perhaps also after 70, Christian faith was spreading in Palestine. In Galilee whole villages, such as Sikhnin, may have become Christian. In the messianically excited atmosphere of Palestine between the two revolts the status of the *desposynoi* as Davidides, leading a movement dedicated to a Davidic Messiah, was not only a liability, as Hegesippus's accounts of Symeon and the grandsons of Jude show, but also no doubt an advantage. It seems the *desposynoi* also extended their missionary work outside Palestine, and in Mesopotamia the evidence for the family tradition of church leadership continues after such evidence is no longer available for Palestine.

Both Jude's letter and the Lukan genealogy of Jesus offer precious evidence of the theological character of the Christianity of the relatives of Jesus and their circle in the first generation. That this evidence relates to the earliest period is all the more important in that the Palestinian Christianity of this period had significance far beyond its own boundaries: it laid theological foundations on which all subsequent Christianity was built. The theological creativity of the Palestinian Christianity of the earliest period – and the debt of all later theological development to it – has begun to be recognized afresh, especially in the crucial area of Christology. But that the circle of the brothers of Jesus played an important role in this first vital phase of Christian theological development has not hitherto been recognized. The letter of Jude and the Lukan genealogy are surviving evidence of their work in this regard (to be placed alongside the letter of James, which we have not studied here). Davidic messianism, 'Enochic' apocalypticism and pesher exegesis could be considered the three major characteristics which these two documents reveal about their theological contribution. It is a theological contribution which should not be undervalued because its thought-forms and procedures are so remote not only from us, but even from the Gentile Christianity of a later period. In its own context it was both learned and relevant.

The fantasy, entertained by some scholars, that Jesus was first considered the messianic 'Son of David' without reference to his ancestry must now be laid to rest. We must now see the family of Jesus as Davidides, conscious, through family tradition, of the hopes of Davidic restoration which had been cherished in their line since Zerubbabel. Their insignificant social status would have made the family tradition of this potent ancestry no less tenacious or significant. The tradition may not have been important to Jesus himself, but it was there to be activated and developed when Jesus' relatives became some of his most convinced and dedicated followers. As they developed the scriptural exegesis to sustain and promote the new faith in Jesus as Messiah, the apparent insignificance of the family, epitomized by its residence at Nazareth, became significant. Isaiah's prophecy of the Branch from the roots of Jesse (Isa 11:1), already a key text for Davidic messianism, was fulfilled in a way the traditional family genealogy could easily illustrate: in a Messiah descended not from the royal line, but by non-royal descent from David, taken by God from a background as insignificant as David's own.

Moreover, by a pesher-type pun the prophecy of the Branch (*nēṣer*) itself alluded to Nazareth. The name Nazarenes, which the Jewish Christian movement gained, was surely not unconnected with the Davidic messianic significance the family of Jesus saw in the family home which they made a major centre of the movement. It should be noticed how our three areas of investigation – the traditions about the relatives of Jesus, the letter of Jude, and the Lukan genealogy – relate very closely at this point. From Jude's letter we know of the elaborate and skilful pesher exegesis practised by at least one of the brothers of Jesus. Knowing from Julius Africanus that the *desposynoi* made Nazareth and Kokhaba the centres for their missionary travels, we may reasonably guess that they did so, in part at least, because allusions to these two places could be found by pesher exegesis in the two most popular texts of royal messianism: the Branch (Isa 11:1) and the Star (Num 24:17). Finally, we can see how one of these texts (Isa 11:1) was indispensable to understanding Jesus as legitimate heir to the throne of David, as presented in the genealogy.

Yet, important as Davidic messianism evidently was for the *desposynoi* (as well as for those who found their leadership in the churches appropriate because of their status as royal family), Davidic messianism is not a sufficient category to characterize the Christology of the brothers of Jesus and their circle. The Lukan genealogy is a sophisticated theological construction which embodies a world-historical scheme, indebted to close study of the Enoch literature, such as Jude's letter also shows us was pursued in his circle. It designates Jesus not only as heir to the throne of David, but also as the climax and completion of the whole of world history. His contemporaries live in the last generation of world history, in which Jesus, the greater than Enoch and the greater than David, will inaugurate the kingdom of God, a new age beyond the generations of this world's history. In its own way this is faithful to the apocalyptic dimension of Jesus' own message. It expects of God through Jesus no mere restoration of national sovereignty under a Davidic king, but the eschatological fulfilment of God's purposes for Israel and the world, transcending all previous history. It adapts the apocalyptic speculations of the Enoch literature in order to make the family genealogy into a vehicle for this apocalyptic christological message. We can see how the genealogy could have played an important role in the missionary preaching of the *desposynoi*, as Julius Africanus indicates it did. Exposition of it could show how Jesus is the one who fulfils all the promises of God and the expectations of his people.

The more arcane elements in the significance of the genealogy were no doubt already lost on Luke. In the form in which they were there expressed, appropriate to the Palestinian Judaism of that time, they did not form part of the christological inheritance which passed to the rest of the church. But the Christology of the genealogy is coherent with the more familiar christological expressions of Jude's letter, focused on the lordship of Jesus. In these we see Christian thinking already more than halfway to the culmination of later christological development in the acknowledgment of Jesus' full divinity. Already God's own divine name, the tetragrammaton represented by κύριος, belongs to Jesus as the one who exercises God's eschatological lordship. Already Jesus represents, to church and world, the exclusive divine lordship of the one God of Israel. It is instructive to see how closely this development relates to the messianic exegesis of the Old Testament and apocryphal literature which was the theological method of this circle of Christian leaders and subsequently of much of early Christianity. It was a method employed with considerable intellectual sophistication, however strange it may sometimes seem to us. The exegetical techniques and the hermeneutical presuppositions were shared with the most learned of current Jewish exegesis and with the apocalyptic literature. But in these Christian hands the method was used to develop the conviction that Jesus of Nazareth, in his recent history, his present lordship and his impending parousia as lord and judge of the world, was the fulfilment of all God's purposes and promises. The results of the exegetical work pioneered in early Palestinian Christianity are to be found throughout the New Testament.

Abbreviations

Abbreviations for Ancient Literature

ActsPet	Acts of Peter
ActsThom	Acts of Thomas
Ap. Const.	Apostolic Constitutions
ApAbr	Apocalypse of Abraham
1ApJas	First Apocalypse of James (CG V,3)
2ApJas	Second Apocalypse of James (CG V,4)
ApMos	Apocalypse of Moses
ApPaul	Apocalypse of Paul
ApPet E	Apocalypse of Peter (Ethiopic version)
AscIsa	Ascension of Isaiah
b. ʿAbod. Zar.	Babylonian Talmud tractate ʿAbodah Zarah
2 Bar	Syriac Apocalypse of Baruch
3 Bar	Greek/Slavonic Apocalypse of Baruch
Barn	Epistle of Barnabas
b. B. B.	Babylonian Talmud tractate Baba Batra
b. Ber.	Babylonian Talmud tractate Berakot
b. B. Meṣ.	Babylonian Talmud tractate Baba Meṣiʿa
b. Giṭṭ.	Babylonian Talmud tractate Giṭṭin
BkThom	Book of Thomas (CG II,7)
b. Qidd.	Babylonian Talmud tractate Qidduši̇n

b. Šabb.	Babylonian Talmud tractate Šabbat
b. Sanh.	Babylonian Talmud tractate Sanhedrin
Cant	Canticles (Songs of Songs)
CD	Damascus Rule
CG	Nag Hammadi codices
1 Chron	1 Chronicles
2 Chron	2 Chronicles
1 Clem	1 Clement
2 Clem	2 Clement
Clem. Alex.	Clement of Alexandria
ClemHom	Clementine Homilies
ClemRec	Clementine Recognitions
Col	Colossians
1 Cor	1 Corinthians
2 Cor	2 Corinthians
3 Cor	Apocryphal correspondence of Paul and the Corinthians
Dan	Daniel
Deut	Deuteronomy
Deut. R.	Midrash Rabbah on Deuteronomy
Did	Didache
Diogn	Epistle to Diognetus
Eccles	Ecclesiastes (Qohelet)
Eccles. R.	Midrash Rabbah on Ecclesiastes
EpApp	Epistle of the Apostles (Epistula Apostolorum)
Eph	Ephesians
EpJer	Epistle of Jeremiah
EpTitus	Epistle of Titus
1 Esd	1 Esdras (LXX)
Esth	Esther
Exod	Exodus
Ezek	Ezekiel
4 Ezra	Apocalypse of Ezra (2 Esdras)
Gal	Galatians

Gen	Genesis
Gen. R.	Midrash Rabbah on Genesis
GHeb	Gospel of the Hebrews
GNaz	Gospel of the Nazarenes
GPet	Gospel of Peter
GPhil	Gospel of Philip (CG II,3)
GThom	Gospel of Thomas (CG II,2)
GTruth	Gospel of Truth (CG I,3 and XII,2)
Hab	Habakkuk
Hag	Haggai
Heb	Hebrews
HistJos	Coptic History of Joseph
Hos	Hosea .
Ign.	Ignatius
InfGThom	Infancy Gospel of Thomas
j. 'Abod. Zar.	Palestinian Talmud tractate 'Abodah Zarah
Jas	James
j. Ber.	Palestinian Talmud tractate Berakot
Jer	Jeremiah
j. Šabb.	Palestinian Talmud tractate Šabbat
Josh	Joshua
Jub	Jubilees
Judg	Judges
LAB	Pseudo-Philo, *Liber Antiquitatum Biblicarum*
LAE	Life of Adam and Eve
LadJac	Ladder of Jacob
Lam	Lamentations
Lam. R.	Midrash Rabbah on Lamentations
Lev	Leviticus
Lev. R.	Midrash Rabbah on Leviticus
LXX	Septuagint
1 Macc	1 Maccabees
2 Macc	2 Maccabees

3 Macc	3 Maccabees
4 Macc	4 Maccabees
Mal	Malachi
Mart. Conon	Martyrdom of Conon
Mart. Justin	Martyrdom of Justin
Matt	Matthew
Mic	Micah
m. Sanh.	Mishnah tractate Sanhedrin
m. Par.	Mishnah tractate Parah
Mur	Muraba'at texts
Nah	Nahum
Neh	Nehemiah
Num	Numbers
Num. R.	Midrash Rabbah on Numbers
OdesSol	Odes of Solomon
Pap. Oxy.	Oxyrhynchus Papyrus
1 Pet	1 Peter
2 Pet	2 Peter
Phil	Philippians
Phlm	Philemon
Polyc.	Polycarp
ProtJas	Protevangelium of James
Prov	Proverbs
Ps, Pss	Psalms
PssSol	Psalms of Solomon
1Q34^{bis}	A Liturgical Prayer from Qumran Cave 1
4Q176, 177, 180, 181, 182, 183	Texts from Qumran Cave 4
4QAmr^b	Visions (or Testament) of Amram from Qumran Cave 4
4QEn$^{a, b, c}$	Aramaic texts of 1 Enoch from Qumran Cave 4
4QEnastr$^{b, d}$	Aramaic texts of the Astronomical Book of Enoch from Qumran Cave 4

4QEnGiants[a]	Enochic Book of Giants from Qumran Cave 4
4QFlor	Florilegium from Qumran Cave 4
1QH	Hodayot (Thanksgiving Hymns) from Qumran Cave 1
1QM	Milḥamah (War Scroll) from Qumran Cave 1
11QMelch	Melchizedek text froim Qumran Cave 11
4QPBless	Blessings of Jacob (Patriarchal Blessings) from Qumran Cave 4
1QpHab	Pesher on Habakkuk from Qumran Cave 1
4QpIsa[a, b]	Pesharim on Isaiah from Qumran Cave 4
4QpNah	Pesher on Nahum from Qumran Cave 4
4QpPs[a]	Pesher on Psalms from Qumran Cave 4
4QPs–Ezek	Apocryphal Ezekiel text from Qumran Cave 4
1QS	Serek Hayyaḥad (Community Rule) from Qumran Cave 1
1QSb	Blessings from Qumran Cave 1
11QT	Temple Scroll from Qumran Cave 11
4QTest	Testimonia text from Qumran Cave 4
11QTgJob	Targum on Job from Qumran Cave 11
Rev	Revelation
Rom	Romans
Ruth R.	Midrash Rabbah on Ruth
1 Sam	1 Samuel
2 Sam	2 Samuel
SibOr	Sibylline Oracles
Sifre Deut	Sifre on Deuteronomy
Sir	Ben Sira (Ecclesiasticus)
TAbr	Testament of Abraham
TAsher	Testament of Asher
TBenj	Testament of Benjamin
Tg.	Targum
Tg. Ps-Jon.	Targum of Pseudo-Jonathan
1 Thess	1 Thessalonians

2 Thess	2 Thessalonians
t. Ḥull.	Tosephta tractate Ḥullin
1 Tim	1 Timothy
2 Tim	2 Timothy
TIss	Testament of Issachar
TJob	Testament of Job
TJos	Testament of Joseph
TJud	Testament of Judah
TLevi	Testament of Levi
TMos	Testament of Moses
TNapht	Testament of Naphtali
t. Par.	Tosephta tractate Parah
t. Soṭa	Tosephta tractate Soṭa
Wis	Wisdom of Solomon
Zech	Zechariah
Zeph	Zephaniah

Abbreviations for Serial Publications

AB	Anchor Bible
AnBib	Analecta Biblica
AnBoll	*Analecta Bollandiana*
ANCL	Ante-Nicene Christian Library
ATR	*Anglican Theological Review*
AzTh	Arbeiten zur Theologie
BeO	*Bibbia e Oriente*
BETL	Bibliotheca ephemeridum theologicarum Lovaniensium
BFCT	Beiträge zur Förderung christliche Theologie
Bib	*Biblica*
BibOr	Biblica et Orientalia
BibS (F)	Biblische Studien (Freiburg)
BibS (N)	Biblische Studien (Neukirchen)
BNTC	Black's New Testament Commentaries
BSac	*Bibliotheca Sacra*
BST	Basel Studies in Theology

BZ	*Biblische Zeitschrift*
BWANT	Beiträge zur Wissenschaft vom Alter und Neuen Testament
BZAW	Beihefte zur *ZAW*
BZNW	Beihefte zur *ZNW*
BZRGG	Beihefte zur *ZRGG*
CBC	Cambridge Bible Commentary
CBQ	*Catholic Biblical Quarterly*
CBQMS	Catholic Biblical Quarterly – Monograph Series
CDios	*Ciudad de Dios*
CGTC	Cambridge Greek Testament Commentaries
CNT	Commentaire du Nouveau Testament
ConB (NT)	Coniectanea Biblica (New Testament Series)
CoTh	*Collectanea theologica* (Warsaw)
CRINT	Compendia Rerum Iudaicarum ad Novum Testamentum
CSCO	Corpus Scriptorum Christianorum Orientalium
CTJ	*Calvin Theological Journal*
DJD	Discoveries in the Judaean Desert
EBib	Études Bibliques
EstBib	*Estudios bíblicos*
EvQ	*Evangelical Quarterly*
Exp	*The Expositor*
ExpB	Expositor's Bible
ExpT	*Expository Times*
FolOr	*Folia orientalia*
FRALNT	Forschungen zur Religion und Literatur des Alten und Neuen Testament
GCS	Griechische christliche Schriftsteller
HC	Hand-Commentar zum Neuen Testament
HeyJ	*Heythrop Journal*

HNT	Handbuch zum Neuen Testament
HTKNT	Herders theologischer Kommentar zum Neuen Testament
HTR	*Harvard Theological Review*
HTS	Harvard Theological Studies
HUCA	*Hebrew Union College Annual*
ICC	International Critical Commentary
JA	*Journal asiatique*
JBL	*Journal of Biblical Literature*
JQR	*Jewish Quarterly Review*
JRS	*Journal of Roman Studies*
JSJ	*Journal for the Study of Judaism in the Persian, Hellenistic and Roman Period*
JSNT	*Journal for the Study of the New Testament*
JSNTSS	Journal for the Study of the New Testament Supplement Series
JSOTSS	Journal for the Study of the Old Testament Supplement Series
JSS	*Journal of Semitic Studies*
JTS	*Journal of Theological Studies*
KEK	Kritisch-exegetischer Kommentar über das Neue Testament
KNT	Kommentar zum Neuen Testament
LCL	Loeb Classical Library
LD	Lectio Divina
MGWJ	*Monatschrift für Geschichte und Wissenschaft des Judentums*
MNTC	Moffatt's New Testament Commentary
MSGVK	*Mitteilungen der schlesischen Gesellschaft für Volkskunde*
Mus	*Le Muséon*
NCeB	New Century Bible
Neot	*Neotestamentica*

NHS	Nag Hammadi Studies
NIGTC	New International Greek Testament Commentary
NLCNT	New London Commentary on the New Testament
Nov T	*Novum Testamentum*
NovTSup	Novum Testamentum Supplements
NTD	Das Neue Testament Deutsch
NTM	New Testament Message
NTS	*New Testament Studies*
OTL	Old Testament Library
ParOr	*Parole de l'Orient*
PC	Proclamation Commentaries
RB	*Revue biblique*
REJ	*Revue des études juives*
RESl	*Revue des études slaves*
RNT	Regensburger Neues Testament
RQ	*Revue de Qumran*
SB	Sources bibliques
SBLDS	SBL Dissertation Series
SBLMS	SBL Monograph Series
SBLSCS	SBL Septuagint and Cognate Studies
SBS	Stuttgarter Bibelstudien
SBT	Studies in Biblical Theology
Scr	*Scripture*
ScrHie	*Scripta Hierosolymitana*
Sem	*Semitica*
SJLA	Studies in Judaism in Late Antiquity
SNTSMS	Society for New Testament Studies Monograph Series
SPB	Studia Postbiblica
SUNT	Studien zur Umwelt des Neuen Testament
SVTP	Studia in Veteri Testamenti Pseudepigrapha
TBC	Torch Biblical Commentaries

TextsS	Texts and Studies
THKNT	Theologischer Handkommentar zum Neuen Testament
TNTC	Tyndale New Testament Commentaries
TOTC	Tyndale Old Testament Commentaries
TQ	*Theologische Quartalschrift*
TRu	*Theologische Rundschau*
TSK	*Theologische Studien und Kritiken*
TU	Texte und Untersuchungen
TynB	*Tyndale Bulletin*
TZ	*Theologische Zeitschrift*
UUÅ	Uppsala Universitetsårsskrift
VC	*Vigiliae Christianae*
VT	*Vetus Testamentum*
WBC	Word Biblical Commentary
WUNT	Wissenschaftliche Untersuchungen zum Neuen Testament
ZAW	*Zeitschrift für die alttestamentliche Wissenschaft*
ZKG	*Zeitschrift für Kirchengeschichte*
ZKT	*Zeitschrift für katholische Theologie*
ZNW	*Zeitschrift für die neutestamentliche Wissenschaft*
ZRGG	*Zeitschrift für Religions- und Geistesgeschichte*
ZWT	*Zeitschrift für wissenschaftliche Theologie*

Bibliography

Aalen, S., 'St Luke's Gospel and the Last Chapters of I Enoch', *NTS* 13 (1966–67) 1–3.

Abbott, E. A., 'On The Second Epistle of St Peter', *Exp* 2/3 (1882) 49–63, 139–155, 204–219.

Abel, E. L., 'The Genealogies of Jesus Ο ΧΡΙΣΤΟΣ', *NTS* 20 (1974) 203–210.

Abraham, M., *Légendes juives apocryphes sur la Vie de Moïse: La Chronique de Moïse – L'Ascension de Moïse – La Mort de Moïse*, Paris: Geuthner, 1925.

Adam, A., 'Erwägungen zur Herkunft der Didache', *ZKG* 68 (1957) 1–47.

Adler, W., 'Enoch in Early Christian Literature', in *SBL 1978 Seminar Papers*, vol. 1, ed. P. J. Achtemeier (Missoula, Montana: Scholars Press, 1978) 271–275.

Albin, C. A., *Judasbrevet: Traditionen Texten Tolkningen*, Stockholm: Natur och Kultur, 1962.

Albright, W. F. & Mann C. S., *Matthew*, AB 26, Garden City, New York: Doubleday, 1971.

Aldama, J. A. de, *María en la patrística de los siglos I y II*, Madrid: La Editorial Católica, 1970.

Alford, H., *The Greek Testament*, vol. 4, London: Rivingtons/Cambridge: Deighton, Bell, [2]1880.

Argyle, A. W., 'Greek among the Jews of Palestine in New Testament Times', *NTS* 20 (1973–74) 87–89.

Aune, D. E., 'Magic, Magician', in *The International Standard Bible Encyclopedia*, ed. G. W. Bromiley, vol. 3 (Grand Rapids: Eerdmans, 1986) 213–219.

Bacchiocchi, S., 'Sabbatical Typologies of Messianic Redemption', *JSJ* 17 (1986) 153–176.

Bacon, B. W., 'Genealogy of Jesus Christ', in *A Dictionary of the Bible*, ed. J. Hastings, vol. 2 (Edinburgh: T. & T. Clark, 1899) 137–141.

Bagatti, B., 'I "Parenti del Signore" a Nazaret', *BeO* 7 (1965) 259–263.

——, *Excavations in Nazareth*, Vol. 1, tr. E. Hoade, Publications of the Studium Biblicum Franciscanum 17, Jerusalem: Franciscan Printing Press, 1969.

——, *Antichi Villaggi Cristiani di Galilea*, Pubblicazioni dello Studio Biblico Franciscano: Collezione minore 13, Jerusalem: Franciscan Printing Press, 1971. (1971A)

——, *The Church from the Circumcision: History and Archaeology of the Judaeo-Christians*, tr. E. Hoade, Publications of the Studium Biblicum Franciscanum 2, Jerusalem: Franciscan Printing Press, 1971. (1971B)

Baldwin, J. G., 'Semaḥ as a Technical Term in the Prophets', *VT* 14 (1964) 93–97.

——, *Haggai, Zechariah, Malachi*, TOTC, Leicester: Inter-Varsity Press, 1972.

Balzer, K., 'Das Ende des Staates Juda und die Messias-Frage', in *Studien zur Theologie der alttestamentliche Überlieferung*, G. von Rad Festschrift, ed. R. Rendtorff and K. Koch (Neukirchen: Neukirchener Verlag, 1961) 33–43.

Barker, M., *The Lost Prophet: The Book of Enoch and its influence on Christianity*, London SPCK, 1988.

Barnett, A. E., 'The Epistle of Jude', in *The Interpreter's Bible*, vol. 12 (New York–Nashville: Abingdon, 1957) 317–343.

Barns, T., 'The Epistle of St. Jude: A Study in the Marcosian Heresy', *JTS* 6 (1905) 391–411.

Bartlet, J. V., *The Apostolic Age: Its Life, Doctrine, Worship and Polity*, Edinburgh T. & T. Clark, 1900.

Bartlett, J. R., 'The use of the word *rōš* as a title in the Old Testament', *VT* 19 (1969) 1–10.

Barton, J., *Oracles of God: Perceptions of Ancient Prophecy in Israel after the Exile*, London: Darton, Longman & Todd, 1986.

Batey, R. A., ' "Is not this the Carpenter?" ', *NTS* 30 (1984) 249–258.

Bauckham, R. J., 'A Note on a Problem in the Greek Version of 1 Enoch i.9', *JTS* 32 (1981) 136–138.

——, *Jude, 2 Peter*, WBC 50, Waco Texas 1983. (1983A)

——, 'The Liber Antiquitatum Biblicarum of Pseudo-Philo and the Gospels as "Midrash" ', in *Gospel Perspectives: III: Studies in Midrash and Historiography*, ed. R. T. France and D. Wenham (Sheffield JSOT Press, 1983) 33–76. (1983B)

——, 'Synoptic Parousia Parables Again', *NTS* 29 (1983) 129–134. (1983C)

——, 'The Two Fig Tree Parables in the Apocalypse of Peter', *JBL* 104 (1985) 269–287.

——, 'The Parable of the Vine: Rediscovering a Lost Parable of Jesus', *NTS* 33 (1987) 84–101. (1987A)

——, 'The Bishops and the Virginal Conception', *Churchman* 101 (1987) 323–333. (1987B)

——, '2 Peter: An Account of Research', in *Aufstieg und Niedergang der römischen Welt*, vol. 2/25/5, ed. W. Haase (Berlin/New York: de Gruyter, 1988) 3713–3752. (1988A)

——'The Letter of Jude: An Account of Research', in *Aufstieg und Niedergang der römischen Welt*, vol. 2/25/5, ed. W. Haase (Berlin/-New York: de Gruyter, 1988) 3791–3826. (1988B)

——'The Apocalypse of Peter: An Account of Research', in *Aufstieg und Niedergang der römischen Welt*, vol. 2/25/6, ed. W. Hasse (Berlin/New York: de Gruyter, 1988) 4712–4750. (1988C)

——'Pseudo-Apostolic Letters', *JBL* 107 (1988) 469–494. (1988D)

——'James, 1 and 2 Peter, Jude', in *It is Written: Scripture Citing Scripture: Essays in Honour of Barnabas Lindars SSF*, ed. D. A. Carson and H. G. M. Williamson (Cambridge: Cambridge University Press, 1988) 303–317. (1988E)

——, 'Jesus Christ, Worship of', forthcoming in *The Anchor Bible Dictionary*, ed. D. N. Freedman, New York: Doubleday, 1992.

——, 'Salome the Sister of Jesus, Salome the Disciple of Jesus and the *Secret Gospel of Mark*' (forthcoming).

Bauer, W., *Das Leben Jesu im Zeitalter der neutestamentlichen Apokryphen*, Tübingen: Mohr (Siebeck), 1909.

——, 'The Picture of the Apostle in Early Christian Tradition: 1. Accounts', in E. Hennecke, W. Schneemelcher & R. McL. Wilson ed., *New Testament Apocrypha*, vol. 2 (London: Lutterworth, 1965) 35–74.

Bauer, W., Arndt, W. F. & Gingrich, F. W., *A Greek–English Lexicon of the New Testament and Other Early Christian Literature*, revised F. W. Gingrich and F. W. Danker from W. Bauer's fifth edition, Chicago/London: University of Chicago Press, 1979.

Beckwith, R. T., 'The Significance of the Calendar for Interpreting Essene Chronology and Eschatology', *RQ* 10 (1980) 167–202.

——, 'Daniel 9 and the Date of the Messiah's Coming in Essene, Hellenistic, Pharisaic, Zealot, and Early Christian Computation', *RQ* 40 (1981) 521–542.

——, *The Old Testament Canon of the New Testament Church and its Background in Early Judaism*, London: SPCK, 1985.

Beker, J. C., 'Jude, Letter of', in *The Interpreter's Dictionary of the Bible*, ed. G. A. Buttrick, vol. 2 (New York-Nashville: Abingdon, 1962) 1009–1011.

Benoît, P., Review of Chaine (1939), *Vivre et Penser* 1 (1941) 134–140.

Benoît, P., Milik, J. T., and de Vaux, R., *Les Grottes de Murabba'ât*, DJD 2, Oxford: Clarendon Press, 1961.

Berger, K., 'Hartherzigkeit und Gottes Gesetz, die Vorgeschichte des anti-jüdischen Vorwurfs in Mc 10⁵', *ZNW* 61 (1970) 1–47.

——, 'Der Streit des guten und des bösen Engels um die Seele: Beobachtungen zu 4QAmr^b und Judas 9', *JSS* 4 (1973) 1–18.

Berridge, J. M., *Prophet, People and the Word of Yahweh: An Examination of Form and Content in the Proclamation of the Prophet Jeremiah*, BST 4, Zurich: EVZ-Verlag, 1970.

Bertrand, D. A., 'Le destin "post mortem" des protoplastes selon la "Vie grecque d'Adam et Ève"', in *La Littérature intertestamentaire: Colloque de Strasbourg (17–19 Octobre 1983)*, Bibliothèque des Centres d'Études Supérieures Specialisés (Paris: Presses Universitaires de Frances, 1985) 109–118.

——, *La vie grecque d'Adam et Ève*, Recherches Intertestamentaires 1, Paris: Maisonneuve 1987.

Best, E., 'I Peter II 4–10 – a Reconsideration', *NovT* 11 (1969) 270–293.

——, *A Commentary on the First and Second Epistles to the Thessalonians*, BNTC, London: A. & C. Black, 1972.

Betz, O., 'The Eschatological Interpretation of the Sinai-Tradition in Qumran and in the New Testament', *RQ* 6 (1967) 89–107.

Beyer, K., *Die aramäischen Texte vom Toten Meer samt den Inschriften aus Palästina, dem Testament Levi aus der Kairoer Genisa, der Fastenrolle und den alten talmudischen Zitaten*, Göttingen: Vandenhoeck & Ruprecht, 1984.

Beyse, K.-M., *Serubbabel und die Königserwartungen der Propheten Haggai und Sacharja: Eine historische aund traditionsgeschichtliche Untersuchung*, AzTh 1/48, Stuttgart: Calwer Verlag, 1972.

Bieder, W., 'Judas 22f.: Οὓς δὲ ἐᾶτε ἐν φόβῳ', *TZ* 6 (1950) 75–77.

Bigg, C., *A Critical and Exegetical Commentary on the Epistles of St. Peter and St. Jude*, ICC 41, Edinburgh: T. & T. Clark, 1901.

Birdsall, J. N., 'The Text of Jude in P⁷²', *JTS* 14 (1963) 394–399.

Bischoff, B., 'Wendepunkte in der Geschichte der lateinischen

Exegese im Frühmittelalter', *Sacris Erudiri* 6 (1954) 189–281.

Bishop, E. F. F., 'Mary (of) Clopas and Her Father', *ExpT* 73 (1961–62) 339.

Black, M., 'Critical and exegetical notes on three New Testament texts, Hebrews xi.11, Jude 5, James i.27', in : *Apophoreta: Festschrift für Ernst Haenchen*, BZNW 30 (Berlin: A. Töpelmann, 1964) 39–45.

——, 'The Christological Use of the Old Testament in the New Testament', *NTS* 18 (1971–72) 1–14.

——, 'The Maranatha Invocation and Jude 14, 15 (I Enoch 1:9)', in *Christ and Spirit in the New Testament: in honour of C. F. D. Moule*, ed. B. Lindars and S. S. Smalley, Cambridge: Cambridge University Press, 1973.

——, 'The Apocalypse of Weeks in the Light of 4Q En^a', *VT* 28 (1978) 464–469.

——, 'Two Unusual Nomina Dei in the Second Vision of Enoch', in *The New Testament Age: Essays in Honour of Bo Reicke*, ed. W. C. Weinrich, vol. 1 (Macon, Georgia: Mercer University Press, 1984) 53–59.

——, *The Book of Enoch or I Enoch: A New English Edition*, SVTP 7, Leiden: Brill, 1985.

Blinzler, J., *Die Brüder und Schwestern Jesu*, SBS 21, Stuttgart: Katholisches Bibelwerk, ²1967.

Bode, E. L., *The First Easter Morning: The Gospel Accounts of the Women's Visit to the Tomb of Jesus*, AnBib 45, Rome: Biblical Institute Press, 1970.

Bonwetsch, G. N., *Hippolyt's Kommentar zum Buche Daniel und die Fragmente des Kommentars zum Hohenliede*, in Hippolytus Werke I: Exegetische und homiletische Schriften, GCS, Leipzig: Hinrichs, 1897.

——, 'Die Mosessage in der slavischen kirchlichen Literatur', *Nachrichten von der Königlichen Gesellschaft der Wissenshaft zu Göttingen: Philologisch-historische Klasse* (1908) 581–607.

Boobyer, G. H., 'Jude', in *Peake's Commentary on the Bible*, ed. M. Black and H. H. Rowley, London: Nelson, 1963.

Bornhäuser, K., *Die Geburt- und Kindheitsgeschichte Jesu: Versuch einer zeitgenössischen Auslegung von Matthäus 1 und 2 und Lukas 1–3*, BFCT 2/23, Gütersloh: C. Bertelsmann, 1930.

Brooke, G. J., *Exegesis at Qumran: 4QFlorilegium in its Jewish Context*, JSOTSS 29, Sheffield: JSOT Press, 1985.

Brown, R. E. *The Gospel according to John*, AB 29–29A, 2 Vols., London: G. Chapman, 1971.

——, *The Birth of the Messiah: A Commentary on the Infancy Narratives in Matthew and Luke*, Garden City, New York: Doubleday, 1977.

——, '"Other Sheep not of this Fold": The Johannine Perspective on Christian Diversity in the Late First Century', *JBL* 97 (1978) 5–22.

——, 'Not Jewish Christianity and Gentile Christianity but Types of Jewish/Gentile Christianity', *CBQ* 45 (1983) 74–79.

Brown, R. E. *et al.*, *Mary in the New Testament: A Collaborative Assessment by Protestant and Roman Catholic Scholars*, ed. R. E. Brown, K. P. Donfried, J. A. Fitzmyer, J. Reumann, Philadelphia: Fortress/New York: Paulist, 1978.

Brown, S. K., 'Jewish and Gnostic Elements in the Second Apocalypse of James (CG V, 4)', *NovT* 17 (1975) 225–237.

Bruce, F. F., *This is That: the New Testament Development of Some Old Testament Themes*, Exeter: Paternoster, 1968.

——, *Men and Movements in the Primitive Church: Studies in Early Non-Pauline Christianity*, Exeter: Paternoster, 1979.

——, 'Jude, Epistle of', in *The Illustrated Bible Dictionary*, rev. ed. N. Hillyer, vol. 2 (Leicester: IVP, 1980) 831–832.

——, *The Epistle of Paul to the Galatians*, NIGTC, Exeter: Paternoster, 1982.

Buchanan, G. W., *Revelation and Redemption: Jewish Documents of Deliverance from the Fall of Jerusalem to the Death of Naḥmanides*, Dillsboro, North Carolina: Western North Carolina Press, 1978.

Buckley, J. J., *Female Fault and Fulfilment in Gnosticism*, Chapel Hill/London: University of North Carolina Press, 1986.

Budge, E. A. W., *Miscellaneous Coptic Texts in the Dialect of Upper Egypt*, London: British Museum, 1915.

——, *The Contendings of the Apostles*, London: Oxford University Press/H. Milford, 1935.

Bultmann, R., *Theology of the New Testament*, tr. K. Grobel, vol. 1, London: SCM Press, 1952.

Burger, C., *Jesus als Davidssohn: Eine traditionsgeschichtliche Untersuchung*, FRLANT 98, Göttingen: Vandenhoeck & Ruprecht, 1970.

Burkitt, F. C., 'Moses, Assumption of', in *A Dictionary of the Bible*, ed. J. Hastings, vol. 3 (Edinburgh: T. & T. Clark, 1900) 448–450.

Busto Saiz, J. R., 'La carta de Judas a la luz de algunas escritos judíos', *EstBib* 39 (1981) 83–105.

Cantinat, J., 'The Catholic Epistles', in *Introduction to the New Testament*, ed. A. Robert and A. Feuillet, New York: Desclee, 1965.

——, *Les épîtres de Saint Jacques et de Saint Jude*, SB, Paris: Gabalda, 1973.

Carmignac, J., 'Le document de Qumran sur Melkisédeq', *RQ* 7 (1969–71) 343–378.

Carr, W., *Angels and Principalities: The background, meaning and development of the Pauline phrase* hai archai kai hai exousiai, SNTSMS 42, Cambridge: Cambridge University Press, 1981.

Carrington, P., *The Early Christian Church*, vol. 1, Cambridge: Cambridge University Press, 1957.

Carroll, R. P., *From Chaos to Covenant: Uses of Prophecy in the Book of Jeremiah*, London: SCM Press, 1981.

——, *Jeremiah: A Commentary*, OTL, London: SCM Press, 1986.

Cavallin, H. C. C., 'The False Teachers of 2 Pt as Pseudo-Prophets', *NovT* 21 (1979) 263–270.

Cerfaux, L., *Receuil Lucien Cerfaux: Études d'Exégèse et d'Histoire Religieuse*, vol. 1, BETL 6, Gembloux: J. Duculot, 1954. (1945A)

——, *Le Christ dans la théologie de saint Paul*, Paris: Cerf, ²1954. (1954B)

Chabot, J. B., 'Notes d'Épigraphie', *JA* 10 (1897) 327–328.

Chaine, J., *Les épîtres catholiques: La seconde épître de Saint Pierre, les épîtres de Saint Jean, l'épître de Saint Jude*, EBib 27, Paris: Gabalda, ²1939.

Charles, R. H., *The Assumption of Moses*, London: A. & C. Black, 1897.

——, *The Book of Enoch*, Oxford: Clarendon Press, 1893.

——, *The Book of Enoch*, Oxford: Clarendon Press, ²1912.

——, *A Critical and Exegetical Commentary on the Book of Daniel*, Oxford: Clarendon Press, 1929.

Charlesworth, J. H., *The Old Testament Pseudepigrapha and the New Testament*, SNTSMS 54, Cambridge: Cambridge University Press, 1985.

Charue, A., 'Les épîtres catholiques', in *La Sainte Bible*, ed. L. Pirot and A. Clamer, vol. 12 (Paris: Letouzey et Ané, 1946) 373–579.

Chase, F. H., 'Jude, Epistle of', in *A Dictionary of the Bible*, ed. J. Hastings, vol. 2 (Edinburgh: T. & T. Clark, 1899) 799–806.

Chazon, E. G., 'Moses' Struggle for His Soul: A Prototype for the *Testament of Abraham*, the *Greek Apocalypse of Ezra*, and the *Apocalypse of Sedrach*', *Second Century* 5 (1985–86) 151–164.

Chilton, B., 'Jesus *ben David*: reflections on the Davidssohnfrage', *JSNT* 14 (1982) 88–112.

Cladder, H. J., 'Strophical Structure in St. Jude's Epistle', *JTS* 5 (1904) 589–601.

Cohen, A., *Midrash Rabbah*, ed. H. Freedman and M. Simon: *Ecclesiastes*, tr. A. Cohen, London: Soncino Press, 1939.

Collins, J. J., 'Testaments', in M. E. Stone, *Jewish Writings of the Second Temple Period*, CRINT 2/2 (Assen: Van Gorcum/Philadelphia: Fortress, 1984) 325–355. (1984A)

——, *The Apocalyptic Imagination: An Introduction to the Jewish Matrix of Christianity*, New York: Crossroad, 1984. (1984B)

Collins, R. F., *Studies on the First Letter to the Thessalonians*, BETL 66, Leuven: Leuven University Press, 1984. (1984C)

Colon, J.-B., 'Jude (Épître de)', in *Dictionnaire de théologie catholique*, ed. A. Vacant, E. Mangenot and É. Amann, vol. 8 (Paris: Letouzey et Ané, 1925) 1668–1681.

Cone, O., 'Jude, The General Epistle of', in *Encyclopaedia Biblica*, ed. T. K. Cheyne and J. S. Black, vol. 2 (London: A. & C. Black, 1901) 2630–2632.

Coppens, J., *Le Messianisme Royal: Ses origines, Son développement, Son accomplissement*, LD 54, Paris: Cerf, 1968.

Cramer, J. A., *Anecdota Graeca e codd. manuscriptis Bibliothecae Regiae Parisiensis*, vol. 2, Oxford: Oxford University Press, 1839.

——, *Catenae Graecorum Patrum in Novum Testamentum*, vol. 8. Oxford: Oxford University Press, 1844.

Cranfield, C. E. B., *I & II Peter and Jude*, TBC, London: SCM Press, 1960.

——, *The Gospel according to Saint Mark*, CGTC, Cambridge: Cambridge University Press, ²1963.

Crossan, J. D., 'Mark and the Relatives of Jesus', *NovT* 15 (1973) 81–113.

Cullmann, O., *The Christology of the New Testament*, tr. S. C. Guthrie and C. A. M. Hall, London: SCM Press, ²1963.

——, 'Infancy Gospels', in E. Hennecke, W. Schneemelcher & R. McL. Wilson ed., *New Testament Apocrypha*, vol. 1 (London: Lutterworth, 1963) 363–417. (1963A)

Dalman, G., *The Words of Jesus considered in the light of post-biblical Jewish writings and the Aramaic language*, tr. D. M. Kay, Edinburgh: T. & T. Clark, 1902.

Dalton, W. J., *Christ's Proclamation to the Spirits: A study of I Peter 3:18–4:16*, AnBib 23, Rome: Pontifical Biblical Institute, 1965.

——, 'Jude', in *A New Catholic Commentary on Holy Scripture*, ed. R. C. Fuller, L. Johnston and C. Kearns (London: Nelson, 1969) 1263–1265.

Daniel, C., 'La mention des Esséniens dans le texte grec de l'épître de S. Jude', *Mus* 81 (1968) 503–521.

Bibliography 397

——, '"Faux Prophètes": surnom des Esséniens dans le Sermon sur la Montagne', *RQ* 7 (1969) 45–79.

Daniélou, J., 'L'Étoile de Jacob et la mission chrétienne à Damas', *VC* 11 (1957) 121–138.

——, *Primitive Christian Symbols*, tr. D. Attwater, London: Burns & Oates, 1964.

Danker, F. W., 'I Peter $1^{24} - 2^{17}$ – A Consolatory Pericope', *ZNW* 58 (1967) 93–102.

——, 'The Second Letter of Peter', in R. H. Fuller, G. S. Sloyan, G. Krodel, F. W. Danker, E. S. Fiorenza, *Hebrews, James, 1 and 2 Peter, Jude, Revelation*, PC (Philadelphia: Fortress, 1977) 81–91.

——, 'Jude, Epistle of', in *The International Standard Bible Encyclopedia*, ed. G. W. Bromiley, vol. 2 (Exeter: Paternoster/ Grand Rapids: Eerdmans, 1982) 1153–1155.

Daube, D., *The New Testament and Rabbinic Judaism*, London: University of London Athlone Press, 1956.

Davids, P. H., 'The Epistle of James in Modern Discussion', in *Aufstieg und Niedergang der römischen Welt*, vol. 2/25/5, ed. W. Haase (Berlin/New York: de Gruyter, 1988) 3621–3645.

Davidson, S., *An Introduction to the Study of the New Testament*, vol. 2, London: Kegan Paul, Trench, Trübner, ^{3}1894.

de Boor, C., *Neue Fragmente des Papias, Hegesippus und Pierius in bisher unbekannten Excerpten aus der Kirchengeschichte des Philippus Sidetes*, TU 5/2, Leipzig: J. C. Hinrichs, 1889.

Dehandschutter, B., 'Pseudo-Cyprian, Jude and Enoch: Some Notes on 1 Enoch 1:9', in *Tradition and Re-Interpretation in Jewish and Early Christian Literature: Essays in Honour of Jürgen C. H. Lebram*, ed. J. W. van Henten, H. J. de Jonge, P. T. van Rooden, J. W. Wesselius, SPB 36, Leiden: Brill, 1986.

Deichgräber, R., *Gotteshymnus und Christushymnus in der frühen Christenheit*, SUNT 5, Göttingen 1967.

Denis, A. M., *Fragmenta Pseudepigraphorum quae supersunt Graeca*, in Pseudepigrapha Veteris Testamenti Graece, vol. 3, ed. A. M. Denis and M. de Jonge (Leiden: Brill, 1970) 45–246. (1970A)

——, *Introduction aux Pseudépigraphes grecs d'Ancien Testament*, SVTP 1, Leiden: Brill, 1970. (1970B)

Delcor, M., *Le Testament d'Abraham*, SVTP 2, Leiden: Brill, 1973.

De Santos Otero, A., 'The Pseudo-Titus Epistle', in E. Hennecke, W. Schneemelcher & R. McL. Wilson ed., *New Testament Apocrypha*, vol. 2 (London: Lutterworth, 1965) 141–166.

Desjardins, M., 'The Portrayal of the Dissidents in 2 Peter and Jude: Does it tell us more about the "Godly" than the "Ungodly"?',

JSNT 30 (1987) 89–102.

Dexinger, F., *Henochs Zehnwochenapokalypse und offene Probleme der Apokalyptikforschung*, SPB 29, Leiden: Brill, 1977.

Dods, M., Reith, G., & Pratten, B. P., *The Writings of Justin Martyr and Athenagoras*, ANCL 2, Edinburgh: T. & T. Clark, 1867.

Draper, J. A., 'The twelve apostles as foundation stones of the heavenly Jerusalem and the foundation of the Qumran community', *Neot* 22 (1988) 41–63.

Dubarle, A.-M., 'Rédacteur et destinataires de L'Épître aux Hébreux,' *RB* 48 (1939) 509–529.

——, 'Le péché des anges dans l'épître de Jude,' in *Memorial J. Chaine* (Lyons: Facultés Catholiques, 1950) 145–148.

Dunn, J. D. G., *Jesus and the Spirit: A Study of the Religious and Charismatic Experience of Jesus and the First Christians as Reflected in the New Testament*, London: SCM Press, 1975.

——, *Unity and Diversity in the New Testament: An Inquiry into the Character of Earliest Christianity*, London: SCM Press, 1977.

——, *Christology in the Making: A New Testament Inquiry into the Origins of the Doctrine of the Incarnation*, London: SCM Press, 1980.

Ehrhardt, A., *The Apostolic Succession in the first two centuries of the church*, London: Lutterworth, 1953.

Elliott, J. H., *The Elect and the Holy: An exegetical examination of I Peter 2:4–10 and the phrase βασίλειν ἱεράτευμα*, NovTSup 12, Leiden: Brill, 1966.

——, 'Peter, Silvanus and Mark in 1 Peter and Acts: Sociological-Exegetical Perspectives on a Petrine Group in Rome,' in W. Haubach and M. Bachmann ed., *Wort in der Zeit: Neutestamentliche Studien* (K. H. Rengstorf Festschrift; Leiden: Brill, 1980) 250–267.

——, *A Home for the Homeless: A Sociological Exegesis of 1 Peter, Its Situation and Strategy*, London: SCM Press, 1982.

Elliott-Binns, L. E., *Galilean Christianity*, SBT 16, London: SCM Press, 1956.

Ellis, E. E., *Paul's Use of the Old Testament*, Edinburgh: Oliver & Boyd, 1957.

——, *Prophecy and Hermeneutic in Early Christianity*, WUNT 18, Tübingen: Mohr (Siebeck), 1978.

Ermoni, V., 'Jude, Épître de saint', in *Dictionnaire de la Bible*, ed. F. Vigoroux, vol. 3 (Paris: Letouzey et Ané, 1910) 1807–1813.

Eybers, I. H., 'Aspects of the Background of the Letter of Jude', *Neot* 9 (1975) 113–123.

Falconer, R. A., 'Is Second Peter a Genuine Epistle to the Churches of Samaria?', *Exp* 6/5 (1902) 459–472; 6/6 (1902) 47–56, 117–127, 218–227.

Fallon, F. T. & Cameron, R., 'The Gospel of Thomas: A Forschungsbericht and Analysis', in *Aufstieg und Niedergang der römischen Welt*, vol. 2/25/6, ed. W. Haase (Berlin/New York: de Gruyter, 1988) 4195–4251.

Farrar, F. W., *The Early days of Christianity*, vol. 1, London ³1882.

Ferguson, E., 'The Terminology of Kingdom in the Second Century', in E. A. Livingstone ed., *Studia Patristica*, Vol. 17 Part 2 (Oxford: Pergamon Press, 1982) 669–676.

Fiey, J. M., *Jalons pour une histoire de l'église en Iraq*, CSCO 310, Louvain: Secrétariat du CorpusSCO, 1970.

Finkel, A., 'The Pesher of Dreams and Scriptures', *RQ* 4 (1963–64) 357–370.

Fishbane, M., *Biblical Interpretation in Ancient Israel*, Oxford: Clarendon Press, 1985.

Fitzmyer, J. A., 'The use of explicit Old Testament quotations in Qumran literature and in the New Testament', 'The Son of David tradition and Mt 22:41–46 and parallels', and 'A feature of Qumran angelology and the angels of I Cor 11:10', in *Essays on the Semitic Background of the New Testament* (London: G. Chapman, 1971) 3–58, 112–126, 187–204.

——, 'The Languages of Palestine in the First Century A.D.', and 'The Semitic Background of the New Testament Kyrios-Title', in *A Wandering Aramaean: Collected Aramaic Essays*, SBLMS 25 (Missoula, Montana; Scholars Press, 1979) 29–56, 115–142.

——, *The Gospel According to Luke I–IX*, AB 28, Garden City, New York: Doubleday, 1981. (1981A)

——, 'The Virginal Conception of Jesus in the New Testament', in *To Advance the Gospel: New Testament Studies* (New York: Crossroad, 1981) 41–78. (1981B)

Fitzmyer, J. A. and Harrington, D. J., *A Manual of Palestine Aramaic Texts (Second Century B.C. – Second Century A.D.)*, BibOr 34, Rome: Biblical Institute Press, 1978.

Flusser, D., 'Palaea Historica: An Unknown Source of Biblical Legends', *ScriHie* 22 (1971) 48–79.

——, '"The House of David" on an Ossuary', *Israel Museum Journal* 5 (1986) 37–40.

Ford, J. M., *My Enemy Is My Guest: Jesus and Violence in Luke*, Maryknoll, New York: Orbis, 1984.

Fornberg, T., *An Early Church in a Pluralistic Society: A Study of*

2 Peter, ConB(NT)9, Lund: Gleerup, 1977.

Fossum, J., The Name of God and the Angel of the Lord: Samaritan and Jewish Concepts of Intermediation and the Origin of Gnosticism, WUNT 36, Tübingen: Mohr (Siebeck), 1985.

——, 'Kyrios Jesus as the Angel of the Lord in Jude 5–7', NTS 33 (1987) 226–243.

Fowler, J. D., Theophoric Personal Names in Ancient Hebrew: A Comparative Study, JSOTSS 49, Sheffield: Sheffield Academic Press, 1988.

France, R. T., Jesus and the Old Testament: His application of Old Testament passages to himself and his mission, London: Tyndale Press, 1971.

Freudenberger, R., 'Die delatio nominis causa gegen Rabbi Elieser ben Hyrkanos', Revue internationale des droits de l'antiquité 15 (1968) 11–19.

Frey, J.-B., Corpus Inscriptionum Iudaicarum: Receuil des inscriptions juives qui vont du IIIe siècle avant Jésus-Christ au VIIe siècle de notre ère, Vol. 1, Vatican City: Pontifical Institute of Christian Archaeology, 1936.

Freyne, S., Galilee from Alexander the Great to Hadrian 323 B.C.E to 153 C.E.: A Study of Second Temple Judaism, University of Notre Dame Centre for the Study of Judaism and Christianity in Antiquity 5, Wilmington, Delaware: M. Glazier/Notre Dame, Indiana: University of Notre Dame Press, 1980.

Fuchs, E. and Reymond, P., La deuxième épître de Saint Pierre; L'Épître de Saint Jude, CNT 2/13b, Neuchâtel: Delachaux et Niestlé, 1980.

Fuller, R. H., A Critical Introduction to the New Testament, London: Duckworth, ²1971.

Funk, F. X., Didascalia et Constitutiones Apostolorum, vol. 1, Paderborn: F. Schoeningh, 1905.

Funk, W.-P., Die zweite Apokalypse des Jakobus aus Nag Hammadi-Codex V, TU 119, Berlin: Akademie-Verlag, 1976.

Furfey, P. H., 'Christ as Tektōn', CBQ 17 (1955) 324–335.

Garitte, G., Le Calendrier Palestino-Géorgien du Sinaiticus 34 (Xe siècle), Subsidia Hagiographica 30, Brussels: Société des Bollandistes, 1958.

Gaster, T. H., Studies and Texts in folklore, magic, medieval romance, Hebrew apocrypha and Samaritan archaeology, vol. 1, London: Maggs, 1925.

Gijsel, J., 'Les "Évangiles Latins de l'Enfance" de M. R. James', AnBoll 94 (1976) 289–302.

Ginzberg, L., *The Legends of the Jews*, tr. P. Radin, vol. 3, Philadelphia: Jewish Publication Society of America, 1911.

Glasson, T. F., *The Second Advent: The Origin of the New Testament Doctrine*, London: Epworth Press, ²1947.

——, *Greek Influence in Jewish Eschatology*, Biblical Monographs 1, London: SPCK, 1961.

Gloag, P. J., *Introduction to the Catholic Epistles*, Edinburgh: T. & T. Clark, 1887.

Goldberg, A., 'Die Namen des Messias in der rabbinischen Traditionsliteratur: Ein Beitrag zur Messianologie des rabbinischen Judentums', *Frankfurter Judaistische Beiträge* 7 (1979) 1–93.

Goodman, M., *State and Society in Roman Galilee, A.D. 132–212*, Totowa, New Jersey: Rowman & Allanheld, 1983.

Goodspeed, E. J., *An Introduction to the New Testament*, Chicago: University of Chicago Press, 1937.

Graetz, H., 'Historische und topographische Streifzüge: Die Römischen Legaten in Judäa unter Domitian und Trajan und ihre Beziehung zu Juden und Christen', *MGWJ* 34 (1885) 17–34.

Green, E. M. B., *The Second Epistle General of Peter and the General Epistle of Jude*, TNTC, London: IVP, 1968.

Grudem, W., *The First epistle of Peter*, TNTC, Leicester: Inter-Varsity Press, 1988.

Grundmann, W., 'Das Problem des hellenistischen Christentums innerhalb der Jerusalemer Urgemeinde', *ZNW* 38 (1939) 45–73.

——, *Der Brief des Judas und der zweite brief des Petrus*, THKNT 15, Berlin: Evangelische Verlagsanstalt, 1974.

Grunewald, W., *Das Neue Testament auf Papyrus: I: Die Katholischen Briefe*, Berlin/New York: de Gruyter, 1986.

Gunther, J. J., 'The Fate of the Jerusalem Church: The Flight to Pella', *TZ* 29 (1973) 81–94.

——, 'The Family of Jesus', *EvQ* 46 (1974) 25–41.

——, 'The Meaning and Origin of the Name "Judas Thomas",' *Mus* 93 (1980) 113–148.

——, 'The Alexandrian Epistle of Jude', *NTS* 30 (1984) 549–562.

Gustafsson, B., 'Hegesippus' Sources and his Reliability', in F. L. Cross ed., *Studia Patristica*, vol. 3 Part 1 (= TU 78; Berlin: Akademie Verlag, 1961) 227–232.

Guthrie, D., *New Testament Introduction*, London: IVP, ³1970.

Haacker K. & Schäfer, P., 'Nachbiblische Traditionen vom Tod des Mose', in *Josephus-Studien: Untersuchungen zu Josephus, dem antiken Judentum und dem Neuen Testament*, O. Michel Festschrift, ed. O. Betz, K. Haacker, M. Hengel (Göttingen: Vandenhoeck &

Ruprecht, 1974) 147–174.

Hahn, F., 'Randbemerkungen zum Judasbrief', *TZ* 37 (1981) 209–218.

Halkin, F., 'Publications récentes de textes hagiographiques grecs', *AnBoll* 53 (1935) 366–381.

——, 'Vie de S. Conon d'Isaurie', *AnBoll* 103 (1985) 5–34.

Halton, T., 'Hegesippus in Eusebius', in E. A. Livingstone ed., *Studia Patristica*, vol. 17 Part 2 (Oxford: Pergamon Press, 1982) 688–693.

Hamerton-Kelly, R., 'The temple and the origins of Jewish apocalyptic', *VT* 20 (1970) 1–15.

Hanson, A. T., *Jesus Christ in the Old Testament*, London: SPCK, 1965.

——, *Studies in th Pastoral Epistles*, London: SPCK, 1968.

Hanson, P. D., *The Dawn of Apocalyptic*, Philadelphia: Fortress, 1975.

Harnack, A. von, *Geschichte der altchristlichen Litteratur bis Eusebius II: Die Chronologie der altchristlichen Litteratur bis Eusebius*, vol. 1, Leipzig: Hinrichs, 1897.

——, *Geschichte der altchristlichen Litteratur bis Eusebius II: Die Chronologie der altchristlichen Litteratur bis Eusebius*, vol. 2, Leipzig: Hinrichs, 1904.

——, *The Mission and Expansion of Christianity in the First Three Centuries*, tr. J. Moffatt, vol. 2, London: William & Norgate, 1908.

Harrington, D. J., 'Interpreting Israel's History: The *Testament of Moses* as a Rewriting of Deuteronomy 32–34', in *Studies on the Testament of Moses*, SBLSCS 4, ed. G. W. E. Nickelsburg (Cambridge, Massachusetts: SBL, 1973) 59–68.

Harris, J. R., *Four Lectures on the Western Text of the New Testament*, London: C. J. Clay, 1894.

Harris, R., *Testimonies*, Part 1, Cambridge: Cambridge University Press, 1916.

——, *The Twelve Apostles*, Cambridge: Heffer, 1927.

Hartman, L., *Prophecy Interpreted: The formation of some Jewish apocalyptic texts and of the eschatological discourse Mark 13 par.*, ConB (NT)1, Uppsala: Almqvist & Wiksells, 1966.

——, *Asking for a Meaning: A Study of 1 Enoch 1–5*, ConB (NT)12, Lund: Gleerup, 1979.

Hartman, L. & Di Lella, A. A., *The Book of Daniel*, AB 23, Garden City, New York: Doubleday, 1978.

Hauck, F., 'Brief des Judas', in *Das Neue Testament Deutsch*, vol.

3/10 (Göttingen: Vandenhoeck & Ruprecht, ³1937) 99–109.

Heer, J. M., *Die Stammbäume Jesu nach Matthäus und Lukas: Ihre ursprungliche Bedeutung und Text-Gestalt und ihre Quellen*, BibS (F) 15/1, Freiburg: Herder, 1910.

Heiligenthal, R., 'Der Judasbrief: Aspekte der Forschung in den letzten Jahrzehnten', *TRu* 41 (1986) 117–129.

Hengel, M., *The Charismatic Leader and His Followers*, tr. J. C. G. Greig, Edinburgh: T. & T. Clark, 1981.

——, *Between Jesus and Paul: Studies in the Earliest History of Christianity*, tr. J. Bowden, London: SCM Press, 1983.

Henkel, K., *Der zweite brief des Apostelfürsten Petrus geprüft auf seine Echtheit*, BibS (F) 9/5, Freiburg: Herder, 1904.

Herford, R. T., *Christianity in Talmud and Midrash*, London: Williams & Norgate, 1903.

Hervey, A., *The Genealogies of our Lord and Saviour Jesus Christ*, Cambridge: Macmillan/ London: Hatchard, 1853.

Hilgenfeld, A., 'Die Psalmen Salomo's und die Himmelfahrt des Moses, griechisch hergestellt und erklärt, B. Die Himmelfahrt des Moses', *ZWT* 11 (1868) 273–309.

Himmelfarb, M., *Tours of Hell: An Apocalyptic Form in Jewish and Christian Literature*, Philadelphia: University of Philadelphia Press, 1983.

Hofmann, J. Chr. K. von, *Die heilige Schrift neuen Testaments*, vol. 7/2, Nördlingen: C. H. Beck, 1875.

Holl, K., *Epiphanius (Ancoratus und Panarion)*, vol. 1, GCS 25, Leipzig: Hinrichs, 1915.

Holladay, W. L., *Jeremiah 1: A Commentary on the Book of the Prophet Jeremiah Chapters 1–25*, Hermeneia, Philadelphia: Fortress, 1986.

Hollman, G., 'Der Brief Judas und der zweite Brief des Petrus', in *Die Schriften des Neuen Testaments*, ed. J. Weiss, vol. 2 (Göttingen: Vandenhoeck & Ruprecht, ²1907) 571–596.

Holtzmann, O., *Das Neue Testament*, vol. 2, Giessen: Töpelmann, 1926.

Horbury, W., 'The Twelve and the Phylarchs', *NTS* 32 (1986) 503–527.

Horgan, M. P., *Pesharim: Qumran Interpretations of Biblical Books*, CBQMS 8, Washington, DC: Catholic Biblical Association of America, 1979.

Howard, G., 'The Gospel of the Ebionites', in *Aufstieg und Niedergang der römischen Welt*, vol. 2/25/5, ed. W. Haase (Berlin/New York: de Gruyter, 1988) 4034–4053.

Hultgård, A., 'Théophanie et présence divine dans judaïsme antique:

Quelque remarques à partir des textes "intertestamentaires"', in *La Littérature Interestamentaire: Colloque de Strasbourg (17–19 Octobre 1983)*, Bibliothèque des Centres d'Études Supérieures Spécialisés (Paris: Presses Universitaires de Frances, 1985) 43–55.

Hurtado, L. W., *One God, One Lord: Early Christian devotion and ancient Jewish monotheism*, Philadelphia: Fortress, 1988.

Huther, J. E., *Critical and Exegetical Handbook to the General Epistles of Peter and Jude*, tr. D. B. Croom and P. J. Gloag, Edinburgh: T. & T. Clark, 1881.

Ilan, T., 'Notes on the Distribution of Jewish Women's Names in Palestine in the Second Temple and Mishnaic Periods', *JJS* 40 (1989) 186–200.

Isser, S. J., *The Dositheans: A Samaritan Sect in Late Antiquity*, SJLA 17, Leiden: Brill, 1976.

James, M. R., *The Testament of Abraham*, TextsS 2/2, Cambridge: Cambridge University Press, 1892.

——, *The Second Epistle General of Peter and the General Epistle of Jude*, Cambridge Greek Testament for Schools and Colleges, Cambridge: Cambridge University Press, 1912.

——, *The Lost Apocrypha of the Old Testament*, London: SPCK, New York: Macmillan, 1920.

——, *The Apocryphal New Testament*, Oxford: Clarendon Press, 1924.

——, *Latin Infancy Gospels*, Cambridge University Press, 1927.

Japhet, S., 'Sheshbazzar and Zerubbabel – Against the Background of the Historical and Religious Tendencies of Ezra-Nehemiah', *JBL* 94 (1982) 66–98; 95 (1983) 219–229.

Jeremias, J., *Unknown Sayings of Jesus*, tr. R. H. Fuller, London: SPCK, 1957.

——, *Jesus' Promise to the Nations*, tr. S. H. Hooke, SBT 24, London: SCM Press, 1958.

——, *Jerusalem in the Time of Jesus*, London: SCM Press, 1969.

Johnson, M. D., *The Purpose of the Biblical Genealogies with special reference to the setting of the genealogies of Jesus*, SNTSMS 8, Cambridge: Cambridge University Press, 1969.

Jülicher, A., *An Introduction to the New Testament*, tr. J. P. Ward, London: Smith, Elder, 1904.

Kaiser, O., *Isaiah 1–12: A Commentary*, OTL, London: SCM Press, 1972.

Kaplan, C., 'Some New Testament Problems in the Light of Rabbinics and the Pseudepigrapha: The Generation Schemes in Matthew I:1–17, Luke III: 24ff.', *BSac* 87 (1930) 465–471.

Kee, H. C., 'The Terminology of Mark's Exorcism Stories', *NTS* 14 (1968) 232–246.

Keil, C. F., *Commentar über die Briefe des Petrus and Judas*, Leipzig: Dörffling & Franke, 1883.

Kellermann, U., *Messias und Gesetz: Grundlinien einer alttestamentlichen Heilserwartung*, BibS (N) 61, Neukirchen-Vluyn: Neukirchener Verlag, 1971.

Kellett, E. E., 'Note on Jude 5', *ExpT* 15 (1903–4) 381.

Kelly, J. N. D., *A Commentary on the Epistles of Peter and of Jude*, BNTC, London: A. & C. Black, 1969.

Kilpatrick, G. D. 'Jesus, His Family and His Disciples', *JSNT* 15 (1982) 3–19.

Klausner, J., *Jesus of Nazareth: His life, times, and teaching*, tr. H. Danby, London: Allen & Unwin, 1925.

Klein, G., *Die zwölf Apostel: Ursprung und Gehalt einer Idee*, FRLANT 59, Göttingen: Vandenhoeck & Ruprecht, 1961.

Klein, S., *Beiträge zur Geographie und Geschichte Galiläas*, Leipzig: R. Haupt, 1909.

——, *Neue Beiträge zur Geschichte und Geographie Galiläas*, Palästina Studien 1, Vienna: Verlag 'Menorah', 1923.

Klijn, A. F. J., 'John xiv 22 and the Name Judas Thomas', in *Studies in John*, J. N. Sevenster Festschrift, NovTSup 24 (Leiden: Brill, 1970) 88–96.

——, 'Jude 5 to 7', in *The New Testament Age: Essays in Honour of Bo Reicke*, ed. W. C. Weinrich, vol. 1 (Macon, Georgia: Mercer University Press, 1984) 237–244.

——, 'Das Hebräer- und Nazoräerevangelium', in *Aufstieg und Niedergang der römischen Welt*, 2/25/5, ed. W. Haase (Berlin/New York: de Gruyter, 1988) 3997–4033.

Klijn, A. F. J. and Reinink, G. J., *Patristic evidence for Jewish-Christian Sects*, NovTSup 36, Leiden: Brill, 1973.

Kmosko, M., 'S. Simeon bar Sabba'e', in *Patrologia Syriaca*, vol. 2 (Paris: Firmin-Didot, 1907) 659–1055.

Knibb, M. A., 'The Exile in the Literature of the Intertestamental Period', *HeyJ* 17 (1976) 253–272.

——, *The Ethiopic Book of Enoch*, vol. 2, Oxford: Clarendon Press, 1978.

Knopf, R., *Die Briefe Petri und Judä*, KEK 12, Göttingen: Vandenhoeck & Ruprecht, [7]1912.

Kobelski, P. J., *Melchizedek and Melchireša'*, CBQMS 10, Washington, D. C.: Catholic Biblical Association of America, 1981.

Koch, K., 'Sabbatstruktur und Geschichte: Die sogenannte Zehn-

Wochen-Apokalypse (I Hen 93 1–10 91 11–17) und das Ringen um die alttestamentlichen Chronologien im späten Israelitentum', *ZAW* 95 (1983) 403–430.

Koester, H., 'ΓΝΩΜΑΙ ΔΙΑΦΟΡΟΙ: The Origin and Nature of Diversification in the History of Early Christianity', *HTR* 58 (1965) 279–318.

———, *Introduction to the New Testament: Volume 2: History and Literature of Early Christianity*, Philadelphia: Fortress/Berlin/New York: de Gruyter, 1982.

Koetschau, P., *Origenes Werke V: De Principiis [ΠΕΡΙ ΑΡΧΩΝ]*, GCS, Leipzig: Hinrichs, 1913.

Kraft, R. A., 'Barnabas' Isaiah Text and the "Testimony Book" Hypothesis', *JBL* 79 (1960) 336–350.

Kramer, W., *Christ, Lord, Son of God*, tr. B. Hardy, SBT 50, London: SCM Press, 1966.

Kreitzer, L. J., *Jesus and God in Paul's Eschatology*, JSNTSS 19, Sheffield: JSOT Press, 1987.

Krodel, G., 'The Letter of Jude', in R. H. Fuller, G. S. Sloyan, G. Krodel, F. W. Danker and E. S. Fiorenza, *Hebrews, James, 1 and 2 Peter, Jude, Revelation*, PC (Philadelphia: Fortress, 1977) 92–98.

Kubo, S., 'Jude 22–23: Two-division Form or Three?', in *New Testament Textual Criticism*, Festschrift B. M. Metzger, ed. E. J. Epp and G. D. Fee (Oxford: Clarendon Press, 1981) 239–253.

Kugelman, R., *James and Jude*, NTM 19, Dublin: Veritas, 1980.

Kühl, E., *Die Briefe Petri und Judae*, KEK 12, Göttingen: Vandenhoeck & Ruprecht, [6]1897.

Kuhn, G., 'Die Geschechtsregister Jesu bei Lukas und Matthäus, nach ihrer Herkunft untersucht', *ZNW* 22 (1923) 206–228.

Kümmel, W. G., *Introduction to the New Testament*, tr. H. C. Kee, London: SCM Press, [2]1975.

Lacocque, A., *The Book of Daniel*, tr. D. Pellauer, London: SPCK, 1979.

Laible, H., *Jesus Christ in the Talmud, Midrash, Zohar, and the Liturgy of the Synagogue* (texts and translation by G. Dalman, with an introductory essay by H. Laible), tr. A. W. Streane, Cambridge: Deighton, Bell, 1893.

Lake, K., *Eusebius: The Ecclesiastical History*, LCL, 2 vols., London: Heinemann/New York: Putnam, 1926, 1932.

Lambrecht, J., 'The relatives of Jesus in Mark', *NovT* 16 (1974) 241–258.

Lane, W. L., *The Gospel according to Mark*, NLCNT, London: Marshall, Morgan & Scott, 1974.

Laperrousaz, E.-M., *Le Testament de Moïse (généralement appelé "As-somption de Moïse": Traduction avec introduction et notes* = Sem 19 (1970) 1–140.

Lawlor, G. L., *Translation and Exposition of the Epistle of Jude*, Nutley N.J.: Presbyterian and Reformed, 1976.

Lawlor, H. J., 'Early Citations from the Book of Enoch', *Journal of Philology* 25 (1897) 164–225.

——, *Eusebiana: Essays on the Ecclesiastical History of Eusebius Pam-phili, ca 264–349 A.D. Bishop of Caesarea*, Oxford: Oxford University Press, 1917, reprinted Amsterdam: Philo Press, 1973.

Lawlor, H. J. and Oulton, J. E. L., *Eusebius Bishop of Caesarea: The Ecclesiastical History and the Martyrs of Palestine*, Vol. 1, London: SPCK, 1927.

Layton, B., *The Gnostic Scriptures*, London: SCM Press, 1987.

Leaney, A. R. C., *The Letters of Peter and Jude*, CBC, Cambridge: Cambridge University Press, 1967.

Leconte, R., 'Épître de Jude', in *Supplément au Dictionnaire de la Bible*, ed. L. Pirot, H. Cazelles and A. Feuillet, vol. 4 (Paris: Letouzey et Ané, 1949) 1288–1291.

——, *Les épîtres catholiques de Saint Jacques, Saint Jude et Saint Pierre*, La Sainte Bible, Paris: Cerf, ²1961.

Lenski, R. C. H., *The Interpretation of the Epistles of St. Peter, St. John and St. Jude*, Commentary on the New Testament 11, Minneapolis: Augsburg, 1966.

Leslau, W., *Falasha Anthology*, Yale Judaica Series 6, New Haven/London: Yale University Press, 1951.

Levey, S. H., *The Messiah: An Aramaic Interpretation*, Monographs of the Hebrew Union College 2, Cincinnati, New York, Los Angeles, Jerusalem: Hebrew Union College/Jewish University of Religion, 1974.

Lévi, I., 'L'Apocalypse du Zorobabel et le roi de Perse Siroès', *REJ* 68 (1914) 129–160; 69 (1919) 108–121; 71 (1920) 57–65.

Lieberman, S., 'Roman Legal Institutions in Early Rabbinics and in the Acta Martyrum', *JQR* 35 (1944–45) 1–57.

Lieu, S. N. C., *Manichaeism in the later Roman Empire and medieval China: A historical survey*, Manchester: Manchester University Press, 1985.

Lightfoot, J. B., *The Apostolic Fathers: Part II: S. Ignatius, S. Poly-carp*, vol. 2 sect. 1, London: Macmillan, 1885.

——, 'The Brethren of the Lord', in *Dissertations on the Apostolic Age* (London: Macmillan, 1892) 1–45, reprinted from *Saint Paul's Epistle to the Galatians* (London: Macmillan, ⁷1881) 252–291.

Lindars, B., *New Testament Apologetic: The Doctrinal Significance of the Old Testament Quotations*, London: SCM Press, 1961.

——, *Jesus Son of Man: A Fresh Examination of the Son of Man Sayings in the Gospels in the Light of Recent Research*, London: SPCK, 1983.

Loewenstamm, S. E., 'The Death of Moses', in *Studies on the Testament of Abraham*, ed. G. W. E. Nickelsburg, SBLSCS 4 (Missoula, Montana: Scholars Press, 1976) 185–217.

Lohmeyer, E., *Galiläa und Jerusalem*, FRLANT 52, Göttingen: Vandenhoeck & Ruprecht, 1936.

Loisy, A., *Remarques sur la littérature épistolaire du Nouveau Testament*, Paris: É. Nourry, 1935.

——, *The Origins of the New Testament*, tr. L. P. Jacks, London: Allen & Unwin, 1950.

Lüdemann, G., 'The Successors of Pre-70 Jerusalem Christianity: A Critical Evaluation of the Pella-Tradition', in *Jewish and Christian Self-Definition: 1: The Shaping of Christianity in the Second and Third Centuries*, ed. E. P. Sanders (London: SCM Press, 1980) 161–173.

Lumby, J. R., 'On the Epistles of St Peter: The Second Epistle', *Exp* 1/4 (1876) 372–399, 446–469.

——, *The Epistles of St. Peter*, ExpB, London: Hodder & Stoughton, ²1908.

McCown, C. G., "Ο ΤΕΚΤΩΝ', in *Studies in Early Christianity: Presented to Frank Chamberlin Porter and Benjamin Wisner Bacon*, ed. S. J. Case (New York/London: Century, 1928) 173–189.

MacDonald, J., *Memar Marqah: The teaching of Marqah*, vol. 2, BZAW 84, Berlin: Töpelmann, 1963.

McDonald, J. I. H., *Kerygma and Didache: The articulation and structure of the earliest Christian message*, SNTSMS 37, Cambridge: Cambridge University Press, 1980.

McGinn, B., *Apocalyptic Spirituality: Treatises and Letters of Lactantius, Adso of Montier-en-Der, Joachim of Fiore, the Franciscan Spirituals, Savonarola*, Classics of Western Spirituality, London: SPCK, 1980.

McHugh, J., *The Mother of Jesus in the New Testament*, London: Darton, Longman & Todd, 1975.

McKane, W., *A Critical and Exegetical Commentary on Jeremiah*, vol. 1, ICC, Edinburgh: T. & T. Clark, 1986.

McNamara, M., 'The Unity of Second Peter: A Reconsideration', *Scr* 12 (1960) 13–19.

McNeile, A. H., *An Introduction to the Study of the New Testament*, revised C. S. C. Williams, Oxford: Clarendon, ²1953.

Maier, F., 'Zur Erklärung des Judasbriefes (Jud 5)', *BZ* 2 (1904) 377–397.

——, 'Ein Beitrag zur Priorität des Judasbrief', TQ 87 (1905) 547–580.

——, *Der Judasbrief: Seine Echtheit, Abfassungszeit und Leser: Ein Beitrag zur Einleitung in die katholischen Briefe*, BibS(F) 11/1–2, Freiburg im B.: Herder, 1906. (1906A)

——, 'Die Echtheit des Judas- und 2. Petrusbriefes: Eine Antikritik, vornehmlich gegen H. J. Holtzmann', *ZKT* 30 (1906) 693–729. (1906B)

Maier, J., *Jesus von Nazareth in der Talmudischen Überlieferung*, Erträge der Forschung 82, Darmstadt: Wissenschaftliche Buchgesellschaft, 1978.

Manns, F., *Essais sur le Judéo-Christianisme*, Studium Biblicum Franciscanum Analecta 12, Jerusalem: Franciscan Printing Press, 1977.

Mansel, H. L., *The Gnostic Heresies of the First and Second Centuries*, London: J. Murray, 1875.

Marshall, I. H., *The origins of New Testament Christology*, Downers Grove, Illinois: InterVarsity Press, 1976.

——, *The Gospel of Luke*, NIGTC, Exeter: Paternoster, 1978.

——, 'Pauline Theology in the Thessalonian Correspondence', in *Paul and Paulinism: Essays in honour of C. K. Barrett*, ed. M. D. Hooker and S. G. Wilson (London: SPCK, 1982) 173–183.

Mastin, B. A., 'The Imperial Cult and the Ascription of the Title θεός to Jesus (John XX.28)', in *Studia Evangelica* 6, ed. E. A. Livingstone, TU 112 (Berlin: Akademie-Verlag, 1973) 352–365.

Mayer, G., *Die jüdische Frau in der hellenistisch-römischen Antike*, Stuttgart: Kohlhammer, 1987.

Mayor, J. B., *The Epistle of St. James*, London: Macmillan, ²1897.

——, 'Brethren of the Lord', in *A Dictionary of the Bible*, ed. J. Hastings, vol. 1 (Edinburgh: T. & T. Clark, 1898) 320–326.

——, 'The Epistle of St. Jude and the Marcosian Heresy', *JTS* 6 (1905) 569–577.

——, *The Epistle of St. Jude and the Second Epistle of St. Peter*, London: Macmillan, 1907.

——, 'The Epistle of Jude', in *The Expositor's Greek Testament*, ed. W. R. Nicoll, vol. 5, London: Hodder & Stoughton, 1910.

Mays, J. L., *Hosea: A Commentary*, OTL, London: SCM Press, 1969.

Mees, M., 'Papyrus Bodmer VII (P⁷²) und die Zitate aus dem Judasbrief bei Clemens von Alexandrien', *CDios* 181 (1968) 551–559.

Meyer, A. and Bauer, W., 'The Relatives of Jesus', in *New Testament Apocrypha*, ed. E. Hennecke, W. Schneemelcher and R. McL. Wilson, vol. 1 (London: Lutterworth, 1963) 418–432.

Meyers, E. M. & Strange, J. F., *Archaeology, the Rabbis and Early Christianity*, London: SCM Press, 1981.

Michaels, J. R., 'Second Peter and Jude – Royal Promises', in G. W. Barker, W. L. Lane, J. R. Michaels ed., *The New Testament Speaks* (New York: Harper & Row, 1969) 346–360.

Michl, J., *Die katholischen Briefe*, RNT 8/2, Regensburg: F. Pustet, ²1968.

Milik, J. T., 'Trois tombeaux juifs récemment découverts au Sud-Est de Jérusalem', *Liber Annuus* 7 (1956–57) 232–267.

——, '4Q Visions de 'Amram et une citation d'Origène', *RB* 79 (1972) 77–97.

——, *The Books of Enoch: Aramaic Fragments of Qumrân Cave 4*, Oxford: Clarendon, 1976.

Miller, J. M. and Hayes, J. H., *A History of Ancient Israel and Judah*, London: SCM Press, 1986.

Mishcon, A. & Cohen, A., *The Babylonian Talmud: 'Abodah Zarah*, London: Soncino Press, 1935.

Moffatt, J., *An Introduction to the Literature of the New Testament*, Edinburgh: T. & T. Clark, ³1918.

——, *The General Epistles: James, Peter and Judas*, MNTC, London: Hodder & Stoughton, 1928.

Montgomery, J. A., *A Critical and Exegetical Commentary on the Book of Daniel*, ICC, Edinburgh: T. & T. Clark, 1927.

Moule, C. F. D., *The Origin of Christology*, Cambridge: Cambridge University Press, 1977.

Mowinckel, S., *He That Cometh*, tr. G. W. Anderson, Oxford: Blackwell, 1956.

Mullins, T. Y., 'Petition as a Literary Form', *NovT* 5 (1962) 46–54.

Mussies, G., 'Parallels to Matthew's Version of the Pedigree of Jesus', *NovT* 28 (1986) 32–47.

Musurillo, H., *The Acts of the Christian Martyrs*, Oxford: Clarendon Press, 1972.

Myers, J. T., *I Chronicles*, AB 12, Garden City, New York: Doubleday, 1965.

Naveh, J. & Shaked, S., *Amulets and Magic Bowls: Aramaic Incantations of Late Antiquity*, Jerusalem: Magnes Press/Leiden: Brill, 1985.

Neusner, J., *A History of the Jews in Babylonia*, vol. 1, SPB 9, Leiden: Brill, 1965.

——, *Eliezer ben Hyrcanus: The tradition and the man*, 2 vols., SJLA 3–4, Leiden: Brill, 1973.

Neyrey, J. H., *The Form and Background of the Polemic in 2 Peter*, unpublished dissertation, Yale University, 1977.

Nicholson, E. W., *Preaching to the Exiles: A Study of the Prose Tradition in the Book of Jeremiah*, Oxford: Blackwell, 1971.

Nickelsburg, G. W. E., 'An Antiochan Date for the Testament of Moses', in G. W. E. Nickelsburg ed., *Studies on the Testament of Moses*, SBLSCS 4 (Cambridge, Massachusetts: SBL, 1976) 33–37.

——, 'Riches, the Rich, and God's Judgment in I Enoch 92–105 and the Gospel according to Luke', *NTS* 25 (1979) 324–344.

——, *Jewish Literature Between the Bible and the Mishnah: A Historical and Literary Introduction*, London: SCM Press, 1981.

Noll, S. F., *Angelology in the Qumran Texts*, unpublished Ph.D. thesis, University of Manchester, 1979.

Noth, M., *Die israelitischen Personennamen im Rahmen der Gemeinsemitischen Namengebung*, BWANT 46, Stuttgart: N. Kohlhammer, 1928.

Oberlinner, L., *Historische Überlieferung und christologische Aussage: Zur Frage der "Bruder Jesu" in der Synopse*, Forschung zur Bibel 19, Stuttgart: Katholisches Bibelwerk, 1975.

Ogilvie, R. M., *The Library of Lactantius*, Oxford: Clarendon Press, 1978.

Oleson, J. P., 'An Echo of Hesiod's Theogony vv 190–2 in Jude 13', *NTS* 25 (1979) 492–503.

Osburn, C. D., 'The Text of Jude 22–23', *ZNW* 63 (1972) 139–144.

——, 'The Christological Use of 1 Enoch i.9 in Jude 14, 15', *NTS* 23 (1976–77) 334–341.

——, 'The Text of Jude 5', *Bib* 62 (1981) 107–115.

——, '1 Enoch 80:2–8 (67:5–7) and Jude 12–13', *CBQ* 47 (1985) 296–303.

Patte, D., *Early Jewish Hermeneutic in Palestine*, SBLDS 22, Missoula, Montana: Scholars Press, 1975.

Payne, D. F., 'Jude', in *A New Testament Commentary*, ed. G. C. D. Howley (London: Pickering & Inglis, 1969) 626–628.

Perrin, N., *The New Testament: An Introduction*, New York: Harcourt Brace Jovanovich, 1974.

Pesch, R., *Das Markusevangelium*, vol. 1, HTKNT 2/1, Freiburg/Basel/Vienna: Herder, 1976.

Pfleiderer, O., *Primitive Christianity: its writings and teachings in their historical connections*, tr. W. Montgomery, vol. 4, London: Williams & Norgate/New York: Putnam, 1911.

Philippi, F., *Das Buch Henoch, sein Zeitalter und sein Verhältnis zum Judasbrief*, Stuttgart: S. G. Liesching, 1868.

Plessis, P. J. du, 'The Authorship of the Epistle of Jude', in *Biblical Essays: Proceedings of the Ninth Meeting of "Die Ou-Testamentiese Werkgemeenskap in Suid-Afrika", and Proceedings of the Second Meeting of "Die Nuwe-Testamentiese Werkgemeenskap van Suid-Afrika"*, (Potchefstroom: Potchefstroom Herald Beperk, 1966) 191–199.

Plummer, A., 'The Second Epistle of St. Peter', and 'The Epistle of St. Jude', in *A New Testament Commentary for English Readers*, ed. C. J. Ellicott, vol. 3, London: Cassell, 1884.

——, *The General Epistles of St. James and St. Jude*, ExpB, London: Hodder & Stoughton, 1891.

——, *A Critical and Exegetical Commentary on the Gospel according to S. Luke*, ICC, Edinburgh: T. & T. Clark, ⁴1901.

Plumptre, E. H., *The General Epistles of St. Peter and St. Jude*, Cambridge Bible for Schools and Colleges, Cambridge: Cambridge University Press, 1879.

Poirier, P.-H., 'Une étymologie ancienne du nom de Thomas l'apôtre at sa source', *ParOr* 10 (1981–82) 285–290.

Pratscher, W., *Der Herrenbruder Jakobus und die Jakobustradition*, FRLANT 139, Göttingen: Vandenhoeck & Ruprecht, 1987.

Priest, J., 'Testament of Moses', in J. H. Charlesworth ed., *The Old Testament Pseudepigrapha*, vol. 1 (London: Darton, Longman & Todd, 1983) 919–934.

Pritz, R. A., *Nazarene Jewish Christianity: From the End of the New Testament Period Until Its Disappearance in the Fourth Century*, SPB 37, Jerusalem: Magnes Press/Leiden: Brill, 1988.

Purvis, J. D., 'Samaritan Traditions on the Death of Moses', in *Studies on the Testament of Moses*, ed. G. W. E. Nickelsburg, SBLSCS 4, Cambridge, Mass.: Scholars Press, 1973.

Reichardt, W., *Die Briefe des Sextus Julius Africanus an Aristides und Origenes*, TU 34/3, Leipzig: Hinrichs, 1909.

Reicke, B., *Diakonie, Festfreude und Zelos in Verbindung mit der altchristlichen Agapenfeier*, UAÅ 1951:5, Uppsala: A. B. Lundequistska/Wiesbaden: O. Harrassowitz, 1951.

——, *The Epistles of James, Peter and Jude*, AB 37, Garden City, New York: Doubleday, 1964.

Renan, E., *Saint Paul*, Paris: M. Lévy, 1869.

Rengstorf, K. H., 'δεσπότης, οἰκοδεσπότης, οἰκοδεσποτέω,' in *Theological Dictionary of the New Testament*, ed. G. Kittel and G. W. Bromiley, vol. 2 (Grand Rapids: Eerdmans, 1964) 44–49.

Reumann, J., '"Jesus the Steward": An Overlooked Theme in

Christology', in *Studia Evangelica* 5/2, ed. F. L. Cross, TU 103 (Berlin: Akademie-Verlag, 1968) 21–29.

Richardson, P. and Shukster, M. B., 'Barnabas, Nerva, and the Yavnean Rabbis', *JTS* 34 (1983) 31–55.

Robinson, F., *Coptic Apocryphal Gospels*, TextsS 4/2, Cambridge: Cambridge University Press, 1896.

Robinson, J. A. T., *Redating the New Testament*, London: SCM Press, 1976.

Robinson, J. M., *The Nag Hammadi Library in English*, Leiden: Brill, 1977.

Robson, E. I., *Studies in the Second Epistle of St Peter*, Cambridge: Cambridge University Press, 1915.

Rohland, J. P., *Der Erzengel Michael, Arzt und Feldherr*, BZRGG 19, Leiden: Brill, 1977.

Rönsch, H., 'Weitere Illustrationen zur Assumptio Mosis', *ZWT* 12 (1869) 213–228.

Rordorf, W., 'Die neronische Christenverfolgung in Spiegel der apokryphen Paulusakten', *NTS* 28 (1982) 365–374.

Rostovtzeff, M., *Caravan Cities*, tr. D. and T. Talbot Rice, Oxford: Clarendon Press, 1932.

Rowland, C., *The Open Heaven: A Study of Apocalyptic in Judaism and Early Christianity*, London: SPCK, 1982.

Rowston, D. J., *The Setting of the Letter of Jude*, unpublished dissertation, Southern Baptist Theological Seminary, Louisville, Kentucky 1971.

——, 'The Most Neglected Book in the New Testament', *NTS* 21 (1974–75) 554–563.

Rubinkiewicz, R., *Die Eschatologie von Henoch 9–11 und das Neue Testament*, Klosterneuburg 1984.

Ruwet, J., 'Clément d'Alexandrie: Canon des Écritures et Apocryphes', *Bib* 29 (1948) 77–99, 240–268, 391–408.

Salmon, G., *A Historical Introduction to the Study of the Books of the New Testament*, London: J. Murray, [7]1894.

Salmond, S. D. F., *Jude*, Pulpit Commentary, eds., H. D. M. Spence and J. S. Exell, London/New York: Funk & Wagnalls, [2]1907.

Saltman, A., *Pseudo-Jerome: Quaestiones on the Book of Samuel*, SPB 26, Leiden: Brill, 1975.

Sanders, E. P., 'Testament of Abraham', in J. H. Charlesworth ed., *The Old Testament Pseudepigrapha*, vol. 1 (London: Darton, Longman & Todd, 1983) 871–902.

Schelkle, K. H., *Die Petrusbriefe, der Judasbrief*, HTKNT 13/2, Freiburg/Basel/Vienna: Herder, 1961.

——, 'Der Judasbrief bei den Kirchenvätern', in *Abraham unser Vater: Juden und Christen im Gespräch über die Bibel: Festschrift für Otto Michel*, O. Betz, M. Hengel and P. Schmidt eds., Leiden: Brill, 1963.

——, 'Spätapostolische Briefe als frühkatholisches Zeugnis', in *Neutestamentliche Aufsätze*, Festschrift for J. Schmid, eds. J. Blinzler, O. Kuss and F. Mussner, Regensburg: Pustet, 1963.

Schlatter, A., *Geschichte Israels von Alexander dem Grossen bis Hadrian*, Stuttgart: Calwer, ³1925.

——, *Die Briefe des Petrus, Judas, Jakobus, der Brief an die Hebräer*, Stuttgart: Calwer, 1964.

Schmidt, C. and MacDermot, V., *The Books of Jeu and the Untitled Text in the Bruce Codex*, NHS 13, Leiden: Brill, 1978.

Schmidt, D., *The Peter Writings: Their Redactors and Their Relationships*, unpublished dissertation, Northwestern University (Evanston, Illinois), 1972.

Schneemelcher, W., 'Acts of Paul', in *New Testament Apocrypha*, ed. E. Hennecke, W. Schneemelcher, R. McL. Wilson, vol. 2 (London: Lutterworth, 1965) 322–390.

Schneider, J., *Die Briefe des Jakobus, Petrus, Judas und Johannes: Die Katholischen Briefe*, NTD 10, Göttingen: Vandenhoeck and Ruprecht, ⁹1961.

Schoeps, H. J., *Theologie und Geschichte des Judenchristentums*, Tübingen: Mohr (Siebeck), 1949.

Schottroff, L. and Stegemann, W., *Jesus and the Hope of the Poor*, tr. M. J. O'Connell, Maryknoll, New York: Orbis, 1986.

Schrage, W., 'Der Judasbrief', in H. Balz and W. Schrage, *Die 'Katholischen' Briefe: Die Briefe des Jakobus, Petrus, Johannes und Judas*, NTD 10, Göttingen: Vandenhoeck and Ruprecht, ¹¹1973.

Schultz, D. R., 'The Origin of Sin in Irenaeus and Jewish Pseudepigraphal Literature', *VC* 32 (1978) 161–190.

Schultz, J. P., 'Angelic Opposition to the Ascension of Moses and the Revelation of the Law', *JQR* 61 (1971) 282–307.

Schulz, S., 'Maranatha und Kyrios Jesus', *ZNW* 53 (1962) 125–144.

Schürer, E., *The History of the Jewish People in the Age of Jesus Christ (175 B.C.–A.D. 135)*, revised by G. Vermes and F. Millar, vol. 1, Edinburgh: T. & T. Clark, 1973.

Schwartz, E., *Eusebius Werke: II: Die Kirchengeschichte*, vol. 1, GCS, Leipzig: Hinrichs, 1903.

Seethalter, P. A., 'Kleine Bermerkungen zum Judasbrief', *BZ* 31 (1987) 261–264.

Sellin, G., 'Die Häretiker des Judasbriefes', *ZNW* 77 (1986) 206–225.

Selwyn, E. C., *The Christian Prophets and the Prophetic Apocalypse*, London: Macmillan, 1900.

——, *St. Luke the Prophet*, London: Macmillan, 1901.

Sevenster, J. N., *Do You Know Greek? How much Greek could the first Jewish Christians have known?*, NovTSup 19, Leiden: Brill, 1968.

Sherlock, T., 'Dissertation I: The Authority of the Second Epistle of St. Peter', in *Discourses preached at the Temple Church, and on several occasions*, vol. 4 (Oxford: Clarendon Press, 1812) 129–149.

Sickenberger, J., 'Engels- oder Teufelslästerer im Judasbriefe (8–10) und im 2. Petrusbriefe (2,10–12)?', in *Festschrift für Jahrhundertfeier der Universität zu Breslau*, ed. T. Siebs = *MSGVK* 13–14 (1911–12) 621–639.

Sidebottom, E. M., *James, Jude and 2 Peter*, New Century Bible, London: Nelson, 1967.

Silver, A. H., *A History of Messianic Speculation in Israel: From the First through the Seventeenth Centuries*, New York: Macmillan, 1927.

Simon, M., *Le Christianisme antique et son contexte religieux: Scripta Varia*, WUNT 23, Tübingen: Mohr (Siebeck), 1981.

——, *Verus Israel: A study of the relations between Christians and Jews in the Roman Empire (135–425)*, tr. H. McKeating, Oxford: Oxford University Press (Littman Library), 1986.

Skarsaune, O., *The Proof from Prophecy: A Study in Justin Martyr's Proof-Text Tradition*, NovTSup 56, Leiden: Brill, 1987.

Slomovic, E., 'Toward an Understanding of the Exegesis in the Dead Sea Scrolls', *RQ* 7 (1969–71) 3–15.

Smallwood, E. M., 'Atticus, Legate of Judaea under Trajan', *JRS* 52 (1962) 131–133.

Smid, H. R., *Protevangelium Jacobi: A Commentary*, Assen: Van Gorcum, 1965.

Smith, M., *Clement of Alexandria and a Secret Gospel of Mark*, Cambridge, Massachusetts: Harvard University Press, 1973.

Smith, R. L., *Micah-Malachi*, WBC 32, Waco, Texas: Word Books, 1984.

Smith, T. V., *Petrine Controversies in Early Christianity*, WUNT 2/15, Tübingen: Mohr (Siebeck), 1985.

Soards, M. L., '1 Peter, 2 Peter, and Jude as Evidence for a Petrine School', in W. Haase ed., *Aufstieg und Niedergang der Römischen Welt*, vol. 2/25/5 (Berlin/New York: de Gruyter, 1988), 3827–3849.

Soden, H. von, *Hebräerbrief, Briefe des Petrus, Jakobus, Judas*, HC 3/2, Freiburg i. B.: Mohr (Siebeck), 1899.

Sparks, H. F. D., *The Apocryphal Old Testament*, Oxford: Clarendon Press, 1984.

Spicq, C., *Les Épitres de Saint Pierre*, SB, Paris: Gabalda, 1966.

Spitta, F., *Der Zweite Brief des Petrus und der Brief des Judas*, Halle a. S.: Buchhandlung des Waisenhauses, 1885.

Spittler, R. P., 'Testament of Job', in J. H. Charlesworth ed., *The Old Testament Pseudepigrapha*, vol. 1 (London: Darton, Longman and Todd, 1983) 829–868.

Stauffer, E., 'Zum Kalifat des Jacobus', *ZRGG* 4 (1952) 193–214.

Stemberger, G., 'Galilee – Land of Salvation?', in W. D. Davies, *The Gospel and the Land: Early Christianity and Jewish Territorial Doctrine*, (Berkeley: University of California Press, 1974) 409–438.

Stokes, W., 'The Irish Verses, Notes and Glosses in Harl. 1802', *Revue Celtique* 8 (1887) 346–369.

Stone, M. E., 'Three Armenian Accounts of the Death of Moses', in *Studies on the Testament of Moses*, ed. G. W. E. Nickelsburg, SBLSCS 4 (Cambridge: Mass.: Scholars Press, 1973) 118–121.

Strack, H. L. and Billerbeck, P., *Kommentar zum Neuen Testament aus Talmud and Midrasch*, vol. 1, Munich: Beck, 1922.

Strange, J. F., 'Diversity in Early Palestinian Christianity: Some Archaeological Evidences', *ATR* 65 (1983) 14–24.

Streeter, B. H., *The Primitive Church*, London: Macmillan, 1929.

Strycker, E. de, *La forme la plus ancienne du Protévangile de Jacques*, Subsidia Hagiographica 33, Brussels: Société des Bollandistes, 1961.

Sundberg, A. C., *The Old Testament of the Early Church*, HTS 20, Cambridge, Massachusetts: Harvard University Press/London: Oxford University Press, 1964.

Swete, H. B., *The Gospel according to St Mark*, London: Macmillan, ³1909.

Swetnam, J., 'Some Observations on the Background of ṣaddîq in Jeremias 23,5a', *Bib* 46 (1965) 29–40.

Symes, J. E., *The Evolution of the New Testament*, London: J. Murray, 1921.

Szewc, E., '"Chwaty" w listach Judy i 2 Piotra ("Les Gloires" dans les épîtres de St. Jude et deuxième de St. Pierre)', *CoTh* 46 (1976) 51–60.

——, '"Doxai" in den katholischen Briefen und die qumranische Literatur', *FolOr* 21 (1980) 129–140.

Taylor, V., 'The Message of the Epistles: Second Peter and Jude', *ExpT* 45 (1933–34) 437–441.

——, *The Gospel according to St Mark*, London: Macmillan, 1952.

Tcherikover, V. A. and Fuks, A., *Corpus Papyrorum Judaicarum*, 3 vols, Jerusalem: Magnes Press/Cambridge, Massachusetts: Harvard University Press, 1957, 1960, 1964.

Testa, E., *Il Simbolismo dei Giudeo-Cristiani*, Pubblicazione dello Studium Biblicum Franciscanum 14, Jerusalem: Franciscan Printing Press, 1962.

——, *Nazaret Giudeo-Cristiana: Riti, Iscrizioni, Simboli*, Pubblicazione dello Studium Biblicum Franciscanum: Collectio minor 8, Jerusalem: Franciscan Printing Press, 1969.

Theissen, G., *The First Followers of Jesus: A Sociological Analysis of the earliest Christianity*, tr. J. Bowden, London: SCM Press, 1978.

Thomas, D. W., *Documents from Old Testament Times*, London: Nelson, 1958.

Tricot, A., 'Deuxième épître de saint Pierre', in A. Vacant, E. Mangenot, É. Amann ed., *Dictionnaire de Théologie Catholique*, vol. 12 (Paris: Letouzey and Ané, 1933) 1775–1792.

Trompf, S. W., 'The First Resurrection Appearance and the Ending of Mark's Gospel', *NTS* 18 (1971–1972) 308–330.

Turdeanu, E., 'La *Chronique de Moïse* en russe', *RESl* 46 (1967) 35–64.

Turner, J. D., *The Book of Thomas the Contender*, SBLDS 23, Missoula, Montana: Scholars Press, 1975.

Unterman, J., *From Repentance to Redemption: Jeremiah's Thought in Transition*, JSOTSS 54, Sheffield: JSOT Press, 1987.

van den Broek, R., 'Der Brief des Jakobus an Quadratus und das Problem der judenchristlichen Bischöfe von Jerusalem (Eusebius, *HE* IV,5,1–3)', in *Text and Testimony: Essays on New Testament and Apocryphal Literature in Honour of A. F. J. Klijn*, eds. T. Baarda, A. Hilhorst, G. P. Luttikhuizen, A. S. van der Woude (Kampen: K. H. Kok, 1988) 56–65.

VanderKam, J. C., 'The Theophany of Enoch I 3b–7, 9', *VT* 23 (1973) 129–150.

——, *Enoch and the Growth of an Apocalyptic Tradition*, CBQMS 16, Washington, D.C.: Catholic Biblical Association of America, 1984.

van de Vorst, C., 'Saint Phocas', *AnBoll* 30 (1911) 252–295.

Vassiliev, A., *Anecdota Graeco-Byzantina*, Moscow: Imperial University Press, 1893.

Vegas Montaner, L., 'Testamento de Moises', in *Apocrifos del Antiguo Testamento*, vol. 5, ed. A. Diez Macho, M. Angeles Navarro, A. de la Fuente and A. Piñero (Madrid: Ediciones Cristiandad, 1987) 217–275.

Vermes, G., *Jesus the Jew: A Historian's Reading of the Gospels*, London: Fontana/Collins, ²1976.

——, *The Dead Sea Scrolls in English*, London: Penguin, ³1987.

Vielhauer, P., 'Jewish-Christian Gospels', in *New Testament Apocrypha*, E. Hennecke, W. Schneemelcher and R. McL. Wilson ed., vol. 1 (London: Lutterworth, 1963) 117–165.

——, *Geschichte der urchristlichen Literatur: Einleitung in das Neue Testament, die Apokryphen und die Apostolischen Väter*, Berlin/New York: de Gruyter, 1975.

Villegas, B., 'Peter, Philip and James of Alphaeus', *NTS* 33 (1987) 292–294.

Vogt, P., *Der Stammbaum Christi bei den heiligen Evangelisten Matthäus und Lukas*, BibS(F) 12/2, Freiburg: Herder, 1907.

von Campenhausen, H., 'Die Nachfolge des Jakobus: Zur Frage eines urchristlichen "Kalifats"', *ZKG* 63 (1950–51) 133–144.

Vrede, W., 'Judas-, Petrus- und Johannesbriefe', in *Die heilige Schrift des Neuen Testaments*, F. Tillmann ed., vol. 4, Bonn: P. Hanstein, 1916.

Wacholder, B. Z., 'Chronomessianism: The Timing of Messianic Movements and the Calendar of Sabbatical Cycles', *HUCA* 46 (1975) 201–218; reprinted in *Essays on Jewish Chronology and Chronography* (New York: Ktav, 1976) 240–257.

Wand, J. W. C., *The General Epistles of St. Peter and St. Jude*, Westminster Commentaries, London: Methuen, 1934.

Wandel, G., *Der Brief Judas exegetisch-praktisch behandelt*, Leipzig: A. Deichert (G. Böhme), 1898.

Weidner, E. F., 'Jojachin, König von Juda, in Babylonischen Keilschrifttexten', in *Mélanges Syriens offerts à Monsieur René Dussard*, vol. 2 (Paris: Geuthner, 1939) 922–935.

Weiss, B., 'Die petrinische Frage: Kritische Untersuchungen: II: Der zweite petrinische Brief', *TSK* 39 (1866) 255–308.

——, *A Manual of Introduction to the New Testament*, tr. A. J. K. Davidson, vol. 2, London: Hodder & Stoughton, 1888.

Wenham, J. W., 'The Relatives of Jesus', *EvQ* 47 (1975) 6–15.

Werdermann, H., *Die Irrlehrer des Judas- und 2. Petrusbriefes*, BFCT 17/6, Gütersloh: C. Bertelsmann, 1913.

Whallon, W., 'Should We Keep, Omit, or Alter the 'OI in Jude 12?', *NTS* 34 (1988) 156–159.

White, W., Jr., 'Peter, Second Epistle of', in M. C. Tenney and S. Barabas ed., *The Zondervan Pictorial Encyclopedia of the Bible*, vol. 4 (Grand Rapids: Eerdmans, 1975) 726–732.

Wiesenberg, E., 'The Jubilee of Jubilees', *RQ* 9 (1961) 3–40.

Wikenhauser, A., *New Testament Introduction*, tr. J. Cunningham, Dublin: Herder & Herder, 1958.

Wikgren, A., 'Some Problems in Jude 5', in *Studies in the History and Text of the New Testament in Honor of K. W. Clark*, B. L. Daniels and M. J. Suggs eds. (Salt Lake City: University of Utah Press, 1967) 147–152.

Wilcox, M., 'Text form', in *It is Written: Scripture Citing Scripture: Essays in Honour of Barnabas Lindars SSF*, ed. D. A. Carson and H. G. M. Williamson (Cambridge: Cambridge University Press, 1988) 193–204.

Williamson, H. G. M., 'Eschatology in Chronicles', *TynB* 28 (1977) 115–154.

———, *1 and 2 Chronicles*, NCeB, Grand Rapids: Eerdmans/London: Marshall, Morgan and Scott, 1982.

———, *Ezra, Nehemiah*, WBC 16, Waco, Texas: Word Books, 1985.

Willmering, H., 'The Epistle of St. Jude', in *A Catholic Commentary on Holy Scripture*, B. Orchard, E. F. Sutcliffe, R. C. Fuller and R. Russell eds. (London: Nelson, 1953) 1191–1192.

Wilson, R. McL., *Studies in the Gospel of Thomas*, London: Mowbray, 1960.

———, *The Gospel of Philip*, London: Mowbray, 1962.

Wilson, R. R., 'The Old Testament Genealogies in Recent Research', *JBL* 94 (1975) 169–189.

———, *Genealogy and History in the Biblical World*, New Haven/London: Yale University Press, 1977.

Windisch, H., *Die katholischen Briefe*, revised H. Preisker, HNT 15, Tübingen: Mohr (Siebeck), [3]1951.

Wisse, F., 'The Epistle of Jude in the History of Heresiology', in *Essays in the Nag Hammadi Texts in Honour of A. Böhlig*, M. Krause ed., NHS 3 (Leiden: Brill, 1972) 133–143.

Wohlenberg, G., *Der erste und zweite Petrusbrief und der Judasbrief*, KNT 15, Leipzig/Erlangen: A. Deichert, [3]1923.

Wolthius, T., 'Jude and Jewish Traditions', *CTJ* 22 (1987) 21–41.

Wordsworth, C., *The New Testament of Our Lord and Saviour Jesus Christ*, vol. 2, London: Rivingtons, [2]1882.

Wright, A. G., *The Literary Genre Midrash*, New York: Alba House, 1967, reprinted from *CBQ* 28 (1966) 105–138, 417–457.

Wuthnow, H., *Die semitischen Menschennamen in grieschischen Inschriften und Papyri des vorderen Orients*, Studien zur Epigraphik und Papyruskunde 1/4, Leipzig: Dieterich, 1950.

Zahn, T., *Forschungen zur Geschichte des neutestamentliche Kanons und der altkirchen Literatur, VI. Teil: I. Apostel und Apostelschüler in der*

Provinz Asien; II. Brüder und Vettern Jesu, Leipzig: A. Deichert, 1900.

——, *Introduction to the New Testament*, tr. M. W. Jacobus et al., vol. 2, Edinburgh: T. & T. Clark, 1909.

Index of Passages Cited

I. OLD TESTAMENT

II. APOCRYPHA

III. NEW TESTAMENT

IV. JEWISH PSEUDEPIGRAPHA

V. DEAD SEA SCROLLS

VI. JOSEPHUS

VII. PHILO

VIII. TARGUMS, RABBINIC AND OTHER LATER JEWISH LITERATURE

IX. CLASSICAL GREEK AUTHORS

X. NAG HAMMADI LITERATURE

XI. EARLY CHRISTIAN LITERATURE

XII. MISCELLANEOUS

Index of Ancient Persons and Places

Index of Modern Authors